GUIDELINES FOR PUBLIC DEBT MANAGEMENT:
ACCOMPANYING DOCUMENT AND SELECTED CASE STUDIES

Prepared by the Staffs of the
International Monetary Fund and the World Bank

International Monetary Fund and The World Bank
Washington, DC

9180248

© 2003 International Monetary Fund

Production: IMF Multimedia Services Division
Cover design: Lai Oy Louie
Typesetting: Grammarians, Inc.

Cataloging-in-Publication Data

Guidelines for public debt management : accompanying document and selected case studies / prepared by the staffs of the International Monetary Fund and the World Bank – Washington, D.C. : International Monetary Fund : World Bank Group, c2003.

p. cm.

Includes bibliographical references.
ISBN 1-58906-194-2
1. Debts, Public. I. International Monetary Fund. II. World Bank.

HJ8015.G687 2003

ISBN 1-58906-194-2

Price: US$31.00

Please send orders to:

International Monetary Fund
Publication Services
700 19th Street, N.W.
Washington, DC 20431, USA
Tel.: (202) 623-7430
Telefax: (202) 623-7201
E-mail: publications@imf.org
Internet: http://www.imf.org

The World Bank
Publications
1818 H Street, N.W.
Washington, DC 20433, USA
Tel.: (800) 645-7247
Telefax: (703) 661-1501
E-mail: books@worldbank.org
Internet: http://www.worldbank.org

Contents

Foreword

A government's debt stock is usually the largest financial portfolio in the country. It often contains complex financial structures and can create substantial balance sheet risk for the government. Several debt market crises have highlighted the importance of sound debt management practices and the need for efficient and sound capital markets. Improved debt management will reduce a country's vulnerability to economic and financial shocks and support the environment for growth.

The *Accompanying Document and Selected Case Studies* complements the IMF and World Bank's *Guidelines for Public Debt Management*, which were endorsed by the International Monetary and Financial Committee and the Development Committee at their spring 2001 meetings. It illustrates the variety of approaches taken by 18 countries from different parts of the world, and at different stages of economic and financial development, to develop their public debt management practices in a manner consistent with the *Guidelines*. The experience of these countries should offer some useful practical suggestions of the kinds of steps that other countries could take as they strive to build their capacity in public debt management.

In line with the process adopted for the *Guidelines*, the preparation of the *Accompanying Document and Selected Case Studies* has sought to ensure that the description of individual country practice and the lessons learned are well grounded. To this end, the case studies were prepared by government debt managers with the coordination of staff from the IMF and the World Bank. IMF and World Bank staffs also prepared Part I of the document, which summarizes key lessons from the case studies. Two formal rounds of consultations were held with the country officials who prepared the case studies, and an outreach conference organized by IMF and World Bank staffs was held in Washington in September 2002 so that the country officials could meet to discuss the lessons drawn from the case studies and the book as a whole.

Anne Krueger
First Deputy Managing Director
International Monetary Fund

Jeffrey Goldstein
Managing Director
The World Bank

Acknowledgments

Guidelines for Public Debt Management: Accompanying Document and Selected Case Studies was prepared by Mats Filipsson and Mark Zelmer of the International Monetary Fund, Tomas Magnusson of the World Bank, and the officials from the 18 countries that prepared the case studies. The project was supervised by Piero Ugolini of the International Monetary Fund and Fred Jensen of the World Bank. Valuable feedback and suggestions for improving this book of case studies were obtained from the country officials who prepared the case studies and staff within the International Monetary Fund and the World Bank. In particular, Stefan Ingves and V. Sundararajan of the Fund and Graeme Wheeler and Ken Lay of the World Bank provided very useful comments.

Special thanks are due to Natalie Baumer, who helped to edit this book; Sandra Marcelino for her help in compiling data and preparing charts and tables; and Stephen Swaray for his help in preparing the box "Applying the Guidelines to the HIPCs." Thanks are also due to William Murray and Sean Culhane of the External Relations Department of the IMF and to Craig Carter of the Public Debt Management Group of the World Bank who managed the production of this document.

Glossary and List of Abbreviations

ADB	Asian Development Bank
ALM	Asset and Liability Management
ALM Branch	Asset and Liability Management Branch (of the National Treasury, South Africa)
BAM	Bank Al-Maghrib (Morocco)
BaR	Budget-at-Risk
BdR	Banco de la República (Colombia)
BESA	Bond Exchange of South Africa
BIS	Bank of International Settlement
BOI	Bank of Italy
BOJ	Bank of Jamaica
BoJ	Bank of Japan
BOJ-NET	Bank of Japan Financial Network System
BOM	Bank of Mexico
BOS	Bank of Slovenia
BOTs	Buoni Ordinari del Tesoro
BPD	Bureau of the Public Debt
BTEs	Buoni del Tesoro (Italy)
BTPs	Buoni del Tesoro Poliennali (Italy)
CaR	Cost-at-Risk
CBB	Central Bank of Brazil
CBI	Central Bank of Ireland
CBISSO	Central Bank of Ireland Securities Settlements Office
CCIL	Clearing Corporation of India Ltd.
CCTs	Certificati di Credto del Tesoro (Italy)
CDP	Cassa Depositi e Prestini (Italy)
Cetes	Certificados de la Tesorería (Mexico)
COI	Obligacje czteroletnie indeksowane oszczędnościowe (Poland)
CP	Commercial Paper
CPSS	Committee on Payment and Settlement Systems (of the central banks of the Group of Ten countries)
CRR	Cash Reserve Ratio
CSE	Copenhagen Stock Exchange

CTEs	Certificati del Tesoro (Italy)
CTOs	Certificati del Tesoro con Opzione (Italy)
CTZs	Certificati del Tesoro Zero-Coupon (Italy)
Dáil	Lower House of Irish Parliament
DCV	Depósito Central de Valores (Colombia)
Diet	The Japanese Parliament
DMFAS	Debt Management and Financial Analisis System (Colombia)
DMO	The U.K. Debt Management Office
DMU	Debt Management Unit (of the Ministry of Finance and Planning, Jamaica)
DNB	Danmarks Nationalbank
DOS	Obligacje dwuletnie oszczędnościowe o stałej stopie procentowej (Poland)
DRMR	Debt and Reserves Management Report (U.K.)
DS	Obligacje dziesięcioletnie o oprocentowaniu stałym (Poland)
DsaR	Debt-Service-at-Risk
DvP	Delivery-versus-Payment
DZ	Obligacje dziesięcioletnie o oprocentowaniu zmiennym (Poland)
ECB	European Central Bank
ECB	External Commercial Borrowing (India)
ECP	Euro Commercial Paper
ECU	European Currency Unit
EEC	European Economic Community
EFFAS	European Federation of Financial Analysts Societies
EMS	European Monetary System
EMTN	Euro Medium-Term Notes
EMU	European Monetary Union
EONIA	Euro Overnight Index Average
ERM II	European Exchange Rate Mechanism II
ESCB	European System of Central Banks
EU	European Union
Euribor	Euro Interbank Offered Rate
Eurostat	Statistical Office of the European Communities
FAA	Financial Administration and Audit
Fed	Federal Reserve System
FILP	Fiscal Investment and Loan Program (Japan)
FMC	Financial Markets Committee
FMS	Financial Management Service
FRL	Fiscal Responsibility Law (Brazil)
FSC	Financial Services Commission
GDCF	Government Debt Consolidation Fund (Japan)
GEMM	Gilt-Edged Market Makers (U.K.)
HIPC	Heavily Indebted Poor Countries
IDB	Interdealer Broker
IG GEMM	Index-Linked Gilt-edged Market Makers (U.K.)
IGCP	Instituto de Gestão do Credito Publico (Portuguese Government Debt Agency)
IGR	Impôt Général sur le Revenu (Morocco)
IMF	International Monetary Fund
IMFC	International Monetary and Financial Committee

IOSCO	International Organization of Securities Commissions
IPAB	Instituto de Protección al Ahorro Bancario (Mexico)
IRS	Interest Rate Swap
IS	Impôt sur les Sociétés (Morocco)
ISDA	International Swap Dealers Association
ISMA	International Securities Market Association
IT	Information Technology
IVT	Intermédiaires en Valeurs du Trésor (Morocco)
JCSD	Jamaica Central Securities Depository
JGB	Japanese Government Bond
LFT	Letras Financeiras do Tesouro (Brazil)
LOA	Lei Orçamentária Anual
LRS	Local Registered Stocks (Jamaica)
LSE	London Stock Exchange
LTN	Letras do Tesouro Nacional
M2	Broad Money 2
MEDIP	The Portuguese acronym for "Special Market for Public Debt"
MEF	Ministry of the Economy and Finance (Italy)
MoF	Ministry of Finance
MP	Multiple-Price
MTN	Medium-Term Notes
MTS	Electronic trading system for fixed-income securities
NBP	National Bank of Poland
NDS	National Depository for Securities
NDS	Negotiated Dealing System
NPV	Net Present Value
NTMA	The National Treasury Management Agency (Ireland)
NTN-C	Notas do Tesouro Nacional - Série C
NZDMO	New Zealand Debt Management Office
OECD	Organization for Economic Cooperation and Development
OK	Obligacje dwuletnie zerokuponowe (Poland)
OPCVMs	Organismes de placement Collectif en valeurs Mobilières (Morocco)
OT	Obrigações do Tesouro (standard fixed-rate treasury bonds, Portugal)
OTC	Over the Counter
PDD	Public Debt Department (of the Ministry of Finance, Poland)
PDD	Public Debt Direction (of the Italian Treasury Department)
PS	Obligacje pięcioletnie o oprocentowaniu stałym (Poland)
R&I	Rating and Investment Information, Inc.
RAPM	Risk-Adjusted Performance Measurement
RBI	Reserve Bank of India
RTGS	Real-Time Gross Settlement
SARB	South African Reserve Bank
SDDS	Special Data Dissemination Standard
SEBRA	Sistema Electrónico de Banco de la República (Colombia)
Secad	Secretaria Adjunta do Tesouro Nacional (Brazil)
SEN	Sistema Electrónico de Negociación de Deuda Pública (Colombia)
SFC	Secretaria Federal de Controle (Brazil)

SLR	Statutory Liquidity Ratio
SNDO	Swedish National Debt Office
SOEs	State-Owned Enterprises
SP	Obligacje pięcioletnie o stałej stopie procentowej (Poland)
SPF	Social Pension Fund
STRIPS	Separate Trading of Registered Interest and Principal of Securities
SWIFT	Society for Worldwide Interbank Financial Telecommunication
TARGET	Trans European Real-time Gross Settlement Express Transfer
TCU	Tribunal de Contas da União (external auditing agency, Brazil)
TES	Treasury Security (Colombia)
TPR	Transfer-Pricing Regime
TZ	Obligacje trzyletnie o oprocentowaniu zmiennym (Poland)
UMS	United Mexican States
UNCTAD	United Nations Conference on Trade and Development
UP	Uniform-Price
USD CP	U.S. Dollar Commercial Paper
VaR	Value-at-Risk
WMAs	Ways and Means Advances
WS	Obligacje dwudziestoletnie o oprocentowaniu stałem (Poland)

EXECUTIVE SUMMARY

Recognizing the important role that public debt management can play in helping countries cope with economic and financial shocks, the International Monetary and Financial Committee (IMFC) requested that staff from the International Monetary Fund and World Bank work together in cooperation with national debt management experts to develop a set of guidelines for public debt management to assist countries in their efforts to reduce financial vulnerability. When the Executive Boards of the IMF and the World Bank endorsed the guidelines in the spring of 2001, they requested that the staff of the two institutions also prepare an accompanying document to the guidelines containing sample case studies to illustrate how a range of countries from around the world and at different stages of economic and financial development are developing their debt management capacity in a manner consistent with the guidelines. The experiences of these countries should offer some useful practical suggestions of the kinds of steps that other countries could take as they strive to build their capacity in public debt management.

The 18 case studies presented in this report clearly illustrate the rapid evolution that is taking place in the field of public debt management. In contrast to 15 or 20 years ago, countries are much more focused on managing the financial and operational risks inherent in the debt portfolio. Also, the way in which the stock of debt is managed is becoming increasingly sophisticated, especially in those countries that have had histories of excessive debt levels or have experienced shocks associated with the reversal of capital flows.

These points are embodied in several overarching themes that emerge from the country case studies.

The first key theme is that the objectives for managing debt and the institutional framework for meeting these objectives are becoming more formalized. All of the countries surveyed have explicit objectives for managing their debt, which focus on managing the need to borrow at the lowest possible cost over a medium- to long-term time frame. Most countries' statements of objectives also make explicit reference to the need to manage risks prudently, but this is not universal. Even so, the reference to managing costs over the medium to long term can be seen as an awareness of the need to avoid taking on dangerous debt structures that might have lower costs in the short run but could trigger much higher debt-service costs in the future. They clearly do not strive to minimize costs in the short run without regard to risk. Avoiding dangerous debt structures is, of course, easier said than done. In some countries, the costs of borrowing domestically by issuing long-term fixed-rate instruments may simply be too prohibitive in the short run because of weak macroeconomic conditions or because this segment of the market is not functioning well. As a result, many countries are dedicating significant effort and resources toward developing the domestic market for government debt so that down the road they can reduce rollover risk and other market risks in the debt stock, even though the benefits of doing so may only emerge over time and entail higher debt service costs in the short run.

Another aspect of the more formal institutional framework can be seen in the organizational structure underpinning debt management. There is a clear trend toward providing a proper legal framework to support debt management, and centralizing debt management activities as much as possible in one entity, even though the preferred entity varies depending on country circumstances. As circumstances permitted, the countries surveyed took steps to separate the conduct of monetary policy from debt management, while ensuring continued adequate coordination at the operational level, so that there is appropriate sharing of information on the government's liquidity flows between debt managers and fiscal and monetary policy authorities, and so that the two activities do not operate at cross-purposes in financial markets. They have also taken a number of steps to clearly specify the roles and responsibilities of those involved in debt management and subject the conduct of debt management activities to appropriate financial and management controls. This has helped to ensure that appropriate safeguards are in place to manage the operational risks associated with debt management.

The more formal institutional framework has also been accompanied by transparency in debt management activities and appropriate accountability mechanisms. Debt managers in all of the case study countries emphasized the need to ensure that the public is fully informed about the government's financial condition, the objectives governing debt management, and the strategies and modalities used by debt managers to pursue these objectives. They also use a variety of communication vehicles, such as regular formal reports and media announcements, to report on their performance in meeting the objectives laid out for them and outline in general terms their plans and priorities for the year ahead. In some countries, their performance in both a financial and a broader stewardship sense is also subject to regular external review. This reflects a general consensus among the countries that markets work best, and debt service costs are minimized, when uncertainty regarding the objectives and conduct of debt management and the state of government finances is kept to a minimum.

A second key theme relates to the high level of awareness of the importance of risk management of public debt and of a growing consensus on the appro-

priate techniques for managing risk. Many of the countries surveyed use cash-flow modeling for analyzing the costs and risks of different debt strategies, where cost is measured as the expected, or most likely, cost of debt service over the medium to long term and risk is the potential increase or volatility in cost over the same period. One rationale for this is that the cost of debt is best considered in terms of its impact on the government's budget, and that cash-flow measures are a natural way of quantifying this impact. A few countries are beginning to experiment with modeling debt service and macrovariables jointly to more directly measure cost and risk of debt relative to the government's revenues and other expenditures—that is, to model the government's assets and liabilities jointly. In a number of other cases, this asset and liability management (ALM) approach has been used in a more limited way by jointly analyzing the risk characteristics of government financial assets (such as foreign exchange reserves) and debt to determine the appropriate structure of debt and assets.

The management of operational risk is also receiving increased attention. In large part, this is addressed by having institutional structures that permit clear assignment of authority and responsibility, operations manuals detailing all important procedures, conflict of interest rules, clear reporting lines, and formal audits. But many debt offices now also have separate middle offices with responsibility for analyzing risk and designing and implementing risk-control procedures. (Some of these same offices also have responsibility for analyzing strategies for managing the costs and risks of debt, although in others, the responsibility for strategic analysis is separate from the risk-control unit.)

Those debt offices, which trade their debt or take tactical risk positions, have particularly strong middle-office control structures. The focus on formal risk analysis and control structures is not universal, however, because it depends largely on country circumstances. In the past, the industrial countries seen as leaders in this field also had large and risky debt structures, including a substantial share of foreign currency debt. Consequently, the benefits of taking a more systematic approach to the financial and risk management of the government's debt were substantial. Others, which have deep and liquid domestic debt markets and consequently little or no foreign currency debt, have a much less risky debt structure and less of a need for a formal strategy for managing debt based on cost/risk trade-offs. However, emerging market and developing countries, many of which also have had risky debt structures, had a later start in building the capacity for managing this risk. Although some of these countries are now using models and systems that are similar to those in industrialized countries, others are still in the process of building this capacity. Good progress has been made, but the experience of the leading practitioners demonstrates that this process can take several years. That said, some countries may not need to build models and systems as sophisticated as those found in the industrial countries because their debt issuance options are narrower and their markets less amenable to statistical analysis. Instead, they should strive to set achievable goals for their models that are limited to the genuinely useful aspects.

It also is clear that a lot of financial resources and management time is being devoted to developing the technology and systems needed to perform these tasks. This speaks to the need to ensure that the systems acquired are appropriate to the government's needs, given a country's stage of development. The systems acquired do not necessarily have to include all of the latest and most sophisticated features—many of the cash-flow simulation models used for cost/risk analysis are spreadsheet based. Countries also have pursued the acquisition of technology in different ways, depending on country-specific circumstances. Some have opted to acquire these systems by purchasing commercially available systems that were designed for private sector financial institutions and customizing them to suit their own needs, and others have opted instead to develop their own systems in-house. Some systems are very basic, focusing on the primary needs of debt recording, reporting, and analysis, and others are integrated with other cash management, accounting, and budget systems. This highlights the fact that the appropriate technology varies considerably depending on country-specific circumstances, and that many countries are still experimenting to find out which systems work best.

A third key theme that emerged from the case studies is the striking convergence in approaches taken by countries to issue debt and promote a well-functioning domestic financial market. Auctions of standardized market instruments are commonly used to issue debt in domestic markets, and debt managers are cognizant of the need to avoid excessive fragmentation of the debt stock if they are to encourage deep and liquid markets for government securities. Where differences exist, they tend to be at the level of execution, such as in terms of the features of instruments issued and the extent to which debt managers are prepared to rely on primary dealers to market their debt to end-investors. Nonetheless, it is important to note that all of the countries surveyed referred to the advantages of working collaboratively with market participants to develop their domestic government securities markets and minimize the amount of uncertainty in the market regarding government financing activities. Over time, this appears to be paying off in the form of more efficient domestic financial markets, and ultimately lower borrowing costs for the government, in that the presence of a thriving domestic market makes it easier for debt managers to achieve a debt-stock structure that embodies the government's preferred cost/risk trade-off.

Fourth, it is important to highlight what sound debt management in and of itself cannot deliver. It is no substitute for sound macroeconomic and fiscal policies, and on its own will not be enough to ensure that a country is well insulated from economic and financial shocks. Developing public debt management in a manner consistent with the guidelines clearly has an important role to play in fostering prudent debt management practices and contributing to the development of a well-functioning market for government securities. However, many countries also stressed the need for a sound macroeconomic policy framework, characterized by an appropriate exchange rate regime, a monetary policy framework that is credibly focused on the pursuit of price stability, sustainable levels of public debt, a sound external position, and a well-supervised financial system. Such a framework is an important underpinning to instilling confidence among financial market participants that they can invest in government securities with a minimum of uncertainty. It is thus an important precondition if debt managers are to succeed in achieving a debt structure that reflects the government's preferred cost/risk trade-off and helping the country at large to minimize its vulnerability to economic and financial shocks. Indeed, through their links to financial markets and their risk management activities, government debt managers are well positioned to gauge the effects of government financing requirements and debt levels on borrowing costs, and to communicate this information to fiscal policy advisers.

Finally, although the examples of debt management practices presented in the case studies and the lessons drawn here offer some practical guidance for policymakers in all countries that are striving to strengthen the quality of their public debt management and reduce their country's vulnerability to economic and financial shocks, they are especially relevant for the heavily indebted poor countries (HIPCs) and developing transition economies. These are at an earlier stage of developing their capacity in public debt management. For them, in addition to continuing to strengthen their budget and cash management functions, an important priority will be to draw from the experiences outlined in the case studies to build a proper foundation for conducting debt management. In this regard, some important first steps for many of these countries are the need to introduce appropriate governance and institutional structures so that the operational and financial risks associated with debt management are properly managed, the need to develop information systems that fully capture the financial characteristics of all of the government's financial obligations and contingent liabilities, and the need to develop a debt strategy that encompasses both domestic and external debt. The last is especially important, and the experiences of the countries covered by the case studies suggest that the development of a domestic debt market can play an important role over time in helping to broaden the range of borrowing opportunities for a country, making it easier for it to achieve its desired cost/risk trade-off.

I

IMPLEMENTING THE GUIDELINES IN PRACTICE

1
Introduction

A government's debt portfolio is usually the largest financial portfolio in the country. It often contains complex financial structures and can create substantial balance-sheet risk for the government. Large and poorly structured debt portfolios also make governments more vulnerable to economic and financial shocks and have often been a major factor in economic crises. Recognizing the important role that public debt management can play in helping countries cope with economic and financial shocks, the International Monetary and Financial Committee (IMFC)[1] requested that staff from the International Monetary Fund and World Bank work together in cooperation with national debt management experts to develop a set of guidelines on public debt management to assist countries in their efforts to reduce financial vulnerability. The IMFC's request, which was endorsed by the Financial Stability Forum, was made as part of a search for broad principles that could help governments improve the quality of their policy frameworks for managing the effects of volatility in the international monetary and financial system.

By involving national debt management authorities in the preparation of the guidelines, the process sought to strengthen countries' sense of ownership of them and helped to ensure that they are in line with sound practice. Government debt managers from about 30 countries provided input to an initial draft that was discussed by the Executive Boards of the IMF and World Bank in July 2000. Following these discussions, more than 300 representatives from 122 countries attended five outreach conferences on the guidelines in Abu Dhabi, United Arab Emirates; Hong Kong Special Administrative Region; Johannesburg, South Africa; London, United Kingdom; and Santiago, Chile.[2] The feedback provided was taken into account in the final version that was approved by the Executive Boards of the two institutions in March 2001, and endorsed by the IMFC and the Development Committee[3] at their meetings in April 2001. Since then, the guidelines have been available on the IMF and World Bank web sites in five languages (English, French, Spanish, Russian, and Arabic), and a hard copy version was published by the two institutions in September 2001.[4] The guidelines are summarized in Appendix I.

In the course of the Board discussions, the Executive Directors of the IMF and the World Bank asked their staff to prepare an accompanying document to the guidelines that would contain sample case studies of countries that are developing strong systems of public debt management. At the same time, the Boards requested that this report should not expand or add to the guidelines, but instead delineate the experiences of various countries in the form of case studies. In response, staff from the IMF and the World Bank have prepared this document, which contains 18 country case studies to illustrate how a range of countries from around the world and at different stages of economic and financial development are developing their capacity in debt management in a manner consistent with the guidelines. The diverse nature of the countries represented in the case studies is illustrated by the economic and financial indicators presented in Table I.1. The experience of these countries should offer some useful practical suggestions of the kinds

of steps that other countries could take as they strive to build their capacity in government debt management.

In line with the process adopted for the guidelines, the preparation of the accompanying document has sought to foster countries' sense of ownership of the product and ensure that the descriptions of individual country practice and the lessons learned are well grounded. The 18 country case studies were prepared by government debt managers coordinated by IMF and World Bank staff. They cover both their domestic debt management and foreign financing activities. After collecting the information and preparing initial drafts of the case studies, the officials involved in preparing the case studies were invited to an outreach conference in Washington in September 2002 to discuss the conclusions drawn from the cases by IMF and World Bank staff, as well as the document as a whole.

Table I.1. Selected Macroeconomic and Financial Indicators for Case Study Countries in 2001

	Nominal GDP per capita (US$)	General government net debt (%GDP)	Broad money (M2) (%GDP)	Stock market capitalization (1999 data) (%GDP)	Standard and Poor's long-term debt ratings		Moody's long-term debt ratings
					Foreign currency	Local currency	
Brazil	2,986	56	25	30	BB–	BB+	B1
Colombia	2,021	47[a]	31	13	BB	BBB	Ba2
Denmark	30,160	39	39	60	AAA	AAA	Aaa
India	466	90	65	41	BB	BBB–	Ba2
Ireland	26,596	25	n.a.[b]	45	AAA	AAA	Aaa
Italy	18,904	104	n.a.[b]	62	AA	AA	Aaa
Jamaica	3,758	130[c]	44	38	B+	BB–	Ba3
Japan	32,637	66	131	105	AA	AA	Aa1
Mexico	6,031	42	29	32	BBB–	A–	Baa2
Morocco	1,147	76	75	39	BB	BBB	Ba1
New Zealand	12,687	18	89	52	AA+	AAA	Aa2
Poland	4,562	36	46	19	BBB+	A+	Baa1
Portugal	10,587	59[a]	n.a.[b]	58	AA	AA	Aa2
Slovenia	10,605	1	52	11	A	AA	A2
South Africa	2,490	43[a]	60	200	BBB–	A–	Baa2
Sweden	23,547	–3	46	156	AA+	AAA	Aa1
United Kingdom	23,765	31	95	203	AAA	AAA	Aaa
United States	36,716	42	53	182	AAA	AAA	Aaa

a. Gross debt as a percent of GDP.
b. M2 data are not available at the national level for members of the European Monetary Union.
c. End of fiscal year 2001–02.
Source: IMF *World Economic Outlook*, Bankscope databases, and IMF staff estimates.

What Is Public Debt Management and Why Is It Important?

Public debt management is the process of establishing and executing a strategy for managing the government's debt to raise the required amount of funding, pursue its cost/risk objectives, and meet any other public debt management goals the government may have set, such as developing and maintaining an efficient and liquid market for government securities.

In a broader macroeconomic context for public policy, governments should seek to ensure that both the level and the rate of growth in their public debt are fundamentally sustainable over time and can be serviced under a wide range of circumstances while meeting cost/risk objectives. Government debt managers share fiscal and monetary policy advisers' concerns that public sector indebtedness remains on a sustainable path and that a credible strategy is in place to reduce excessive levels of debt. Debt managers should ensure that the fiscal authorities are aware of the impact of government financing requirements and debt levels on borrowing costs.[5] Examples of indicators that address the issue of debt sustainability include the public sector debt-service ratio and ratios of public debt to GDP and to tax revenue.[6]

Every government faces policy choices concerning debt management objectives, its preferred risk tolerance, which part of the government balance sheet those managing debt should be responsible for, how to manage contingent liabilities, and how to establish sound governance for public debt management. On many of these issues, there is increasing convergence in the global debt management community on what are considered prudent sovereign debt management practices that can also reduce vulnerability to contagion and financial shocks. These include (a) recognition of the benefits of clear objectives for debt management; (b) weighing risks against cost considerations; (c) the separation and coordination of debt and monetary management objectives and accountabilities; (d) a limit on debt expansion; (e) the need to carefully manage refinancing and market risks and the interest costs of debt burdens; (f) the necessity of developing a sound institutional structure and policies for reducing operational risk, including clear delegation of responsibilities and associated accountabilities among government agencies involved in debt management; and (g) the need to carefully identify and manage the risks associated with contingent liabilities.

Public debt management problems often originate in the lack of attention paid by policymakers to the benefits of having a prudent debt management strategy and the costs of weak macroeconomic management and excessive debt levels. In the first case, authorities should pay greater attention to the benefits of having a prudent debt management strategy, framework, and policies that are coordinated with a sound macropolicy framework. In the second, inappropriate fiscal, monetary, or exchange rate policies generate uncertainty in financial markets regarding the future returns available on local currency–denominated investments, thereby inducing investors to demand higher risk premiums. Particularly in developing and emerging markets, borrowers and lenders alike may refrain from entering into longer-term commitments, which can stifle the development of domestic financial markets and severely hinder debt managers' efforts to protect the government from excessive rollover and foreign exchange risk. A good track record of implementing sound macropolicies can help to alleviate this uncertainty. This should be supplemented with appropriate technical infrastructure—such as a central registry and payments and settlement systems—to facilitate the development of domestic financial markets.

In addition, poorly structured debt in terms of maturity, currency, or interest rate composition and large and unfunded contingent liabilities has been important factors in inducing or propagating economic crises in many countries throughout history. For example, irrespective of the exchange rate regime, or whether domestic or foreign currency debt is involved, crises have often arisen because of an excessive focus by governments on possible cost savings associated with large volumes of short-term or floating-rate debt. This has left government budgets seriously exposed to changing financial market conditions, including changes in the country's creditworthiness, when this debt has to be rolled over. Foreign currency debt also poses particular risks, and excessive reliance on foreign currency debt can lead to exchange rate or monetary pressures or both if investors become reluctant to refinance the government's foreign currency debt. By reducing the risk that the government's own portfolio management will become a source of instability for the private sector, prudent government debt management, along with sound policies for managing contingent liabilities, can make countries less susceptible to contagion and financial risk.

The size and complexity of a government's debt portfolio often can generate substantial risk to the government's balance sheet and to the country's financial stability. As noted by the Financial Stability Forum's Working Group on Capital Flows, "recent experience has highlighted the need for governments to limit the build-up of liquidity exposures and other risks that make their economies especially vulnerable to external shocks."[7] Therefore, sound risk management by the public sector is also essential for risk management by other sectors of the economy "because individual entities within the private sector typically are faced with enormous problems when inadequate sovereign risk management generates vulnerability to a liquidity crisis." Sound debt structures help governments reduce their exposure to interest rate, currency, and other risks. Sometimes these risks can be readily addressed by relatively straightforward measures, such as lengthening the maturities of borrowings and paying the associated higher debt-servicing costs (assuming an upward-sloping yield curve), adjusting the amount, maturity, and composition of foreign exchange reserves, and reviewing criteria and governance arrangements for contingent liabilities.

There are, however, limits to what sound debt management policies can deliver in and of themselves. Sound debt management policies are no panacea or substitute for sound fiscal and monetary management. If macroeconomic policy settings are poor, sound sovereign debt management may not by itself prevent any crisis. Even so, sound debt management policies can reduce susceptibility to contagion and financial risk by playing a catalytic role for broader financial market development and financial deepening.

Purpose of the Guidelines

The guidelines are designed to assist policymakers in considering reforms to strengthen the quality of their public debt management and reduce their country's vulnerability to domestic and international financial shocks. Vulnerability is often greater for smaller and emerging market countries because their economies may be less diversified, have smaller bases of domestic financial savings (relative to GDP), and less developed financial systems. They could also be more susceptible to financial contagion, if foreign investor exposures are significant, through the relative magnitudes of capital flows. As a result, the guidelines should be considered within a broader context of the factors and forces more generally affecting a government's liquidity and the management of its balance sheet. Governments often manage large foreign exchange reserves portfolios, their fiscal positions are frequently subject to real and monetary shocks, and they can have large exposures to contingent liabilities and to the consequences of poor balance-sheet management in the private sector. However, irrespective of whether financial shocks originate within the domestic banking sector or from global financial contagion, prudent government debt management policies, along with sound macroeconomic and regulatory policies, are essential for containing the human and output costs associated with such shocks.

The guidelines cover both domestic and external public debt and encompass a broad range of financial claims on the government. They seek to identify areas in which there is broad agreement on what generally constitutes sound practices in public debt management. The guidelines focus on principles applicable to a broad range of countries at different stages of development and with various institutional structures of national debt management. They should not be viewed as a set of binding practices or mandatory standards or codes, nor should they suggest that a unique set of sound practices or prescriptions exists that would apply to all countries in all situations. The guidelines are mainly intended to assist policymakers by disseminating sound practices adopted by member countries in debt management strategy and operations. Their implementation will vary from country to country, depending on each country's circumstances, such as its state of financial development. Heavily indebted poor countries (HIPCs) face special challenges in this regard.[8] The terms and conditions surrounding debt relief provided to them typically include provisions that focus on the need to improve debt management practices in ways that are consistent with the guidelines (see Box I.1).

Building capacity in sovereign debt management can take several years, and country situations and needs vary widely. Their needs are shaped by the capital market constraints they face; the exchange rate regime; the quality of their macroeconomic, fiscal, and regulatory policies; the effec-tiveness of the budget management system; the institutional capacity to design and implement reforms; and the country's credit standing. Capacity building and technical assistance therefore must be carefully tailored to meet stated policy goals, while recogniz-ing the policy settings, institutional framework, technology, and human and financial resources that are available. The guidelines should assist policy advisers and decision makers involved in designing

---

Box I.1. Applying the Guidelines to the HIPCs

The HIPC Initiative was launched by the World Bank and the IMF in 1996 (and later enhanced in 1999) as a compre-hensive effort to eliminate unsustainable debt in the world's poorest, most heavily indebted countries. Through the pro-vision of debt relief to eligible HIPCs that show a strong track record of economic adjustment and reform, the initiative was designed to help these countries achieve a sustainable debt position over the medium term. Insufficient attention paid to public debt management is widely thought to have been one of the most important factors that contributed to the accu-mulation of unsustainable levels of debt in these countries. Together with sound overall macroeconomic policy settings, prudent debt management in the HIPCs remains central to ensuring a durable exit from the unsustainable debt burden.

A recent survey by staff of the World Bank and the IMF revealed that several very important weaknesses continue to exist in key aspects of debt management in the HIPCs, notably in the design of their legal and institutional frameworks, coor-dination of debt management with macroeconomic policies, new borrowing policy, and the human and technical require-ments for performing basic debt management functions.[a] In the area of the legal framework, although most HIPCs have an explicit legal instrument governing the debt office and its functions, the legal framework is not always clearly defined and adequately implemented. In addition, transparency and accountability in debt management, including public access to debt information, require strengthening. Institutional responsibilities for debt management in many HIPCs are also not clearly defined and coordinated. Moreover, their debt management activities are undermined by a number of institutional weaknesses and low implementation capacity due to insufficient human, technical, and financial resources. To overcome these difficulties, a first step could be to implement clear and transparent legal and institutional frameworks. The guide-lines and the governance lessons drawn from the case studies can help HIPCs strengthen their legal and institutional frameworks for debt management. For example, they highlight some ways in which borrowing authority can be delegated from the parliament and the council of ministers to debt managers with appropriate accountability mechanisms, the mer-its of centralizing debt management activities in a single unit, and some ways in which appropriate controls can be intro-duced to manage the operational risks associated with debt management activities. They also illustrate how some countries have taken steps to obtain more control over contingent liabilities issued in the name of the government.

Regarding policy coordination, the survey showed that fewer than half of the HIPCs have in place a comprehensive, forward-looking strategy focused on medium-term debt sustainability. Many do not regularly conduct a debt sustain-ability analysis, and very little coordination of information between debt offices and other agencies involved in macroeconomic management takes place. Clearly, coordination of debt management with macroeconomic policies, as well as regular conduct of debt sustainability analysis, are critical, not only as part of the requirements for the HIPC Initiative process, but also if these countries are not to relapse into an unsustainable debt position. In particular, close coordination among the budget, cash management, and planning functions and the debt management office is essen-tial. Again, the guidelines and the lessons drawn from the case studies provide some insights into how they can develop debt management strategies that pay attention to the medium- to long-term implications of economic poli-cies and the resulting implications for debt sustainability. For example, they show how various countries have built linkages among debt managers, cash managers, and monetary and fiscal policymakers to ensure that relevant infor-mation is regularly shared and their respective policies and operational activities are appropriately coordinated.

(*Box continues on the following page.*)

Box I.1. (continued)

Unsustainable debt burdens in the HIPCs have also resulted from unsound policies regarding new borrowing even after benefiting from concessions, including rescheduling. To date, up to two-thirds of these countries still do not have in place a sound policy framework for new borrowing, a direct consequence of the fact that they have yet to develop a comprehensive debt strategy, and many lack complete information on the total debt they have incurred or guaranteed. Moreover, even though domestic debt is becoming an important aspect of fiscal sustainability in some low-income countries, including the HIPCs, underdeveloped domestic financial markets seriously limit the role of domestic debt in most HIPCs. If they are to ensure long-term sustainability beyond the HIPC Initiative completion point, however, they need to develop borrowing strategies that are clear, transparent, and enforceable and begin to develop a domestic debt market so that they can broaden the range of borrowing options available to them. The guidelines and the case studies offer some lessons on how they could implement a framework that they could not only use to develop an overall debt management strategy—including sound new borrowing policies—and develop their domestic debt markets, but also allow debt managers in these countries to identify and manage the trade-offs between the expected costs and risks in the government debt portfolio. For example, they highlight the benefits of using an asset and liability management (ALM) approach to assessing the debt service costs of different borrowing strategies in tandem with the financial characteristics of government revenues, expenditures, and financial assets. They encourage debt managers to stress test the results obtained so that debt strategy decision makers have an understanding of how the chosen strategy will perform in a variety of economic and financial settings. They also note how increased transparency in debt management activities and the choice of borrowing instruments can be used to promote the development of a liquid market for domestic government securities.

To be able to develop strong systems for debt management in a manner consistent with the guidelines, the HIPCs will continue to need technical assistance to build their debt management capacity. Long-term debt sustainability should be viewed not only in relation to the debt burden but also in terms of the structures, processes, and management information services required to manage the debt burden effectively. The HIPC Initiative process itself recognizes this by focusing on, among other things, the technical assistance requirements of HIPCs reaching the decision point. At the same time, the countries themselves must supplement the assistance efforts by ensuring that there are adequate numbers of motivated staff in debt offices that could benefit from technical assistance. In addition, full political support is critical to the success of any efforts to strengthen debt management capacity.

In general, the guidelines and the lessons drawn from the case studies should be useful for all countries striving to develop their policy frameworks and capacity for debt management, but they are particularly relevant for the HIPCs. For them, the guidelines and lessons drawn can not only facilitate achievement of the decision and completion points of the HIPC Initiative process, but, more important, they can help ensure that debt sustainability is maintained for many years to come.

a. See International Development Association, "External Debt Management in Heavily Indebted Poor Countries," Board Discussion Paper IDA/ SecM2002-0148, (Washington), 2002.

---

debt management reforms as they raise public policy issues that are relevant for all countries. This is the case whether the public debt comprises marketable debt or debt from bilateral or multilateral official sources, although the specific measures to be taken will differ, to take into account a country's circumstances.

Notes

1. The IMFC is an advisory body that reports to the IMF's Board of Governors on issues regarding the management of the international monetary and financial system.

2. In addition, staff from the IMF and the World Bank participated in a seminar on debt and fiscal management in Whistler, Canada, attended by representatives from Western Hemisphere countries, which included a discussion of the draft guidelines.

3. The Development Committee of the Boards of Governors of the IMF and the World Bank advises the two Boards on critical development issues and on the financial resources required to promote economic development in developing countries.

4. International Monetary Fund and the World Bank, 2001, *Guidelines for Public Debt Management* Washington.

5. Excessive levels of debt that result in higher interest rates can have adverse effects on real output. See, for example, A. Alesina, M. de Broeck, A. Prati, and G. Tabellini, "Default Risk on Government Debt in OECD Countries," *Economic Policy: A European Forum* (October 1992), pp. 428–63.

6. *Guidelines for Public Debt Management*, p. 1. For a discussion of indicators of external vulnerability for a country, see International Monetary Fund, *Debt- and Reserve-Related Indicators of External Vulnerability*, SM/00/65 (Washington), 2000.

7. Financial Stability Forum, *Report of the Working Group on Capital Flows*, (Basel), April 5, 2000, p. 2.

8. Forty-one countries are considered to be HIPCs. A list of the HIPCs and an overview of the HIPC Initiative can be found in International Monetary Fund and the World Bank, *Debt Relief for Poverty Reduction: The Role of the Enhanced HIPC Initiative* (Washington), 2001.

2
Lessons from the Country Case Studies

This chapter pulls together the main lessons from the 18 country case studies contained in Part II of the document plus the results of a survey of debt management practices, summarized in Table I.2, to show how many countries at different stages of economic and financial developments are developing their public debt management practices in a manner consistent with the guidelines. The aim is to highlight the different ways in which countries can improve their debt management activities by illustrating the variety of ways that the key principles contained in the guidelines have been implemented in practice. References to specific practices contained in the case studies demonstrate how the guidelines are applied; further details on individual country practices can be found in the country case studies in Part II of the document. Implications of these practices for countries seeking to improve their own debt management capabilities are also discussed. The conclusions are grouped in accordance with the six sections of the guidelines: objectives for debt management and coordination with fiscal and monetary policies, transparency and accountability for debt management activities, institutional framework governing debt management activities, debt management strat-

egy, the framework used for managing risks, and developing and maintaining an efficient market for government securities.

Debt Management Objectives and Coordination

The guidelines in this section address the main objectives for public debt management, the scope of debt management, and the need for coordination among debt management and monetary and fiscal policies. They encourage authorities to consider the risks associated with dangerous debt strategies and structures when they set the objectives for debt managers and suggest that debt management should encompass the main financial obligations over which the central government exercises control. Given the importance of ensuring appropriate coordination among debt management and fiscal and monetary policies, they recommend that authorities share an understanding of the public policy objectives in these domains. They also promote the sharing of information on the government's current and future liquidity needs, but argue

Table I.2. Survey of Debt Management Practices

	Yes		No	
Institutional framework				
Annual borrowing authority	14	78%	4	22%
Debt ceiling limit	10	56%	8	44%
Domestic and foreign currency debt programs managed together	13	76%	4	24%
Separate debt agency	4	22%	14	78%
Separate front and back offices	15	83%	3	17%
Separate risk management unit (middle office)	12	67%	6	33%
Formal guidelines for managing market and credit risk	10	56%	8	44%
Annual debt management reports	15	83%	3	17%
Regular external peer reviews of debt management activities	10	63%	6	38%
Annual audits of debt management transactions	16	89%	2	11%
Code-of-conduct and conflict of interest guidelines for debt management staff	12	67%	6	33%
Business recovery procedures in place	11	69%	4	25%
Portfolio management				
Stress test of market risk exposures	10	59%	7	41%
Trading conducted to profit from expected movements in interest or exchange rates	5	29%	12	71%
Government cash balances managed separately from debt	11	65%	6	35%
Foreign currency borrowing integrated with foreign exchange reserves management	5	31%	11	69%
Specialized management information technology in place for risk management	9	56%	7	44%
Primary market structure for government debt				
Auctions used to issue domestic debt	18	100%	0	0%
UP = uniform price	10	56%	8	44%
MP = multiple price	15	83%	3	17%
Fixed-price syndicates used to issue domestic debt	5	28%	13	72%
Benchmark issues for domestic market	16	89%	2	11%
Preannounced auction schedule	17	94%	1	6%
Central bank participates in the primary market	6	33%	12	67%
only on a competitive basis	6	43%	8	57%
Primary dealer system	13	72%	5	28%
Universal access to auctions	10	56%	8	44%
Limits on foreign participation	1	6%	17	94%
Collective action clause, domestic issues	0	0%	18	100%
Collective action clause, external issues	6	33%	12	67%
Secondary market for government debt				
Over-the-counter (OTC) market	15	88%	2	12%
Exchange-traded market mechanism	14	82%	3	18%
Clearing and settlement systems reflect sound practices	17	94%	1	6%
Limits on foreign participation	1	6%	17	94%
Portfolio management statistics: strategic benchmarks				
Duration	11	65%	6	35%
Term-to-maturity	12	71%	5	29%
Fixed-floating Ratio	12	71%	5	29%
Currency composition	14	88%	2	13%
Are benchmarks publicly disclosed?	8	50%	8	50%
Use of derivatives	9	56%	7	44%

Note: Percentages are computed on the basis of the number of responses to each question because some countries did not answer all of the questions.

that where the level of financial development allows, there should be a separation of debt management and monetary policy objectives and accountabilities.

Application

Objectives

The objectives governing debt management in all 18 countries emphasize the need to ensure that the government's financing needs and its payment obligations are met at the lowest possible cost over the medium to long run. However, although most countries' statement of objectives makes explicit references to the need to manage risks prudently, this is not universal. For example, the goals governing debt management in the United States emphasize the need to "meet the financing needs of the government at the lowest cost over time." Similarly, Jamaica's objectives are defined as "to raise adequate levels of financing on behalf of the Government of Jamaica at minimum costs, while pursuing strategies to ensure that the national public debt progresses to and is maintained at sustainable levels over the medium term." Even though no explicit reference is made to the need to manage risks in a prudent fashion, these countries do not simply strive to minimize costs in the short run without regard to risk.

Many countries also promote the development and maintenance of efficient primary and secondary markets for domestic government securities as an important complementary objective for debt management. In the short run, governments may have to accept higher borrowing costs as they seek to develop a domestic market for their securities. However, most governments are willing to incur these costs because they expect that over time they will be rewarded with lower borrowing costs as the domestic market matures and becomes more liquid across the yield curve. In turn, this also should help them achieve a less risky debt stock, because a well-functioning domestic market would enable them to issue a larger share of their debt in longer-term, fixed-rate, domestic currency–denominated securities and thus reduce interest rate, exchange rate, and rollover risks in the debt stock.[1] For example, countries such as Brazil,

Jamaica, Morocco, and South Africa have focused on the need to develop the domestic debt market as a means of lessening dependence on external sources of financing. And even when this objective is not explicitly included in the list of objectives governing debt management, in practice debt managers play an active role in developing the domestic government securities market. An example in this regard is the active role played by debt managers in many countries in working with market participants to introduce electronic trading in their domestic government debt markets.

Developing the market for government securities can also help to stimulate the development of domestic markets for private securities. For example, in Japan the development of the secondary market for government securities is considered to be an important objective for debt management because this market, by virtue of being a low credit risk, serves as the foundation for domestic financial markets and is by far the most actively traded segment of the domestic bond and debenture market.

Scope

Debt management activities in most countries surveyed encompass the main financial obligations over which the central government exercises control. Where differences arise, they tend to be over the extent to which debt managers play a role in managing retail debt issued directly to households (e.g., nonmarketable savings instruments), contingent liabilities, and debt issued by subnational governments, and also on the extent to which foreign currency debt management is integrated with domestic debt management. For example, in the United Kingdom, the wholesale and retail debt programs are managed by separate agencies, but in the United States, both debt programs are managed by a single group. In Ireland, the management of explicit contingent liabilities is handled by the Ministry of Finance (Exchequer), and wholesale debt funding is managed by the debt management agency, whereas in Colombia and Sweden, debt managers play an active role in the management of explicit contingent liabilities. The Colombian approach reflects, in part, a response to past experience where these obligations had grown rapidly as a result of weak oversight and inappropriate pricing. In the latter two countries, involving debt managers in the valuation of explicit contingent liabilities enabled governments to tap the expertise needed to price them in a more rigorous fashion.

Most national debt managers do not play a role in the management of debt issued by other levels of government, because the national governments typically are not liable for debts incurred by those governments. The United States is a good example in this regard. However, in Colombia and India, debt managers are actively involved in the management of debt at both national and subnational levels of government. In Colombia, difficulties encountered by some other Latin American countries due to excessive borrowing by subnational governments led federal debt managers to set limits on subnational government borrowing to ensure that the financial condition of these governments does not undermine the health of federal finances. In India, the involvement of the central bank in the management of the debts of the states is a voluntary contractual arrangement that enables the states to access the debt management expertise and resources that exist within the central bank.

Even if national debt managers are not directly involved in the management of debt issued by other levels of government, recent financial crises have shown that these debts can contribute to financial instability. Thus, the national government in some countries, such as Italy, requires other levels of government to provide it with information on their borrowing activities. In addition, situations can arise where the national government may need to play a role in managing these debts even if it does not directly involve the national debt managers. For example, when the Brazilian central government refinanced debts issued by Brazilian states in 1997 and municipalities in 1999, as a condition of these refinancing programs, the Brazilian Treasury established contracts with these subnational borrowers. These contracts have strict rules on subnational spending and new borrowings. Adherence to these rules and those governments' fiscal situations are regularly monitored by the treasury.

Coordination with monetary and fiscal policies

The industrial countries have advanced the furthest in separating the objectives and accountabilities of debt management from those of monetary policy and introducing appropriate mechanisms for sharing information between debt managers and the central bank on government cash flows. This is most evident for those countries surveyed that are members of the European Economic and Monetary Union (EMU), because monetary policy is conducted by the European System of Central Banks (ESCB), and debt management is conducted by the national authorities, thereby minimizing the risk of possible conflicts of interest between debt management and monetary policy. Provisions in the Maastricht Treaty, which prevent governments from borrowing from their national central banks, and debt limits, which foster debt sustainability, reinforce the separation of debt management from monetary policy in the EMU. Also, there are appropriate information-sharing mechanisms in place to ensure that the national central banks have the information they need on their governments' liquidity flows so that they and the European Central Bank can work together to manage the amount of liquidity circulating in the eurosystem. For example, in Italy, debt managers from the Italian Treasury continuously monitor and formulate projections of expected government cash flows, taking into account the usual annual cyclical and extraordinary patterns of revenues and expenditures. In addition, debt managers and the Bank of Italy regularly exchange information on the movements of cash in and out of the cash account that the treasury holds with the bank, through which most government cash flows are channeled. To ensure proper financial control over the government's finances, only the treasury is authorized to transact through this account.

The industrialized countries surveyed have also taken steps to ensure that debt managers and central banks coordinate their activities in financial markets so that they are not operating at cross-purposes. In the United Kingdom, for example, the Debt Management Office (DMO) avoids holding auctions at times when the Bank of England is conducting money market operations, and it does not hold reverse repo tenders at the 14-day maturity range. It also does not conduct ad hoc tenders on days when the bank's Monetary Policy Committee is announcing its interest rate settings. However, these restrictions do not apply to bilateral operations conducted by the DMO because of their relatively low market profile compared with auctions. An example of what can happen when there is insufficient coordination at an operating level was cited by one country at the outreach conference. It admitted that a past failure to coordinate activities between the central bank and debt managers in financial markets led to an awkward situation where the ministry of finance was repaying foreign currency debt at the same time as the central bank was in need of foreign exchange reserves.

Industrial countries have also found ways to deal with the potential conflicts that can arise between central banks and debt managers when central banks seek to use government securities in their open market operations. This issue is especially acute when government borrowing requirements are modest or nonexistent, but the central bank needs a large volume of low-risk assets for use in implementing monetary policy. In the EMU, for example, the ESCB has developed a broad list of public and private securities that it is willing to use in its open market operations so as to avoid the need to rely strictly on government securities. Similar steps have also been taken by central banks in the other industrial countries surveyed.[2]

The coordination challenges are more acute for emerging market and developing countries that do not have well-developed financial markets. The lack of central bank independence and the absence of well-developed domestic markets make it difficult for them to wean governments from central bank credit. This also makes it difficult to separate debt management and monetary policy objectives, because both activities often need to rely on the same market instruments and are forced to operate at the short end of the yield curve.

Many countries, such as Poland, have also experienced difficulties in projecting government revenues and expenditures[3] and establishing appropriate coordination mechanisms and information-sharing arrangements between the ministry of finance and the central bank.[4] Nonetheless, some

have taken important steps toward ensuring proper coordination between debt management and monetary policy activities. For example, in Brazil and Colombia, debt managers and central bankers regularly meet to share information and construct projections of the government's current and future liquidity needs.[5] In Mexico, debt management, fiscal policy, and monetary policy are formulated using a common set of economic and fiscal assumptions. Moreover, the Mexican central bank acts as the financial agent of the government in many transactions. This helps to cement a continuous working relationship in Mexico among fiscal, debt management, and monetary policy authorities and foster the appropriate sharing of information. In Slovenia, the central bank is given an opportunity to comment ahead of time on the annual financing program contained within the fiscal documents, and the government is legally prohibited from borrowing directly from the central bank. In addition, under a formal agreement, the Slovenian Ministry of Finance supplies the central bank with regularly updated forecasts of projected day-to-day cash flows of all government revenues and expenditures over one- and three-month horizons. Officials from both institutions also meet regularly to share information on the technical details regarding the implementation of their respective policies.

Among other emerging market countries—in Jamaica, for example—the transfer of debt management activities from the central bank to the Ministry of Finance and Planning has resulted in greater coordination of fiscal policy and debt management activities, and, as in many countries, it has also allowed for a more clearly defined set of debt management objectives that are determined independently of monetary policy considerations. At the policy level, there are regular meetings between senior officials of the planning authorities—the Ministry of Finance and Planning, the Bank of Jamaica, the Planning Institute of Jamaica, and the Statistical Institute of Jamaica—to ensure consistency in the government's economic and financial program. At the technical level, there are regular weekly meetings where information is shared on the government's liquidity requirements and borrowing programs, as well as on current monetary conditions and developments in financial markets. In India, the requisite coordination among debt management, fiscal, and monetary policies is achieved through various regular meetings within the central bank, as well as through regular discussions between central bank and Ministry of Finance staff on the government's fiscal situation and the implications for borrowing requirements. In addition, debt management officials attend the monthly monetary policy strategy meeting, and there is an annual pre-budget exercise that seeks to ensure consistency between the monetary and fiscal programs (at both the central and state government levels). However, the Indian authorities believe that a formal separation of debt management from monetary policy in the future would depend on the development of domestic financial markets, the achievement of reasonable control over the fiscal deficit, and legislative changes. In Morocco, the Treasury and External Finance Department, which is responsible for debt management, participates actively in defining the orientations of the budget law, particularly the level of the budget deficit and the resources to cover it.

Implementation considerations

The introduction of appropriate, well-articulated objectives for debt management is an important step that can be introduced by any country regardless of its state of economic and financial development. Indeed, in recent years, many countries have introduced objectives that explicitly mention the need to manage risks as well as achieve low funding costs for the government, or at least make clear that the focus on costs is over a medium- to long-run horizon so that debt managers are not tempted to pursue short-term debt-service cost savings at the expense of taking on dangerous debt structures that expose them to a higher risk of sovereign default. Highlighting the cost/risk trade-off in the objectives can be a useful way of anchoring ensuing discussions on debt management strategy and the execution of borrowing decisions.

Country circumstances, such as the state of domestic financial markets and the degree of central bank independence, play an important role in determining the range of activities that are handled by debt management, as well as the extent to which debt management and monetary policy objectives and

instruments can be separated. Coordination between the budget management and debt management functions is crucial. This is particularly the case in transition and developing economies, where the lack of capacity to accurately forecast government revenues and expenditure flows means that coordination on government liquidity requirements and day-to-day cash flows needs to be frequent and well structured. Nonetheless, as shown above, there are many steps that countries can take to build appropriate coordination mechanisms over time, regardless of their state of economic and financial development.

Particularly for developing and emerging market countries, it is important to have good coordination between the fiscal policy advisers and the debt management function. The debt managers' role here is to convey their views not only on the costs and risks associated with government financing requirements, but also the financial market's views on the sustainability of the government's debt levels.

Transparency and Accountability

The guidelines in this section argue in favor of disclosing the allocation of responsibilities among those responsible for executing different elements of debt management, the objectives for debt management, and the measures of cost/risk that are used. They also encourage countries to disclose materially important aspects of debt management operations and information on the government's financial condition and its financial assets and liabilities, and highlight the need to ensure that debt management activities are audited to foster proper accountability.

Application

Clarity of roles, responsibilities, and objectives of financial agencies responsible for debt management

In many industrial countries, the objectives for debt management and the roles and responsibilities of the institutions involved are explicitly stated in the laws governing debt management activities. This information also is often published in annual reports prepared by debt management authorities and on official web sites. Indeed, as indicated in Table I.2, 15 countries reported that they produce annual debt management reports. Among emerging market and developing countries, there are less formal ways to disclose these items. In Morocco, for example, the Minister of Economy and Finance announces the objectives for debt management each year at an annual press conference, whereas Slovenia announces the goals and instruments for debt management in the annual Financing Program and other policy documents, which are available on government web sites.

Not all countries in the survey set specific targets for risk (such as targets for duration and currency composition)—the results in Table I.2 suggest that about one-third, including Japan and the United States, do not—but most of those that do set targets, disclose them. For example, Brazil's benchmark targets are publicly disclosed in the government's annual borrowing program, which also provides a comprehensive overview of debt management activities and the government's financial situation. Denmark publishes its targets in a special announcement to the stock exchange and as part of its annual report, and Sweden's targets are published in the annual debt management guidelines given to the Swedish National Debt Office (SNDO) by the government (cabinet) before the start of the fiscal year. In Italy, public disclosure of strategic cost/risk analysis is at an early stage of development; however, current versions are available on the Italian Treasury's web site.

Public availability of information on debt management policies

All countries disclose materially important aspects of their debt management operations and information on the government's financial condition and its financial assets and liabilities. The Italian Treasury, for example, maintains an extensive web site that includes information on the government's annual auction calendar, the quarterly issuing program, tender announcements, auction results, and information on government securities and the primary dealers in Italian government securities markets.

Among emerging market countries, the Jamaican government's debt strategy is presented to Parliament at the start of the fiscal year in the form of a Ministry Paper that has widespread public distribution and is available on the ministry's web site. Comprehensive information on Jamaica's debt is also available on the ministry's web site. In addition, the rules for participating in primary debt auctions are widely disclosed, and notices for future domestic debt issues and auction results are reported through print and electronic media and on the ministry's web site. In India, an auction calendar was introduced in April 2002, which has improved the transparency of the borrowing program. In addition, the Reserve Bank of India regularly issues statistical information on the primary and secondary markets for government securities, and it began issuing data on trades in government securities on a real-time basis through its web site in October 2002. In Morocco, the Minister of Economy and Finance's annual press conference also includes a presentation on the key results and statistics on government debt for the previous year plus an overview of the measures and actions to be implemented in the coming year. Moroccan authorities also issue monthly announcements on the results from the previous month's auctions and details of upcoming auctions, and they hold regular meetings with market participants to enhance their understanding of debt management activities.

Accountability and assurances of integrity by agencies responsible for debt management

Almost all countries' debt management activities are audited annually by a separate government-auditing agency that reports its findings to parliament. The data in Table I.2 indicated that 16 countries have annual debt management audits, and 10 have regular external peer reviews. For example, in Ireland, the annual accounts are audited by the state auditor (Comptroller and Auditor General), even though the Irish debt management agency engages a major international accounting firm to undertake an internal audit of all data, systems, and controls. In Denmark, the state auditor (Auditor General) audits government debt management with the help of the central bank's internal audit department. In India, however, separate financial accounts for the debt management operations at the central bank are not prepared and thus cannot be subjected to a formal audit. Although accounting for government debt is done by the government's Controller General of Accounts, the accounts are subject to audit by the Comptroller and Auditor General of Accounts, a constitutional body. The relevant central bank departments are also subjected to an internal management audit and concurrent audit.

Implementation considerations

All countries surveyed issue a wide range of information on their debt management objectives, issuance procedures, and financial requirements to market participants and the general public, and the level of disclosure does not appear to be overly dependent on a country's state of economic and financial development. This process has been helped immeasurably by the introduction of the Internet, which provides a vehicle for issuing this information in a cost-effective manner to a worldwide audience. However, as noted in Box I.1 for HIPCs, for many developing countries, an important step toward improving transparency in their debt management activities is obtaining complete and reliable data on their debt obligations. Such a step is a necessary precondition to operating in a manner consistent with the disclosure requirements of the guidelines.

Institutional Framework

The guidelines in this section address the importance of sound governance and good management of operational risk. They recommend that the authority to borrow and undertake other transactions related to debt management as well as the organizational framework be clear and well specified. To reduce operational risk, they highlight the need for well-articulated responsibilities for staff and a system of clear monitoring and control policies and reporting arrangements. They also stress the importance of separating the execution of market transactions (front office) from the entering of transactions into the accounting systems (back office). The development of an accurate and comprehensive management information system, a code of conduct, conflict-of-interest guidelines, and sound business recovery procedures is also encouraged.

Application

Governance

In all of the countries surveyed, the legal authority to borrow in the name of the central government rests with the parliament or congressional legislative body. However, practices differ with respect to the delegation of borrowing power from the parliament to debt managers. In most of the countries, legislation has been enacted authorizing the ministry (or minister) of finance (or its equivalent) to borrow on behalf of the government. In some others, that power has been delegated to the council of ministers (the cabinet) and, in one case (India), directly to the central bank. Whether the delegation is to the council of ministers, the ministry, or the minister of finance seems to be more of a formality that recognizes country conventions regarding the decision making within the government than a practical matter.

The mandate to borrow is usually restricted, either by a borrowing limit expressed in net or gross terms or by a clause regarding the purpose of the borrowing. Most countries surveyed rely on borrowing limits (Table I.2) defined in terms of a debt ceiling or an annual borrowing limit. The most common structure is that the parliament sets an annual limit in connection with the approval of the fiscal budget, which then functions as a means for it to control the budget. With the "purpose" clause, the mandate is restricted to certain borrowing purposes, the main ones being to finance the budget deficit and refinance existing obligations. In practice, the parliament has significant control over the debt, even when the borrowing is restricted to certain purposes. The main purpose is always to cover any budget deficit, which the parliament influences when it approves the expenditures and tax measures contained in the budget. If the deficit deviates significantly from the path projected in the budget, it is possible for the parliament to intervene, either during the fiscal year or by modifying the budget for subsequent fiscal years.

Another example of a legislative debt ceiling is the one used by Poland, a prospective EMU member.

Poland has inserted into its Constitution a requirement that total government debt, augmented by the amount of anticipated disbursements on guarantees, is not allowed to exceed 60 percent of GDP, the debt limit stipulated by the Maastricht Treaty. Denmark and the United States are examples of other countries that also have legislative limits on the stock of debt outstanding.

The country with the most open mandate is the United Kingdom, where the National Loans Act of 1968 permits the Treasury to raise any money that it considers expedient for the purpose of promoting sound monetary conditions and in such manner and on such terms and conditions as the Treasury sees fit. However, the U.K. Parliament has an indirect influence on the size of the deficit, and hence the debt level, in that it approves tax rates and the government's spending plans. Moreover, in the current fiscal policy framework, the government has the stated objective to limit net debt to a maximum of 40 percent of GDP.

Delegation of debt management authority from the council of ministers or the ministry of finance to the unit responsible for the debt management is usually stipulated in the form of either a governmental ordinance or a power of attorney. However, most countries surveyed ensure that the government or the ministry retains the power to decide on the debt management strategy, normally after considering a proposal from the debt managers. Most countries, especially those with a separate debt agency, have adopted formal guidelines for that purpose. At the outreach conference, it was noted that it is important to ensure that decision makers are fully informed about the consequences of their chosen debt management strategy. In one country, the failure to do so left its debt managers exposed to criticism when the debt strategy did not achieve the expected results. In addition, some other countries admitted that in the past, the lack of clear objectives and weak governance arrangements led to political pressure on them to focus on achieving short-term debt-service cost savings at the expense of leaving the debt portfolio exposed to the risk of higher debt-service costs in the future. In one country, this also led to an awkward situation where political interference in the timing of debt issues forced the debt managers to raise a sig-

nificant amount of the annual borrowing requirement toward the end of the fiscal year, after it became apparent that interest rates were not going to evolve as expected.

The details contained in these guidelines differ across countries. In Sweden, for example, the guidelines are set each year by the Council of Ministers, and they specify targets for the amount of foreign currency debt, inflation-linked debt, and nominal domestic currency debt. They also indicate the government's preferred average duration for total nominal debt, the maturity profile of the total debt, and rules for the evaluation of the debt management. In Portugal, which also has a separate debt agency, the guidelines are determined by three different decisions. First, the Minister of Finance sets long-term benchmarks for the composition of the debt portfolio. These reflect selected targets concerning the duration, currency risk, and refinancing risk, and they are used to evaluate the cost and performance of the debt portfolio. Second, the government (Council of Ministers) specifies annually which debt instruments are to be used and their respective gross borrowing limits. Finally, the Minister of Finance annually approves guidelines for specific operations, such as buybacks; repos; the issuing strategy in terms of instruments, maturities, timing, and placement procedures; measures regarding the marketing of the debt; and the relationship with the primary dealers and other financial intermediaries.

The case studies reveal a clear trend toward centralizing public debt management functions. Most countries have placed them in the ministry of finance. For example, as mentioned previously, Jamaica centralized the core debt management functions in the Debt Management Unit of the Ministry of Finance and Planning in 1998. Before then, they had been divided between the ministry and the central bank. In the same year, Poland also centralized its domestic and foreign debt management in the Public Debt Department of the Ministry of Finance. Brazil plans to centralize all aspects of debt management within the Treasury in September 2003; the central bank currently handles the front office activities associated with international capital market borrowings, and domestic debt management is handled by the Treasury. Four countries (Ireland, Portugal, Sweden, and the United Kingdom) have located their debt agencies outside the Ministry of Finance in that these agencies are from an organizational point of view not directly part of the ministry (Table I.2). These agencies also have some independence regarding staffing policies, and they are physically located in offices outside the ministry. However, they report to and their activities are evaluated by the Council of Ministers or the Ministry of Finance. For example, Portugal consolidated its debt management functions into a separate debt agency in 1997. Before then, this activity had been split between the Treasury Department (external debt and treasury bills) and the Public Credit Department (domestic debt, excluding the treasury bills). In two countries (Denmark and India), the debt management unit is located in the central bank. In Denmark's case, this reflects a consolidation of activities that had previously been split between the ministry and the central bank. In India, the central bank manages domestic debt, and the Ministry of Finance has responsibility for external debt.

All countries with a debt management unit in the ministry of finance, except Slovenia, use the central bank to conduct auctions in the domestic debt market. This stands in contrast to those with separate debt agencies, where all market contacts, including the conduct of auctions, are handled by the agency. In Sweden, even the acquisition of foreign currencies in the market needed to service the external debt has been shifted to the debt agency from the central bank, starting in July 2002.

The rationale behind the different organizational structures differs across countries. For example, although the United Kingdom and Denmark both delegate the management of foreign currency debt and foreign exchange reserves to the central bank, they have taken different approaches in the management of domestic debt. The United Kingdom, which shifted domestic debt management from the central bank to a debt agency in 1998, believes it is important to have separate objectives for monetary policy and domestic debt management to mitigate any perception that the debt management might benefit from inside knowledge over the future path of interest rates. Denmark, which moved debt management functions from the Ministry of Finance to the central bank in 1991, has in place strict fund-

ing rules between debt management and monetary policy, and found that the move to the central bank has helped to centralize the retention of knowledge of most aspects of financial markets within a single authority. Moreover, because Danish interest rates are largely determined by interest rate developments in the euro area, the involvement of the Danish central bank in domestic debt management is unlikely to generate a perception that domestic debt management benefits from inside information on the future path of interest rates.

Ireland and Portugal, which both created separate debt agencies (in 1990 and 1996, respectively), highlighted the need to attract and retain staff with the relevant skills and centralize all debt management functions in one unit. Sweden, whose separate debt agency was founded in 1789, notes the historical reason and that the system provides a clear distribution of responsibilities between the parties concerned. However, it also reflects a long-standing tradition in Sweden of working with small ministries responsible for policy decisions and delegating operational functions to agencies that have separate management teams and are at arm's length from the ministries.

Poland placed debt management activities in the public debt department of the Ministry of Finance on the grounds that at the very early stage of development of its domestic financial market, when the transition to the free market economy had just begun, that department had more instruments to support development of the market, cooperate with other regulatory institutions, and prepare an efficient legal and infrastructure environment. New Zealand, which also chose to set up a unit within the Ministry of Finance (the New Zealand Debt Management Office [NZDMO]) instead of a separate debt agency, suggested that important linkages would otherwise be lost. In addition to debt-servicing forecasts for the budget and other fiscal releases, the NZDMO provides a range of capital markets advice to other sections of Treasury.

The role of the parliament or congress in the management of the debt, apart from delegating its borrowing power, differs among the countries. In Sweden, for example, the Parliament has stated the objective of the central government debt management in an act, and the Council of Ministers is obliged to send an annual report to the Parliament evaluating the management of the debt. In Mexico, the Congress approves the annual limit for net external and domestic borrowing as well as the debt strategy; the latter is scrutinized closely, because debt management issues have been a contributing factor to past financial crises in Mexico. At the end of the year, the Mexican Congress also (through its auditing organization) reviews the accounts and other specific topics that are of interest to its members. In Ireland and the United Kingdom, the chief executive of the debt agency reports directly to the Parliament in the presentation of the accounts.

Management of internal operations

Fifteen countries have separate front and back offices for the management of the debt (Table I.2). Twelve countries, including all of the countries that actively trade to profit from expected movements in interest rates or exchange rates, have a separate middle office, too (Table I.2). From an operational risk point of view, it is useful to have a separate middle office in a debt unit where many transactions are being conducted regularly. Its main functions are to ensure that all transactions done by the front office are within predetermined risk limits, assess the performance (where relevant) of the front office's trading against a strategic benchmark portfolio, set proper operational procedures and ensure that they are followed, and, in some countries, play a leading role in the development of the debt management strategy.

Most of the surveyed countries have code-of-conduct and conflict-of-interest guidelines for the debt management staff and business recovery procedures in place (Table I.2). Brazil has also created an Ethics and Professional Conduct Committee.

Some countries, such as Ireland, New Zealand, Portugal, Sweden, and the United Kingdom, have boards that provide external input on specific areas of expertise. In Ireland, the board assists and advises the National Treasury Management Agency (NTMA) (the Irish debt agency) on matters referred to it by the NTMA. In New Zealand, the board has a quality assurance role. It oversees the NZDMO's activities, the risk management framework, and the business

plan, and reports directly to the Secretary of the Treasury. In Portugal, it plays an advisory role on strategic matters. Sweden has a decision-making board, chaired by the Director General of the SNDO. Of the external members, four are members of Parliament and the other three have professional experience as economists. In the United Kingdom, the board advises the DMO's senior management on strategic, operational, and management issues, but only in an advisory capacity because it has no formal decision-making role.

Many debt managers noted that they are confronted with significant challenges in attracting and retaining staff because of intense competition for such staff from the private sector. As described above, in some cases, this has been one of the driving forces behind the transfer of the debt management function from the ministry of finance to either the central bank or to a separate debt agency. To alleviate this problem, many countries have sought to offer their staff challenging and interesting tasks, good training, and further education. Brazil, for instance, offers a graduate course in debt management. Slovenia also supports postgraduate education through time-off allowances and payment of tuition fees.

In all of the cases where management information systems were discussed (Colombia, Denmark, Ireland, Morocco, New Zealand, and Portugal), countries have experimented with different approaches. Some have developed their own systems, and others purchased off-the-shelf systems and customized them to meet their particular needs. For example, New Zealand relied on its own internally developed system until the mid-1990s, when it acquired a commercial system. However, significant customization was required, and work on it has continued over the years to meet the NZDMO's evolving requirements.

Portugal provides an example of a strategy to reduce operational risk. When the Portuguese debt agency was created, an analysis of operational risk led to the adoption of an organizational structure based on the financial industry standard of front, middle, and back office areas with clearly segregated functions and responsibilities. It has since been a focus of attention by means of three main initiatives, namely a significant investment in information technology

(IT) (including the purchase of a management information system), followed by the development of a manual of internal operating procedures, and finally attracting and retaining specialized expertise. In the future, these measures will be supplemented with an internal auditing function to complement the external auditing that is already done by the Audit Court.

Implementation considerations

The case studies show that only four countries (Ireland, Portugal, Sweden, and the United Kingdom), all highly developed and with well-functioning domestic capital markets, have created separate debt agencies for the management of the central government debt. However, in other countries, there are ongoing discussions about the merits of such an agency. One argument, which is often mentioned in favor of a separate agency, is that it provides for more focused debt management policy, in part because there is a top management whose main responsibility is debt management, not fiscal or monetary policy, and thus has the time to focus on debt management issues. When debt management is part of the ministry of finance or central bank, there is a risk that debt management policy could be a secondary consideration. This focus fosters professionalism and gives debt management staff attention from top management, which together with competitive salaries, makes it easier to hire and retain skilled staff. However, as noted by some countries at the outreach conference, if one goes down this path, the introduction of a separate debt agency should be accompanied by strong internal governance, accountability, and transparency mechanisms to ensure that the agency performs as expected and is held accountable for decisions within its remit.

This is not to say that every country should have a separate debt agency. A common argument for placing the debt office in the ministry of finance is the importance of maintaining key linkages to other parts of the government, such as budget and fiscal policy. Especially in countries with less developed financial markets, coordination of debt management policy with that of fiscal and monetary policy is of such importance that centralization of responsibilities either in the ministry of finance or the central bank often makes sense. Moreover, even when separate, the debt agency always reports to the council of ministers (cabinet) or ministry of finance, which decides on the debt management strategy and evaluates the work of the debt agency. To fulfill these duties, the ministry of Finance may also find it advantageous to have some staff skilled in debt management.

The role of the parliament or congress differs among the countries, partly because of historical reasons. However, if the legislature is the political body that approves tax and spending measures, which is normally the case, one could argue that it should also approve overall borrowing by the government as well as broad debt management policy issues, such as debt limits and the objectives for managing debt, given that the management of debt ultimately has significant repercussions for future tax and spending levels. Within these limits and policy objectives, the council of ministers and debt managers should have sufficient authority to implement the approved policies as they deem appropriate, subject to being held accountable for their actions by the legislature.

Debt Management Strategy

The guidelines in this section stress the importance of monitoring and assessing the risks in the debt structure, and they recommend that the financial and other risk characteristics of the government's cash flows be considered when setting the desired debt structure. In particular, the debt manager should carefully assess and manage the risks associated with foreign currency and short-term or floating-rate debt, and ensure there is sufficient access to cash to avoid the risk of not being able to honor financial obligations when they fall due.

Application

Debt managers' risk awareness is high, and most have formal guidelines for managing market and credit risk (see Table I.2). However, the risks that countries focus on vary depending on country-specific circumstances. For example, Colombia aims to limit the exposure of its foreign currency debt portfolio to market shocks and international crises, whereas Italy concentrates its efforts on reducing both interest rate risk and rollover risk after having experienced government indebtedness levels that reached 124 percent of GDP in 1994. Recent financial crises in Latin America and Russia have shown that the management of rollover risk is an especially important task for many developing and emerging market countries. An inability to roll over debt when markets are turbulent can severely compound the effects of economic and financial shocks.

The cases also show a trend toward using an ALM framework, at least conceptually, to assess the risks and cost of the debt portfolio by evaluating the extent to which debt-service costs are correlated with government revenues and noninterest expenditures.[6] One issue that arises is how to measure cost/risk. In Portugal, for example, one of the objectives, stated in the Portuguese Public Debt Law, is to ensure a balanced distribution of debt costs over several years. Against that background and with the focus on budget volatility, the Portuguese debt agency has found it useful to measure market risk on a cash-flow basis. However, it is still working on the development and implementation of an integrated budget-at-risk (BaR) indicator for the debt portfolio. In Sweden, the SNDO is using a cost-to-GDP ratio in its analysis of the costs for different debt portfolios. This is a step in the direction of ALM because the assumption here is that the budget balance covaries with GDP via both tax and expenditure channels. A debt portfolio with a relatively stable cost-to-GDP ratio will thus contribute to deficit (tax) smoothing.

Some countries also explicitly incorporate specific government assets and liabilities (such as foreign exchange reserves and contingent liabilities) into an overall risk management framework. Countries using this approach, or which have started to look at it, are Brazil, Denmark, New Zealand, and the United Kingdom. They have found, for example, that usage of such a framework highlights the benefits of coordinating the maturity and currency composition of foreign currency debt issued by the government with that of the foreign exchange reserves held by either the government or the central bank so as to hedge the government's exposure to interest rate and exchange rate risk. Indeed, in the United Kingdom,

foreign exchange reserves and foreign currency borrowings are managed together by the Bank of England using an ALM framework.

The debt management section of the Danish central bank also manages the assets of the Social Pension Fund. In managing interest rate risk, it integrates assets and liabilities and monitors the duration of the net debt. As a result, a reduction in the duration of net debt can be achieved by raising the duration of the asset portfolio. New Zealand, which has been using the ALM approach for more than a decade, created an Asset and Liability Management Branch in the Treasury in 1997, of which the NZDMO constitutes one part. The ALM strategy is implicitly incorporated into the NZDMO's strategic objective to maximize the long-term economic return on the government's financial assets and debt in the context of the government's fiscal strategy, particularly its aversion to risk. The objective has regard to both the balance sheet and fiscal implications of the debt strategy. Going forward, debt strategy in New Zealand is likely to be influenced by an analysis that is under way in the Treasury and aimed at understanding the financial risks that exist throughout the government's operations, and how its balance sheet is likely to change through time.

Debt management strategies, such as the selection of debt maturities and the choice between raising funds in domestic or foreign currencies, depend to a large degree on the special circumstances in the countries, such as the characteristics of the debt portfolio, the vulnerability of the economy to economic and financial shocks, and the stage of development of the domestic debt market. Brazil, for example, which before the Asian financial crisis sought to lengthen the average term-to-maturity of its debt by issuing longer fixed-rate securities, switched in October 1997 to floating-rate and inflation-indexed securities to achieve a quicker reduction in rollover risk. At that time, investors were more willing to invest for the longer term if the securities in question carried floating-rate or inflation-indexed coupons than if they were fixed for the tenor of the instrument. However, the reduction in rollover risk came at the expense of making Brazil's debt dynamics more sensitive to changes in interest rates. Before the onset of financial market turbulence in 2002, it also sought to reduce its vulnerability to interest rate fluctuations by extending the domestic yield curve and building up cash reserves.

Mexico's experience underlines the need for sound macroeconomic policies, fiscal discipline, and a prudent and consistent debt management policy. In the wake of the 1994–95 financial crisis, when its public finances were undermined by excessive reliance on short-term, foreign currency–linked debt, the government has been actively promoting the development of the domestic debt markets by introducing new instruments and making the necessary regulatory adjustments to reduce its dependence on short-term domestic debt and foreign currency (and foreign currency–linked) debt. Today, Mexico's debt management strategy aims to reduce rollover, interest rate, and exchange rate risks by issuing a combination of domestic currency, medium-term, floating-rate notes and medium- to long-term fixed-rate instruments. The issuance of the floating-rate debt helps to reduce rollover risk. Over time, the issuance of domestic currency fixed-rate instruments at increasingly longer tenors should reduce rollover risk further and, at the same time, lower interest rate and exchange rate risk.

In Morocco, debt managers have sought to reduce debt-service costs of the external debt by exercising debt-equity swap options, triggering cancellation and prepayment rights to retire onerous debt, and by refinancing or revising interest rates as permitted by the loan agreements. They also have a policy of promoting the development of the domestic debt market so that more financing needs can be met in domestic currency.

Turning now to the most developed countries, the United States, for example, has sought to minimize debt-service costs over time by championing a deep and liquid market for U.S. Treasury securities. This has involved taking steps to ensure that treasury securities maintain their consistency and predictability in the financing program, issuing across the yield curve to appeal to the broadest range of investors, and aggregating all the financing needs of the central government into one debt program. Portugal, a participant in the euro area, has a strategy of building a government yield curve of liquid bonds (at least 5 billion outstanding for each series) along different

maturity points. Since 1999, every year the priority has been to launch a new 10-year issue and, second, to launch a new 5-year issue. As part of this strategy, priority has been given to the development of efficient primary and secondary treasury debt markets. At the highest level, New Zealand's strategy regarding domestic debt management is to be transparent and predictable. The NZDMO maintains a mix of fixed- and floating-rate debt and a relatively even maturity profile for debt across the yield curve. It has taken steps to develop the market for domestic government securities, including a derivatives market, which the commitment to transparency, predictability, and evenhandedness supports.

Participation in European Exchange Rate Mechanism II (ERM II) for Denmark and prospective EMU membership for Slovenia are important factors in managing the exchange rate risk of debt issued by these countries. Since 2001, all of Denmark's foreign currency exposure is in euros. In Slovenia, more than 90 percent of its foreign currency exposure is in euro. Slovenia also issues euro-denominated bonds in its domestic market to support the pricing of long-term instruments issued by other Slovenian borrowers.

Although all countries pay close attention to the cost/risk trade-off, some countries with stable macroeconomic conditions, strong fiscal positions, and well-developed domestic debt markets are in a better position than others to pursue cost savings at the expense of some increase in the riskiness of the debt. Sweden, for instance, has decided to have a 2.7-year duration target for its nominal debt, and Denmark has shortened the duration of its debt from 4.4 years at the end of 1998 to 3.4 years at the end of 2001. In both countries, these actions reflect, first, a significant decline in their debt loads in recent years; second, a view that debt-service cost savings can be realized over time in an upward-sloping yield curve environment; and third, a view that these countries are generally well insulated from economic and financial shocks because of their strong macroeconomic policy frameworks.

The benefit of having well-functioning domestic currency markets is also shown in cash management. Most of the countries hold cash balances so that they can honor their financial obligations on time, even when their ability to raise funds in the market is temporarily curtailed or very costly. However, Sweden is sufficiently secure in its ability to access markets at any time that it has opted not to hold cash balances, but instead rely completely on its ability to raise funds in the market. To do that, it is also important to have complete control over the government cash flows, so that the timing of these flows can be managed accordingly.

As will be discussed in more detail below, almost all the surveyed countries are building up, or plan to build up, liquid benchmark securities in their domestic currency markets (Table I.2). The most common methods used to reduce the rollover risk associated with large benchmark securities are buyback or bond-switching operations near the maturity dates.

Countries typically adjust the financial characteristics of their debt portfolios by adjusting the mix of securities issued in their borrowing programs or by repurchasing securities before they mature and replacing them with new ones that better reflect its cost/risk preferences. In addition, as indicated in Table I.2, half of the countries use financial derivatives, mainly interest rate swaps and cross-currency swaps, to separate funding decisions from portfolio management decisions and adjust the risk characteristics of their debt portfolios. However, this is not an option available to all countries. Those with under-developed domestic markets may not have access to domestic derivatives markets, and those with weak credit ratings may not be able to access global derivatives markets at a reasonable cost. Moreover, there is a need for careful management of the counter-party risks associated with derivatives transactions. Denmark, New Zealand, and Sweden, for example, noted that they use credit exposure limits and collateral agreements to reduce the credit (counter-party) risks associated with these transactions.

Implementation considerations

The debt management strategies pursued by countries generally reflect their particular circumstances and their own analysis of the risks associated with their debt portfolios. Thus, it is not surprising that the strategies pursued differ considerably across countries. However, one element that seems to be common across all countries, regardless of their stage of development, is the focus on developing or maintaining the efficiency of the domestic debt market as a means of reducing excessive reliance on short-term and foreign currency-linked debt. Another aspect worthy of note is the move toward using an ALM framework to assess the risks and costs of debt and determine an appropriate debt structure.

Particularly for developing and emerging market countries, the level of the debt and the soundness of the macroeconomic policies are important constraints on the amount of discretion that countries have in setting and pursuing their debt management strategies. Regarding the debt level, decisive factors are the central government's capacity to generate tax revenues and savings, as well as its sensitivity to external shocks.

Risk Management Framework

The guidelines in this section recommend that a framework should be developed to enable debt managers to identify and manage the trade-offs between expected costs and risks in the government debt portfolio. They also argue in favor of stress tests of the debt portfolio as part of the risk assessment, and that the debt manager should consider the impact of contingent liabilities. In addition, they discuss the importance of managing the risks of taking market positions.

Application

The framework used to trade off expected costs and risks in the debt portfolio differs across countries. Most seem to use rather simple models, based on deterministic scenarios, and judgment. However, new risk models are under development in many countries. Only a few (Brazil, Denmark, Colombia, New Zealand, and Sweden) use stochastic simulations. For example, New Zealand developed a stochastic simulation model to improve its understanding of the trade-off between the cost/risk associated with different domestic debt portfolio structures. Most countries also use stress testing as a means to assess the market risks in the debt portfolio and the robustness of different issuance strategies. Stress testing is particularly important for the assessment of debt sustainability.

Consistent with the ALM framework discussed above, most countries measure cost on a cash-flow basis over the medium to long term. This facilitates an analysis of debt in terms of its budget impact. Risk is typically measured in terms of the potential increase in costs resulting from financial and other shocks. Some countries, such as Brazil, Portugal, and Sweden, are experimenting with measures such as cost-to-GDP or concepts such as BaR to reflect the explicit incorporation of a joint analysis of debt and GDP or budget flows to shocks.

Four countries (Brazil, Colombia, Denmark, and New Zealand) use "at-risk" models to quantify the market risks. For example, Colombia uses a debt-service-at-risk (DsaR) model to quantify the maximum debt-service cost of the debt portfolio with 95 percent likelihood. The methodology takes into consideration the exposure to different market variables, such as interest rates, exchange rates, and commodity prices (24.5 percent of the debt is price indexed). For managing the cost/risk dimensions of the debt portfolio, the middle office presents a monthly report of funding alternatives based on DsaR analysis. This report compares the cost of the expected scenario with the 95 percent risk scenario for each of the different funding alternatives. Denmark uses a cost-at-risk (CaR) model to quantify the interest rate risk by simulation of multiple interest scenarios. The model analyzes different strategies, such as the issuing strategy, the amount of buybacks, and the duration target.

Scope for active management

Among the countries in this survey, only Ireland, New Zealand, Portugal, and Sweden actively manage their debt portfolios to profit from expected movements in interest rates and exchange rates. New Zealand and Sweden limit the positions taken to the foreign currency portfolios, but Ireland and Portugal, being relatively small players in the euro area, are prepared to trade the euro segment of their debt. The arguments for position taking vary, and it is worth noting that these countries have centralized their debt management activities outside the central bank. It might be difficult for debt managers in the central bank to take active positions in the market because of concerns that such actions may be seen to convey signals with respect to other policies that affect financial markets. New Zealand argues that temporary pricing imperfections sometimes occur, making it possible to generate profit from tactical trading. In addition, it believes that tactical trading helps to build debt managers' understanding of how various markets operate under a variety of circumstances, which improves the NZDMO's management of the overall portfolio. For example, it suggested that tactical trading enables it to develop and maintain skills in analysis, decision making under uncertainty, deal negotiations, and deal closure. The immediate benefit is a reduced risk of mistakes when transacting and the projection of a more professional image to counter-parties. However, it is important to make sure that tactical trading activities are properly controlled. At the outreach conference, it was noted that one country had used swaps to speculate on an expected convergence in European interest rates in the early 1990s. This strategy led to losses when the European Exchange Rate Mechanism broke down in the autumn of 1992.

To mitigate the market risk associated with the tactical trading, New Zealand uses both value-at-risk (VaR) and stop-loss limits, the determination of which is aided by stress tests of the portfolio. The VaR is measured at a 95 percent confidence level relative to notional benchmark portfolios or subportfolios, which embody the approved strategy. Trading performance is measured on a risk-adjusted basis, using a notional risk capital for market, credit, and operational risk use. The risk-adjusted performance return is defined as the net value added divided by the notional risk capital.

Even if only a few countries are actively taking positions in the market, most of them do try to take advantage of pricing anomalies in the market. The most common approach is to buy back illiquid bond issues, financed through new issues in liquid benchmark securities. Another similar method, noted by Morocco, is to refinance onerous bank loans by exercising prepayment rights in the loan agreements and refinancing the prepayments through new loans with more favorable terms. Other examples include using the swap market to achieve lower borrowing costs. Ireland, for example, obtains cheaper short-term domestic currency funding by issuing commercial paper denominated in U.S. dollars and swapping the proceeds into euros, instead of raising euro-denominated funds.

Contingent liabilities

Most of the case studies did not comment on the management of contingent liabilities.[7] Among the countries that did, only Colombia, Morocco, New Zealand, and Sweden seem to have an organizational structure within the debt management unit or ministry of finance that facilitates the coordination of the management of explicit financial guarantees with the management of the debt. Such coordination is essential, because government guarantees have been significant contributors to the public debt burden in many developing and transition economies. At the outreach conference, some countries noted that the level of these guarantees is typically determined elsewhere in the government, and their contingent nature makes them very difficult to quantify. However, others argued that although their valuation is difficult, they should not be ignored. Consequently, they recommended that these guarantees be borne in mind when setting debt strategy, especially when conducting stress tests of prospective strategies.

None of the countries surveyed appear to involve debt managers in the management of implicit contingent liabilities. The latter finding is not too surprising, because these claims often arise in response to weaknesses in prudential supervision and regulation—areas that are usually outside the scope of debt management. Nonetheless, these claims can pose major risks for governments, as evidenced by the costs imposed on several countries in Asia and Latin America in the 1990s, when governments were forced to recapitalize failed banking systems. Thus, they need to be judged in conjunction with other macroeconomic risk factors. Similarly, national governments in Argentina and Brazil found themselves unexpectedly taking on significant liabilities when they had to assume the liabilities of subnational governments that had borrowed excessively. In Brazil's case, controls have since been placed on subnational government borrowings, and these governments are repaying the amounts refinanced by the national government. As noted previously, the latter issue has led countries such as Brazil and Colombia to set limits on subnational government borrowing, and others regularly monitor these borrowings and ensure that the subnational governments in question have independent sources of revenue to service their obligations.

Implementation considerations

Most of the countries in the case studies rely on fairly simple models to assess the trade-offs between expected costs and risks in the debt portfolios. Some countries may lack enough data needed to run more complicated models. It is also important to bear in mind that the usefulness of all models depends to a large degree on the quality of the data used as inputs and the assumptions that underpin the model. The latter may behave differently in extreme situations, can change over time, and can be influenced by policy responses. Thus, the parameters and assumptions underpinning these models should be regularly reviewed, and it is important to be aware of the limitations and underlying assumptions of the model. These should be carefully described and understood when results are applied in the decision-making process.

Developing and Maintaining an Efficient Market for Government Securities

Most of the guidelines in this section focus on the benefits of governments raising funds using market-based mechanisms in a transparent and predictable fashion, and the merits of a broad investor base for their obligations. Others discuss the benefits of governments and central banks working with market participants to promote the development of resilient secondary markets and the need for sound clearing and settlement systems to handle transactions involving government securities. Further information on the steps that countries can take to develop a domestic government debt market can be found in a handbook published by the World Bank and the IMF in 2001.[8]

Application

Primary market

Most of the countries surveyed use similar techniques for issuing government securities in the domestic market in that all of them except Denmark use pre-announced auctions to issue debt. Most also use multiple-price auction formats for conventional securities and, in some cases, uniform-price formats to issue inflation-indexed instruments, although the U.S. Treasury now issues all of its securities using uniform-price auctions. It shifted away from multiple-price auctions after evidence showed that the range of successful bidders tended to be broader in uniform-price auctions, and that bidders tend to bid more aggressively as a result of a reduction in the so-called winner's curse (the risk that a successful bidder will pay more than the common market value of the security in the postauction secondary market).

The advent of the euro has led to significant changes in the debt management practices of some smaller EMU members. For example, Portugal now uses syndications to launch the first tranche of each new bond, because this tranche corresponds to around 40 percent of the targeted final amount to be issued. It believes that as a small player in the euro government bond market, syndications help it to achieve more control over the issue price and help to foster a broader diversification of the investor base. Auctions are then used for future issues of the same security.

When borrowing in foreign markets, most countries rely on underwriting syndicates to help them price and place securities with foreign investors, because these borrowings are usually not undertaken in sufficient volume or on a regular enough basis to warrant the use of an auction technique. However, some countries, such as Sweden and the United Kingdom, have found it more cost-effective to separate funding decisions from portfolio decisions by using financial derivatives and raise foreign currency funds by issuing more domestic currency debt and swapping it into foreign currency obligations—a technique that has the added benefit of helping to maintain large issuance volumes in domestic markets when domestic borrowing requirements are modest. The largest industrial countries—the United States and Japan—have a long-standing policy of issuing only domestic currency–denominated securities in their domestic markets and avoid raising funds offshore. Potential EMU members, such as Poland and Slovenia, and the ERM II participant, Denmark, prefer to issue euro-denominated securities when raising external financing, because these would ultimately become domestic currency instruments if they join the EMU.

Most countries have taken steps to increase the transparency of the auction process in the domestic market to reduce the amount of uncertainty in the primary market and achieve lower borrowing costs. Almost all countries preannounce their borrowing plans and auction schedules (Table I.2) so that prospective investors can adjust their portfolios ahead of time to make room for new issues of government securities, and the rules and regulations governing the auctions and the roles and responsibilities of primary dealers are publicly disclosed so that market participants fully understand the rules of the game. For example, in Brazil and Poland, the basic rules for treasury bills and bond issuance are covered by ordinances issued by the minister of finance, and the details of specific issues are described in Letters of Issue published on the ministry's web site. Dates of auctions are announced at the beginning of each year in Poland and monthly in Brazil, and a calendar is maintained on the ministry's web site. Two days before the tender in Poland, detailed information on the forthcoming auction is made available on the web site and through Reuters.

Auction processes are also becoming more efficient as countries automate their auction processes and explore the possibility of using the Internet to issue securities. For example, Ireland and Portugal conduct their auctions using the electronic Bloomberg auction system, which has reduced the lag between the close of bidding to the release of auction results to less than 15 minutes. Among emerging market and developing countries, India and Jamaica have moved to introduce electronic bidding in their debt auctions, and Brazil, besides using electronic bidding in its debt auctions since September 1996, began issuing securities to small investors over the Internet in January 2002.

Countries are also taking steps to remove regulations that have created captive investor classes and distorted auction outcomes, and only one country reported limits on foreign participation in auctions (Table I.2). Such regulations have been a particular problem in many emerging market and developing countries, especially where prudential regulations required some institutions to hold a prescribed portion of their assets in government securities. As a result, Morocco and South Africa, for example, took steps to gradually remove these requirements and broaden the base of investors that hold government securities. Although the removal of these requirements may result in interest rates moving up in the short run to market-clearing levels, the ensuing broadening of the investor base should bring about a deeper and more liquid domestic market for government securities. This should result in debt-service cost savings over time as the government is better positioned to implement its preferred debt structure.

One issue of debate is over the merits of using primary dealers to support the issuance of securities in the domestic market.[9] According to Table I.2, 13 countries surveyed have introduced primary dealer systems on the grounds that these institutions help to ensure that auctions are well bid, that there is a regular source of liquidity for the secondary market, and they have found that primary dealers can be a useful source of information for debt managers on market developments and debt management policy issues. Moreover, at the outreach conference, some countries suggested that a primary dealer system offering special privileges can help to encourage market participants to play a role in the development of the market as a whole, especially when the market is at an early stage of development. However, there are several industrial countries—Denmark, Japan, and New Zealand—that have not found it necessary to introduce a primary dealer system. Indeed, at the outreach conference, one country noted that its borrowing costs declined significantly after it abolished its primary dealer system. Similarly, some developing and emerging market countries have questioned the benefits of introducing primary dealer systems because their markets are too small, and the number of mar-

ket participants too few, to warrant such a system. Thus, they have been prepared to let the secondary market participants themselves determine which of them can profit from playing the role of market maker in the secondary market. Moreover, some countries that have primary dealer systems, such as the United States, do not restrict access to the auctions to primary dealers, but also allow other market participants to bid, provided they have a payment mechanism in place to facilitate settlement of their auction obligations. Consequently, each country needs to evaluate its own situation in deciding whether the potential benefits of a primary dealer system outweigh the costs. The trade-off will likely depend on the state of financial market development, and some countries may not need to offer special privileges to encourage market participants to take the lead in developing the market.

To foster deep and liquid markets for their securities, most governments have taken steps to minimize the fragmentation of their debt stock. Sixteen countries reported that they strive to build a limited number of benchmark securities at key points along the yield curve (Table I.2). They generally use a mixture of conventional treasury bills and coupon-bearing bonds that are devoid of embedded option features. These benchmark securities are typically constructed by issuing the same security over the course of several auctions ("reopenings") and, in some cases, by repurchasing older issues before maturity that are no longer actively traded in the market. Extending the yield curve for fixed-rate instruments beyond a limited number of short-term tenors has posed a major challenge for countries that have had a history of weak macroeconomic policy settings. Consequently, Brazil, Colombia, Jamaica, and Mexico, for example, have sought to extend the maturity of their debt by initially offering securities that are indexed to inflation or an exchange rate until such time as they can develop investor interest in longer-term fixed-rate securities.

Despite the desire to minimize the fragmentation of the debt stock, some industrial countries plus South Africa have been working hard to develop a market for government securities that are indexed to inflation. In contrast to emerging market and developing countries, where such instruments are thought to be a useful device for extending the yield curve, the attraction of these instruments for industrial countries and South Africa is that they have enabled some of them to reduce borrowing costs by avoiding the need to compensate investors for the inflation uncertainty premium that is thought to exist in nominal bond yields. This was especially true when these programs were first launched, because, in many cases, the spread between nominal and inflation-indexed yields at that time (an indicator of the market's expectations for future inflation) tended to be above the central bank's stated inflation objective, even though the inflation-indexed securities were less liquid than their nominal counterparts. They also help to reduce the total risk embedded in the debt stock, because the debt-service costs of inflation-indexed securities are not highly correlated with those for conventional securities.[10] That said, most countries have found it difficult to develop a liquid secondary market for inflation-indexed securities, implying that the yields paid by governments may include a premium to compensate investors for their lack of liquidity.

In situations where domestic borrowing requirements are modest or declining over time in response to fiscal surpluses, debt managers in Brazil, Denmark, Ireland, New Zealand, South Africa, Sweden, the United Kingdom, and, to a lesser extent, the United States have repurchased securities that are no longer being actively traded in the market to maximize the size of new debt issues, and they will often offer to exchange older securities for newly issued benchmark securities of similar terms-to-maturity. This helps to minimize debt-stock fragmentation and concentrate market liquidity in a small number of securities, thereby helping to ensure that they can still be actively traded even though the total debt outstanding may be on the decline. The United Kingdom has also sought to maintain new issuance volumes in the bond market in a period of fiscal surpluses by allowing its holdings of financial assets to rise temporarily when it received an unexpectedly large injection of cash from the sale of mobile phone licenses. In addition, Denmark, Sweden, and the United Kingdom offer market participants a facility to borrow temporarily or obtain by repo specific securities that are in short supply in the market, albeit at penalty inter-

est rates, to ensure that the government securities market is not unduly affected by pricing distortions in the market.

The countries surveyed also maintain an active investor relations program, whereby they meet regularly with major market participants to discuss government funding requirements and market developments and examine ways in which the primary market can be improved. Such a program, with appropriate staff and a public presence, has proven to be very helpful in assisting countries manage their debt in times of stress and in conveying messages on the government's economic and financial policies to domestic and foreign creditors. For example, South African authorities operate an investor relations program in which debt management officials conduct road shows to meet investors, primary dealers, and other financial institutions and explain developments in the South African market and government finances. Similarly, Japan and Denmark's investor relations programs enable debt managers to maintain regular and close contact with the financial community. This is considered to be an important channel in both countries for building investor understanding of the government's financial situation and debt management operations, and the programs are given high priority in these countries' debt management activities. Market participants in both countries are given an opportunity through regular meetings with debt management officials to discuss the management of the government debt, including the potential need for changes to or the introductions of new financial instruments.

In the wake of Argentina's debt default in 2001, one issue that has emerged is whether government debt instruments should also have renegotiation or collective action clauses covering the coupon and repayment terms, such as majority voting rules, attached to them. Indeed, as indicated in its September 28, 2002, communiqué, the IMFC encouraged the official community, the private sector, and sovereign debt issuers to continue work on developing collective action clauses and promote their use in international sovereign bond issues. According to the data presented in Table I.2, six countries (Brazil, Denmark, Slovenia, Sweden, Poland, and the United Kingdom) have introduced them for some securities issued in international markets, but none have attached them to their domestic debt. The ability of a country to attach collective action clauses to its international debt issues depends on the practice and laws in the market where the security is issued. For example, Slovenia and Sweden have attached these clauses to debt issued in the eurobond market, which is governed by British law. However, these clauses are not attached to securities issued in some other markets, such as Germany and the state of New York.

Secondary market

Debt managers in many countries actively work with market participants and other stakeholders to improve the functioning of the secondary market for government securities. For example, authorities in Italy, Poland, Portugal, Sweden, and the United Kingdom have introduced primary dealer systems and have worked closely with market participants to promote electronic trading of government securities. In addition, debt managers in India and Italy have worked with other interested parties to alleviate distortions caused by the tax treatment of returns on government securities. And those in Japan, New Zealand, South Africa, and the United Kingdom have worked with market participants to develop ancillary markets, such as futures, repo, and strips markets that help to deepen the government securities market.

Given the importance of sound clearing and settlement systems to the functioning of the government securities market, it is not surprising to find that many debt managers have been working with the relevant stakeholders to improve the systems in their countries. For example, in Brazil, Japan, and Poland, debt managers helped champion the introduction of real-time gross settlement for government securities transactions. In India, the central bank helped establish a central counter-party for the settlement of outright and repo transactions in government securities, which is expected to lead to substantial growth in trading activity in these markets. Also, to increase the efficiency of secondary market trading, the Jamaican authorities are working with market participants to dematerialize government securities within the central depository.

Implementation considerations

Although the preceding discussion suggests that there are a number of steps that governments can take to develop the primary and secondary markets for their securities, the sequencing of reforms and speed of deregulation will depend on country-specific circumstances. Nonetheless, the experience of developing these markets in many countries demonstrates the importance of having a sound macroeconomic and fiscal policy framework in place so that investors are willing to hold government securities without fear that their investment returns will be unexpectedly eroded by inflation or debt sustainability concerns.

Countries seeking to develop their domestic markets should also take heed that attempts to develop a market for government securities across the yield curve may entail some short-term costs for governments as debt managers strive to develop an investor base for their securities. For example, the yield curve could be very steep as a result of weak macroeconomic conditions, and, in some situations, the effect on debt sustainability of incurring extra debt-service costs could be very severe, or investors may simply be unwilling to purchase this debt. Thus, debt managers need to decide on a case-by-case basis whether the benefits outweigh the costs. In addition, to ensure a well-functioning market, debt should be issued in a predictable fashion, using standardized instruments and practices, so that the issuer's behavior does not disrupt market activity and investors can become accustomed to the instruments that are traded. Of course, situations may arise where it is costly for the government to honor a commitment or where it might be tempting to seek out short-term cost savings by manipulating the outcome of an auction. However, a demonstrated commitment to the development of the market should, over time, contribute to increased market liquidity and lower borrowing costs.

Notes

1. Developing a well-functioning domestic financial market also helps to improve the conduct of monetary policy. See A. Carare, A. Schaechter, M. Stone, and M. Zelmer, "Establishing Initial Conditions in Support of Inflation Targeting," IMF Working Paper 02/102 (Washington: International Monetary Fund), 2002.

2. Issues surrounding the securities used by industrial countries' central banks in their open market operations and held on their balance sheets are discussed in M. Zelmer, "Monetary Operations and Central Bank Balance Sheets in a World of Limited Government Securities." IMFPolicy Discussion Paper 01/7 (Washington: International Monetary Fund), 2001.

3. At the outreach conference, one country noted that a past failure to take account of the uncertainty in fiscal projections led it to issue too much short-term debt. This debt ultimately had to be rolled over into longer-term debt in the middle of a financial crisis when interest rates were high.

4. Information on the Polish experience can be found in P. Ugolini, 1996. *National Bank of Poland: The Road to Indirect Instruments*, IMFOccasional Paper No. 144 (Washington: International Monetary Fund), 1996.

5. In Brazil, the central bank also has an opportunity to comment ahead of time on the annual financing program, and the government is legally prevented from borrowing directly from the central bank.

6. Further information on ALM in the context of public debt management can be found in: G. Wheeler, and F. Jensen *Sound Practice in Sovereign Debt Management.* (Washington: World Bank), forthcoming.

7. Further information on the management of contingent liabilities in a sovereign context can be found in H.P. Brixi and A. Schick, eds., *Government at Risk: Contingent Liabilities and Fiscal Risk*(Washington: World Bank), 2002.

8. World Bank and International Monetary Fund, *Developing Government Bond Markets: A Handbook* (Washington), 2001.

9. Primary dealers are a group of dealers in government securities designated by the authorities to play a role as specialist intermediaries between the authorities and investors. They are usually granted special bidding privileges in primary auctions of government securities (and, in some cases, access to central bank credit) in exchange for agreeing to ensure that the auctions are fully subscribed and perform market-making functions in the secondary market.

10. A useful side benefit of issuing inflation-indexed securities is that central banks in countries that have such securities have found that the spread between yields on nominal and inflation-indexed debt can be a useful indicator of expected inflation for the conduct of monetary policy. However, the reliability of this indicator requires that the market for inflation-indexed securities be sufficiently liquid so that prices are not distorted by technical factors associated with individual transactions, or at least that the distortions be fairly stable over time. Further information on the benefits and design of inflation-indexed securities can be found in R.T. Price, 1997. "The Rationale and Design of Inflation-Indexed Bonds," IMF Working Paper 97/12 (Washington: International Monetary Fund), 1997.

II

COUNTRY CASE STUDIES

This part of the document contains the 18 country case studies prepared by government debt managers. Each case study focuses on the steps taken by the country to improve public debt management practices in recent years and their connection with the *Guidelines for Public Debt Management.*

1

Brazil[1]

The Brazilian government has been implementing several measures to improve the conduct of public debt management. This document provides an overview of the main guidelines currently followed by Brazilian public debt officials, drawing comparisons to those proposed by the IMF and the World Bank in their joint report, *Guidelines for Public Debt Management.*

The first section, "Developing a Sound Governance and Institutional Framework," covers a broad array of issues. It starts with a brief discussion of the objectives and scope of public debt management in Brazil and its coordination with monetary and fiscal policies. Following is a description of the main measures to enhance transparency and accountability by means of well-defined roles and attributions for debt management, comprehensive information disclosure, and frequent examination of debt management activities by external auditors. Concluding the section, the most relevant events regarding governance and the management of internal operations, including recent institutional reforms, are presented.

The second section, "Establishing a Capacity to Assess and Manage Cost and Risk," focuses on the guidelines that have been considered in determining optimal strategies for keeping the cost and risk of the

public debt at sustainable levels. Along with an illustration of the recent behavior of several debt management indicators, this section describes the implementation of an ALM framework and strategies envisaging reductions in refinancing and market risks. The main features of the risk management models currently in place and under development are also described.

The third and concluding section covers the actions that have been taken for developing the markets for government securities. Emphasis is given to the description of some noteworthy measures released by the Brazilian Treasury and central bank in November 1999 and to the continuous effort to stimulate the demand for long-term securities.

Developing a Sound Governance and Institutional Framework

Debt management objectives and coordination

Objectives

In line with the guidelines suggested by the IMF and the World Bank, the basic directive pursued by the

Brazilian government for public debt management is cost minimization over the long term, taking into consideration the maintenance of judicious levels of risks. As a secondary and complementary objective, the Brazilian Debt Management Unit has been taking actions toward the development of its domestic public securities market.

Although debt management officers strive to implement strategies aiming at cost minimization of the Brazilian government debt, special attention is given to the risks embodied in each strategy. Government efforts in the establishment of a solid reputation with creditors, respecting contracts, and avoiding an opportunistic approach in its relationship with the market are also of importance.

Emphasis has been given to the monitoring of refinancing and market risks, most specifically the former. In this respect, the Brazilian Treasury, as reported in greater detail below, has successfully extended the average maturity of the debt and achieved a smoother redemption profile. Close attention is paid to the amount of debt maturing in the short term (12 months), reducing the treasury's exposure to undesirable events that may occur.

The gradual replacement of floating-rate securities for fixed-rate securities represents another major guideline pursued by the Brazilian debt management office. Nevertheless, although it is an important measure to reduce market risk, changing the composition of debt toward greater concentration of fixed-rate instruments has often diverged from the objective of maintaining refinancing risk at comfortable levels. This dilemma occurs as a result of the still limited demand for long-term fixed-rate bonds. As the demand for these securities becomes more pronounced and macroeconomic policies are kept sound and stable, a more aggressive strategy in favor of those securities will follow.

Finally, the Brazilian Treasury seeks the development of the secondary market as a main venue to achieve these objectives. Some measures are already in effect (see the third section, "Developing the Markets for Government Securities"), such as

- improvement of the term structure of interest rates,
- standardization of financial instruments, and

- fungibility for floating-rate securities.

Scope

The scope of Brazilian public debt management is also in line with the IMF and World Bank guidelines. It encompasses the main financial obligations over which the central government exercises control, which include both marketable and nonmarketable debts, domestic and foreign currency debts, and contingent liabilities.[2] Given that the Brazilian Treasury has adopted an integrated ALM framework, asset characteristics are also taken into account in the conduct of public debt management.

Coordination with monetary and fiscal policies

Relative to the coordination with fiscal policy, borrowing programs are based on fiscal projections established by the federal budget and approved by parliament. The treasury also elaborates and publishes a detailed Annual Borrowing Plan that is submitted to the revision and approval of the minister of finance.

In the coordination with monetary policy, there is close interaction between treasury and central bank officials. Regular meetings with members of both institutions are held, and information on the government's current and future liquidity needs is shared. Moreover, although the final decisions regarding public debt financing strategies are under the responsibility of the national treasury, officials from the Central Bank of Brazil (CBB) are always consulted in advance to measure the potential impact of such strategies on the conduct of monetary and exchange rate policies.

An important step taken in Brazil is that as of May 2002, the CBB is no longer allowed by the Fiscal Responsibility Law (FRL) to issue its own securities.[3] Monetary policy is now conducted through secondary market operations with treasury securities, enhancing the transparency between fiscal and monetary policy.

Transparency and accountability

Brazilian debt management authorities seek transparency and accountability by publicly disclosing the roles and responsibilities for debt management and providing the public with information regarding debt management policies and statistics. In addition, external auditors frequently examine and evaluate the activities of public debt management.

Roles and responsibilities for debt management

The roles and responsibilities for debt management are clearly and formally defined by legal instruments. A summary of legislation is available at the treasury's web site.[4] Foreign and domestic public debt management is handled by the ministry of finance and, in turn, within the ministry of finance by the National Treasury Secretariat (that is, the Public Debt Office). Similarly, all regulations related to debt management are disclosed, including those on the activities of primary and secondary markets, and on clearing and settlement arrangements for trade in government securities.

Public availability of information

Information on debt management policies and operations is publicly disclosed by means of a regular calendar of auctions and regular report publications, all available on the treasury's web site. Besides publishing its Annual Borrowing Plan, which includes the main guidelines and strategies to be pursued over the year, the National Treasury Secretariat provides detailed public debt statistics through two monthly reports: the *Federal Government Domestic Debt Report* (in cooperation with the CBB) and the *National Treasury Fiscal Results*.

External auditing

Debt management activities are audited annually by external auditors. Two entities are commonly in charge of such attribution: the Secretaria Federal de Controle ([SFC] internal auditing agency—executive branch) and the Tribunal de Contas da União ([TCU] external auditing agency). These agencies are, respectively, affiliated with the executive and legislative branches of the federal government. Although the SFC plays an important role by conducting a preliminary audit of public debt manage-

ment activities, the TCU is responsible for ultimately approving them.

In addition, some reports required by parliament are related to debt management activities, among which are *Report on Fiscal Management*—follow-up of debt limits,[5] and *Account Balance of the Federal Government*—a description of all federal expenses throughout the year, forwarded annually to parliament and the TCU.

Institutional framework

Governance

The National Treasury Secretariat has implemented a new debt management organizational framework since November 1999, based on the international experience of the DMO. The Public Debt Office comprises three main branches:

- The back office, which is in charge of the registry, control, payment, and accounting of both domestic and foreign debts.
- The middle office, which is responsible for the development of medium- and long-term strategies aiming at reductions of debt cost and risk, macroeconomic follow-up, and investor relations.
- The front office, which is responsible for the design and implementation of short-term strategies related to bond issuances in domestic markets. Front office activities associated with international capital market borrowings are currently handled by the CBB, but will be transferred to the treasury in September 2003.

The new institutional arrangement resulted in a substantial improvement in debt management allowing for the standardization of operational controls, monitoring of risks, and separation of functions concerning long-term (strategic) and short-term (tactical) planning. Currently, approximately 90 financial analysts compose the Public Debt Office.

Management of internal operations

To strengthen internal operations and in response to an increasing number of nonintegrated data systems—making the process of gathering information cumbersome, time-consuming, and highly exposed to operational risk—the treasury has engaged in a cooperative program with the World Bank. The program contemplates three modules:

- IT system development;
- control, internal auditing and security standards, governance and organizational structure; and
- risk management.

Although these modules are interrelated, focus has been given to the development of the IT system. The project is, therefore, mainly directed to the establishment of an integrated platform that will enhance the efficiency and reliability of public debt accounting and reporting, improving the treasury's capacity and transparency in the conduct of public debt management.

The new institutional framework, mentioned previously, also represents an important step toward the reduction of operational risks. Front and back office functions have been clearly separated, and the middle office has been established to respond to the setting and monitoring of risk analysis independently from the area responsible for executing market transactions. Registry and auction services are presently provided by the CBB, for which a formal agreement has been recently formulated.

The process of hiring personnel was subject to some improvements enacted in the face of competition among different careers within the executive branch. Although there is still some degree of competition with other institutions from both the private and public sectors, the treasury has managed to hire and keep qualified staff by restructuring the career of treasury financial analysts and implementing a strict selection process mostly directed to professionals with strong backgrounds in economics and finance. Considerable resources have also been spent in specialized training for the debt management staff, such as a graduate course in debt management.

Another step taken toward the improvement of debt management was the establishment of a Code of Conduct for Public Debt Managers in February 2001, which contemplates some directives related to their conduct—for example, the prohibition on buying public bonds—and the creation of an Ethics and Professional Conduct Committee of Public Debt Managers.

Legal framework relating to borrowing

The main legislation regarding borrowing can be basically specified in four instruments: (1) the Brazilian Constitution—limits on public debt, (2) the FRL regulatory framework for fiscal policy, (3) the Budget Guidelines Law, and (4) the Annual Budget Law (the amount borrowed throughout the year cannot exceed the total established in the specific budgetary sources included in the LOA). Furthermore, a ceiling on new external debt borrowings is determined by a senate resolution.

Among the legal instruments mentioned above, the FRL constitutes a milestone in public finance at all levels of government. By means of a set of rules, it imposes limits on the government's payroll spending and the amount of outstanding debt,[6] requiring higher transparency of public accounts, stricter rules for elected officials of the executive branch at the end of their mandates, and administrative and penalty sanctions on administrators who fail to comply with fiscal legislation.

The FRL reinforced the "golden rule" established in Article 167-III of the Brazilian Federal Constitution, which states that it is forbidden to carry out credit transactions that exceed the amount of capital expenses. It also imposes restrictions on credit operations among government entities, including the national treasury and the CBB, and established that the CBB, as of May 2002, would no longer be allowed to issue its own securities in the primary market.

Establishing a Capacity to Assess and Manage Cost and Risk

Debt management strategy

Brazilian debt management strategy follows guidelines that are initially prepared by the Public Debt Office and submitted for the approval of the secretary of the national treasury and the minister of finance.

The treasury has been gradually moving toward an ALM framework. In this context, the risks inherent in the current debt structure are evaluated, taking into account the characteristics of assets, tax revenues, and other cash flows available to servicing the debt. Net exposures in the balance sheet of the central government are identified by selecting financial assets and liabilities, including guarantees, counterguarantees, and contingent liabilities.

Results of such analysis under an ALM framework suggest that in Brazil (as is usual in most countries), debt managers should seek a debt composition with heavier reliance on fixed-rate and inflation-indexed instruments. The main mismatches between assets and liabilities of the Brazilian central government, as of December 2001, are presented in Figure II.1.1.

Note that the main mismatches concern those related to interest rate and exchange rate exposures. Although there are several difficulties in achieving a debt portfolio that matches the characteristics of assets in the short and medium term, debt management officials find this type of ALM analysis

extremely valuable in setting long-term strategies for reaching optimal debt composition.

Along with the objective of gradual minimization of the interest rate and exchange rate exposures, the Brazilian government, in line with IMF and World Bank guidelines, has established among its priorities the reduction of refinancing risk. These objectives, however, are often conflicting, given the still limited demand for long-term fixed-rate and inflation-indexed securities. Meanwhile, the national treasury and the CBB have concentrated efforts in developing secondary markets and stimulating operations with long-term fixed-rate and inflation-indexed instruments. These measures have proven to be helpful in paving the way to a more appropriate composition of the public debt in the future.

Cash management represents another important aspect of the debt management strategy currently adopted by the Brazilian government. The treasury has been keeping enough cash reserves to allow greater flexibility in the pursuit of its financing strategies and,

Figure II.1.1. Assets and Liabilities Imbalances, December 2001
(In billions of reais)

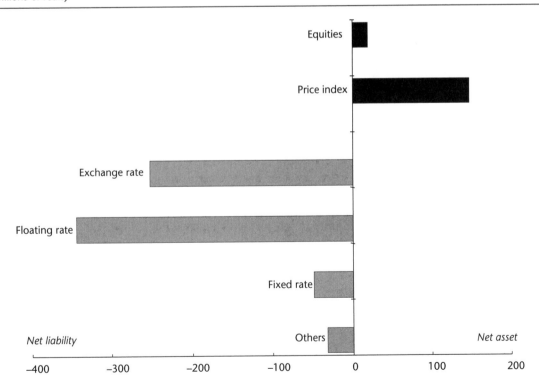

most important, reduce the risk of rolling over the debt under temporarily unfavorable conditions.

The debt management guidelines, which emphasize the reduction in refinancing risk and follow an ALM framework, have already reached good results. With the intent of illustrating the main achievements of such a strategy, and keeping in mind the still long way to attaining a more appropriate debt structure, the recent behavior of several debt management indicators and some of the lessons learned by Brazilian debt management officials over the past years are presented below.

Lengthening of debt average maturity to reduce refinancing risk

The average term of the outstanding domestic securities debt reached 35 months in December 2001, up from 27 months in December 1999. Behind such an achievement are the efforts to extend the maturity of securities issued through auctions, which represent approximately 70 percent of the domestic debt.[7] Figure II.1.2 reports the outstanding increase in the average maturity of these securities, growing from 4.6 months in July 1994 to approximately 29 months in December 2001. This rise is linked to the objective of reducing refinancing risk and can be mainly explained by long-term issues of floating-rate (LFT) and inflation-indexed bonds (NTN-C).

Improving the redemption profile

The percentage of public securities maturing in 12 months, which was reduced from 53 percent in December 1999 to 26 percent in December 2001, is a

Figure II.1.2. Average Maturity—Auction Issued Debt National Treasury
(In months)

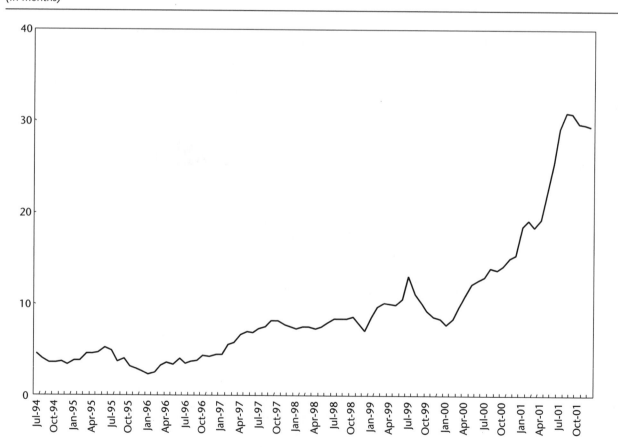

remarkable advance in the Treasury's financing policy, as shown in Figure II.1.3.

Gradual replacement of floating-rate securities for fixed-rate securities

In mid-1995, the national treasury started a process aimed at redefining its debt composition. One of the main measures contemplated was the public debt deindexation by means of a gradual increase in the share of fixed-rate debt. The graphs in figures II.1.4 and II.1.5 illustrate the strategy of gradual replacement of floating-rate (LFT) for fixed-rate (LTN securities. Note that fixed-rate securities were issued with increasing maturities up to the wave of crises that hit emerging markets starting in October 1997. Until then, the treasury had been able to suspend new issues of LFT.

Figures II.1.4 and II.1.5 also show the change in focus of debt management strategy in Brazil toward the reduction of refinancing risk and the adoption of a sustainable strategy of issuance of fixed-rate instruments. To reach these goals, starting in 1999, the treasury has implemented benchmark issues of long-term fixed-rate securities issued periodically and has decided to extend the maturity of the debt by issuing floating-rate securities of much longer terms than those observed historically

Debt composition

The composition of the domestic debt has changed dramatically over the past seven years (see Figure II.1.6). The substantial increase in the fixed-rate instruments pursued in the first few years of economic stabilization, which followed the launch of the

Figure II.1.3. Percentage of Central Government Internal Debt Maturing in 12 Months

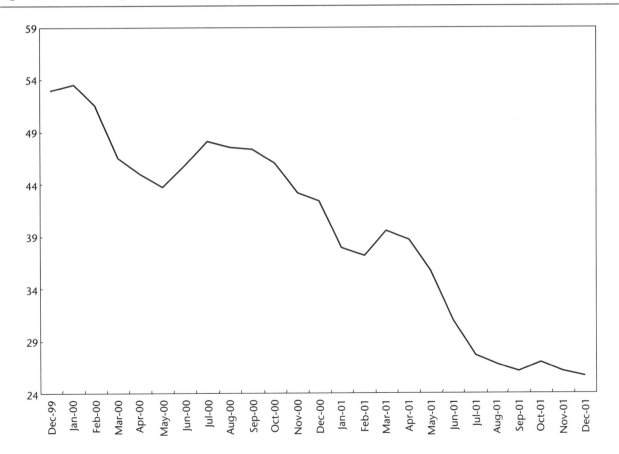

Figure II.1.4. Maximum Maturity at Issuance—Fixed-Rate Securities (LTN), in Months

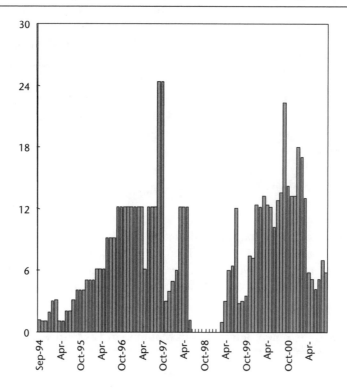

Figure II.1.5. Maximum Maturity at Issuance—Floating-Rate Securities (LFT), in Months

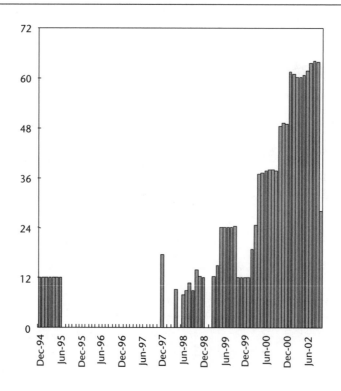

Figure II.1.6. Debt Composition per Index

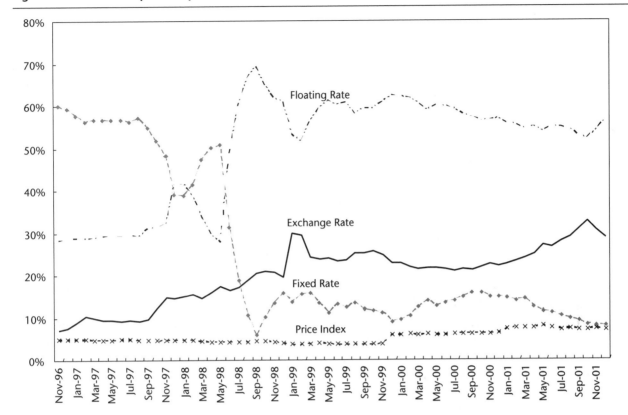

Real Plan in July 1994, proved to be unsustainable as emerging market economies faced a period of strong turbulence after October 1997. In the new economic environment, the Brazilian government had to accept an increase in the floating-rate share, and a consequent reduction in the fixed-rate portion, to avoid an increase in rollover risk.

Implicit in the discussion presented so far is a very important lesson drawn from the Brazilian debt management experience. Allied to the need for sound and stable macroeconomic policies, as a precondition for developing high-quality debt management, the development of (long-term) debt markets is also of fundamental importance. In this respect, the measures recently taken to enhance liquidity in the secondary markets and the already mentioned implementation of benchmark issues of long-term fixed-rate and inflation-indexed securities represent important steps toward a sustainable improvement in the debt composition.

External debt

In 1995, after 15 years out of the market, the Brazilian government restored its presence in the international capital market, issuing sovereign bonds with great success. Since then, the main measures underlying the Brazilian government strategies regarding the international capital markets have been

- consolidation of Brazilian yield curves in strategic markets (U.S. dollar, euro, yen) with liquid benchmarks,
- paving the way for other borrowers to access long-term financing, and
- broadening of the investor base in Brazilian public debt.

Since 1996, the Brazilian government has also pursued a strategy of buying back restructured debt (the Brady bonds) and replacing them with new bonds.

Figures II.1.7 and II.1.8 illustrate the new money and exchange operations held since 1995, totaling US$25.5 billion of sovereign debt issued in diversified markets. Note that the Brazilian government implemented seven exchange operations from May 1997 to March 2001 that helped to reduce the participation of Brady bonds in external bonded debt from 95.1 percent in December 1996 to 36.5 percent in December 2001.

Risk management framework

Within the ALM framework, risk analysis is conducted in a model that allows debt managers to project expected and potential costs of the debt under several different refinancing strategies in the medium and long term. Key debt management indicators, such as average maturity, duration, and debt composition, are generated for each strategy, allowing senior management to decide which is the more appropriate strategy to pursue. The main risks monitored are refinancing risk, market risk, and credit risk

(most federal government assets are composed of credits from states and municipalities).

A new risk management system customized according to the needs of the risk management group was implemented in the first semester of 2002. Besides allowing the same type of analysis that was conducted, this new system allows for a more integrated examination of assets and liabilities characteristics and the adoption of several types of at-risk models, such as CaR, cash-flow-at-risk, and BaR. At the present time, the risk management group conducts risk analysis based on deterministic and stochastic scenarios. Stress scenarios analysis is also used as a complement.

Besides improving its risk management systems, the Brazilian debt management office has been concentrating efforts in developing the skills of its personnel by means of training, external contacts, and hiring advisers. With this purpose, the aforementioned cooperation with the World Bank contemplates a risk management module that will provide an extensive background on international experience

Figure II.1.7. Foreign Bond Issuance in the International Capital Market
(In Millions of US$)

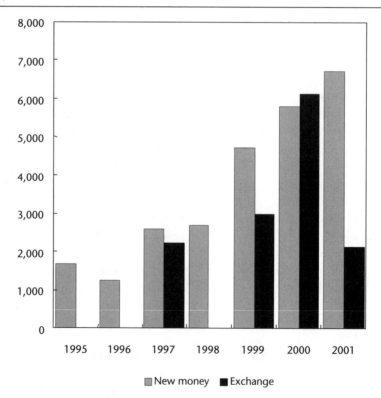

New money ▪ Exchange

Figure II.1.8. External Bonded Debt—Federal Government
(In Billions of US$)

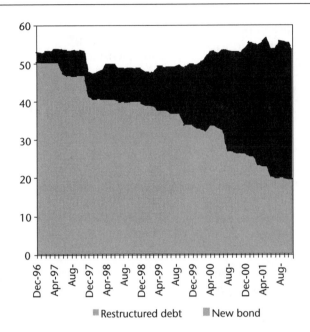

related to best practices of leading sovereign debt offices. The primary objective is to build capacity in assessing and managing the financial risks for a sovereign debt portfolio, and it will initially focus on an ALM framework. The participants will be trained in the various techniques used by the debt offices, and they will learn about future path modeling for market variables. To the extent that several of these techniques are already being developed in parallel by the Brazilian staff, a deeper examination of the risk management tools adopted in other countries will allow useful and valuable comparisons.

Developing the Markets for Government Securities

Improvement measures for the government securities market

During the second semester of 1999, the Brazilian Treasury and the CBB designated a working group with the objective of preparing a diagnosis of the problems related to the markets of public debt securities.

Since then, some procedures have been reorganized, and new instruments and norms were introduced, aiming at the recovery of securities market dynamism. The working group also discussed strategies that could enhance the demand for long-term government securities and released several measures, products, and projects directed to the public debt in primary and secondary markets. Some of these actions include:

- reduction in the number of outstanding series of domestic securities debt,
- use of the reoffer and buyback mechanisms,
- implementation of firm bid (price discovery) auctions for issuing long-term fixed-rate securities,
- release of a monthly schedule of auctions of treasury securities,
- regular and comprehensive information disclosure of public debt policies and statistics, and
- regular meetings with dealers, institutional investors, risk-rating agencies, and others.

The firm bid auctions comprise two stages. In the first stage, only primary dealers are allowed to submit bids, committing themselves to buying the securities auctioned at the prices and quantities specified in their bids. This does not guarantee, however, that these institutions have won the auction. The treasury determines the amount of securities to be auctioned at the final phase and releases such information along with the corresponding cutoff price observed in the first stage, acting as a price reference for the second stage. A discriminatory price auction with the participation of all financial institutions is then conducted. This auction procedure plays an important role in reducing the uncertainty regarding the pricing of fixed-rate long-term bonds issued by the treasury, given that references in the Brazilian market for these bonds are still incipient.

Measures undertaken for the development of the government securities market have been favorable. The noticeable improvements in the term structure of interest rates and the establishment of fungibility for floating-rate and inflation-indexed securities have contributed to stimulating negotiations in the secondary market. As a consequence of this latter measure, a reduction was observed in the number of outstanding series of floating-rate (LFT) and fixed-rate (LTN) securities, illustrated in Table II.1.1.

Improvement of term structure

The interest rate and inflation-indexed term structures have improved as a consequence of the treasury's strategy of building benchmark issues of long-term instruments. At the present time, there are parameters for price index curves up to 30 years, whereas price references for fixed-rate instruments reach 18 months.

Sales through the Internet

As part of the recent actions toward the development of the market for government securities, in January 2002, the Treasury began conducting sales of public debt instruments through the Internet. With low minimum and maximum buying limits (approximately US$80 per transaction and US$80,000 per month, respectively), this measure is mainly directed to small investors and tries to stimulate long-term domestic savings.

As shown in Table II.1.2, the amount issued through the Internet as of July 2002 was around US$11 million, of which 77 percent were fixed-rate securities. The number of investors totaled more than 4,000, from 24 of 27 Brazilian states.

Table II.1.1. Number of Series Outstanding

	Floating-rate securities (LFT)[a]	Fixed-rate securities (LTN)	Inflation-linked securities (NTN-C)	Total
Oct. 1999	47	21	2[b]	70
Dec. 2000	49	12	3	64
Dec. 2001	40	14	6	60

a. Only for LFTs issued through auctions.
b. As of December 1999.

Table II.1.2. Internet Sales
(As of July 31, 2002)

	R$	US$
Total amount sold	32,502,739	10,834,246
Floating-rate (%)	8	
Fixed-rate (%)	77	
Price index (%)	15	
Total number of investors	4,481	
Average amount per investor	7,254	2,418

Note: US$1.00 = R$3.00.
Source: Brazilian authorities.

Figure II.1.9. Yield Curve—NTN-C
(Duration in Months)

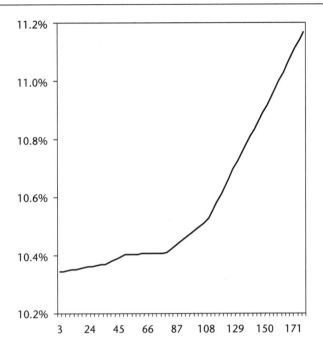

Figure II.1.10. Yield Curve—LTN
(Duration in Months)]

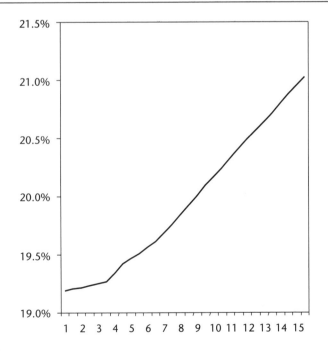

As of December 31, 2001.

Notes

1. The case study was prepared by the Debt Management Unit/Secad III of the Brazilian National Treasury.

2. For debt management purposes, the national treasury considers the contingent liabilities that have not yet materialized and for which there is a legal or contractual obligation or both, such as government guarantees on foreign exchange borrowings and government programs, among others.

3. In anticipation of this measure, the CBB stopped issuing its own securities in October 2001.

4. www.tesouro.fazenda.gov.br.

5. Debt limits were established by the FRL and are currently being discussed by parliament and the executive branch. The treasury secretary will regularly report to parliament on these limits.

6. These limits are based on the relation between the debt outstanding and net current revenue.

7. Besides issuing securities through auctions, the Brazilian Treasury is sometimes required by law to issue debt directly to specific creditors, mainly as a result of debt securitization.

2

Colombia[1]

Developing a Sound Governance and Institutional Framework

Objective

The main objective of debt management is to ensure that financing needs are met with a low funding cost in a long-term perspective, within a sustainable path, and with a prudent level of risk. The risks considered are refinancing, market, credit, operational, and legal.

Scope of debt management activities

Debt management covers both internal and external debt. In addition to funding, debt management also includes management of outstanding debt and contingent liabilities, the latter especially related to infrastructure and public credit operations.

Coordination with monetary and fiscal policies

The 1991 Constitution states that Banco de la República (BdR), the central bank, will be the independent agent responsible for monetary and foreign exchange policy, and the ministry of finance will be responsible for fiscal policy. The DMO, Dirección General de Crédito Público (Directorate General of Public Credit), is situated within the ministry.

Issues that require coordination with the BdR regarding monetary policy, debt management, and the macroeconomic agenda are discussed in the regular biweekly meetings of the board of the central bank, of which the minister of finance is member. The BdR is also in charge of the settlement and clearing of the domestic debt market, which involves coordination between fiscal and monetary authorities in the management of the domestic public debt.

Two officials from the BdR are also members of the Debt Advisory Committee, which determined the guidelines for debt management and the debt issuing program.

Legal framework

The legal framework for debt management is included in Decree 2681 of 1993, which covers

- Public credit transactions that involve new funding and, therefore, increasing the debt stock.

49

- Debt management transactions that reduce portfolio risk and do not increase debt stock. These transactions include hedging operations such as cross-currency swaps, interest rate swaps, debt exchanges, refinancing, debt conversions, and the like.

Institutional structure

As mentioned, the ministry of finance is responsible for debt management, and the DMO (Dirección General de Crédito Público) is a division of the ministry. The ministry of Finance has six divisions:

- Superior (minister, deputy ministers, general secretary),
- Macroeconomic Policy Division,
- National Treasury (Tesoro Nacional),
- Budget Division,
- Subnational Governments Division, and
- Dirección General de Crédito Público.

The DMO is in charge of debt management, and the National Treasury is in charge of cash and asset management. Coordination and communication with the treasury is essential. Although the DMO works closely with the treasury to create synergies between the two areas, communication could be vastly improved by merging these two divisions. No doubt, this merger would also improve ALM. However, at present, there are no plans for a merger.

Management of internal operations

The DMO adopted a new internal structure in May 2001, following recommendations from the World Bank. The new structure, including responsibilities, is the following:

- front office—local and external funding,
- middle office—analysis of portfolio risks and strategy, and
- back office—operational issues.

Besides these three sections, the DMO also includes the legal affairs office and the IT office.

The new structure improves communication and coordination among front, middle, and back offices, thereby reducing operational risk. Completion of a document describing the DMO procedures has also reduced operational risk.

Debt management decisions and actions must be based on accurate and updated information about the debt portfolio. To improve databases and analysis tools, DMFAS software from the United Nations Conference on Trade and Development (UNCTAD)[2] is currently in the process of being implemented. This software is especially designed to strengthen the technical capacity to record, manage, and analyze external and internal debt. It also provides facilities for the recording and monitoring of bond issues, on-lending, and private nonguaranteed debt. After the software is adjusted for the Colombian requirements, it is expected to

- reduce operational risks,
- simplify procedures,
- produce debt profiles and financial risk quantification in real time,
- improve capacity to evaluate statistical models,
- be compatible with other information systems,
- increase accuracy of exercises,
- allow Internet operability, and
- provide a proactive alarm system, which will alert management if the portfolio reaches any debt management policy limits, such as the stated currency or interest rate composition of the debt.

Retain qualified staff with financial market skills

Staff members receive continual training, allowing them to acquire important market skills, while helping the DMO attract and retain qualified staff. This is particularly true in the middle office, where staff receive ongoing training in portfolio analysis and strategy. Individuals are often attracted to this benefit of acquiring knowledge in these areas, thus making the DMO a good working environment. This is especially important because salaries in the public sector often are not competitive with those in the private sector.

Incentives and guidelines to ensure implementation of strategies

A benchmark for external debt has been established since 1997. Although there is no legal obligation or economic incentive that will ensure that debt management is implemented prudently, historically the benchmarks have been met. Internal debt benchmarks have not been formally adopted; however, according to present plans, the authorities approved a benchmark for the internal debt in June 2002.

Transparency

Transparency of the debt figures is achieved through the yearly report of the ministry of finance. This report includes a summary of the previous year's agenda as well as the state of the economy and debt portfolio. Two web sites are also available for debt figures, www.minhacienda.gov.co and www.coinvertir.org.co.

Debt Management Strategy and Risk Management Framework

Reducing the country's vulnerability

During the mid- and late 1990s, the main concern was minimizing the exposure of the external debt portfolio to market shocks and international crisis. As a consequence of this concern, the Public Debt Advisory Committee (Comité Asesor de Deuda Pública) was created on April 21, 1997, integrated by officials from the ministry of finance and the BdR. The main objectives of the committee are to analyze and discuss guidelines for the internal and external indebtedness and propose risk management guidelines.

In 1997, the ratio of internal debt to external debt was approximately the same as it is today. In contrast to the external debt, the internal debt was considered as carrying less risk, because it was made up mainly of liabilities with the public sector. Therefore, the main concern was minimizing the exposure of the external debt portfolio to market shocks and international crisis. As a consequence, benchmarks for the external public debt were established as ref-erence points for the central government and for the eight public entities with the highest outstanding external debt. The benchmarks cover refinance risk, interest rate risk, currency risk, and duration and have been an important tool in controlling and minimizing the exposure to external shocks. The amortization profile has never exceeded the 15 percent limit a year, considerably reducing refinancing risk, and the portfolio has met the currency and interest rate composition in the benchmarks, thereby minimizing market risk.

Because the characteristics of the domestic capital market are different from those of the international capital market, it is not possible to use the external debt benchmark for the internal debt portfolio. For management of the internal debt portfolio, risk management guidelines have been taken into consideration but no explicit benchmark has been adopted. However, the Public Debt Advisory Committee approved a benchmark for the internal debt in June 2002.

Main risks in the government's domestic and foreign debt portfolio

To reduce vulnerability, the DMO focuses on refinancing and market risks. The benchmark for the share of internal debt is 67 percent and 33 percent for external debt.

Since 1997, the Public Debt Advisory Committee has established benchmarks for external debt. These benchmarks have been updated yearly and were reviewed in May 2002. The benchmarks for the external debt are

- Refinancing: No more than 15 percent of the total external debt can mature in any given year. The ideal is 10 percent. (The rationale behind these figures is that market conditions may require executing a funding strategy that exceeds the 10 percent limit, but never the 15 percent limit.)
- Currency composition: U.S. dollar, 83 percent; euro, 13 percent; and yen, 4 percent.
- Interest rate composition: fixed and semifixed rate ≥ 70 percent, floating rate ≤ 30 percent.

- Modified duration: 3.5 years.

For the internal debt, the following benchmarks were approved at the meeting of the Public Debt Advisory Committee in June 2002. The new benchmarks will guarantee that future funding programs will be in line with debt guidelines. The benchmarks for the domestic debt are

- Refinancing: No more than 20 percent of the total internal debt can mature in any given year. The ideal is 15 percent.
- Fixed and price-indexed: Colombian peso, fixed, 92–96 percent; price-indexed, 4–8 percent.
- Interest rate composition: Because local debt instruments are either fixed, price-indexed, or U.S. dollar–indexed, there is no interest rate benchmark for the internal debt.

How different risks are quantified and balanced

Two methods are used to quantify the portfolio risk. The first method compares the actual portfolio with the benchmarks. The second method, called debt-service-at-risk (DsaR), is currently used. DsaR allows the DMO to quantify the maximum debt-service cost of the debt portfolio with 95 percent likelihood. The methodology takes into consideration the exposure to different market variables, such as interest rates, exchange rates, and commodity prices. For managing the cost and risk dimensions of the debt portfolio, the middle office presents a monthly report of funding alternatives based on DsaR analysis. This report compares the cost of the expected scenario with the risk scenario of the different funding alternatives.

The funding strategy takes the benchmarks into consideration. The front office analyzes the market situation and different funding alternatives. If the funding strategy requires exceeding one or more limits established in the benchmarks, the possibility of a hedging transaction is analyzed.

Reducing the risk of losing access to domestic and international financial markets

To have access to financial markets, control over both refinancing and market risk is essential. As previously mentioned, since 1997, the amortization profile of external debt has never exceeded the 15 percent limit, considerably reducing refinancing risk. Recent crises in Russia, Brazil, Turkey, and Argentina have emphasized the importance of monitoring these two risks.

Refinancing in advance, when the conditions of the external capital markets are favorable, has been a successful strategy. It allows the ministry of finance to guarantee the funding needs at a low cost, while anticipating future market shocks. The view of the market is a combination of judgments of parameters such as political conditions, falling spreads, tighter yields, and investors' demand for bonds, in addition to various bank surveys.

For domestic debt, it is important to remember that the local market for public debt is only five years old. Moreover, investors are only progressively demanding longer-term instruments. The first issues were securities with one-, two-, and three-year maturities. Therefore, the amortization profile historically showed concentrations in the first and second years. Now, when the daily volume traded has increased considerably and inflation has reached one-digit levels, fixed-rate securities with longer maturities (5, 7, and 10 years) have been successfully introduced. Securities with longer-term maturities (10 and 15 years) are price indexed.

Several voluntary debt swaps have also been executed recently:

- In June 2001, an internal voluntary debt swap was conducted. Short-term (2001–05) amortizations were reduced by US$2.4 billion, and the refinancing risk was reduced considerably.
- In January and March 2002, two internal voluntary debt swaps took place. US$512 million of short- and mid-term amortizations of U.S. dollar–denominated TES were exchanged for 10-year tenor, fixed-rate peso-denominated TES, considerably reducing exchange rate and refinancing risk.
- In May 2002, another voluntary swap took place, exchanging US$589 million of external bonds (euro- and U.S. dollar–denominated) maturing between 2002 and 2005 for 10-year TES maturing in 2012.
- In June 2002, an external voluntary debt swap was executed. External bond short-term

(2002–05) amortizations were reduced by US$255 million, considerably reducing refinancing risk.

- Other small internal debt exchanges are held regularly.

Management of risks associated with embedded options

So far, the Colombia has issued eight bonds with options, two of which have already been exercised (a "knock-out" yen option and a put option). Management of the risks associated with these options has been conservative. For budgetary purposes, all bonds with put options are always registered as if all the investors exercised the option. This allows the republic to have funds on hand to cover the option.

Strategies to generate returns

The DMO does not engage in active debt management strategies. Transactions such as interest rate and currency swaps have only a hedging purpose. However, by following interest and currency rates, transactions that could reduce debt service are considered if favorable market opportunities occur.

Management of contingent liabilities

The DMO middle office is responsible for explicit contingent liabilities. The responsibilities of the DMO are to verify the methodologies used by the public entities that generate these liabilities. With these models, the DMO structures a contributed payment plan to create a fund, which will be managed by a fiduciary. This fund allows having liquidity to pay the liabilities when the contingency occurs.

In addition, the DMO operates by

- implementing and developing methodologies for quantifying contingent liabilities on guarantees offered by the government to private agents in concession projects of state-owned infrastructure (highways, electricity generation, water, and communications),
- developing methodologies for quantifying contingent liabilities in public credit transactions

(guarantees of the central government on external or internal debt of municipal governments and public entities), and

- creating methodologies for credit risk analysis of municipal public entities.

The procedure of contingent liabilities management includes appointments with investment banks and public entities, developing simulation models for risk assessment, and developing a schedule for the contingent liabilities payouts (including the probability of payouts).

Management information systems used to assess and monitor risk

The IT office created a database that has been in use since 1997. This software allows inquiries about the current debt portfolio; however, it does not have a risk-monitoring module. For risk quantification, the middle office uses its own models based on Excel spreadsheets.

As previously described, more sophisticated DMFAS software will be implemented in 2003. A team is currently working on the transition process. Besides allowing for the possibility for consultation of debt information, the new software will provide analysis of the exposure of the debt portfolio to volatility in interest rates and exchange rates and have the capacity to make simulations of new funding strategies.

Development in markets for private sector debt

The DMO has been one of the most important agents involved in the development of the local capital markets. The treasury bond market has become a model for private debt issuers. This means that the private sector takes into account all developments in the public debt market.

Developing the Markets for Government Securities

Development of the primary market

The DMO is the only agency that issues central government debt. The central bank no longer issues bonds for monetary policy purposes. The DMO is also responsible for updating the database of the public debt, which includes debt of the central government plus other public institutions and subnational governments.

The profile of the internal debt portfolio has changed since 1997. Today, 76 percent of the internal portfolio consists of treasury bonds and notes (exposed to market risks), compared with more than 90 percent five years ago. In 1997, 34 percent of outstanding treasury bonds and notes were liabilities with private investors; today, the ratio has increased to 40 percent.

The DMO issues 1- to 10-year fixed-rate instruments, and 5-, 7-, and 10-year instruments are issued as price-indexed securities. U.S. dollar–indexed securities in 2-, 3-, 5-, and 8-year maturities are issued only when the exchange rate of the Colombian peso to the U.S. dollar undergoes periods of considerable volatility or those that are not part of the normal funding program. To diversify the debt stock across the yield curve, the DMO considers the amortization profile, market conditions, funding cost, and bond liquidity when deciding on the issuing plan.

Treasury securities in the domestic market are issued by two mechanisms. In 2002, weekly primary Dutch auctions counted for 40 percent of internal funding. The remaining 60 percent of internal funding in 2002 was covered by direct placement to public entities. Direct placements (mandatory and agreed-upon) are made with public entities that have cash surpluses. These public entities are price takers in the market.

In the international market, bonds are issued in the U.S. dollar, euro, and yen markets. Borrowing is also executed by loans from multilateral credit agencies and syndicates, as well as other commercial loans.

The ministry of finance issues official press releases with information on bond (local and external) placements as well as agreed loans. These releases are available on the web site, www.minhacienda.gov.co.

Development of the secondary market

Since 1997, one of the objectives of the DMO has been the development of the local public debt market. For this purpose it has established the Programa de Creadores de Deuda Pública (Public Debt Market Maker Program). In this program, 24 of the most important financial institutions, of which 22 are private and 2 are public, participate in weekly primary auctions of treasury bills, notes, and bonds.

Contacts with the financial community

Communication between the DMO and the financial institutions is regarded as very important. Meetings between representatives of the financial institutions and officials from the DMO take place at least every quarter. In the local market, there is constant communication with financial institutions, members of the market maker program, and important investors such as pension funds, fiduciary funds, and insurance companies. For the external market, it is important to keep close contact with various financial institutions that provide market feedback, promote trading of instruments, and have direct contact with key investors.

Clearing and settlement

The following systems are used to settle and clear local debt market transactions:

- DCV (Depósito Central de Valores), the electronic central depository that handles all of the public local debt;
- SEN (Sistema Electrónico de Negociación de Deuda Pública), the system that handles the electronic local public debt market; and
- SEBRA (Sistema Electrónico de Banco de la República), the electronic settlement system used for primary auctions for public local debt.

Tax treatment of government securities

Government securities are tax free only for the profits on the principal of stripped securities. Nonstripped government securities have the same tax treatment as corporate securities.

Notes

1. The case study was prepared by Gustavo Navia, Jorge Cardona, and Carlos Eduardo León, from the Directorate General of Public Credit of the Ministry of Finance and Public Credit.

2. UNCTAD is the principal organ of the United Nations General Assembly to deal with trade, investment, and development issues.

3
Denmark[1]

Developing a Sound Governance and Institutional Framework

Objectives

The overall objective of Denmark's government debt policy is to achieve the lowest possible long-term borrowing costs, consistently with a prudent degree of risk. The authorities pursue this objective while taking various factors into account, including the objective of a well-functioning domestic financial market. Recently, more emphasis has been placed on the discipline of risk management.

Scope of debt management

The debt of the central government is compiled as the nominal value of domestic and foreign debt minus the central government's account with the central bank, Danmarks Nationalbank (DNB), and the assets of the Social Pension Fund (SPF). All administrative functions related to government debt management are undertaken by the DNB.

Two conditions establish a dividing line between fiscal and monetary policy in Denmark. First, government borrowing is subject to a set of funding rules based on an agreement between the government and the DNB. Second, the prohibition on monetary financing in the Maastricht Treaty regulates the central bank's role as a fiscal agent and bank to the government.

Since the early 1980s, central government borrowing has been subject to funding rules for both domestic and foreign borrowing. The present funding rules were stipulated in a 1993 agreement between the government and the central bank, which replaced the informal agreement from the early 1980s, when the Danish fixed exchange rate regime was implemented.

In overall terms, the domestic rule ensures that domestic borrowing in Danish kroner matches the central government's gross domestic financing requirement for the year. Thus, the domestic rule sterilizes the liquidity impact from government payments for the year as a whole. The rule for foreign borrowing states that new foreign loans are normally raised to refinance the redemptions on the foreign debt. If the level of foreign exchange reserves is considered inappropriate, a decision can be made to reduce or increase the level of foreign debt. Foreign exchange reserves are owned by the DNB, and the central government's DNB account provides the link between government foreign debt and foreign exchange reserves.

In accordance with the Maastricht Treaty's prohibition of monetary financing, the central government's account with the DNB may not show a deficit. The government's borrowing is therefore planned to ensure an appropriate balance on its account.

The central government receives interest on its account with the DNB. This interest rate is equal to the discount rate set by the central bank. The discount rate is equivalent to the current-account rate (folio rate), which is the interest rate for the banks' and mortgage-credit institutions' current-account deposits with the DNB. This arrangement implies, together with the fact that the surplus of the central bank after reserve allocations is transferred to the government, that the government receives an interest rate on the account that is comparable to what would be obtained if the account were placed in a commercial bank.

Legislative basis for central government borrowing

The legal authority for the central government to borrow is stipulated in legislation enacted in 1993. It allows the minister of finance to borrow in the name of the government. It also empowers the minister of finance to raise loans on behalf of the central government, up to a maximum of DKr 950 billion, which is the limit for the total domestic and foreign government debt. Moreover, it empowers the minister of finance to transact swaps and other kinds of financial instruments.

Before the beginning of a new fiscal year, a finance bill is adopted by parliament. It authorizes the minister of finance to raise loans to finance the central government's projected gross financing requirement, which is the sum of the current central government deficit plus redemptions on domestic and foreign debt. The borrowing is obtained according to the domestic and foreign norm. During a fiscal year, changes may occur in the gross financing requirement. This happens primarily because of

changes in the central government deficit or because of buybacks that increase the amount of redemptions. Changes in the gross financing requirement are similarly financed by government loans. These loans are authorized by an act of supplementary appropriation of the finance bill at the end of the year or by the Financial Committee of the Parliament during the year.

Besides the government debt, the central government guarantees the borrowing and financial transactions related to the borrowing of a number of public entities. The entities are mainly related to infrastructure projects, for example, the Great Belt Bridge and subway construction in Copenhagen. The board of directors and the management of the individual entity are responsible for the financial transactions of the entity, but the central government establishes borrowing limits and guidelines for the borrowing activities. The guidelines are determined in a set of agreements between the DNB and the ministry of finance or the ministry of transport and between the relevant ministry and the individual entity. The agreement between the central bank and the relevant ministry sets out the main tasks and responsibilities of the parties involved. The set of agreements also includes a list of acceptable types of loans. The list describes which kind of financial transactions and currency exposure the entity is allowed to incur.

The entities publish their own annual report and are covered by the general legislation applied to private firms.

The Danish debt office is placed within the central bank

The responsibility to parliament for central government borrowing rests with the ministry of finance. Since 1991, the central bank has undertaken all administrative functions related to government debt management. The division of responsibility is set forth in an agreement between the ministry of finance and the DNB. By power of attorney, DNB officials are authorized to sign loan documents on behalf of the minister of finance.

Before 1991, the debt office was part of the ministry of finance. In 1991, the debt office was moved to the central bank—the structural change occurring partly as a consequence of a report prepared by the public auditors. The report indicated that most of the assignments related to the central government debt were already carried out by the DNB, but duplication of assignments occurred between the central bank and the ministry of finance. Furthermore, the report suggested that a stronger coordination between the management of the foreign exchange reserve in the DNB and the central government's foreign debt would be beneficial. Finally, it suggested that attracting and maintaining staff with the relevant skills for the debt office would be easier if the debt office were placed in the central bank. The move to the central bank has helped to centralize the retention of knowledge of most aspects of financial markets within a single authority.

The relation between the debt office and the ministry of finance

At quarterly meetings, the ministry of finance and the DNB determine the overall strategy for government borrowing on the basis of written proposals from the DNB. The adopted strategy is authorized and signed by the ministry of finance. In December each year, the overall strategy for the next year is determined, as well as the detailed strategy for the first quarter of the next year. At the following quarterly meetings, amendments to and specifications of the main strategy for the subsequent quarter are decided.

The strategy specifies the expected domestic and foreign borrowing requirements and includes a set of decisions for the next year. Among the decisions are

- bands for duration of the central government debt,
- a list of on-the-run issues for the domestic debt,
- the borrowing strategy for foreign debt,
- a list of government securities eligible for buybacks or switch operations,
- a list of government securities in the securities lending facility, and
- maximum amounts of buybacks and use of interest rate swaps.

The first four items are published after the meeting in December. If changes in these decisions occur

during the year, these are published as well. Maximum amounts of buybacks and use of interest rate swaps are not made public.

On the basis of these conclusions, the central bank handles the necessary borrowing transactions and the ongoing management of the debt. Besides the formal meetings, the DNB is in regular contact with the ministry of finance, and ad hoc adjustments in the strategy may occur during the year.

Structure of the debt office within the central bank

Within the DNB, four departments are involved in the management of the central government debt—the Government Debt Management unit of the Financial Markets Department, the Market Operations Department, the Accounting Department, and the Internal Audit Department. The division of the management of government debt into a front, middle, and back office structure was implemented in 1996 to diminish operational risk.

The Government Debt Management unit is responsible for middle office functions and constitutes the Danish debt office. It formulates the principal aspects of the debt management strategy and carries out analysis and risk management. The unit also formulates guidelines for the Market Operations Department on sale of domestic bonds, buybacks, swap transactions, and the amount of foreign borrowing.

The Market Operations Department is responsible for front office functions, such as sale of securities and issuance of foreign loans. Responsibility for back office functions, such as settlement and bookkeeping, is handled in the Accounting Department and Government Debt Accounting.

The Internal Audit Department in the central bank assists the Auditor General (the national audit office) in the auditing of government debt management. In handling the government debt, the departments involved in the process also draw on resources from other departments in the central bank, for example, the legal experts.

Information policy

The Danish government debt strategy is aiming at a high degree of transparency toward the general public and the financial markets. Therefore, the DNB compiles and publishes a wide and frequent range of information on central government borrowing and debt.

The information policy is based on several announcements to the public. Some of them follow a fixed annual schedule. The most important announcements and publications are the following:

- Before the beginning of each half year, normally in June and December, the central bank sends an announcement to the Copenhagen Stock Exchange (CSE) and market participants with details of central government benchmark issues concerning July and January, respectively. The announcement also presents more general information on the plans for the central government's domestic borrowing.

- Before the opening of new government securities series, an announcement is sent to the CSE with details of the coupon, maturity, and opening day of the new loan.

- On the first banking day of each month, the DNB sends an announcement to the CSE and other interested parties on the sale and buyback of domestic government securities during the preceding month. On the second banking day of each month, the DNB issues a press release with details of the government's actual borrowing requirements and other important financial details of the preceding month.

- Details of the sale and buyback of domestic government securities are issued daily via the DNB's web site[2] and an electronic information system (DN News). Most of this information is reproduced directly by Reuters, for example. Further information on prices and circulating amounts of government bonds is available from the CSE.

- Terms and conditions for treasury bill auctions and results are announced via the CSE and the electronic auction system.

- The ministry of finance regularly publishes information on the development in the government budget.

- Other information on Danish government borrowing and debt appears in the DNB's annual report.

The DMO in the central bank publishes an annual report (*Danish Government Borrowing and Debt*), usually in February. The annual report is the cornerstone of the implementation of the information policy. The report informs the public, market participants, parliament, and ministry of finance about all activities related to Danish debt management in the preceding year. Since 1998, the report has also been published in English. The report describes considerations and factors concerning borrowing and debt management. It also includes sections on special topics of relevance to government debt management. Finally, it includes a comprehensive appendix of tables with detailed central government borrowing and debt statistics, including a list of all government loans.

Enhancing quality and reducing operational risk

Procedures manual

A procedures manual ensures proper government debt administration for the relevant units in the departments working with government debt. The manual describes authorities and obligations of the unit. The central bank's Audit Department is responsible for any changes to the written procedures, which are then passed on to the ministry of finance. Developing and maintaining the procedures manual is a key element in enhancing quality and reducing operational risk, and it is thus an area of high priority in debt management.

Work descriptions are used in daily work as a supplement to the procedures manual. A work description is a detailed description of a particular task that is regularly carried out. For example, there are work descriptions for such factors as the opening of a new government bond, a buyback auction, calculations of duration and CaR, and monthly releases of public information on the government debt. The use of work descriptions contributes to consistency and accuracy in the administration of the government debt.

Guidelines for acceptable loan categories are set out for the central government's foreign borrowing. The guidelines stipulate requirements of the overall loan structure, including both the underlying loan and any related derivatives. The purpose of these guidelines is to minimize the political, legal, and operational risks.

Codes of conduct

The DNB staff must adhere to internal codes of conduct based on the guidelines on speculation set by the Danish Financial Supervisory Authority and the legislation against insider trading. In short, this means that the staff is allowed to invest only personal capital and only in nonspeculative investments.

Recruiting and maintaining highly skilled staff

The placement of the DMO within the central bank has helped the office in recruiting highly skilled staff. Contributing to this is the fact that the DMO is a part of a larger environment, where finance, financial markets, and policy are major areas. Therefore, it is able to recruit both internally from other departments and externally, offering new employees an opportunity to be part of a large and highly skilled organization that is well known to the public.

The staff in the Government Debt Management unit (middle office) consists of a mix of senior staff, who have worked with debt management for a number of years, have worked in other areas of the bank, or both, and young economists recently employed in the DNB.

Including employees working in the front and back offices, around 20 staff are working mainly with tasks related to the central government debt.

Management information system and use of IT

Strong and reliable IT systems are crucial to limiting operational risk. In the Danish DMO, the current IT strategy is primarily built upon a specially developed back office system (System Statsgæld) combined with the use of other software. All borrowing and swap transactions for the central government debt enter System Statsgæld. Transactions are controlled by the back office.

The back office system generates information on payments to be made or received; input to the central bookkeeping system, which covers all government entities; and data for analytical purposes.

During 2002, the plan was to implement a new middle office system. The purpose of this system is to automate important calculations used on a regular basis, for example, duration calculations, market value, and various risk factors on the debt. The new system will draw data directly from the back office system. The implementation of the new middle office system will further reduce operational risks.

Debt Management Strategy and the Risk Management Framework

Limiting country vulnerability

The objective and strategy for government debt management focuses on reducing the risk of negative spillover effects from the government debt to the surrounding economy. In that respect, interest rate risk and exchange rate risk are considered the most important risk factors.

To reduce country vulnerability, it is important to limit interest and exchange rate risk. In Denmark, this is done primarily through steering the duration and redemption profile on the debt and by borrowing only in euros or Danish kroner.

Borrowing strategy

Domestic debt

The strategy for domestic borrowing involves building up large government security series in the internationally important 2-, 5-, and 10-year maturity segments. The liquidity premium resulting from this strategy contributes to low borrowing costs for the central government. A range of government debt instruments is applied to ensure large liquid benchmark issues. This includes domestic interest rate swaps, buybacks, and swaps from Danish kroner to euros. The domestic borrowing strategy also includes a treasury bills program with monthly issues of bills with maturity up to 12 months.

Given that the central government is a dominant issuer on the domestic bond market, the measurement of performance does not encompass comparison of the cost relative to that of a specific benchmark portfolio constructed on the basis of domestic bond issues.

The Danish domestic government bonds are priced on a competitive financial market, which consists of both domestic and international investors. Furthermore, the bonds are comparable to other domestic and foreign bonds and are issued in the internationally most important maturity segments. In that respect, the pricing is based on market conditions.

In the case of buybacks, the government determines whether buybacks are advantageous as seen from a broad government debt perspective. Buybacks are used to concentrate government debt in liquid bonds, in cash management, and to control the redemption profile. Buybacks take place at market prices. Comparing prices with theoretical prices calculated on the basis of zero-coupon yield curves drawn from the market ensures that buybacks will be purchased at the market price.

Over the years, there has been a gradual change in the domestic borrowing strategy toward a concentration of borrowing on a reduced number of benchmark bonds and an increase in the use of interest and currency swaps. The changes have been carried out to ensure the outstanding amount and the liquidity in the bonds in a time with reduced borrowing needs as a result of budget surpluses since 1997.

The issuance of bonds takes place only in the 2-, 5-, and 10-year maturity segments. The 5- and 10-year bonds are on average open for issuance for 2 years, and the 2-year bonds are open for about 1 year. The issuance in the 30-year segment was effectively stopped by the end of 1997. By the end of 2001, 99 percent of the total outstanding amount in domestic bonds and treasury bills were distributed on 11 bonds and 4 treasury bills. The bonds are among the leading bonds on the CSE. Three of these bonds are considered benchmarks; the benchmark in the 10-year segment is the most important.

Foreign debt

All foreign borrowing takes place directly in euros or via loans swapped to euros. All central government foreign currency exposure, including swap transactions, is in euros. In 2002 and the coming years, the borrowing strategy is now based on raising primarily bigger loans, preferably directly in euros. The strategy is supplemented by the opportunity to issue domestic bonds combined with currency swaps to euros.

The strategy for foreign borrowing has changed gradually over the years, from small loans and, in some cases, structured loans to a mixture of smaller and bigger loans with end exposure in euros. The present strategy, focusing on bigger bullet loans directly in euros, is in line with this development toward a more standardized foreign borrowing.

When foreign exchange reserve considerations entail an immediate need for foreign currency borrowing, the central government may issue short-term commercial paper (CP). The central government can use short-term CP programs in periods when the balance of the central government's account with the DNB is expected to be low.

The euro interbank offered rate (Euribor) serves as a reference in the assessment of borrowing costs for the foreign government debt. In addition, the cost of different instruments is compared, for example, direct borrowing in euros is compared with borrowing in other currencies swapped to euros. The borrowing costs for the foreign debt are also compared with the levels achieved by peer countries.

Main types of risk

The main risks for the government debt portfolio are interest rate, exchange rate, credit, and operational risks:

- Interest rate risk is the risk that the development in interest rates will lead to higher borrowing costs. The concept of interest rate risk also covers refinancing risk, which is the risk that existing debt will have to be refinanced at a time with unfavorable market conditions or particularly unfavorable borrowing terms for the central government. Interest rate risk is relevant for the domestic debt and the foreign debt.
- Exchange rate risk is the risk that the value of the debt will increase as a consequence of development in exchange rates.
- The central government undertakes a credit risk when it enters into swap transactions. A swap is an agreement between two parties to exchange payments during a predetermined period. Thus, there is a risk that the counter-party will default on its obligations. Credit exposure is included in

the management of the credit risk as soon as the swap is transacted.

- The central government is also exposed to other risks, such as the risk of error in the administration of the debt by itself or by counter-parties.

Managing the risks

As described above, the government debt comprises four subportfolios: the domestic debt, the foreign debt, SPF assets, and the central government account with the DNB.

The four subportfolios that make up the government net debt are all subject to management by the central bank as an agent of the central government.

Interest rate risk

Management of interest rate risk is based on the net debt as a whole. This is a direct consequence of the subportfolios being more and more integrated. An example of more integration among the portfolios is the use of currency swaps from Danish kroner to euros to raise foreign loans, which at the same time affect the interest rate risk on domestic and foreign debt.

Interest rate risk is primarily managed by a duration target and a duration band for the total central government debt (net). Historically, each subportfolio had a separate duration target, but this practice was abolished by the end of 1999.

One important consequence of targeting only the duration on the net debt is that a reduction in duration may be achieved by, for example, using either domestic or foreign interest rate swaps. A reduction in duration on the net debt can also be achieved by an increase in the duration of the central government asset portfolio. Therefore, targeting only the duration of the net debt brings higher flexibility to the management of the duration.

Smoothing the redemption profile is also a part of the interest rate risk management, and this is applied separately to domestic and foreign debt. Ensuring a smooth redemption profile, whereby a more or less constant proportion of the debt is redeemed each year, reduces the risk of being obliged to refinance the debt at a time when market conditions in general are unfavorable or when the borrowing terms for the central government are particularly unfavorable.

The SPF portfolio, which is a subasset portfolio of the net government debt, contains mortgage bonds. These mortgage bonds can be redeemed at par value at any time, that is, they include an option. For these bonds, an option-adjusted duration is used in the calculation of the duration on the government net debt.

Exchange rate risk

The Danish exchange rate policy is based on maintaining a stable rate for the Danish krone against the euro within the ERM II framework. As a result of this policy, the exchange rate risk on the foreign government debt is handled by taking only foreign loans with an end risk in euros (that is, borrowing takes place directly in euros or via loans that are swapped to euros).

From 1991 to 2000, the exchange rate risk on the foreign government debt was handled together with the exchange rate risk on the foreign exchange reserve in the central bank in a formalized set-up. In this way, the exchange rate risk for the government debt and the central bank was measured on a net basis. The formalized set-up was abolished by end of 2000 as a result of the decision that all foreign government debt should be in euros. Also, the central bank has only a very small amount of exchange reserves in currencies other than the euro, thus there was no need for a formalized arrangement by the end of 2000.

Credit risk

Credit risks exist on the swap portfolio of the central government. Therefore, risk principles for credit risk management of the portfolio have been laid down. Significant elements of credit risk management are high ratings for the counter-parties and credit exposures within relatively tight credit lines. New transactions take place only with counter-parties that have signed a collateral agreement. By the end of 2001, 80 percent of the swap portfolio consisted of collateralized agreements.

Cash management risk

As mentioned above, the government has an account with the DNB. According to the Maastricht Treaty, the government is not allowed to overdraw this account. To ensure that this requirement is fulfilled, there is a minimum deposit requirement for the government's account of DKr 10 billion (1.3 billion), and, at certain times, the requirement is higher. Every year, a detailed forecast of the government's payments in the next year is made. On the basis of this forecast, an estimate is made concerning the daily deposits to the government's account in the DNB. Because redemptions on the government debt are usually placed toward the end of the year, liquidity on the government's account is front loaded during the first part of the year to meet the redemption requirements. The amount of front-loading is reduced by buybacks of bonds redeemed in the current year.

Operational and legal risks

The separation of the various debt management functions (front, middle, and back offices) is a measure against administrative errors and operational risks. As described above, procedure manuals and internal procedures ensure a clear division of authority and responsibility allocated to the three functions. The use of simple, well-known, debt management instruments also contributes to minimizing the operational risks. Finally, the central government debt management area is subject to audit by the Auditor General. Legal risk is minimized by using standardized contracts.

Risks in relation to state guaranties

The government guarantees the borrowing and the financial transactions of a number of public entities. This implies a risk for the government. This risk is limited by setting up guidelines for the borrowing activities of the entities (see the first section of this case study for a discussion of the legislative basis for central government borrowing).

In 2001, the government-guaranteed entities obtained greater access to relending of government loans through the central government. Relending assures the government-guaranteed entities of a cheaper way of funding compared with a situation where they raise all funding individually. The loans offered to the entities are identical to existing government loans, including bonds, which are not benchmark issues. Relending increases the central government's gross financing requirement and is financed by on-the-run issues. This improves consolidation of the borrowing of the public sector.

Determining the level of risks

At the meetings of the ministry of Finance and the Government Debt Management unit, the overall objective for the interest rate risk of the government debt is determined by weighing borrowing costs against the risk.

In this process, a CaR model is used as a support in selecting the preferred issuing strategy and duration target. In the CaR model, different approaches to issuing strategy, amount of buybacks, and duration target are analyzed. The results are presented to and discussed with the ministry of finance.

The CaR model is developed in-house by the Government Debt Management unit. The model is used to quantify the interest rate risk by simulation of multiple interest rate scenarios, but it is also used as a scenario model in which specific scenarios are analyzed and discussed more thoroughly. The horizon of the analysis is up to 10 years.

Analyzing specific scenarios has played a major role in determining the overall strategy for the government debt during the last years. By using a scenario model, future developments in the outstanding amount of different bonds, redemption profiles, and the time path for the duration can be analyzed very thoroughly. This can determine whether a certain strategy is feasible, given some exogenous assumptions. Among the most important assumptions in this kind of analysis is the development in the government budget.

The duration target for central government debt has been reduced in the last few years. This reduction is primarily the result of falling debt and reduced interest costs, which have increased the willingness to take on risk. The nominal net debt has fallen from DKr 601 billion in 1997 to DKr 514 billion by the end of 2001, a drop from 54 percent to 38 percent of GDP.

From end-1998 to end-2001, the duration of the central government debt has been reduced from 4.4

to 3.4 years. The exact development in the duration during the previous year is made public in the annual report, which is published in February.

In the process of determining risks and borrowing strategy, normally neither domestic nor foreign borrowing is based on a particular interest rate outlook. Therefore, the managers do not in general actively try to generate excess returns—for example, by having views on the future interest development, which is different from market expectations.

Developing the Markets for Government Securities

Background

The Danish bond market is among the largest in Europe. The market value of the volume of bonds in circulation at the CSE was DKr 2.198 trillion at nominal value by the end of 2001. Besides government bonds, the Danish market has a large volume of mortgage-credit bonds. The large proportion of these bonds is explained by the long-standing tradition of financing construction and private housing by issuing mortgage-credit bonds. All domestic government securities are listed on the CSE. Government bonds make up one-third of the volume, and mortgage-credit bonds make up the remaining two-thirds.

The government bond yield curve

The Danish bond market is relatively large and mature, and, as mentioned above, government bonds make up only one-third of the outstanding value. Issuing bonds along the curve in many different maturity segments is therefore not a necessity under Danish policy to maintain a well-functioning capital market. Instead, in past years, the main focus has been on ensuring liquidity in government bonds by using a strategy of issuing fewer bonds with longer maturities, mainly because of a surplus on the government budget. Furthermore, buybacks have for some time been an important instrument in the Danish policy. Partly as a way of increasing the borrowing needs during the year, and partly as a way of reducing the outstanding amounts in old, non-market-conforming securities

(for example, old bonds with a high coupon), the buybacks are made in a time with surpluses.

In the domestic market, treasury bills are issued in 3-, 6-, 9-, and 12-month maturities and bonds in 2-, 5-, and 10-year maturities. All bonds are bullet loans with a fixed coupon. By the end of 1998, the government had ceased issuing 30-year bonds as a result of low borrowing needs and a reduction in the duration target for the government debt. Government bonds are used as benchmarks on the Danish bond market. Index bonds are not an instrument in the Danish government debt strategy because of their relatively low liquidity: The Danish strategy focuses on liquidity.

If government debt continues to fall, it is expected that mortgage bonds can play a benchmark role again, as was the situation until the beginning of the 1990s.

Issuing mechanisms

Issuing domestic debt

Government bonds and treasury notes are issued on tap by the central bank on behalf of the central government via the electronic trading system, Saxess, of the CSE. All licensed traders on the CSE may purchase government bonds directly from the DNB via the Saxess system.

Tap sales signify that government securities are issued when a borrowing requirement exists. Normally, the DNB does not underbid itself within the same day or within a few days. The sale of government securities on the preceding day is published daily.

The use of tap sales has a long tradition in the Danish mortgage bond market; therefore, it was natural to choose this issuing method when the government bond market was established. The use of tap sales gives the government a flexible system with the opportunity to issue bonds daily. It is the general assessment that tap sales are an appropriate way of issuing domestic government bonds in the Danish bond market.

The planning of tap sales for the year is based on selling nearly the same amount in each remaining month. This means that by the beginning of the year, the assumed expectation with respect to monthly sales is an evenly distributed sale during the year. This strategy is implemented by authorizing the front office to target a specified amount of issuance each month. The target is supplemented by a minimum and a maximum for each individual sale. The front office handles the tap sale within these boundaries. After each month, the expected monthly sale for the rest of the year is updated. Within the month, the dealers at the front office handle the tap sale. It is aimed to "tap" the market when market demands are high. Views on the future development in the interest rates are generally not a part of the planning of the tap sale.

The licensed traders on the CSE are obliged to report transactions that take place outside the Saxess platform. Transactions should be reported within five minutes. Of the total turnover, 10 percent are reported to the CSE and take place over the Saxess system. The remaining 90 percent are transacted by telephone sale between the market participants. Telephone sales are based on price indications from an electronic system at the CSE.

Treasury bills are sold at monthly auctions via an electronic system at the central bank. All licensed traders on the CSE and the DNB's monetary policy counter-parties may bid at the auctions. Bids are made for interest rates. All bids at or below the fixed cutoff interest rate are met at the cutoff interest rate (uniform pricing). Bids at the cutoff interest rate may be subject to proportional allocation.

Issuing foreign currency debt

Foreign loans have normally been established on the basis of concrete approaches from foreign investment banks, which are in contact with investors with special placement requirements. The currency swaps from Danish kroner to euros are established on the basis of competitive bidding from different investment banks.

As described above, the foreign strategy for 2002 and beyond focuses primarily on obtaining larger syndicated loans directly in euros, using one or more lead managers.

Primary dealers, market makers, and lending schemes

Primary dealers are not used in issuing domestic government securities in Denmark. All licensed traders

on the CSE may buy government bonds and treasury notes directly from the DNB via Saxess on the CSE. Licensed stock exchange traders and the DNB's monetary policy counter-parties may participate in the treasury bill auctions.

There are two voluntary market maker schemes for government securities under the auspices of the CSE and the Danish Securities Dealers Association, respectively. Participants in these schemes are obliged to quote two-way prices for a certain amount of appropriate bonds at any time. Under the CSE, scheme prices are set only in the 10-year benchmark, whereas the scheme of the Danish Securities Dealers Association comprises other liquid government securities as well. The central bank does not take part in the market maker plans.

To support liquidity, securities lending schemes have been set up. Two lending schemes exist, one held by the central government and one held by the SPF. A lending scheme supports the liquidity in the government bond market because situations involving any shortage of bonds are prevented. The lending scheme held by the government was introduced in 1998, and the SPF lending scheme was introduced in 2001. In both plans, Danish government bonds are accepted as collateral.

The lending scheme held by the government comprises mainly benchmark issues not held by the SPF. The SPF lending scheme consists of government bonds in the portfolio of the government bullet-loan type. The two lending schemes do not overlap with respect to bonds. Together, they consist of lending in most government bonds, including treasury bills.

Financial market contact

A regular and close contact with the financial market community is important for the government debt policy and is therefore given high priority. In regular meetings, different aspects of the management of the central government debt are discussed with market participants. At these meetings, market participants get the opportunity to discuss the management of the government debt with representatives of the Government Debt Management unit, including discussion of the potential need for changes or introduction of new financial instruments.

Clearing and settlement system

Government bonds, treasury notes, and treasury bills have been registered electronically in the Danish Securities Center (VP-system) since 1983. Danish government securities may also be registered in Euroclear and Clearstream. A direct link between Euroclear and VP-system aids easy transfer of securities between them without loss of trading days. Government securities trades are normally settled in VP-system, but may also be settled in Euroclear and Clearstream. Foreign loans are registered in Euroclear or Clearstream. All three systems adhere to the principles set forth in the Committee on Payment and Settlement Systems (CPSS)–International Organization of Securities Commissions (IOSCO) standards of November 2001 on securities settlement systems. The DNB as overseer conducted a formal assessment of VP-system against these standards during the first half of 2002.

Tax issues and effects on trading off government securities

Danish government bonds are treated equally to other bonds on the Danish bond market. No discriminatory tax rules exist. This means that the general legislation for taxation of bonds applies to government bonds. Foreigners investing in Danish bonds do not pay withholding tax.

For noncorporate investors who pay taxes to the Danish government, a minimum coupon rule exists for domestic bonds. This rule implies that capital gains on bonds with a coupon higher than the minimum coupon are free of taxation. The minimum coupon is normally revised semiannually according to the development in the general interest rate level.

Notes

1. The case study was prepared by the Government Debt Management Office of Danmarks Nationalbank.
2. www.nationalbanken.dk.

4
India[1]

India operates under a fiscal regime, with the Constitution of India specifying the fiscal responsibilities for the central and the state governments through the three lists: the Union List, the State List, and the Concurrent List. According to current budgetary practice, there are three sets of liabilities of the government that constitute public debt: internal debt, external debt, and "other liabilities."

Total outstanding liabilities of the central government as a proportion of GDP reached the peak level of 65.4 percent at the end of March 1992, after which it recorded a significant consolidation over the first half of the 1990s and declined to 56.4 percent by the end of March 1997 (see Table A.1 in the Appendix). In the next period, however, it showed an increasing trend, reaching 65.3 percent of GDP by the end of March 2002 and is projected to be around 67 percent by the end of March 2003.

As in the case of the central government, the debt-GDP ratio of state governments first recorded an improvement, falling from 19.4 percent at the end of March 1991 to 17.8 percent by the end of March 1997; later, the ratio increased significantly, reaching 24.1 percent by the end of March 2001 (see Table A.2 in the Appendix) in the revised estimates. According to the budget estimates of the state governments, the debt-GDP ratio was estimated to be 23.9 percent at the end of March 2002. Concomitantly, the interest payments–GDP ratio of the states increased from 1.5 percent in 1990–91 to a budgeted level of 2.6 percent in 2001–02.

The combined central and state governments liabilities had similar trends and stood at 72.9 percent of GDP at the end of March 2001 (see Table A.2 in the Appendix) and were estimated to be about 76 percent at the end of March 2002, significantly higher than 63.5 percent at the end of March 1997. The sharp increase in the debt-GDP ratio in 2001–02 is mainly attributable to the increase in the total liabilities of the central government. The continuing high level of public debt leads to increasing interest payments, which in turn necessitate higher market borrowings and put pressure on the fiscal deficit.

Until the early 1990s, India used a development strategy based on its predominant role in the public sector. Large statutory preempts and borrowing from the Reserve Bank of India (RBI), the central bank of the country, provided the government the ability to finance the large fiscal deficits. Lower administered yields on government securities coupled with high cash and liquidity reserve requirements resulted in a repressed financial system with very little scope for active debt management.

Reorientation of the debt management strategy began under the overall process of financial sector reforms that were started in the early 1990s. The authorities preferred a gradual approach for this purpose, wherein sequencing the policy initiatives was given the utmost importance.

The first initiative in the reforms process was to allow market-determined rates in the primary issuance market for government securities through auctions (1992). To compensate to some extent for the escalation in the cost of borrowing, and in view of the market preference under the new regime as well as the expectation that interest rates would experience downward trends over the years, the maturity profile of the debt issuance was shortened. The tenor of new loans issued during the next few years after moving toward price discovery mechanism was restricted to 10 years. The move was also prompted by the recommendations of the Committee to Review the Working of the Monetary System. This was followed by a stoppage of automatic monetization of the fiscal deficit and gradual withdrawal of the central bank's support to finance the government budget at subsidized rates.

The role of net market borrowing in financing gross fiscal deficit gradually increased from 21 percent in 1991–92 to 66.2 percent at present. This has happened even while statutory preempts were being reduced. Reserve requirements were brought down. The statutory liquidity ratio (SLR), which requires banks to invest a certain percentage of their liabilities in government securities, was brought down from a peak of 38.5 percent in 1990 to 25 percent in 1997. (At present, the SLR continues to be at 25 percent, which is the statutory minimum.) The cash reserve ratio (CRR), which requires banks to keep a certain proportion of their liabilities in the form of cash with the RBI, was also brought down from a high of 25 percent in 1992 (including the CRR on incremental liabilities) to 5 percent in June 2002.

Debt management strategy began to focus, on the one hand, on the interest rate and refinancing risks inherent in managing public debt and, on the other hand, on monetary policy objectives so that the debt management policy would be consistent with the objectives of the monetary policy. This strategy, in turn, required the authorities to develop the institutional, infrastructure, legal, and regulatory framework for the government securities market.

Developing a Sound Governance and Institutional Framework

Objective

The objective of the debt management policy has changed over the years. It first focused on minimizing the cost of borrowing, but now the objective is minimizing the cost of borrowing over the long run, taking into account the risk involved, and ensuring that debt management policy is consistent with monetary policy.

Scope

Under the current Indian budgetary classifications, three sets of liabilities constitute central government debt: internal debt, external debt, and "other liabilities."

Internal debt and external debt constitute the public debt of India and are secured under the Consolidated Fund of India, as reported under "Consolidated Fund of India—Capital Account" in the *Annual Financial Statement of the Union Budget.* Article 292 of the Indian Constitution provides for placing a limit on public debt secured under the Consolidated Fund of India but precludes "other liabilities" under the Public Account There is also a similar provision in Article 293 with respect to borrowings by the states, wherein the state legislature has the power to set limits on state borrowings upon the security of the Consolidated Fund of the state. However, a state's power to borrow is limited to internal debt, and a state is required to obtain prior consent of the government of India as long as the state has outstanding loans made by the government of India.

Internal debt includes market loans; special securities issued to the RBI; compensation and other bonds; treasury bills issued to the RBI, state governments, commercial banks, and other parties; as well as nonnegotiable and non-interest-bearing rupee securities issued to internal financial institutions. The internal debt is classified into market loans, other long- and medium-term borrowing, and short-term borrowing and is shown in the receipt budget of the union government. External debt represents loans received from foreign governments and bodies. The liabilities other than internal and external debts include other interest-bearing obligations of the government, such as post office savings deposits, deposits under small savings schemes, loans raised through post office cash certificates, provident funds, interest-bearing reserve funds of departments such as railways and telecommunications, and certain other deposits.

The "other liabilities" of the government arise in the government's accounts more in its capacity as a banker than as a borrower. Hence, such borrowings, not secured under the Consolidated Fund of India, are shown as part of the Public Account. Furthermore, some of the items of other liabilities, such as small savings, are more in the nature of autonomous flows, which to a large extent are determined by public preference and the relative attractiveness of these instruments. Nevertheless, it should be emphasized that all liabilities are obligations of the government.

Provisional Actual Budget data for the year 2001–02 show that the gross fiscal deficit of the central government at 6 percent of GDP was financed by domestic market borrowings to the extent of 69.4 percent and through other liabilities to the extent of 26.1 percent. External financing accounted for only 1.6 percent of the gross fiscal deficit. According to budget estimates for 2002–03, the gross fiscal deficit of the central government is targeted at 5.3 percent of GDP and is to be financed by domestic market borrowings to the extent of 70.7 percent and by other liabilities to the extent of 28.7 percent; external financing would contribute only 0.6 percent.

Coordination with monetary and fiscal policies

The RBI acts as the government's debt manager for marketable internal debt. Because the RBI is also responsible for monetary management, there is a need for coordination between the monetary and debt management policies, especially in view of the large market borrowing program to be completed at market-related rates. At the time the budget is prepared, there are consultations between the government of India and the RBI on the overall magnitude of the market borrowing program of the central government and the aggregate market borrowings of all the states.

The coordination among debt management and fiscal and monetary policies is achieved through

- the Financial Markets Committee (FMC) within the RBI (the heads of departments responsible for debt management, monetary policy, and foreign exchange reserves management), which meets daily to assess the markets, liquidity, and other financial considerations that might arise;
- involvement of the debt management functionaries in the monetary policy strategy meeting, which is held at least once a month;
- the Standing Committee on Cash and Debt Management (with representatives from the RBI responsible for debt management and operations as banker to the government and the ministry of finance (MoF), which meets once a month; and
- the annual pre-budget exercise of dovetailing the monetary budget with government finances, including the finances of subnational governments.

During the first stages of market development, especially for countries such as India with large net market borrowing (3 to 4 percent of GDP in the recent period), having the central bank responsible for both debt management and monetary management has the advantage of appropriate policy coordination. During this early period, however, as the markets develop, the economy opens up for capital flows and the private sector starts contributing more to the economic activity, and there is a need for independent monetary management and separation of the debt management function from the central bank. Under the Fiscal Responsibility and Budget Management Bill (currently before parliament) and as a first step toward separation of debt management from monetary management, it is proposed that within three years, RBI participation in the primary market for government securities will be eliminated.

The approach of separation of the debt management function from the central bank has in principle been accepted. However, separation of the two functions would be dependent on the fulfillment of three preconditions: reasonable control over the fiscal deficit, development of financial markets, and necessary legislative changes. The actual separation of debt management functions would depend on the extent and speed with which the fiscal deficit can be brought down. The large borrowing requirements of the government and the need to minimize the impact of such borrowing requirements on interest rates has necessitated private placements of securities with the RBI from time to time or participation in the primary issuance market as a noncompetitive bidder with the later sale of such securities to the market as conditions improve. Elimination of RBI participation in the primary market is perceived as the first step in separating the function of debt management from monetary management. A lower fiscal deficit is thus envisaged as a required precondition for ensuring that the government borrowings are not disrupting the financial markets and enabling a smooth transition to the separation of the debt management function. In the development and integration of the financial markets, significant progress has been made with the introduction of new instruments and participants, strengthening of the institutional infrastructure, and greater clarity in the regulatory structure. On the legislative front, two important changes are (a) the proposed amendment in the RBI Act of 1934 to take away the mandatory nature of public debt management by the RBI, vesting the discretion with the central government to undertake the management either by itself or to assign it to some other independent body; and (b) the proposed Fiscal Responsibility and Budget Management Bill, which is expected to rein in the fiscal deficit.

Legal framework

The Constitution of India gives the executive branch the power to borrow upon the security of the Consolidated Fund of India, or that of the respective state, within such limits, if any, as may from time to time be fixed by law by parliament or the respective state legislature.

Although parliament or the state legislature gives the authority to borrow by approving the budget, the RBI as an agent of the government (both union and the states) implements the borrowing program.

The RBI draws the necessary statutory powers for debt management from the RBI Act of 1934. The management of the union government's public debt is an obligation of the RBI, but the RBI undertakes the management of the public debts of the various state governments by agreement.

The procedural aspects in debt management operations are governed by the Public Debt Act of 1944 and the Public Debt Rules framed hereunder. Considering the technological changes and other developments taking place in the government securities market, the authorities are interested in replacing the 1944 act with an updated proposed Government Securities Act.

Amendments to the RBI Act have been proposed to remove the mandatory nature of public debt management by the RBI and allow the government to entrust the public debt management function to any agent. This would remove a legal hurdle for separation of debt management functions from the RBI.

Organizational structure

All debt management functions for marketable internal debt are currently undertaken in the RBI, albeit in different departments. The middle office functions relating to decisions on the maturity profile and timing of issuance are undertaken in consultation with the MoF.

As regards management of the external debt, several territorial divisions in the Department of Economic Affairs of the MoF, such as the IMF-World Bank Division, the European Central Bank (ECB) Division, ADB Division, EEC Division, and Japan Division, in addition to the RBI, act as the front offices. The External Debt Management Unit of the MoF acts as the middle office, and the Office of the Controller of Aid Accounts and Audit of the MoF acts as the back office.

The RBI is vested with the powers of managing government debt, of both the union and the state governments, under the provisions of the RBI Act of 1934. Management of debt of the union statutorily devolves upon the RBI, but management of the debt of the states has been undertaken by the RBI through mutual agreements between the central bank and the respective states. Thus, the RBI is responsible for managing the market borrowing program of the union and state governments.

Within the RBI, the Internal Debt Management Unit performs the debt management function. The main functions comprise formulation of a core calendar for primary issuance, deciding the desired maturity profile of the debt, designing the instruments and methods of raising resources, deciding the size and timing of issuance, and other critical decisions, taking into account the government's needs, market conditions, and preferences of various segments while ensuring that the entire strategy is consistent with the overall monetary policy objectives. The Unit also conducts auctions.

The actual receipt of bids and settlement functions are undertaken at various offices of the RBI. Various public debt offices also manage the registry and depository functions and keep securities accounts, including the book entry form of ownership. The central accounts are maintained by the Department of Government and Bank Accounts.

Decisions on the implementation of the borrowing program, based on proposals made by the Unit and market preference, are periodically made by the Standing Committee on Cash and Debt Management, made up of MoF and RBI officials. This represents a formal working relationship between the MoF and the RBI, and it is complemented by regular discussions between the ministry's Budget and Expenditure Divisions and the RBI.

Another standing committee is the Technical Advisory Committee on Money and Government Securities Market, which advises the RBI on development and regulation of the government securities market. This committee is made up of eminent people from the financial sector, representatives of market associations such as the Primary Dealers Association of India, the Fixed Income Money Markets and Derivatives Association of India, mutual funds, academia, and the government.

The operations of the debt management functions are subject to the statutory audit that takes place at the RBI, which covers all the functions of the RBI. The concerned departments within the RBI are also subjected to internal audit, including management audit and concurrent audit. Separate financial accounts of the debt management operations at the RBI are not prepared, hence there is no scope for subjecting these operations to a formal audit. However, although accounting for the debt management operations is done by the government's Controller General of Accounts, the accounts are subject to the audit by the Comptroller and Auditor General of Accounts, a constitutional body.

The internal debt management functions are reported in the *Annual Report* of the RBI, which is a statutory report and is placed before parliament, and the external debt management functions are reported in the *Annual Status Report on External Debt* presented to parliament by the minister of finance.

Risk Management Framework and Debt Management Strategy

Risk management framework

In view of the large fiscal deficits of the central government—in the range of 5-7 percent of GDP in the 1990s—there is a need to ensure a long-term stable environment for facilitating economic growth with price stability. As regards management of external debt, the Indian government has adopted a cautious and step-by-step approach toward capital account convertibility. It has initially liberalized non-debt-creating financial flows followed by liberalization of long-term debt flows. There is partial liberalization of external commercial borrowing, but only for the medium-term and long-term maturities. There is tight control on short-term external debt and a close watch on the size of the current account deficit. In fact, the government of India does not borrow from external commercial sources, and there is no short-term external debt on the government account. There is a high share of concessional debt, amounting to nearly 80 percent of sovereign external debt at the end of March 2002. The maturity of government debt is also concentrated toward the long end for the debt portfolio.

These policies have paid dividends. Capital account restrictions for residents and modest short-term liabilities helped India to protect itself during the East Asian economic crisis from 1997 to 2000. There has been significant improvement of external debt indicators over the years. The World Bank's *Global Development Finance* now classifies India as a low-indebted country. The incidence of external debt burden, as measured by debt-to-GDP ratio, was reduced to 20 percent at the end of December 2001, from the peak level of 38.7 percent at the end of March 1992. Similarly, the burden of debt service as a proportion of gross current receipts on external account declined from a peak of 35.3 percent in 1990–91 to 16.3 percent in 2000–01. With the steady contraction in the stock of short-term debt, the ratio of short-term to total external debt declined from a peak of 10.2 percent at the end of March 1991 to 3.4 percent at the end of March 2001. At the same time, with a substantial increase in foreign exchange reserves, short-term debt as a proportion of foreign exchange assets declined from a high of 382 percent to 8.8 percent.

As regards internal debt, there is a natural incentive to focus on long-term sustainability of interest rates, keeping in view the fiscal scenario and other macroeconomic developments, while planning the maturity pattern of debt and the component of fixed- and floating-rate and external debt. There has been a conscious attempt to avoid issuance of floating-rate and short-term debt and foreign currency–denominated debt.

During the early years of the move to market-determined rates, keeping in sight the investors' preference, the average maturity of new debt (issued during a year) was between 5.5 and 7.7 years during the period 1992–93 to 1998–99. As inflationary conditions receded and markets developed, keeping in view the redemption pattern of existing debt stock, the need to smooth the maturity pattern of the debt stock, and the need to minimize the refinancing risk, debt management policy has consciously attempted to extend the maturity pattern of the debt. Thus, the average maturity of new debt issued after 1998–99 (issued during a year) was above 10 years, and for the year ending December 2001, the average maturity of loans issued during the year stood at about 14 years. The average maturity of the total debt stock, which was about 6 years in March 1998, stood at about 8.20 years at the end of December 2001.

The trade-off between market timing (which involves carrying cost) and the just-in-time pattern (which involves the risk of uncertain markets) is taken into account while tapping the market. Within the year, to ensure that the markets do not become volatile as a result of the large volume of borrowings made by the government or uncertainties in the foreign exchange markets, the RBI at times subscribes to the primary issuances through private placements of debt with itself. These are later sold in the secondary market when liquidity conditions ease and uncertainty diminishes. To minimize the risk arising from occasional RBI participation in primary auctions, which results in an increase in reserve money, the RBI undertakes active open market operations adjusted to the needs of liquidity in the system using domestic and external operations.

However, the major risk in debt management is the size of the debt itself and the pressures of servicing the debt. Hence, as part of its advisory role and as debt manager, the RBI has been urging the government of India to enforce a ceiling on overall debt. It has also provided the technical inputs in formulating the Fiscal Responsibility and Budget Management Bill to ensure that the country's vulnerability is minimized. Currently before parliament, the Fiscal Responsibility and Budget Management Bill envisages targeted reduction in the fiscal deficit, especially revenue deficit and total debt as a share of GDP, as well as elimination of RBI participation in the primary issuance of debt.

Strategy

Given the size of the market borrowing program of the union and the states, the approach to risk management has been one of minimizing the cost of raising debt subject to refinancing risk. Thus, the decisions on composition and maturity of debt reflect a risk-averse preference in the context of the prevailing fiscal deficit and likely fiscal deficits in the future. It comprises three tenets:

- minimizing refinancing risk,
- minimizing external debt, and
- minimizing floating-rate debt.

Simultaneously, the focus has been on ensuring that the interest rates are sustainable over time.

As regards external debt, the focus has been on relatively concessional loans and highest maturity. Recently, the government of India also adopted the policy of prepaying a part of the debt taken from multilateral institutions and other countries. In some cases, maturity and interest rates of these expensive loans have been restructured by the lending institutions or countries.

Avoiding external sovereign debt and floating-rate debt has considerably reduced the country's vulnerability. According to the revised estimates for 2001–02, internal debt constituted about 61 percent of the total liabilities, and other internal liabilities constituted 24 percent of total outstanding liabilities of the central government (see Table A.2 in the Appendix). External debt (at current exchange rates), which consists mostly of debt to multilateral institutions and other countries, constituted about 15 percent of the total liabilities. The nonmarketable debt, including mainly the small savings mobilizations, is managed by the government. The refinancing risk is very well recognized. The debt management policy focuses on managing the maturity profile of the debt and deciding on the share of 364-day treasury bills in the total borrowing program as well as the share of floating-rate debt.

The process of debt consolidation—involving the reopening and reissuance of existing stock—has helped in more or less containing the number of bonds to the prevailing level at the end of 1999 (fiscal year). The results of the process of consolidation may be gauged from the fact that of the 110 outstanding loans,[2] 43 loans (39 percent) account for 77 percent of the marketable debt stock. However, in view of the large and growing net borrowings by the government, there has been a need to extend the maturity profile of government debt to minimize the refinancing risk. The loans maturing within the next 5 years account for 31 percent of the total debt stock,[3] another 37 percent of the loans mature between the sixth and tenth year. Thus, about 32 percent of the loans mature after 10 years. The weighted average maturity of the debt stock was about 8.20 years as of the end of 2001, compared with about 6 years as of March 31, 1998.

Reopenings through price-based auctions (as opposed to earlier yield-based auctions) began in 1999 and have greatly improved market liquidity and helped the emergence of benchmark securities in the market. In addition, such reopenings also have helped the price discovery process, acting as a proxy for the when-issued market.

Callbacks of numerous existing loans in exchange for a few benchmark stocks have not been considered worthwhile because of administrative, cost, and legal considerations. In the absence of budget surpluses and a call provision for existing stocks, this form of active consolidation would be difficult to achieve.

However, during 2001–02, the government had prepaid a part of expensive external debt from multilateral institutions and restructured some costly external debt from other countries. The government has also allowed selected public sector enterprises to prepay a part of their expensive external debt, which was guaranteed by the government. These policies have helped to reduce sovereign external debt, as well as contingent liabilities of the government, to some extent.

Cash management

In a landmark development in 1994, the government of India entered into an agreement with the RBI to phase out the system of automatic monetization of budget deficits within three years. Accordingly, the system of financing the government through creation of ad hoc treasury bills was abolished effective April 1, 1997. Under a new arrangement, a scheme of ways and means advances (WMAs) was introduced to help the government of India to address the temporary mismatches in its cash flows. According to this scheme, a limit was fixed for WMAs, so that when the government reached 75 percent of the limit, the RBI could enter the market on behalf of the government to raise funds. This arrangement meant that the government has to fund its budget requirements at market-related rates. Keeping in view the trends in the government's cash flows, the limit for WMAs for the second half of the year is kept lower than that for the first half of the year. The introduction of the WMAs scheme demanded greater skills in active debt management on the part of the RBI. It also brought up the government's need for efficient cash management. Accordingly, surplus funds, if any, in the government's account are invested in its own securities available in RBI's portfolio, thus reducing the net borrowing from the RBI as well as the cost.

The RBI also provides WMAs to the states. The limits are fixed through a formula linked to their revenue receipts and capital expenditure. Once the limits are reached, the accounts go into overdraft, and they are not only limited in size to the WMA bound but also not allowed to continue beyond 12 working days. Beyond this point, payments are stopped on behalf of the respective state government.

Surplus funds of states are invested in special intermediate treasury bills of the central government. Because these instruments can be instantly rediscounted whenever required, the interest rate is fixed at the bank rate minus 1 percent. At the request of the state governments, the RBI also invests their surplus funds in dated securities offered by the government of India from its investment portfolio at prices prevailing in the secondary markets.

Contingent liabilities

Contingent liabilities of the central government arise because of the government's role in promoting private savings and investment by issuing guarantees. Contingent liabilities of the central government could be both domestic and external contingent liabilities and could also be explicit or implicit in nature. Domestic contingent liabilities of the central government are made up of direct guarantees on domestic debt, recapitalization costs for public sector enterprises, or unfunded pension liabilities. External contingent liabilities are made up of direct guarantees on external debt, exchange rate guarantees on external debt such as Resurgent India Bonds and

Indian Millennium Deposits, and counter-guarantees provided to foreign investors participating in infrastructure projects, particularly for electric power. Although from the accounting point of view, contingent liabilities do not form part of the government debt, they could pose severe constraints on the fiscal position of the government in the event of default.

The total outstanding direct credit guarantees issued by the central government on both domestic and external debt remained stable around Rs 1 trillion from the end of March 1994 to the end of March 1999. Domestic guarantees increased modestly during the corresponding period, but there was an absolute decline in the guarantees on external debt. As a proportion of GDP, however, both domestic guarantees and external guarantees registered a decline of 3 percent from 1993 to 1999. Thus, the total guaranteed debt of the central government declined steadily, from 11.8 percent of GDP in 1993–94 to 5.9 percent 1998–99.

In addition, the exchange rate guarantee on external debt has implications for the finances of the central government. For example, for Resurgent India Bonds, according to the agreement, exchange rate loss in excess of 1 percent on the total foreign currency, or the equivalent of US$4.2 billion, would have to be borne by the government of India. The extent of such a loss, since August 1998, when Resurgent India Bonds were first issued, would depend on the exchange rate prevailing at the time of redemption in 2003. A similar exchange rate guarantee was provided on the amount of US$5.5 billion raised through India Millennium Deposits from October to November 2000. Counter-guarantees provided to foreign investors participating in infrastructure projects bring about similar risk for the government exchequer. There is also a growing volume of implicit domestic contingent liabilities in pension funds.

Legal ceilings on government debt and contingent liabilities

Given the legacy of huge public debt and interest burden due to a long history of high fiscal deficits, which has increasingly constrained maneuverability in fiscal management, the central government introduced the Fiscal Responsibility and Budget Management Bill (2000) in parliament. The bill aims at ensuring intergenerational equity in fiscal management and long-term macroeconomic stability. This would be accomplished by achieving sufficient revenue surplus; eliminating fiscal deficit; removing fiscal impediments in the effective conduct of monetary policy and prudential debt management consistent with fiscal sustainability through limits on central government borrowings, debt, and deficits; and establishing greater transparency in fiscal operations. The specific target for debt management in this regard is to ensure that the total liabilities of the central government (including external debt at the current exchange rate) is reduced during the next 10 years and does not exceed 50 percent of GDP. Simultaneously, the central government will not borrow from the RBI in the form of subscription to the primary issues by the RBI.

The bill also attempts to check the contingent liability by restricting guarantees to 0.5 percent of GDP during any financial year. In particular, transparency in budget statements would involve disclosure of contingent liabilities created by way of guarantees, including guarantees to finance exchange risk on any transactions, and all claims and commitments made by the central government that have potential budgetary implications.

Developing the Markets for Government Securities

Need and approach

The development of deep and liquid markets for government securities is of critical importance to the RBI in facilitating price discovery and reducing the cost of government debt. Such markets also enable the effective transmission of monetary policy, facilitate introduction and pricing of hedging products, and serve as a benchmark for other debt instruments. Hence, as the monetary authority, the RBI has a stake in the development of debt markets. Liquid markets imply more transparent and correct valuation of financial assets; they also facilitate better risk management and are therefore extremely useful to the RBI as a regula-

tor of the financial system. As the system integrates with the global markets, it is necessary to ensure low-cost financial intermediation in domestic markets or the intermediation will move offshore. This reinforces the argument for development of domestic debt markets.

Therefore, since the early 1990s, the RBI has been focusing on development of the government securities markets through carefully and cautiously sequenced measures within a clear agenda for primary and secondary market design, development of institutions, enlargement of participants and products, sound trading and settlement practices, dissemination of market information, and prudential guidelines on valuation, accounting, and disclosure.

Primary dealers

In 1996, the structure of primary dealers was adopted for developing both the primary and the secondary markets for government securities in India. The objective of promoting an institutional mechanism for primary dealers is to ensure development of underwriting and market-making capabilities for government securities outside the RBI, so that the latter will gradually shed these functions; the purpose is also to strengthen the infrastructure in the government securities market to make it vibrant, liquid, and broad-based. The intermediate goals include improving the secondary market trading system, which would contribute to price discovery, enhance liquidity and turnover, encourage voluntary holding of government securities among a wider investor base, and make primary dealers an effective conduit for conducting open market operations.

Among their obligations are giving annual bidding commitments to the RBI, to underwrite the primary issuance and offer two-way quotes in select government securities. The annual bidding commitments are determined through negotiations between the RBI and the primary dealers. Serious bidding is ensured through a stipulation of a success ratio (40 percent) linked to the bidding commitments. In return, the dealers are extended a liquidity support by the RBI. This support, which was entirely a standing facility in the initial years (linked to their bidding commitments and secondary market activity with a cap, a certain ratio of their net worth), is being gradually withdrawn. The primary dealers, along with banks, are allowed to participate in the Liquidity Adjustment Facility of the RBI, whereby the RBI operates in the market through repos and reverse repos.

Primary dealers are essentially well-capitalized, nonbanking finance companies, set up as subsidiaries of banks and financial institutions or as corporate entities, and they are predominant players in the government securities market. Currently, 18 primary dealers are authorized by the RBI.

The RBI also envisaged the institutional mechanism of satellite dealers to further the efforts of the primary dealers with a main objective of developing a retail market for government debt. As their name suggests, they were to establish a link with a primary dealer, and thus the RBI did not extend them the same benefits as those extended to primary dealers. This lack of access to the call money market and the impediments in transacting in the repo market (including prohibition of sale of securities purchased under repos and prohibition of short sale) have restricted the operations of the satellite dealers. Thus, the system has never succeeded. Although some of the satellite dealers later became primary dealers, others have been active only as brokers.

Brokers

Although banks are encouraged to deal directly without involving brokers, they can undertake trades in government securities through the member brokers of the National Stock Exchange, the Bombay Stock Exchange, and the Over-the-Counter Exchange of India. About 35 percent of trades are OTC trades. The remaining trades are negotiated through brokers who are members of the exchanges and are reported on the exchanges. After irregularities in the securities market that involved fraudulent links between the brokers and banks, banks were advised by the RBI not to trade more than 5 percent of their transactions through a single broker.

Instruments

In the early 1990s, there was experimentation with issuing a variety of instruments, such as zero coupon bonds, stocks for which investors could pay in installments, floating-rate bonds, and capital-indexed bonds, in addition to fixed-rate bonds.

The requirements of the various segments of the market, the need to smooth the redemption pattern across different years, and the need to focus on issuing new securities in key benchmark maturities are all factors that have resulted in issuing relatively longer dated securities in the last few years. To the greatest possible extent, the RBI endeavors to issue securities across the yield curve. Although the extended maturity profile has benefited long-term investors such as insurance companies and pension or provident funds, it has resulted in asset liability mismatches for the banking sector, which continues to be the major final investor in, and holder of, government securities. Recognizing this, the RBI is attempting to develop the separate trading of registered interest and principal of securities (STRIPS) market in government securities. The consultative paper on STRIPS has been placed on the RBI web site for wider consultation.[4]

Further, to facilitate interest rate risk management, the RBI has reintroduced floating-rate bonds in a modest way (the first issuance of floating-rate bonds was made in 1995). The outstanding floating-rate bonds account for less than 1.5 percent at present. Bonds with callable options have not been experimented with, taking into account the size of the overall debt, new issuance programs, and refinancing risk.

Issuance procedures

Government stock is normally sold through auction. Sometimes it is sold through a tap system with a fixed coupon. The salient features of the issuance procedures have been codified and are placed in the public domain through a government notification called "general notification." The public is notified of the details of each issuance, generally three to seven days before the flotation or auction.

Issuance of a calendar has to address the trade-off between certainty for the market and flexibility for the issuer in terms of market timing. The uncertain trends in the cash-flow pattern of the government also greatly constrain the publication of the issuance calendar. An indicative calendar for issuance of marketable dated securities by the government of India was introduced in April 2002 for the first half of the fiscal year. It was followed by an announcement of an indicative borrowing calendar for the second half of the year in September 2002. This practice of announcing the calendar twice a year is expected to continue, to enable institutional and retail investors to better plan their investments and provide further transparency and stability in the government securities market. There is already a preannounced issuance calendar for treasury bills auctions.

For the states, the RBI normally prefers a preannounced coupon method, and the yields are fixed about 25 basis points above the rate prevailing in the market for a union government stock of similar maturity.

The auctions of government securities are open for individuals, institutions, pension funds, provident funds, nonresident Indians, overseas corporate bodies, and foreign institutional investors. Individuals and small investors such as provident and pension funds and corporations can also participate in auctions on a noncompetitive basis in certain specific issues of dated government securities and in treasury bill auctions. Noncompetitive bidding has been allowed since January 2002, and up to 5 percent is allocated to noncompetitive bidders at weighted average cutoff rates. Bids are received through banks and primary dealers. A multiple-price auction format has been the predominant method used for the auctions. However, the RBI of late has started using the uniform-price auction method on an experimental basis.

Whenever there is an urgent need for the government to raise resources from the market, and sufficient time is not available to prepare the market for a public issuance, the RBI takes a private placement (at market-related rates based on the secondary market rates) and such acquisitions are off loaded in the secondary market during appropriate market conditions. The tap method is also used when the demand is uncertain and the RBI and the government do not want to take on the uncertainty of auctioning the security. This approach is widely used in the case of state government loans.

Technological development and settlement mechanism

The RBI developed a negotiated dealing system (NDS), which became operational in February 2002.

The NDS facilitates electronic bidding in auctions and offers a straight-through settlement, because it connects with the public debt offices and banks' accounts with the RBI. Banks, primary dealers, and other financial institutions, including mutual funds, can negotiate deals in government securities through this electronic mode on a real-time basis and report all trades to the system for settlement. The details of all trades are transparently available to the market on the NDS. In October 2002, the RBI also began disseminating data on trades in government securities reported on the NDS on a real-time basis through its web site.

The delivery-versus-payment system (DvP), introduced in 1995 for the settlement of transactions in government securities, has greatly mitigated the settlement risk and facilitated growth in the volume of transactions in the secondary market for government securities. Completion of the ongoing projects and launching of the associated functions and products relating to the Clearing Corporation of India Ltd. (CCIL), the NDS, electronic funds transfer, and the Real-time gross settlement (RTGS) system, as well as the proposed Government Securities Act (in lieu of the existing Public Debt Act of 1944), would further augment the efficiency and safety of the government securities market.

A clearing corporation, the CCIL, was introduced simultaneously with the NDS in February 2002. The CCIL acts as a central counter-party in the settlement of outright and repo transactions in government securities. The settlements through the CCIL are guaranteed by the corporation through a settlement guarantee fund within the corporation, which is funded by the members. The establishment of the CCIL is seen as a major step in the development of the government securities market, and the repo market is expected to witness significant growth.

Work on the RTGS system has already begun, and it is expected to bring about further improvement in the payment and settlement system.

Retail market

The RBI has been encouraging wider retail participation in government securities. As part of these efforts, the RBI has been promoting the gilt mutual funds to develop a retail market for government securities.

Gilt funds are mutual funds with 100 percent of their investments in government securities; the fund in turn sells its units to investors. The RBI offers a limited liquidity support to the mutual funds in the form of repos to promote an indirect retail market for government securities.

The RBI allows retail participation at the auctions on a noncompetitive basis up to a maximum of 5 percent of the notified amount. Banks and primary dealers operate the scheme.

To bring about efficient and easy retail transactions in government securities, an order-driven, screen-based system is proposed to be implemented through the stock exchanges with adequate safeguards for settlement.

Coordination between public debt management and private sector debt

Together with active debt management of marketable government debt, the RBI has been focusing on the need to rationalize the continuing administered interest rates and tax regime on small savings and contractual savings, such as provident and pension funds, not only to minimize the effective cost of overall debt but also to align the interest rates on these liabilities with market-determined rates. Public financial institutions, or long-term development banking institutions, are the largest issuers of debt in the nongovernmental sector, and guidelines have been issued to them for ensuring that the interest rates on debt they issue do not go beyond certain spreads over government securities of similar tenor. Corporate debt is not governed by the RBI and while communicating to the government of India (MoF) the acceptable level of total market borrowing, the RBI takes into account the needs of the corporate sector that have to be met from both credit market and capital (debt) markets.

Laws and regulations

The existing Public Debt Act of 1944 is expected to be replaced by a new government securities bill. The proposed legislation seeks to streamline and simplify procedures in the handling of public debt of the central and state governments and will reflect the changes in the operating and technological environment.

Under the amendments in March 2000 to the Securities (Contracts) Regulation Act, powers have been clearly delegated to the RBI for regulating the dealings in the government securities market.[5]

Short selling of securities is not permitted under the current regulatory framework.

Tax treatment

Government securities are not subject to withholding tax. Gains are treated as both income and capital gains, depending on the nature of the transaction, and investors are allowed to pay tax on both a cash and an accrual basis. Such a treatment, however, could cause distortions in the market when the STRIPS market on government securities comes into existence. The Central Board of Direct Taxes has amended the guidelines on tax treatment of zero-coupon bonds or deep discount bonds by requiring that for tax purposes, the mark-to-market gains in the relevant year will be reckoned. The tax incentive on nonmarketable debt, such as small savings, has tended to distort the market for government securities and a committee under the Deputy Governor of RBI recently recommended rationalization of tax treatment on such instruments.

Adherence to CPSS-IOSCO standards

A detailed examination of CPSS-IOSCO standards is being undertaken separately. Nevertheless, the broad adherence to the standards can be described:

- Presettlement risk: Currently, all trades between direct market participants are confirmed directly between the participants on the same day and are settled either on the same day or on the next day, thereby minimizing presettlement risk. For trades undertaken through members of the exchanges, confirmation is done on T+0, but settlement can be done up to T+5.

- Settlement risk: All trades undertaken by banks, financial institutions, primary dealers, and mutual funds having "scripless" accounts with the RBI in its Public Debt Office are settled under a gross trade-by-trade DvP system with queuing up to the end of the day, when funds settlement is eventually known. At this time, if there is shortage of securities or funds, trades are considered "failed." Such failure constituted only around 0.01 percent of the total number of trades in 2001 and about 0.3 percent of the total value of trades in 2001. Both the presettlement and settlement risks were minimized with the setting up of the CCIL and its ability to provide guaranteed settlement by various risk management systems, including the constitution of the settlement guarantee fund.

- Legal risk: Several of the legal safeguards recommended for securing safe settlement systems—including rights of central counter-parties to the settlement guarantee fund in the event of, for example, insolvency of members—are yet to be put in place. However, pending detailed legislative changes, the legality of various aspects of the settlement process has been achieved through the framing of mutual agreements under contract law and through the use of concepts such as novation for ensuring legality of netting.

Notes

1. The case study was prepared by Usha Thorat and Charan Singh from the Reserve Bank of India and Tarun Das from the Ministry of Finance.

2. These results are as of the end of 2001.

3. These figures also occurred as of the end of 2001.

4. www.rbi.org.in.

5. The Securities and Exchanges Board of India is the capital market regulator. A High-Level Committee on Capital Market coordinates both the regulators.

Appendix

Table A.1. Outstanding Liabilities of the Central Government
(In Rs 10 million)

Year	Internal liabilities (3+4)	Internal debt	Other internal liabilities	External debt[a]	Total outstanding liabilities (2+5)	External debt adjusted[b]	Total outstanding liabilities adjusted[b] (2+7)
1	2	3	4	5	6	7	8
1990–91	283,033	154,004	129,029	31,525	314,558	66,314	349,347
1991–92	317,714	172,750	144,964	36,948	354,662	109,685	427,399
1992–93	359,654	199,100	160,554	42,269	401,923	120,987	480,641
1993–94	430,623	245,712	184,911	47,345	477,968	127,808	558,431
1994–95	487,682	266,467	221,215	50,929	538,611	142,514	630,196
1995–96	554,984	307,869	247,115	51,249	606,233	148,398	703,382
1996–97	621,438	344,476	276,962	54,238	675,676	149,564	771,002
1997–98	722,962	388,998	333,964	55,332	778,294	161,418	884,380
1998–99	834,551	459,696	374,855	57,255	891,806	177,934	1,012,485
1999–2000	962,592	714,254	248,338	58,437	1,021,029	186,791	1,149,383
2000–01	1,111,081	803,698	307,383	65,945	1,177,026	189,990	1,301,071
2001–02 (RE)	1,274,369	909,052	365,317	67,899	1,342,268	222,780	1,497,149
2002–03 (BE)	1,444,248	1,021,739	422,509	68,520	1,512,768	n.a.	n.a.
(As percent of GDP)							
1990–91	49.8	27.1	22.7	5.5	55.3	11.7	61.4
1991–92	48.6	26.5	22.2	5.7	54.3	16.8	65.4
1992–93	48.1	26.6	21.5	5.6	53.7	16.2	64.2
1993–94	50.1	28.6	21.5	5.5	55.6	14.9	65.0
1994–95	48.2	26.3	21.8	5.0	53.2	14.1	62.2
1995–96	46.7	25.9	20.8	4.3	51.0	12.5	59.2
1996–97	45.4	25.2	20.2	4.0	49.4	10.9	56.4
1997–98	47.5	25.5	21.9	3.6	51.1	10.6	58.1
1998–99	47.9	26.4	21.5	3.3	51.2	10.2	58.2
1999–2000	49.9	37.0	12.9	3.0	52.9	9.7	59.6
2000–01	53.2	38.5	14.7	3.2	56.4	9.1	62.3
2001–02 (RE)	55.6	39.7	15.9	3.0	58.6	9.7	65.3
2002–03 (BE)	56.9	40.3	16.6	2.7	59.6	n.a.	n.a.

a. At historical exchange rate.
b. Converted at year-end exchange rates.
Source: Indian authorities.

Table A.2. Combined Outstanding Liabilities of the Central and State Governments
(In Rs 10 million)

Year	Central government			State govt. debt	Combined central and state governments		
	Domestic	External[b]	Total	Domestic	Domestic	External[b]	Total
1	2	3	(2+3)	5	6	7	(6+7)
1990–91	283,033	66,314	349,347	110,289	319,432	66,314	385,746
1991–92	317,714	109,685	427,399	126,338	360,787	109,685	470,472
1992–93	359,654	120,987	480,641	142,178	410,579	120,987	531,566
1993–94	430,623	127,808	558,431	160,077	489,546	127,808	617,354
1994–95	487,682	142,514	630,196	184,527	557,294	142,514	699,808
1995–96	554,984	148,398	703,382	212,225	638,296	148,398	786,694
1996–97	621,438	149,564	771,002	243,525	719,390	149,564	868,954
1997–98	722,962	161,418	884,380	281,207	836,207	161,418	997,625
1998–99	834,551	177,934	1,012,485	341,978	978,018	177,934	1,155,952
1999–2000	962,592	186,791	1,149,383	420,132	1,145,905	186,791	1,332,696
2000–01	1,111,081	189,990	1,301,071	504,248	1,333,156	189,990	1,523,146
2001–02 (RE)	1,274,369	222,780	1,497,149	n.a.	n.a.	222,780	n.a.
2002–03 (BE)	1,444,248	n.a.	n.a.	n.a.	n.a.	n.a.	n.a.
			(As percent of GDP)				
1990–91	49.8	11.7	61.4	19.4	56.2	11.7	67.8
1991–92	48.6	16.8	65.4	19.3	55.2	16.8	72.0
1992–93	48.1	16.2	64.2	19.0	54.9	16.2	71.0
1993–94	50.1	14.9	65.0	18.6	57.0	14.9	71.9
1994–95	48.2	14.1	62.2	18.2	55.0	14.1	69.1
1995–96	46.7	12.5	59.2	17.9	53.7	12.5	66.2
1996–97	45.4	10.9	56.4	17.8	52.6	10.9	63.5
1997–98	47.5	10.6	58.1	18.5	54.9	10.6	65.5
1998–99	47.9	10.2	58.2	19.6	56.2	10.2	66.4
1999–2000	49.9	9.7	59.6	21.8	59.4	9.7	69.1
2000–01	53.2	9.1	62.3	24.1	63.8	9.1	72.9
2001–02 (RE)	55.6	9.7	65.3	n.a.	n.a.	9.7	n.a.
2002–03 (BE)	56.9	n.a.	n.a.	n.a.	n.a.	n.a.	n.a.

a. At historical exchange rate.
b. Converted at year-end exchange rates.

5
Ireland[1]

The management of the national debt in Ireland was delegated to the National Treasury Management Agency (NTMA) by legislation enacted in 1990. This delegated authority includes issuance, secondary market activity, and all necessary ancillary activity, such as, for example, arranging for clearing and settlement.

Debt Management Objectives and Coordination

Objectives of debt management

The key objectives of the NTMA in managing the national debt are, first, to protect liquidity to ensure that the exchequer's funding needs can be financed prudently and cost effectively and, second, to ensure that annual debt-service costs are kept to a minimum, subject to containing risk within acceptable limits. It must also have regard to the absolute size of the debt insofar as its actions can affect it (deep discounts and currency mix).

Although the broad objectives of debt management have remained more or less unchanged, the emphasis on how best to achieve these objectives has changed, particularly in response to Ireland's adoption of the euro.

Scope

Debt management activity covers both the issue and the subsequent management of the central government's short-term and long-term debt as well as the management of its cash balances. The management of the debt is concerned with both the annual cost of debt service, in the traditionally understood sense of measuring and controlling the total value of interest and debt issuance costs each year, as well as with the economic impact, over the life of the debt, of all debt management activity. This latter aspect of debt management is captured by measuring the net present value (NPV) of the debt and comparing it with a benchmark.

Coordination with monetary and fiscal policy

The annual debt service cost, in terms of cash flows, is a major part of the overall expenditure in the budget of the ministry of finance (MoF) and is framed to be consistent with the general level of borrowing or surplus envisaged by that budget. Monetary policy is the prerogative of the European Central Bank (ECB), and before the introduction of the euro, it was under the control of the Central Bank of Ireland (CBI). Debt management policy is not coordinated with the ECB's monetary policy. Before 1999, neither was there any formal coordination of debt management policy with the monetary policy of the central bank, even though there was a nonstatutory exchange of information and views with the CBI on the main thrust of debt management policy. In managing the debt, the NTMA was conscious of the need to avoid any conflict with the central bank's monetary and exchange rate policies. The advent of the euro in 1999 ended the scope of and need for such policy sensitivity.

Treasury service and advice to other arms of government

The debt management activity of the NTMA relates only to the debt of the central government. The debt of other arms of the government, such as local government authorities, regional health boards, and state bodies, remains the responsibility of those bodies, subject to approvals and guidelines issued by the department of finance. The NTMA has been empowered, however, to offer a central treasury service, in the form of deposit and loan facilities, as well as treasury advice to a range of designated local authorities, health boards, and local education committees. It has also been authorized to advise ministers on the management of funds under their control and, where the requisite authority is delegated, to manage such funds on behalf of those ministers. The NTMA currently manages the assets of the Social Insurance Fund under such delegated authority. It has also been mandated to manage the National Pensions Reserve Fund under the direction of the National Pensions Reserve Fund Commissioners, who are appointed by the minister of finance.

Transparency and accountability

Relationship with the minister of finance

The minister of finance approves the budget for annual debt-service costs, and the NTMA is obliged under legislation to achieve that budget as near as may be. Its performance relative to this budget is reported to the MoF, as is the performance in NPV terms against a benchmark portfolio. However, all debt-service payments, including redemptions, are a first charge on the revenues of the government and, under the provisions of the legislation that authorizes the raising of debt, are not subject to annual approval by the minister or by parliament. The NTMA also reports to the MoF on the very broad outlines of its borrowing plans for each year, indicating how much it intends borrowing in the currency of the state and how much in other currencies. The minister gives directions to the NTMA each year in the form of widely drawn and prudentially intended guidelines covering the major policy areas, such as the mix of floating- and fixed-rate debt, the maturity profile, foreign currency exposure, and other financial data. The public auditor, the comptroller and auditor general, carries out an audit each year on the agency's compliance with these guidelines.

Role of debt managers and the central bank

The debt managers and the CBI have distinct and nonoverlapping roles from both a legal and an institutional perspective in that the central bank has no role in debt management policy. The introduction of the euro in 1999 did not essentially alter the relationship, except to the extent that it removed the necessity for the degree of informal exchange of information and views that had existed before that date in the interest of the smooth operation of both monetary policy and debt management policy. At present, the NTMA cooperates with the central bank's actions in implementing the liquidity management policy of the ECB by maintaining an agreed level of funds in the exchequer account in the central bank each day. The CBI also maintains the register of holders of Irish government bonds. In December 2000, the clearing and settlement function for Irish government bonds was transferred from the central bank to Euroclear.

Open process for formulating and reporting of debt management policies

The NTMA's annual report and accounts include a full statement of its accounting policies. In addition, it publishes at the beginning of each year a calendar of its bond auctions for that year, together with a statement of the total amount of issuance planned for the year. The NTMA's bond auctions are multiple-price auctions and are carried out by means of competitive bids from the recognized primary dealers. At present, there are seven such dealers who are obliged to quote electronically indicative, two-way prices in designated benchmark bonds within maximum bid/offer spreads for specified minimum amounts from 8:00 a.m. to 4:00 p.m. each day. In addition, primary dealers are required to be market makers in Irish government bonds on the international electronic trading system, Euro MTS, and on the domestic version of it, MTS Ireland.

Public availability of information on debt management policies

The government's budgetary forecasts for the coming year and the two following years are published annually in December. These forecasts include figures for the overall budget surplus or deficit of the government for each year. The preliminary out-turn for the current year is also shown. In addition, the finance accounts published each year by the government contain detailed information on the composition of the debt, including the type of instrument, the maturity structure, and the currency composition. During the course of the year, the MoF publishes detailed information on the evolution of the budgetary aggregates at the end of each quarter, together with an assessment of the outlook for the remainder of the year. The NTMA publishes an annual report that contains its audited accounts as well as a description of its main activities. It also publishes information during the year on the details of all the markets on which it operates and the amount outstanding on the various debt instruments used in these markets. Also, information on the amount outstanding on each of the bonds it has issued is released each week to the public.

Accountability and assurances of integrity

The NTMA has a control and a compliance officer who reports to the chief executive. It also engages a

major international accounting firm to undertake an internal audit of all data, systems, and controls. In addition, the annual accounts are audited by the state auditor, the comptroller and auditor general, before their presentation to parliament within a statutory deadline of six months after the end of the accounting year. The comptroller and auditor general reports the findings to parliament.

Institutional framework

Governance

The National Treasury Management Agency Act of 1990 provided for the establishment of the NTMA "to borrow moneys for the Exchequer and to manage the National Debt on behalf of and subject to the control and general superintendence of the Minister for Finance and to perform certain related functions and to provide for connected matters."

The 1990 Act enabled the government to delegate the finance minister's borrowing and debt management functions to the NTMA, such functions to be performed subject to such directions or guidelines as he or she might give. Obligations or liabilities undertaken by the NTMA in the performance of its functions have the same force and effect as if undertaken by the minister.

The chief executive, who is appointed by the MoF, is directly responsible to the minister and is the accounting officer for the purposes of the Dáil's (lower house of parliament) Public Accounts Committee. The NTMA has an advisory committee, comprising members from the domestic and international financial sectors and the MoF, to assist and advise on such matters as are referred to it by the NTMA.

The main reasons behind the decision to establish the NTMA were outlined as follows by the minister of finance when he introduced the legislation to the parliament in 1990:

> ... debt management has become an increasingly complex and sophisticated activity, requiring flexible management structures and suitably qualified personnel to exploit fully the potential for savings.

… it has become increasingly clear that the executive and commercial operations of borrowing and debt management require an increasing level of specialization and are no longer appropriate to a Government Department. Also, with the growth of the financial services sector in Dublin, the Department [of Finance] has been losing staff that are qualified and experienced in the financial area and it has not been possible to recruit suitable staff from elsewhere.

… [in the agency] there will be flexibility as to pay and conditions so that key staff can be recruited and retained; in return, they will be assigned clear levels of responsibility and must perform to these levels: the agency's staff will not be civil servants.

It was considered that locating all debt management functions within one organization, which had a mandate to operate on commercial lines and had the freedom to hire staff with the requisite experience, would lead to a more professional management of the debt than would be possible within the constraints of the civil service system.

To ensure the complete independence of the NTMA from the civil service, the legislation establishing it expressly precludes its staff from being civil servants. However, political accountability is maintained by having the NTMA's chief executive report directly to the minister of finance and by making the chief executive the accounting officer responsible for the NTMA's activity before the Public Accounts Committee of parliament.

The overall borrowing and debt management powers of the minister have been delegated to the NTMA and further annual parliamentary or legislative authority to borrow or engage in other debt management activities is not required. However, the NTMA is required to present to the MoF each year a statement setting out how much it intends to borrow in the currency of the state and in other currencies during the course of the year. Broadly speaking, it is empowered to use transactions of a normal banking nature for the better management of the debt. This broad power includes the use of derivatives as well as power to buy back debt or, where the borrowing instrument permits, to redeem it early.

Structure within the debt office

The NTMA's structure reflects the fact that it has a number of other functions in addition to debt management, namely the management of the National Pensions Reserve Fund, under the direction of the National Pensions Reserve Fund Commissioners, and the processing of personal injury and property damage claims against the state, in which role the NTMA is known as the state claims agency.

Directors report to the chief executive on funding and debt management and IT, risk and financial management, legal and corporate affairs (including retail debt), the National Pensions Reserve Fund, and the state claims agency. The NTMA also has an advisory committee, appointed by the MoF, to advise on the chief executive's remuneration and such matters as are referred to it by the NTMA.

The separation of the front office function (funding and debt management) from the middle office function (risk management) and the back office function (financial management) is in accordance with best practice and ensures an appropriate separation of powers and responsibilities.

The NTMA retains key staff through its employment contracts and remuneration packages, which are flexible and designed to attract qualified permanent or temporary personnel as required. This freedom to recruit and pay staff in line with market levels was a key element in the government's decision to establish the NTMA. Because the NTMA is a relatively small organization, the training of staff is generally outsourced as the most efficient option. Its IT department has built the back office IT support systems to provide straight-through processing of trades from front office to back office and also to generate the required management reports. Temporary IT expertise was contracted as necessary to achieve this objective. The NTMA is a member of the Society for Worldwide Interbank Financial Telecommunication (SWIFT) and the TransEuropean Real-Time Gross Settlement Express Transfer (TARGET), which enables real-time processing of payment transactions.

Management of internal operations

Internal operational risk is controlled by rigorous policies and procedures governing payments and the separation of duties, in line with best practice in the financial sector generally, including:

- Segregation of duties between front office and back office functions: This practice is enforced by logical and physical controls over access to computer systems and by the application of office instructions and product descriptions.
- Office instructions describe detailed procedures for key functions and assign levels of authority and responsibility.;
- Product descriptions set out a description of the particular product and detailed processing instructions and highlight inherent risks.
- Bank mandates are established with institutions with whom dealing is permitted.
- Third-party confirmations are sought for all transactions.
- Reconciliations and daily reporting.
- Monitoring of credit exposures arising from deposits and derivative transactions, which are managed within approved limits.
- Voice recording of certain telephones.
- Head of control function/internal audit/external audit.
- Code-of-conduct and conflict-of-interest guidelines

Disaster recovery plans are also in place that would enable the NTMA to resume its essential functions from a back-up site within one to four hours. This plan is tested regularly and is made possible by the arrangements for complete back-up of all computer data and their storage off-site three times each day.

Debt Management Strategy and Risk Management Framework

The overall debt management strategy is to protect liquidity so as to ensure that the exchequer's funding needs can be financed prudently and cost effectively and at the same time ensure that the annual costs of servicing the debt are kept to a minimum, subject to an acceptable level of risk.

Risk management

The main risks associated with managing the debt portfolio, apart from operational risk, which has been discussed, are credit risk, market risk, and funding liquidity risk.

Credit risk

Credit limits for each counter-party are proposed by the risk management unit and approved by the chief executive. The credit exposures are measured each day, and any breach is immediately brought to the attention of the chief executive.

In setting credit limits for individual counter-parties, there is a single limit on the consolidated business with the counter-party—that is, all businesses are brought together under one limit. Each limit is divided into short-term (up to one year to maturity) and long-term (more than one year to maturity). In determining the maximum size of an exposure to a counter-party that the NTMA is willing to undertake, account is taken of the size of the counter-party's balance sheet and the return on capital, as well as the credit rating and outlook assigned by Moody's, Standard and Poor's, and Fitch, the major credit-rating agencies. The market value of derivatives is used in measuring the credit risk exposures. The credit risks are also assessed by reference to potential changes in the exposures as a result of market movements and the position is kept under continuous review.

Market risk

The NTMA manages the cost and risk dimensions of the debt portfolio from a number of perspectives, including (a) managing the performance of the actual portfolio relative to the benchmark portfolio on an NPV basis and (b) managing the debt-service budget. Both interest rate risk and currency risk are controlled, measured, and reported on.

The benchmark reflects the medium-term strategic debt management objectives of the exchequer and encapsulates the NTMA's appetite for market risk. When the benchmark has been agreed upon with its external advisers, it is then approved by the minister of finance. The minister decides whether it is consistent with his or her overall guidelines on the management of the debt. Revisions to the benchmark are made from time to time (subject to approvals by the NTMA's external advisers and the Department of Finance) to take account of significant changes in structural economic relationships but not in response to short-term market movements.

The benchmark portfolio is a computer-based notional portfolio representing an appropriate target interest rate, currency mix, maturity profile, and duration for the portfolio. The benchmark is based on a medium-term cost/risk trade-off derived from simulation analysis. Cost is defined in terms of the mark-to-market value of the debt, and risk is defined in terms of the likelihood that debt-service costs will exceed the budget provision of the minister of finance. The simulations lead to the choice of a benchmark portfolio, which is robust under a range of possible out-turns rather than highly dependent on one set of assumptions regarding the future evolution of interest rates and exchange rates.

One of the major risks that must be controlled is the possibility that the annual debt-service cost will fluctuate wildly from year to year and exceed the target level set out by the minister of finance. In tandem with this, the benchmark seeks to minimize the overall cost of the debt in terms of its mark-to-market value. In constructing the benchmark, the simulation exercises seek to find a portfolio that minimizes the mark-to-market value (the cost) while ensuring that the annual debt-service cost is at the minimum level consistent with not fluctuating wildly from year to year. The stability of the debt-service budget over time is more important than minimizing the cost in any one year. Overall, the benchmark seeks to strike a balance between the potentially conflicting objectives of minimizing the NPV of the debt while maintaining the lowest possible stable debt-service costs over the medium term.

Reports

The fiscal budget for annual debt-service costs is sensitive to exchange rate and interest rate risks. Each month, two estimates are produced and reported to quantify the level of this risk:

- Sensitivity of the fiscal budget to a 1 percent movement in interest rates: The interest composition of the outstanding debt and the expected funding requirements are taken into consideration while assessing the possible gains or losses that could be incurred were interest rates to move by 1 percent.
- Sensitivity of the fiscal budget to a 5 percent movement in exchange rates: This takes into consideration the currency composition of the debt. It looks at the possible gains or losses to the debt-service budget in the event of exchange rate movements.

A set of internal monthly fiscal risk limits is put in place early each year. These limits reflect the prudent risk limit for the fiscal budget. The sensitivity reports are compared to these limits to check for compliance.

The main reports for the ongoing management of the debt-service budget are:

- Monthly update of the debt-service forecast for the current year: The forecast is broken down by the various debt instruments and includes a monthly profile of the full year's debt-service budget.
- An analysis of the variances between the debt-service out-turn and the debt-service forecast.
- Monthly report on the debt-service budget, analyzing the effect of possible exchange rate and interest rate movements: This report is done for both current year's fiscal budget sensitivities and future years' fiscal budget sensitivities.

Benchmarking of the domestic portfolio

When the Irish government debt management operations were carried out in the context of an Irish pound (punt) market, before the introduction of the euro, the benchmarking of performance on the domestic debt portfolio was much more difficult than benchmarking the foreign portfolio. Nevertheless, it was considered beneficial to benchmark domestic performance to provide appropriate incentives for the debt portfolio managers. The benchmarking system was devised to give credit for any structural improvements in the domestic bond market brought about by the portfolio managers (e.g., the introduction of the primary trading system and the concentration of liquidity into a smaller number of benchmark issues). The benchmark was also used to assess the effectiveness of the domestic debt managers in achieving their funding target within previously agreed duration limits. The managers were free to vary the timing of their funding actions compared with the benchmark, depending on their interest rate view. Thus, at all times, the debt managers were required to have a view on interest rates when deciding on their issuance policy.

With the development of a relatively uniform euro-area government bond market, Ireland became a very small part of a large liquid market and thus the benchmarking of the domestic debt management operations became more straightforward.

Funding liquidity risk

The NTMA prepares and manages a detailed multi-year funding plan that shows the amount and timing of funding needs, including the effect of the projected surpluses or deficits on the government's budget. In light of this plan, it determines the size and timing of its long-term debt issuance and manages its short-term liquidity positions through the issuance of short-term paper or the use of short-term cash balances.

The main reports for the ongoing maintenance of the exchequer's funding and liquidity requirements are

- the weekly updating of the NTMA's overall funding plan, which includes a review of its underlying assumptions and a review of immediate liquidity requirements; and
- regular reports on the main features of the developments in the government's overall budgetary position to date, and a review of the current outlook.

With the introduction of the euro, the NTMA took a number of steps to enhance the marketability of its bonds and thus reduce funding risk. Broadly speaking, the technical characteristics of Irish government bonds (e.g., day-count convention) have been changed to bring them into line with the bonds of the large, core euro-area issuers. In addition, a number of bond exchange and bond buyback programs have been executed with the objective of concentrating liquidity into a smaller number of large, liquid benchmark issues. At present, virtually all the marketable, long-term, euro-denominated debt with more than one year to maturity is concentrated into five bonds. The NTMA also promotes the openness, predictability, and transparency of the market in Irish government bonds through announcing in advance its schedule of bond auctions, by having a primary dealing system to support the market in the bonds, and by arranging for the listing of the bonds on one of the main electronic trading platforms used for trading euro-area sovereign debt. The deep liquidity thus generated for the market in Irish government bonds reduces the funding risk by making the bonds more attractive to a wider pool of investors. Given that Ireland represents a very small proportion of the total euro-area government debt market (about 1 percent), the NTMA has little difficulty in raising short-term funds to smooth the funding requirement around the time of the redemption of bonds, whose size is quite large by historical standards.

Medium-term focus of debt management

A number of approaches are adopted to ensure that the NTMA's debt management activities are not focused on short-term advantage at the cost of potential longer-term cost. First, each year, the minister of finance issues a set of guidelines covering policy issues such as the mix of floating- and fixed-rate debt, the maturity profile, the foreign currency exposure, the permissible extent of discounted issues, and the credit rating of counter-parties. These guidelines are drawn relatively broadly and are designed as prudential limits, which the NTMA must observe. Second, the NTMA's performance in managing the debt is measured by reference to an independent and externally approved and audited benchmark portfolio. This benchmark performance measurement system takes account not just of current cash flows but also of the NPV of all liabilities; in effect, it calculates the impact of the NTMA's debt management activities not only in the year under review but also their projected impact over the full life of the debt. Under the NPV approach, all future cash flows (both interest and principal) of the notional benchmark debt portfolio and of the actual portfolio are marked to market at the end of each year and discounted (based on the zero-coupon yield curve) back to their respective NPVs. If the NPV of the liabilities in the actual portfolio is lower than the NPV of the notional benchmark portfolio's liabilities, then the NTMA is deemed to have added value in economic terms. This performance against the benchmark is reported to the MoF and published in the NTMA's annual report.

Limitations on activities to generate a return

The managers of the debt portfolio are free to manage the debt within certain risk limits relative to the agreed benchmark. The limits are expressed in terms of the possible change in the market value of the portfolio. Value-at-risk (VaR) and interest and currency sensitivity analysis are used to measure the short-term deviations from the benchmark on a weekly basis (or more frequently, if required). Any position that exceeds the agreed limit relative to the benchmark portfolio is immediately brought to the attention of the chief executive.

In managing the debt relative to a benchmark it is necessary to take views on movements in interest rates, unless one wishes to passively track the benchmark. However active daily trading simply to generate a profit does not take place. The trades entered into by the NTMA are for the purpose of managing the debt, and in the course of this certain arbitrage opportunities may arise. For example, one area of arbitrage that is exploited by the debt managers is the issuance of commercial paper, mainly in U.S. dollars but also in other foreign currencies, and the swapping of these currencies into euros for an overall lower cost of funds than could be achieved by direct borrowings in the euro-denominated commercial paper markets.

Strict limits are placed on the activities of the debt managers in availing of arbitrage opportunities between different markets. Although it is generally feasible for the debt managers to raise funds in the short-term paper markets at lower interest rates than

could be obtained in placing those funds on deposit in the market, the general policy of the NTMA is that borrowing activity will be related to the funding needs of the exchequer. It is, however, desirable to maintain a continuous and predictable presence in the government debt markets, and, in addition, cash surpluses will emerge from time to time on the exchequer account because of mismatches between the timing of government receipts and payments. The surpluses that arise in this way can be placed on deposit in the markets, subject to the constraints of the limits on counter-party credit risk.

The main reports for performance measurement against the benchmark portfolio are

- daily performance results and positions, which are electronically circulated to the dealers' desks;
- monthly VaR analysis to ensure that all risk limits are complied with; and
- quarterly detailed reports on the attribution of performance.

Models to assess and monitor risk

To assess and monitor risk, the NTMA uses models developed in-house and models purchased externally; the latter are used particularly for mark-to-market valuations as part of the risk assessment process. These systems are used mainly to measure and report on market risk and counter-party credit risk exposures on a daily basis.

Contingent liabilities

The NTMA is not responsible for the government's contingent liabilities. These contingent liabilities that arise from government guarantees of the borrowings of state companies or other state bodies are monitored and managed by the Department of Finance.

Developing the Markets for Government Securities

Filling out the yield curve

The NTMA issues the following debt instruments:

- Commercial paper is issued directly to investors or via intermediate banks. The commercial paper is available in all currencies, with tenors not normally exceeding a year.
- Exchequer notes are treasury bills with a maturity range from one day to one year. Each day, the NTMA issues the notes directly through an "open window" facility to a broad range of institutional investors, including corporate investors and banks. The NTMA is prepared to buy back exchequer notes before maturity. At present, there is just a small secondary market. The NTMA is examining the possibility of improving the secondary market by having the notes traded on an electronic trading platform.
- Section 69 notes: In Section 69 of the Finance Act of 1985, the MoF provided for the issue of interest-bearing notes to foreign-owned companies in Ireland. The interest on these notes would not be subject to tax in Ireland. This incentive was introduced to encourage these companies to keep their surplus cash in Ireland rather than repatriate funds to their overseas parent companies. Section 69 notes can be issued in any currency (minimum 100,000) for any tenor.
- Fixed-rate, euro-denominated bonds with maturities up to 14 years are issued by auctions. The bonds are listed on the Irish Stock Exchange and supported in the market by seven market makers (primary dealers).

Foreign and domestic currency debt

Although issuing debt in foreign currencies is now regarded as appropriate for Ireland, because of the advent of the euro with its deep liquid capital market, it is important to remember that conditions for a small open economy such as Ireland were very different in the 1980s.

The problem essentially arose as a result of the oil crisis of 1979 and the subsequent worldwide recession that, along with the prevailing high international interest rates, had severe adverse consequences for Ireland in terms of

- low growth and higher unemployment levels,
- high fiscal deficits,

- high domestic interest rates, and
- fear of "crowding out" on the domestic capital market.

These factors, coupled with the underdeveloped nature of the domestic Irish bond market, led to large-scale foreign borrowing, with a rapid growth in overall indebtedness. In 1991, the position was that foreign currency debt accounted for 35 percent of the national debt and nonresidents held a further 15 percent denominated in Irish currency. Thus, nonresidents held 50 percent of the total national debt.

The NTMA faced a much-changed domestic and international borrowing environment with the gradual abolition of currency controls and the relaxation of the primary and secondary liquidity ratios on banks. During the 1980s, these controls (although hindering the development of the domestic capital market) had ensured something of a "captive market" for Irish government bonds and paper. The NTMA now faced a more competitive environment for attracting investors. Internationally, sovereign names were moving away from the traditional syndicated loans toward capital market instruments.

Priorities for the early years of the NTMA

In the early 1990s, the NTMA identified the following priorities for its borrowing program:

- expanding, broadening, and diversifying the investor base through such ideas as marketing Ireland's name abroad and keeping it visible through road shows and presentations to influential investors (Japanese yen Samurai, CHF private placement, and U.S. dollar Yankee markets were very important for Ireland in the early days of the NTMA);
- tapping new markets;
- keeping access to retail and institutional investors;
- lengthening the duration of the debt and creating a more balanced maturity profile;
- targeting upgrades in Ireland's credit ratings (campaigns to get upgrades ahead of time or that were forward looking);

- marketing campaigns to improve the international image of Ireland (emphasizing the rarity value of Ireland's name); and
- opportunistic approach to foreign borrowing.

The payoff from this approach was that Ireland was very successful in terms of pricing new issues and regularly achieved tighter or keener pricing than similar or more highly rated sovereign borrowers.

In response to the need to diversify the sources of funding, because all markets are not open at the same time, and to broaden and deepen the range and quality of instruments available for debt management, Ireland put in place standardized medium-term notes (MTNs), euro medium-term notes (EMTNs), euro commercial paper (ECP), and U.S. dollar commercial paper (USD CP) programs. By mid-1992, the NTMA had put in place facilities in a range of currencies totaling about US$3 billion, which allowed Ireland immediate and cost-effective access to short- and medium-term funds with maximum flexibility.

These facilities showed their worth in the autumn of 1992, when, because of the shock of the huge extra borrowing needs of sovereign names caused by the turmoil in the exchange rate mechanism of the European Monetary System, large syndicated loans and capital market issues became particularly expensive as spreads widened.

Although in the early years of the NTMA's existence, there was more focus on achieving cash savings on the debt-service cost because of government budgetary pressures, the liquidity risk due to the uneven maturity profile also required urgent attention.

Moves to smooth the maturity profile occurred in 1991. In 1995, the NTMA arranged a 7-year US$500 million, backstop, multicurrency revolving credit facility to support the issuance of commercial paper. Moreover, it arranged the syndication itself to cut down on fees and achieved the tightest pricing ever by a sovereign.

The NTMA also took steps to ensure that derivative instruments (such as interest rate swaps, cross-currency swaps, caps, floors, futures, and foreign currency forward contracts) as well as spot transactions in foreign currencies were available to be used in the management of the debt. The great advantage of recent financial innovations is not that they can help to lower the cost of funds, but rather that these instruments can help to protect the portfolio against different kinds of risks by, for example, shortening or lengthening the average effective duration of the outstanding debt.

The various strategies produced a positive mix of

- cost savings through cheaper funding,
- greater flexibility in funding and hedging,
- more fiscal certainty on debt service, and
- reduced liquidity and rollover risk and greater availability of instruments to deal with market risk more efficiently and dynamically.

The NTMA took the view that the most sophisticated debt managers are not those who achieve the lowest possible cost of borrowing. The goal needs to include minimizing exposure to risk as well as minimizing costs. It is worth paying more to create debt structures that cushion, rather than amplify, the impact of negative shocks. These developments proved positive for credit ratings, investors, and the spreads on Irish sovereign debt as they reduced the relative risk premium.

In 1998, the NTMA decided that, with the imminent introduction of the euro and the relatively positive outlook for government finances, the large euro-area bond and money markets would more than adequately meet Ireland's funding needs for the foreseeable future; therefore, it was no longer necessary to retain exposure to non–European Economic and Monetary Union (EMU) currencies in the portfolio. Consequently, all noneuro debt, with the exception of a residual 6 percent that was left in pounds sterling, was swapped back into euros during late 1998 and early 1999. This remains the policy today.

The pound sterling exposure was maintained not on the basis of a cost/risk trade-off for debt management purposes, but rather as a macroeconomic hedge for public finances in the event of a sudden and significant weakening of the pound sterling exchange rate. This decision was taken on the basis of a study of the economic links with the U.K. economy of a considerable number of firms whose output is based on relatively low-skilled labor and whose profit margins tend to be low. These firms compete with

U.K. firms on the domestic market, the U.K. market, and third markets. Any substantial weakening of pound sterling would lead to a loss of competitiveness and consequential redundancies in this sector, resulting in higher social welfare support payments by the exchequer. This would have been offset to some degree by the lower cost, in Irish pound and euro terms, of servicing the sterling-denominated debt. However, the NTMA is currently reviewing this policy, and it has reduced the pound sterling exposure to about 4 percent of the national debt.

Reduction of fragmented debt stock and issuance of consolidated debt

Securities exchange program

With the objective of reducing borrowing costs for the government, a number of initiatives have been taken by the NTMA over the years to improve liquidity in the Irish bond market. After the launch of the euro, the NTMA decided that a major initiative was required to ensure that Irish bonds traded effectively in the new, euro-denominated, pan-European market. The initiative taken was the securities exchange program. The rationale underlying the program was the NTMA's belief that to be competitive in the new euro environment, Irish government bonds that are "on the run" must have a relatively large issue size and technical characteristics analogous to those in other euro-area markets.

In May 1999, the NTMA addressed the above issues, within the constraints of the overall limited size of the Irish government bond market, by launching a securities exchange program that consolidated about 80 percent of the market into four bonds, each with outstanding amounts of 3–5 billion, with coupons around current market yields and technical characteristics similar to bonds in other European markets. In the absence of such an initiative, there was a risk that the bonds would trade at yields inappropriate to Ireland's credit rating.

Execution of the program

The exchange program was launched in May 1999, with the majority of the transactions taking place in

three phases—that is, on May 11, 17, and 25. On completion of the third phase, more than 91 percent of the outstanding amount of old bonds covered by the program had been exchanged for new bonds.

As a result of the exchange program, the ratio of general government debt (based on nominal value) to GDP was increased by some 5 percentage points. However, because of the effect of the very rapid growth in GDP, the ratio, which was 55.1 percent at the end of 1998, had fallen to 49.6 percent at the end of 1999, including the effects of the exchange program. The program did not affect the economic value of the outstanding debt. Cash-flow savings represented by the lower annual coupons on the new bonds offset the addition to the capital stock of the debt. The bonds bought back under the program were trading above par, because they had been issued at a time when interest rates were very much higher than in 1999. However, the bonds issued under the program were priced very close to par. Hence, the nominal value of the debt increased as a result of the program.

Bond switching program, 2002

In January 2002, the NTMA conducted its first major bond switch since the 1999 securities exchange program. Two of Ireland's existing benchmark bonds (the 3.5 percent 2005 and the 4 percent 2010) were now "off the run" in terms of their euro-area peer group.

The NTMA wished to launch two new benchmark bonds that would have a good shelf life and would be of sufficient critical mass (€5 billion) to join the Euro MTS electronic trading system by mid-2002. The intention was that the two new bonds would be reopened by way of auctions in 2002. The best way to achieve these strategic aims was to offer the market switching terms out of the former 2005 and 2010 bonds into to new benchmark issues (a 2007 and a 2013 bond).

The switch was successfully conducted via the NTMA's primary dealers. The 2005 and 2010 bonds ceased to be designated as benchmarks, because, under NTMA rules, once 60 percent or more of the amount in issue has been bought back, a bond loses its benchmark status. This stipulation acts as in incentive for investors via the primary dealers to take part in the switch, because most investors do not wish to be in non-benchmark stocks with the resultant price illiquidity.

Bond issuance procedures

Regular auction schedule
Between February and November 2002, subject to normal market conditions prevailing, the NTMA has held a bond auction on the third Thursday of each month. Each auction is normally in the €500 million–700 million range and involves the new 2007 and 2013 benchmark bonds (and the 2016 bond, which was first issued in 1997). The primary dealers have exclusive access to the auctions, which add further depth and liquidity in these issues. Five business days before each auction, the NTMA announces to the market the bond to be auctioned and the amount through Bloomberg and Reuters. The Bloomberg auction system is used to conduct the auction. This reduces the time between the close of the bidding and the release of the auction result to about three minutes, thus reducing the risk for bidders.

Auction results
The auction results are published on Bloomberg (page NTMA, menu item 2) and Reuters (page NTMB) simultaneously within about three minutes of the cutoff time for bids.

Noncompetitive auctions
Up to 48 hours after the announcement of the auction results, the NTMA will accept bids in a noncompetitive auction from primary dealers at the weighted average price in the competitive auction. The amount on offer in the noncompetitive auction will not exceed the equivalent of 20 percent of the amount sold to the primary dealers in the current competitive auction.

Structure of the Irish Government Bond Market

Primary dealer system

The Irish government bond market is based on a primary dealer system to which the NTMA is committed. Seven primary dealers recognized by the NTMA make

continuous two-way prices in designated bonds in minimum specified amounts and within maximum specified spreads. There are also a number of stockbrokers who match client orders. However, the primary dealers account for about 95 percent of turnover. This system, which was introduced at the end of 1995, has brought improved depth and liquidity to the market while the bond repo market has grown in tandem, adding to the liquidity in the bond market. Primary dealers are members of the Irish Stock Exchange, and government bonds are listed on the exchange.

With the switch to electronic trading and the listing of the new 2007 and 2013 benchmark bonds on the Euro MTS in the middle of 2002, the current system has been augmented by six new institutions, which are purely price makers in the new 2007 and 2013 bonds. These new institutions are not to be primary dealers and do not have access to supply at the monthly auctions.

The liquidity of the Irish government bond market is underpinned by the primary dealer system. However, to further enhance the liquidity of the market, the NTMA provides these facilities to primary dealers:

- a continuous bid to the market in Irish government benchmark bonds,
- switching facilities between the benchmark bonds, and
- repo and reverse repo facilities in benchmark bonds.

Buybacks

To enhance the liquidity of the market, the NTMA is prepared to buy back amounts of illiquid, nonbenchmark, euro-denominated Irish government bonds that have relatively insignificant amounts outstanding. It is also prepared to buy back amounts of foreign currency–denominated Irish government bonds as opportunities arise in the market. This improves the debt profile, eliminates certain off-the-run and illiquid bonds, and facilitates greater issuance in the liquid benchmark bonds.

Secondary trader

The NTMA maintains a secondary trading function to trade in its bonds with other market participants.

The role of the secondary trader is to provide liquidity to the market and act as a source of market intelligence for the NTMA. The secondary trader is mandated to deal as a retail customer with market makers and brokers in Irish government bonds. The secondary trading is separated from the primary bond desk activity by means of "Chinese walls."

Move to electronic trading of Irish bonds

The NTMA listed the new benchmark 4.5 percent 2007 and 5 percent 2013 Irish government bonds on the Euro MTS electronic trading system at the end of June 2002. A domestic version of MTS was established at the same time, on which the existing 2016 benchmark bond is listed; this bond does not yet meet the 5 billion issue size requirement for listing on the main Euro MTS system. The listing of the bonds on these systems has greatly enhanced turnover, price transparency, and liquidity, and it ensures that Irish bonds are maintained in the mainstream of the euro-area government bond market.

Standard market conventions

All Irish benchmark bonds have a day-count convention based on actual number of days (actual/actual). The bonds trade on a clean price basis, with prices quoted in decimals. The business days for trading are TARGET operating days, and bond dealings settle in full on a T+3 basis, but deferred settlement can be arranged upon request. These are standard features of euro-area bond markets. Irish government bonds are eligible for use as collateral in ECB money market operations.

Settlement

In December 2000, the settlement of Irish government bonds was transferred from the domestic settlement system, the Central Bank of Ireland Securities Settlements Office (CBISSO), to Euroclear, Brussels. Ireland was the first European country to transfer the settlement of government bonds from its central bank to an international securities depository. The CBI remains the registrar.

The objectives of the transfer to Euroclear were

- increased liquidity of Irish government bonds in the international capital markets as a result of improved access to a broader range of investors;
- a simplified and cost-effective settlement infrastructure, in which safekeeping and settlement of domestic and cross-border transactions are centralized within the same entity;
- optimized settlement efficiency, due to the integration of the settlement activity into an international real-time settlement environment; and
- access to a wide range of markets for the former CBISSO members through the Euroclear system.

Inclusion in indices

The following indices have an Irish Government bond component:

- Bloomberg/EFFAS,
- J.P. Morgan Irish Government Bond Index,
- Lehman Brothers Global Bond Index,
- Merrill Lynch Global Government Bond Index 11, and
- Salomon Smith Barney World Government Bond Index.

Credit rating

Ireland has the top long-term credit rating of AAA from Standard and Poor's, Moody's, Fitch, and the Japanese credit rating agency, Rating and Investment Information, Inc. (R&I). Ireland also has the top short-term credit ratings of A-1+, P-1, F1, and A-1+ from Standard and Poor's, Moody's, Fitch, and R&I, respectively.

Tax treatment of Irish government bonds

There is no withholding tax on Irish government bonds. Nonresident holdings are exempt from all Irish taxation. However, the provisions of the European Union (EU) Savings Directive may affect this position in relation to nonresident personal investors. The objective of the EU directive is to ensure a minimum of effective taxation of savings income in the form of interest payments within the EU. The directive applies to individuals (not corporations) who are resident in an EU member state and receive interest income from their investments in another member state. Each member state would be obliged to provide information on such interest payments to the member state in which the beneficial owner of the interest resided.

Indexed debt

To date, Ireland has not issued any index-linked debt.

Establishing and maintaining contacts with the financial community

Despite all the technical and market innovations of the last two decades, financial markets are still a people-driven business, and by maintaining and developing strong contacts, Ireland has traditionally been able to obtain more favorable borrowing costs than one might have expected, given its credit rating. This active engagement with the market has also helped the staff of the NTMA enhance and deepen their knowledge and understanding of market developments and keep abreast of the latest financial market innovations. Provision of accurate and timely information is also part of Ireland's strategy to keep its name visible in capital markets. To this end, the NTMA makes active use of the following:

- the NTMA web site (www.ntma.ie), which is updated regularly with the latest available information;
- an Ireland Information Memorandum published and distributed annually in March and available on the NTMA web site;
- The NTMA annual report, which is published annually in June;
- regular press conferences and relevant press releases to update the market on important developments;
- the NTMA Reuters pages (ntma/b/c);
- an annual reception in December for all NTMA's banking contacts;
- credit lines for financial institutions;
- regular road shows and marketing campaigns to keep Ireland's name visible, particularly in advance of any major issuance program;

- regular contact with the credit-rating agencies (Ireland has the top, AAA rating from Moody's, Standard and Poor's, R&I, and Fitch.);
- active use of the Bloomberg messaging system to seek quotes in non-price-sensitive instruments such as deposits and foreign exchange forward points (This ensures both optimum pricing and that every bank the NTMA has a line with has a chance to quote.); and
- listing Irish government bonds on the major electronic trading platform, Euro MTS.

CPSS and IOSCO standards

The IMF Financial Sector Assessment Program mission reported, "Ireland observes the CPSS core principles for systemically important payment systems. The only systemically important payment system is IRIS, the Irish real-time gross settlement system. This is facilitated by ECB actions to ensure that national payment systems participating in the Trans-European Real-time Gross Settlement Express Transfer (TARGET) embody all the features necessary for the smooth functioning of cross-border transactions." The NTMA operates a securities settlement system as issuer, registrar, and settler of its exchequer note program in accordance with the core principles of the IOSCO standards. The CBI is the registrar for Irish government bonds, which are settled at Euroclear. Both the CBI and Euroclear operate in accordance with the core principles of the IOSCO standards.

The challenge of the euro

The EMU and the advent of the euro have led to a greater degree of intra-euro-area portfolio diversification as the disappearance of foreign exchange risks and transaction costs and deregulation of the various domestic euro-area member domestic markets have resulted in an ever-greater redistribution of assets within euro-area portfolios. Hence, in the case of Ireland, nonresident holdings of Irish government bonds have risen from about 21 percent to 60 percent in June 2002 as domestic investors who were heavily invested in the Irish bond market diversified and were replaced by new, predominantly fellow euro-area investors.

With no exchange risk, unidirectional yields, and lower spreads stemming from convergence (due to more equalization in the sovereign credit ratings of member countries of the euro area), investors' motivations may be reduced to questions of price liquidity, transparency, and market efficiency.

Note

1. The case study was prepared by Oliver Whelan, Funding and Debt Management, National Treasury Management Agency.

6
Italy[1]

The public debt management policy in Italy, as conducted in the last decade, has followed the prescriptions of the Maastricht Treaty, which created a monetary union and the single currency, the euro, among those European countries respecting the criteria of economic stability and fiscal discipline.

Since 1992, the Italian Treasury has undergone a process of profound change in the structure of its liabilities. The main goals to be reached at the end of this process were, in brief:

- the reversion in the growth path of general government consolidated gross debt, as defined according to the specification of the excessive deficit procedure related to the European Monetary Union (EMU);
- the overall reduction of the pressure on capital markets due to excessive supply of bonds;
- the reduction of the exposure to interest rate fluctuations; and
- the creation of a deep and liquid market for government securities.

The strong commitment to the attainment of these goals has been expressed in the legislation passed from 1992 on and in the organizational and structural reforms in the field of public debt management.

Developing a Sound Governance and Institutional Framework

Debt management objective and scope

Objectives

The strategic guidelines for 2002 and 2003 define the objective of public debt management as "...to ensure that the financing needs of the State and its repayments obligations are met, minimizing the cost of debt, the level of risk being equal."

Scope

Referring to the legal framework of responsibilities, the Public Debt Direction (PDD) of the Italian Treasury Department is directly responsible for the issuance and management of public debt domestic securities.

The PDD is also responsible for issuance and management of all other securities. This includes borrowing and other activities in the international capital market, such as issuing syndicated loans and commercial paper and activity on the swap market. The PDD also manages the public debt sinking fund and the cash account (*conto disponibilità*) at the Bank of Italy (BOI) (both dating back to 1993).

The PDD also exercises surveillance over access to financial market funding of public entities, local authorities, and companies controlled by the state that have or do not have a state guarantee

Coordination with monetary and fiscal policies

Coordination between fiscal and monetary policies and debt management activities is a priority for Italian authorities. The division of responsibility and specialization of tasks among the different institutions is clearly stated. The PDD has the responsibility of the issuance and management of public debt. The Italian Treasury Department is responsible for the management of the state treasury and monitoring the financing needs of the central government. The BOI—as a member of the European Central Bank (ECB)—is in charge of monetary policy and surveillance over the Italian financial system.

The set of rules and constraints and the different tasks assigned to each of the acting departments (PDD, treasury department, BOI, and also general government entities) require a deep and constant coordination in activities to prevent the breaking of legal rules and ensure the orderly functioning of state activities (collection of revenues and distribution of payments).

As it is for all members of the EMU, the issue of coordination of debt management with monetary policy in Italy must be seen in the framework of the Maastricht Treaty. The treaty establishes a prohibition against monetary authorities financing the state deficit by buying government securities on the primary market. This provision of the treaty was reflected in national legislation in 1993, which prohibited the BOI from participating in government bond auctions. Regarding the conduct of monetary policy, the PDD has never had any privileged information, because the setting of official interest rates

was an exclusive privilege of the BOI until 1998 and of the ECB thereafter.

The legal framework ensures a complete separation of objectives and accountability for monetary policy and debt management. The BOI is fully independent from the government and acts as an independent authority, or an institution performing its activities with no interference and deriving its powers from specific legislation, without any possibility of intervention or influence by the government onging to specified categories. However, according to the BOI statute, the majority of shares must be in the hands of public entities or companies owned by public entities. As of December 31, 2000, there were 86 shareholders (80 with voting rights).

In addition, Italian law, in accordance with Article 101 of the treaty establishing the European Community as modified by the Maastricht Treaty, forbids all overdraft facilities of the state with the BOI or the ECB, in any form and amount. Since 1993, the direct purchase of public debt instruments from the BOI is forbidden by law. The system also includes the cash account of the treasury at the BOI, implying the removal of any overdraft facility for the treasury. According to the law, this account has to show an average positive balance of €15.49 billion.

However, even though Italy has implemented a clear separation of roles between the treasury and the BOI, these two institutions have always maintained a close dialogue on public debt management issues. First, they exchange views in regular meetings in which issuance policy matters such as amount and instrument mix to be offered are discussed. Second, the BOI is usually involved in workgroups that are occasionally established to work on specific innovations or questions that are relevant for debt management, such as the creation of the strip market, the definition of new facilities, and the like. Third, a close exchange of information is maintained on the issuance activity in foreign currency, given its implications on reserves management and the fact that the BOI is the fiscal agent of the republic.

The smooth functioning of the borrowing activity of the PDD requires constant monitoring of the financing needs of the state in coordination with the direction of the treasury department. This constant monitoring is also done by means of estimates and forecasts of the possible future trends in those needs, taking into account the usual annual cyclical and extraordinary patterns of cash expenses and revenues (typically, revenues from direct and indirect taxation, expenses for salaries, and the like). Finally, the financing requirements need to take into account the maturity and reimbursement profile of outstanding debt.

A close exchange of information is also maintained on the balance of the cash account that the treasury holds at the BOI, through which most payments of the republic are channeled. Although this account is established at the BOI, only the treasury is entitled to order any payment or receipt. However, the two institutions keep close contact on the balance on account because of its implications for liquidity in the system and therefore on monetary policy.

Institutional framework

Governance

The budget law (*legge finanziaria*), passed annually by parliament, sets the binding limit for the net borrowing of the state and for the market borrowing activity during the financial year. The latter represents, in brief, the total amount of gross issuance of public debt.

The legal framework for public debt management activity is defined first by the state law, which has recently created the new ministry of the economy and finance (MEF). The MEF is assigned—among others—the competencies related to the "... funding of Government's financing needs and of Public Debt. ..."

A secondary regulation defines the concrete organization and division of competencies assigned to the treasury department within the MEF, and in particular to the PDD.

The PDD is responsible for the issuance and management of domestic and external public debt, the management of public debt sinking fund, and surveillance of market financing activities of other local and public entities. This surveillance over public and especially local entities is a sensitive issue for the PDD. The obligations of the state related to the excessive deficit procedure are to be met at the general government level—for example, taking into account the funding activity of the local entities and of all entities included in the general government sector.

The particular legislative framework, together with the hierarchy of legislative sources, entails a sound assurance that Italian government stands behind any transactions the PDD managers enter into. The officials of the PDD are civil servants; the managers of the various offices that form the PDD are subject to accountability principle, implying civil, administrative, accounting, and criminal law responsibility.

The PDD produces four main documents illustrating its activities and strategic plans for the future:

- The annual strategic guidelines are drafted internally after extensive discussions among the various offices of the department. The director general of the PDD coordinates the preparation of the document and is responsible for presenting it to the director general of the treasury, who approves the draft. There is no formal presentation to parliament or direct control by the minister of the economy.
- The semiannual report to the Supreme Audit Court (*Corte dei Conti*).
- The quarterly bulletin of public debt.
- The public debt section within the quarterly public sector cash balance and borrowing requirement report.

The last two documents are also provided under the Special Data Dissemination Standard (SDDS) program of the IMF.

The nature of public debt management activity is recognized as essentially governmental. Options for alternative institutional arrangements have been considered in the past, such as an independent office or agency operating in a civil law environment. Although a precise analysis of costs and benefits and an evaluation of the project have never been conducted in an exhaustive manner, the current deputy minister of economy and finance has been put in charge of exploring the possibility of establishing an independent agency for public debt management. For the moment, this remains an issue for academic discussion and research.

Management of internal operations

The management of operational risk is conducted by means of sound practices developed during several years of activity and, in particular, starting from 1991, when the present organizational structure of the PDD was outlined. This process was completed in 1997, when all activities related to public debt management were brought under the authority and responsibility of the PDD.

The legislative division of labor in public debt management makes a clear distinction between the treasury department and the BOI, thus avoiding any conflict of interest between the two entities. There is a tradition of cooperation between the two institutions and the smooth functioning of the auction and settlement procedures, and all operations connected to the secondary market activity, is the result of the successful public debt management reforms in Italy. In particular, an auction procedure manager (at the BOI), of secondary market autonomous trading platforms,[2] and an independent depository institution (Monte Titoli SpA) ensure that the responsibilities are clearly separated and provide full accountability.

Staff

A great effort has been made in in human resources management to ameliorate and renew the human capital endowment of the PDD. The main effort is addressed toward strengthening information technology (IT) and foreign language skills in Italian public administration. The advancements made are considerable and connected with a broader effort of Italian public administration as a whole.

Compared with private institutions, the turnover rate of staff is low. Most of the mobility involves people moving from one department of the MEF to another, from one office of the PDD to another, or retiring. Nevertheless, recently more staff have been moving to international or private institutions (mostly financial institutions). The Italian legislative framework does not provide flexibility in salaries and incentives, except for a few top managers (generally department heads or general directors). The recent legislative reforms, however, try to sketch a more flexible and dynamic framework, especially for man-

agers (the level immediately below general directors), allowing for temporary contracts and some "weak form" of performance-related bonuses. Nonetheless, the PDD, among the other administrations, can offer to its staff training and the development of skills comparable to those offered by the private sector.

A specific code of conduct does not exist, but PDD officials are subject to normal provisions for public officials. The Italian administrative and criminal laws meet all of the criteria of impartiality and help to avoid any conflict of interest.

Audit procedures

The public debt management activity is subject to the control of the accounting department of the MEF and of the Italian Supreme Audit Court.

The formal control by the MEF accounting department is continuous and conducted only on a documentary basis for the whole administration and for a limited number of activities specified by law. This means that the auditing procedures examine and certify the ex ante conformity to the law and accounting regularity of the documentary evidence.

The Supreme Audit Court performs formal controls based in specific laws. Some documents and activities (e.g., purchase agreements above a specified amount) require ex ante legal and accounting approval by the Supreme Audit Court. The Supreme Audit Court's ex post nonformal control of the yearly activity is conducted by sampling the entire Italian administration and, therefore, does not regularly cover the PDD's activity.

In addition, the PDD submits a biannual public debt management activity report to the Supreme Audit Court, detailing the evolution in the composition of public debt and describing the operations undertaken during the semester. This document is not made public. Its main aim is to deepen the knowledge and comprehension of public debt management activity. The examination of numerical results—routinely made by the Supreme Audit Court—is enlarged to include evaluation and explanation of strategies and actions in connection, for instance, with trends in the international capital markets.

Transparency

Transparency is a strategic priority for the Italian Treasury and the PDD, and the commitment to it is very strong. The PDD's web site (www.tesoro.it/publicdebt) is updated daily and fully available in English. The web site is the result of the great importance attached to communication with the vast audience of international and domestic investors.

A document describing the strategic guidelines for public debt management is published yearly on the web site. The strategic guidelines disclose the objectives of the PDD in terms of risk management, portfolio composition, liquidity of the securities on the secondary market, and forecasts of possible gross issuances and of the number of new bonds and treasury bills to be placed on the market. The public disclosure of strategic cost/risk analysis and objectives is at an early stage, but has been provided in the latest strategic guidelines document.

Also available on the web site are

- the annual auction calendar,
- the quarterly issuing program,
- the quarterly bulletin of the PDD,
- the offering announcements for treasury bills and bonds,
- the results of the latest auctions of all bonds and treasury bills, and
- specific sections devoted to
  - specialists on Italian government bonds,
  - public debt statistics,
  - the Italian public debt sinking fund,
  - a listing and description of Italian Treasury securities, and
  - other information and news (e.g., new legislation on fiscal treatment of bonds and treasury bills).

The administrative and organizational framework for debt management is designed primarily through the Italian law and the regulations of the MEF.

The regulations and the procedures for the primary distribution of public debt securities are made clear to the participants through

- the legislative framework,

- the annualdiffusion of the rankings of specialists (on the web site), and
- the public availability of the criteria for evaluation by specialists (on the web site).

As regards the auction framework for Italian public debt securities, the law provides a set of rules, and the electronic procedure for public auctions ensures a clear carrying out of all operations (sending of bids, opening, ranking, and assignment of quantities). Manual or semielectronic recovery procedures are provided in case of IT failure. Since 1988, the secondary market for public debt has been conducted through an electronic platform (MTS.

The reform process of the secondary market ended in 1998, when a law and two decrees were passed to regulate the framework of the secondary market and the role of the MTS electronic platform in the wholesale market for Italian and foreign government bonds.

Information about the flow and stock of government debt is sent to the market with the availability of final data. The PDD releases a quarterly bulletin of the public debt market, showing

- the results of the latest auctions of Italian public debt securities,
- the outstanding amount of benchmark securities,
- the quarterly issuance program of new securities,
- the breakdown by instrument of outstanding government debt,
- historical data on average life of government debt,
- redemptions of outstanding bonds,
- redemptions of the next 12 months, and
- the trading volumes and average bid/offer spreads observed in the secondary market (MTS).

In addition, the Italian Treasury Department provides, when needed, information about changes in fiscal treatment of public debt securities. This has happened with the recent innovations in the taxation regime (withholding tax) for nonresidents: The explanatory notes on the reform and an application form have been published on the PDD web site.

As regards the financing needs of the public sector, a partial disclosure of summary data referring to those aggregates is provided monthly by the Italian Treasury Department. No official forecasts are provided to the public because of the fluctuations and uncertainty of these data.

Debt Management Strategy and the Risk Management Framework

Italy has one of the largest debt stocks among advanced economies, both in nominal terms and as a percentage of GDP. The debt-to-GDP ratio, which stood at 97.2 percent in 1990, reached a peak of 124.3 percent in 1994, when it started to decline as a result of a major fiscal consolidation. Such an enormous debt burden undermined the financial stability of the country and conditioned the government's action in the political economy domain. Throughout the 1980s and the first half of the 1990s, Italy was facing increasingly large expenditure outlays due to the debt service to the point that, in 1993, interest payments on the public debt absorbed 22.6 percent of total expenditure. To service its debt, the republic needed to keep taxes at a high level, and there was very little room for maneuvering to use fiscal policy as a countercyclical tool. Doing so would result in a relaxed fiscal policy that would soon exacerbate the balance of the country's fiscal accounts. Even the independent conduct of monetary policy, which was fighting inflation through a restrictive stance on official rates, could have a negative impact on public finance through an increase in the cost of debt. However, because Italy was not overly exposed to foreign currency–denominated debt (only 3.5 percent of total debt was denominated in foreign currency in 1993), there were not large implications of the large stock of debt on reserves management. As recently as 1994–95, the spread between Italian and German 10-year bonds was still oscillating between 250 and 600 basis points, and it became clear that such a wide spread was unsustainable over the long term.

In this context, although up to the early 1980s the PDD's main concern was to raise the necessary cash to fund the government's operations, the PDD decided to better define its mission and put together a more precise strategy to guide its action. Therefore, even though a set of constraints remained, which made it difficult to shift away from the risky treasury bill market, the treasury department began to put forward some basic concepts to be followed in debt management policy.

A general objective of debt management policy was then considered of minimizing the cost of funding. However, to avoid excessive risks in the presence of specific market conditions, it was decided that this objective should be achieved in a context of careful control of the interest rate risk and refinancing risk. The rationale was that the objective of minimization of the funding cost was not sufficient in itself to prevent the budget from possible shocks. For example, in a situation of declining interest rates, this objective could have led to an excessive issuance of short-dated securities. Although this strategy could indeed save money in the short term, it could also lead the government to assume an unnecessary exposure to the risk that interest rates would rise in the future and determine a sharp increase in the cost of debt.

The work undertaken to better evaluate the main risks faced by the PDD was instrumental in defining the mission of debt management activity. Throughout the 1990s, because of the size and composition of its debt, Italy was largely exposed to two main risks:

- Interest rate (market) risk: Because of the very short duration of the public debt, the cost of debt was very sensitive to changes in interest rates.
- Refinancing (rollover) risk: The average life of public debt was only 2.6 years in 1990. This implied that every year, the Italian authorities had to roll over massive amounts of securities, overloading the market with frequent and large auctions.

The approach to interest rate (market) risk

The need to contain the interest rate risk required the PDD to engage in an active debt management policy with the aim of modifying the composition and increasing the duration of the stock of debt.

The beginning of the fiscal consolidation and the reduction in the inflation rate created a better environment for investors to buy long-term securities. The increased demand made it possible to issue *certi-*

ficati di credito del tesoro ([CCTs] 7-year floating-rate bills) and *buoni del tesoro poliennali* ([BTPs] 3-, 5-, 10-, and 30-year bonds) in higher amounts. In 1990, short-term and floating-rate notes accounted for 73 percent of the total debt, declining to 49 percent in 1995 and reaching 30 percent by 2000. At the same time, the duration of the debt portfolio increased from 1.7 years in 1993 to 3.7 years in 2000.

As a result, the exposure to fluctuations in interest rates declined significantly. Given the current composition of the debt, the impact of a 1 percent shift in the yield curve would determine an increase in interest expenditure of about one-third lower with respect to 1996.

The approach to refinancing (rollover) risk

An even bigger challenge for Italy was that of reducing rollover risk. The structure of the public debt was, until recently, such that the short average life caused a constant need to roll over maturing debt. For example, in 1995, the public debt to be reimbursed amounted to 50 percent of the total debt outstanding. There was also a high concentration of maturities on specific dates, and consequently the recourse to the market had to be particularly large to meet those redemptions.

The strategy to address this risk was based on two pillars. First, the objective was to increase the average life of the public debt. During the 1990s, the average life more than doubled from 2.6 years in 1990 to 5.7 years in 2000. Second, the aim was for a smoother distribution of maturities during the year. Although the borrowing requirement maintained a pronounced seasonality, the PDD strived to spread out maturities more evenly across the various months.

The operative framework to address market and rollover risk

The quest to reduce these two risks went on for most of the 1980s and 1990s, when Italy adopted an active debt management policy and explored all possible avenues to educate investors to buy securities other than short-term treasury bills, which were the backbone of the portfolio of any Italian investor. Moreover, there was a need to diversify the range of instruments used to raise funds, so as not to depend excessively on a specific segment of the market. The PDD launched innovations on both the primary and the secondary markets. In the primary market, the action concentrated mainly on two lines, the diversification of instruments and the introduction of new issuance procedures.

In terms of diversification of instruments, there was a policy aimed at increasing the types of securities to be offered so that the treasury could target a wider range of investors, increase the average maturity of the debt, and obtain a smoother redemption profile. Several new types of securities were introduced:

- The CCT: In a constant struggle to reduce the recourse to short-term treasury bills, in 1978 Italy introduced the CCTs with the aim of lengthening the average life of its debt. However, because of the then prevailing reluctance to invest in long-dated, fixed-rate Italian securities, the PDD decided to index the coupon payments to the current treasury bill rate. This new instrument (whose maturity initially varied but stabilized at seven years in the early 1990s) was extremely successful, especially with households, and accounted for more than 40 percent of the total debt in 1990. In this way, the PDD was able to substantially reduce refinancing risk, but remained exposed to variations in the interest rate level.

- The *certificati del tesoro*(CTEs) denominated in European currency units (ECU): With the CTE, launched in 1982, Italy was among the first issuers to offer securities denominated in the European unit of account, the basket of currencies that was to generate the euro. In doing so, the PDD was able to attract new investors to longer maturities, preventing the fears of devaluation of the Italian lira from discouraging them.

- The *buoni del tesoro* (BTEs) denominated in ECU: Similar to CTEs, but with shorter maturities, these were introduced in 1987.

- The *certificati del tesoro con opzione* (CTOs): These securities, introduced in 1988, were six-year fixed-rate bonds embedding the option for the holder to request advance reimbursement after three years.

- The first 30-year BTP was launched in 1993 with the objective of increasing the duration of the public debt.
- The funding program in foreign currency: Starting in 1984, the Italian government launched bonds denominated in foreign currencies to attract those investors that were not willing to invest in a currency characterized by high inflation. Eventually, Italy became one of the main issuers in the Eurobond market and subsequently complemented this activity with the inclusion of sources of financing other than benchmark bonds, such as the euro medium-term notes (EMTNs) program launched in 1999.

For issuance procedures, several changes have been adopted over the years to improve placement techniques, especially for medium- and long-term bonds. Until the 1980s, medium- and long-term bonds were placed through a syndicate of major domestic banks. To avoid excessive market fluctuations, the PDD would indicate the amount and price of securities to be sold . In 1985, in light of the growing number of intermediaries that could access the Italian market, and with a view to standardizing its placement procedures, the PDD started to test the uniform-price auction and began to make this a standard practice in 1988. By 1990, all treasury securities except foreign currency bonds and treasury bills were placed via uniform-price auction, and in 1992, the requirement of a base price was removed.

As for *buoni ordinari del tesoro* (BOTs), treasury bills of varying maturities, the decision to remove the indication of a base price for the auction (which came in 1988 for 3-month bills and in 1989 for 6-month and 12-month bills) was a very important move, which favored a more precise separation of roles between the treasury and the BOI. The indication of a base price for treasury bills was regarded as extremely important by market participants, who tried to extract from it a signal of the direction of official interest rates. This approach favored a confusion of roles between the treasury and the BOI and would sometimes generate uncertainty in monetary policy expectations.

Another important step in issuance procedures concerned the introduction of reopening auctions for medium- and long-term bonds in 1990. This decision responded to the need to boost the liquidity of the newly established on-screen secondary market (MTS). Transactions on this market could not pick up momentum as expected because of the large number of bonds outstanding, none of which was liquid enough to absorb large transactions. Benchmark bonds would change very frequently, and the market remained fragmented. Therefore, the PDD started to conduct several auctions over time on the same bonds, reducing the number of bonds issued on the same maturity, initially for a period of two to three months, and then for progressively longer periods. Today, a 10-year bond can remain open for more than 6 months and a 30-year bond for more than 1 year. This allows the bonds to reach an optimal outstanding amount, and there is evidence that the introduction of reopening auctions contributed to reducing the cost of debt because investors were more willing to buy liquid securities. This reform was also key to the development of an efficient secondary market.

More recently, the PDD also announced a finalized program to exchange securities nearing maturity with securities in the process of being issued (exchange offers). The objective is to make the profile of maturities more uniform. By means of exchange offers, the PDD will retire old bonds with a short remaining maturity and exchange them for newly issued securities with a longer maturity. The benefit will be twofold:

- On refinancing: By retiring old bonds with a short remaining maturity, the PDD can smooth out the redemption profile for the near term (usually the securities to be repurchased have a maturity up to one year). The securities are usually replaced by new medium- and long-term bonds, which help in spreading out maturities over a longer time horizon.
- On market liquidity: In general, bonds nearing maturities are no longer liquid, therefore they tend to not being actively traded on the secondary market, resulting in an increased burden for primary dealers if they are obliged to quote them. Through the exchange offer facility, the primary dealers are given a window to swap illiq-

uid bonds with highly liquid ones, such as those used by the PDD to execute the exchange offers.

The exchange offers, which were executed for the first time in early 2002, can be carried out according to two procedures:

- through auction, by following the same procedure used for buyback operations made with the proceeds of privatization. (These transactions will preferably be made in the middle of the month, concurrent with three- and five-year BTP auctions.); and
- at a later stage, by operating directly on the regulated secondary market through bilateral transactions.

In both cases, these transactions are reserved for specialists in government bonds, because they are the most active operators on the secondary market and those on whom the treasury relies to maintain high liquidity and efficiency in the secondary market.

Information systems

Given the sophistication that characterizes today's markets, the development of adequate information systems is key to a smooth functioning of debt management. Over the past 10 years, the PDD has worked to improve its systems by focusing on three areas: pricing systems, forecasting systems, and risk management systems.

Pricing systems are instrumental for the front office, because they enable the PDD to have a better understanding and evaluation of the trades that are entered into. The need to develop such systems first arose for liability management purposes, when the PDD started to directly negotiate derivatives contracts with its counterparts; later, such systems were used for issuance activity and other operations on the domestic debt as well. Rather than develop in-house models, the PDD chose to draw upon the experience of investment banks in this field. Therefore, it benefited from their advice in setting up and customizing the pricing tools needed in debt management operations. These models are used for a wide range of purposes, from simple calculation operations such as

discount rates, to pricing of complex structures or determination of the fair value of bonds to be repurchased on the secondary market.

Forecasting systems are being developed for the PDD to have its own views on the evolution of key variables for debt management, such as interest expenditure, stock of debt outstanding at future dates, and so on.

The other area under development is that of risk models, which are gaining importance for reporting and accountability purposes. Here, work is under way to refine the models that allow the PDD to accurately measure its exposure at any given time. Most existing models are based on customizing the value-at-risk (VaR) models, which are the most widely used by investment banks. However, because of the peculiar nature of the fund-raising activity and the accounting methodology for recording debt, the PDD is also working to develop more tailored indicators, such as models calculating the sensitivity of the interest expenditure to variations of interest rates or to changes in the composition of the debt outstanding. The interest expenditure, given its impact on Italian public finances, is a variable that needs to be closely monitored, and it is one for which the PDD can take very little risk. For this reason, many of the simulations that are regularly run at the PDD concern the testing of various compositions of the debt portfolio to see how the interest rate expenditure would react under different market circumstances. The results of such simulations are also the basis for strategic planning of the issuance activity.

Developing the Markets for Government Securities

Italy has invested extensive resources to develop an efficient securities market. Given the heavy financing needs managed by the PDD, the need to create a dependable mechanism for raising funds was one of the top priorities during the 1980s. Work was carried out to develop both the primary and the secondary markets.

Since then, the Italian financial system has undergone constant and rapid development—mostly in the field of IT trading, settlement, and depository systems. Separate institutions were created during the 1990s to operate the secondary market for public debt securities. A wholesale market to trade Italian government securities, MTS SpA, by means of a screen-based system was introduced in 1988. In 1994, MOT, a retail market for securities was created as a branch of Borsa Italia SpA. The latest innovation, started in August 2001, is BondVision (a division of MTS SpA), an Internet-based, multidealer-to-client, wholesale, fixed-income market.

In parallel, since 1991, a number of laws have been passed, ensuring the modernization of the financial markets and institutional investors–related legislation.

Domestic government securities

In the domestic market, the PDD today issues the following instruments:

- BOTs (3-, 6-, and 12-month treasury bills);
- BTPs (3-, 5-, 10-, 15-, and 30-year bonds);
- *certificati del tesoro zero-coupon* ([CTZs] 24-month zero-coupon bills); and
- *certificati di credito del tesoro* ([CCTs] 7-year floating-rate bills).

Primary market

To place its debt, the Italian government uses very standardized and reliable mechanisms. Traditionally, domestic debt has been issued via auctions and foreign debt via syndication of banks. Today, these remain the most important mechanisms, even though, as new products are developed, some other channels may gain ground. The methods can be summarized as follows:

- Treasury bills: competitive auction without any indication of the base price. Investors can submit up to three bids, each of which is assigned the price requested. There is a cutoff price to avoid speculative bids.
- Medium- and long-term bonds: marginal auction, whereby each request is assigned at the marginal price, which is determined by accepting higher bids until the total amount of bids

accepted equals the amount offered. There is a cutoff price to avoid speculative bids.
- Bonds denominated in foreign currency: syndication.
- Commercial paper: direct quote on various networks and over the telephone.

Besides issuing marketable debt, the Italian government also guarantees the debt of the *Cassa Depositi e Prestiti* (CDP), which is placed through the post offices. The CDP is a public institution in charge of funding local authorities or specific projects for public infrastructure. However, to ensure that the borrowing of the CDP is done on similar terms to the funding managed by the PDD, the minister of the economy and finance, who is responsible for debt management, is given the authority to set the financial conditions under which the CDP can issue debt.

Auctions

Issuance procedures have been continuously enhanced in transparency and effectiveness. At the end of 1994, to improve transparency and predictability of issuance policy, the PDD started to disclose an advance calendar of the auction dates for the following year, along with a quarterly issuance program that gives more detail about the bonds and the amounts to be issued in the coming quarter. In this way, all market participants are given detailed information, which is key to accurate planning of their activity for the next year or quarter.

Since 1995, the auctions have been carried out via a completely automated procedure at the BOI. As a result of constant improvement, the lag between the collection of the bids and the announcement of the results has been reduced to a few minutes. The number of institutions allowed to participate in the auctions has been increased over time, and today an average of 40 institutions submit bids at each auction, including foreign institutions, who can submit bids even if they are not resident in Italian territory.

Supplementary auctions

Supplementary auctions take place at the end of every regular auction of medium- and long-term bonds.

Only specialists are allowed to participate in this part of the auction. Each specialist who has been assigned bonds during the regular auction is entitled to submit voluntary bids for an extra allotment of bonds. The extra allotment equals 25 percent of that offered at the regular auction if it concerns a newly opened line of bond (i.e., the first tranche); otherwise, it is 10 percent. The price for the supplementary auction is the same as the regular auction price (the weighted average for treasury bill auctions or the marginal price for uniform-price auctions). This privilege, which transfers the market risk to the treasury (if only for a few hours), is valued highly by the selected institutions.

Bids for the supplementary auction can be submitted until noon of the business day following that of the regular auction, and they follow the same procedure as the regular auction. Each specialist is entitled to be allotted a share of the supplementary auction equal to the ratio between the total amount assigned to the specialist in the last three auctions and the total amount assigned to all specialists in the same three auctions.

By means of supplementary auctions, the PDD has found a way to increase the amounts issued at each auction without committing in advance to larger amounts, which might have proved difficult to place. Instead, the possibility to increase the amount being issued is left in part to the market conditions. If the market yields are decreasing, specialists will find it convenient to participate in the supplementary auctions and the issued amount will rise. Conversely, nothing will happen if market conditions deteriorate in the hours following the regular auction.

Specialists in government bonds

A very important innovation concerned the establishment of the specialists in government bonds. This category of operators, introduced in 1994, was selected from among the primary dealers operating in the Italian-regulated on-screen market (MTS) with a view to enhancing the demand at auctions of Italian government bonds, increasing liquidity of the secondary market, and assisting the treasury with advice on debt management policy issues.

The specialists in government bonds are granted the exclusive right to participate in supplementary auctions and have also been exclusively entitled to participate in the buyback operations launched by the treasury to reduce the public debt outstanding.

Strategic guidelines

In 2000, a strategic guidelines document was introduced, outlining the principles to be followed in debt management policy for the coming year and released at the end of each year. This document is published to disclose as much information as possible on the reasoning behind the decisions that guide the PDD's action in debt management. In this way, market participants are offered useful tools to help them form their expectations on issuance activity for the year to come.

Secondary market

On the secondary market the key reform was the establishment in 1988 of MTS, the on-screen market for government bonds. The MTS model was based on a very simple concept, that is, to provide easy, low-cost access for market makers to the Italian government bond market and facilitate transactions as much as possible. These conditions helped enormously to build up liquidity and favored the stability of the market, because investors could always count on an efficient tool to divest their positions, and such circumstances attracted new investors to the Italian market. Today, the Italian secondary market is one of the most liquid in the world, with very high trading volumes and tight bid/ask spreads. Moreover, the on-screen market is very reliable in times of severe crises. Because of their discretionary nature, transactions based on over-the-counter systems tend to diminish in volume in times of uncertainty or disruption in the financial markets. However, it is standard practice that market makers undertake specific commitments to show two-way quotes on the on-screen market. This commitment is very valuable to the issuer, who can benefit from the information (however little it may be when liquidity tends to dry up) that on-screen systems continue to provide, even during periods of distress.

Tax treatment

Another sector that was key to developing the Italian market was the fiscal treatment of government securities. In the mid-1980s, it was decided to put an end to the long-standing policy of tax exemption on Italian government bonds and enforce a 12.5 percent withholding tax on new bonds. This measure determined a fragmentation of the market, because it introduced the practice of quoting the yield on a net-versus-gross basis, depending on the tax treatment of the holder. Moreover, it hampered the appeal of Italian bonds for foreign investors, because the Italian authorities decided to establish a quite complex procedure to avoid double taxation. Such a procedure would require foreign investors to pay the withholding tax as if they were subject to tax and then apply for a refund. Given the long period that was usually required to process the applications, for some time, there was extensive arbitrage activity on Italian bonds based on this mechanism. Therefore, the PDD started a process that was initially aimed at streamlining the procedure for reimbursement of the withholding tax and eventually (in 2001) implemented a major reform that granted fiscal exemption to virtually all nonresident investors, provided they are not resident in fiscal havens. This reform responds to the assumption that in debt management—and in particular, in fiscal issues associated with debt management—the simpler, the better.

Investor relations

The reform of the taxation for nonresidents was one of the by-products of a closer and more frequent dialogue established by the PDD with investors, and in particular international investors, who may not have been aware of the opportunities offered by the Italian market. For example, because of the technicalities related to the management of the withholding tax, those involved in debt management could gain a good understanding of the problems outstanding because of direct contacts with the interested investors. Based on this experience, the PDD has expanded this type of activity. Today, regular meetings are held with market makers to gain better input on market trends, the treasury conducts road shows to bring new products or market innovations to the attention of investors, and videoconferences are organized as requested to favor exchange of views, preferences, and information between the PDD and investors.

Dealing with exceptional events and financial crises

The system of auction, settlement, and trading for Italian government securities has shown a good resilience to financial crises or disruption at the continental or world level. For instance, in 1992, when the Italian lira was devalued and forced out of the fixed-rate regime of the European Monetary System (EMS), causing continuing pressure on the Italian financial market and the widening of the interest rate spread with major sovereign issuers, the market proved to be efficient and continued to price Italian government securities, despite some problems with the auction procedures.

Another important and decisive test came in 1995, when, after the Mexican crisis of 1994, the framework of primary dealers and specialists and new criteria for quoting securities on MTS proved to be a welcome resilience during major international crises. On that occasion, the benefits were transferred from the secondary to the primary market, where no disruptions were observed in the auction mechanism. The treasury department could continue to place its bonds without any adverse effect.

More recently, on the occasion of the terrorist attacks of September 11, 2001, the treasury department and the PDD continued their activity on the primary market and fulfilled all their plans of auction. In that case, the smooth functioning of the secondary market was ensured by the combination of continental-scale intervention (especially from the ECB) and a well-tested market infrastructure.

Lessons

Based on these experiences, there are a few lessons that can be drawn. First, developing the market may require the issuer to pay a price initially. For example, when the PDD decided to increase the maturity of the public debt, it did so mainly by issuing floating-rate bills (CCTs) in the beginning. This instrument, because of its peculiarity in the indexation of the coupon, was considered by some analysts to be too costly for the treasury. However, the commitment demonstrated by the PDD to develop the market for

CCTs determined a comfortable pickup in liquidity and allowed the treasury to initiate a process of lengthening the maturity of the public debt.

Second, it is advisable that debt managers do not engage in the proposal of too complex or sophisticated securities ahead of time. For example, in 1988, when the treasury department started to issue long-term bonds with an embedded option (CTOs), the market was not yet able to correctly price the value of the option. Because investors were not accustomed to such securities, pricing models were not as widespread as they are today, research on volatility was not developed and available, and investors were treating these bonds as if they were bullet bonds, ignoring the value of the option. This implied that the issuer, while incurring the risk of advance reimbursement associated with the option, could not monetize the premium associated with it.

Third, there may be a trade-off between the requirements for the establishment of an efficient market and short-term gains. To ensure smooth functioning, an efficient market must be organized with simple and standardized practices, so that the issuer's behavior is predictable and does not come as a disruption to normal activity. Italy has followed these prescriptions by adopting, for example, a yearly calendar of government bond auctions, disseminating formal guidelines that anticipate for each year the innovations in debt management policy, and publishing quarterly calendars that detail the characteristics of any new bonds to be sold. A consequence of such a level of disclosure is that the PDD may face situations in which it is costly to honor a commitment. However, credibility is a highly important attribute of the issuer: in the long run, there is a payoff from the commitments that are undertaken, even if a mere short-term perspective may indicate that some costs are being incurred.

Notes

1. The case study was prepared by Domenico Nardelli and Gianluca Colarusso from the Public Debt Management Department of the Italian Treasury.

2. MTS, MOT, and BondVision, described in the section "Developing the Government Securities Market."

7
Jamaica[1]

Jamaica faces serious challenges to long-term growth and development imposed by a substantial debt overhang. Like many other Latin America and Caribbean countries, Jamaica emerged from the 1980s with a heavy external debt burden. The focus then had been the effective management of the external debt portfolio. The combination of external factors—such as low export earnings, reduced access to long-term loans on concessionary terms, and the internal developments of weak output performance and low revenue intake—saw the government relying on domestic financing. Consequently, by the 1990s, the high levels of external debt and attendant issues combined with the cost of rehabilitating the financial sector after the crisis in the financial sector in the mid-1990s resulted in high and rising levels of domestic debt, high interest rates, and fiscal deficits.

Jamaica has taken steps to ensure that sound economic fundamentals are in place to address these issues. A major thrust of the government's economic program has been the reduction of the overall debt. Given that the high levels of public debt and debt service severely limit the government's ability to invest in physical and social infrastructure necessary to promote investment and growth, since the second half of the 1990s, the major challenge to the government of Jamaica has been the management of debt dynamics. Emphasis has been placed on management of the domestic debt, the larger and more expensive share of the public debt.

Macroeconomic Policy Framework

Jamaica accelerated its structural reform program in the early 1990s with, among other developments, the liberalization of the foreign exchange market, the removal of price controls, reduction in trade barriers, and the reform of the tax system. The containment of inflation and the maintenance of relative stability in the foreign exchange market became the focus of the macroeconomic stabilization program introduced in 1991. This was to be achieved through a combination of tight monetary and fiscal policies.

The government succeeded in reducing inflation to single-digit levels and maintaining relative stability in the foreign exchange market. However, one of the costs of the stabilization was the marked increase in the level of the domestic debt, beginning in fiscal year 1994/95.

In addition to deficit financing, the increase in the stock of domestic debt was incurred largely to provide assistance to the central bank, the Bank of Jamaica (BOJ), in its liquidity management objectives and cover the BOJ's losses. Increases were also due to the assumption of debt obligations of parastatal entities. The debt problem was exacerbated by the financial sector crisis, which emerged in 1996, and the cost to the government of rehabilitating and restructuring the sector. All outstanding contingent liabilities that resulted from the rehabilitation and restructuring of the sector (approximately 35 percent of GDP) were assumed by the government as of April 1, 2001.

Jamaica's public debt–GDP ratio amounted to 130 percent at the end of fiscal year 2001/02 compared with 110 percent at the end of fiscal year 1994/95. Domestic debt as a percentage of GDP increased from 32.6 percent at the end of fiscal year 1994/95 to 63.9 percent at the end of fiscal year 2000/01. With the government's assumption of the remaining liabilities associated with the rehabilitation and restructuring of the financial sector, the domestic debt increased to 87.5 percent on April 1, 2001. By the end of fiscal year 2001/02, domestic debt stood at 77.5 percent of GDP. Debt servicing accounted for 66.1 percent of budgetary expenditure for fiscal year 2001/02, with domestic debt-servicing costs accounting for 54.8 percent of budgeted expenditure.

Over the last 10 years, considerable progress has been made in reducing the level of external indebtedness and the attendant debt-service burden. Jamaica's external debt has been reduced from 109.3 percent of GDP at the end of fiscal year 1991/92 to 52.4 percent of GDP at the end of fiscal year 2001/02. Jamaica's external debt-service ratio (total debt service as a percentage of exports of goods and services) has fallen from 29.2 percent in fiscal year 1990/91 to 12.3 percent in fiscal year 2001/02.

The steady decline in the external debt and the improvement in Jamaica's external debt indicators led to the World Bank's 1999 reclassification of Jamaica from a severely indebted to a moderately indebted country. This achievement crowns a series of advances that includes

- Jamaica's exit from commercial bank restructuring in 1990,

- its "graduation" from Paris Club bilateral rescheduling in the mid-1990s, and

- its reentry into the international capital markets in 1997, which was subsequently buoyed by credit ratings from Moody's Investors Service (Ba3) and Standard and Poor's (B) in 1998 and 1999, respectively. Standard and Poor's upgraded Jamaica's credit rating to B+ in May 2001.

Despite these positive developments, Jamaica continues to face a heavy debt burden, the result of the acceleration in the rate of domestic debt accumulation. Thus, although the composition of the debt has changed markedly over the decade, with the share of domestic debt increasing from 26 percent at the end of fiscal year 1990/91 to 60.7 percent at the end of fiscal year 2001/02, the overall debt burden remains onerous.

Cognizant of the importance of reducing the debt to sustainable levels, the authorities took the necessary steps to strengthen Jamaica's debt management capability and embarked on a path toward the implementation of debt reduction strategies and prudent debt management practices. In addition, steps were taken to facilitate the development of the domestic capital market.

Centralization of debt management functions

The need for institutional building and improvements in the government's debt management capability was critical to the formulation and implementation of credible debt management strategy and policies. Since April 1998, there has been a centralization of the debt management functions in the debt management unit (DMU) of the ministry of finance and planning. Before that, the debt management functions were shared by the ministry and the central bank.

Responsibility for the core debt management functions—debt policy and strategy formulation and analyses, debt-raising activities, and the registrar and payment function for government securities and debt recording and monitoring—now fully resides within the DMU. The BOJ, in its agency capacity, is responsible for effecting external debt payments, conducting primary market issues, and issuing and redeeming treasury bills. The accountant general department, a department of the ministry of finance and planning, has responsibility for treasury operations, including the servicing of the debt.

At the operational level, the centralization of the core debt management functions within a single unit in the ministry of finance and planning has led to considerable strengthening of debt strategy implementation. Several factors explain this, foremost of which are increased capacity in debt management expertise, greater clarity of debt management objectives, and improved consolidation of debt management information.

Debt management objectives and coordination

Clear debt management objectives have been developed. The principal debt management objective is to raise adequate levels of financing on behalf of the Government of Jamaica at minimum costs, while pursuing strategies to ensure that the national public debt progresses to and is maintained at sustainable levels over the medium term.

The influences of debt management on and by monetary and fiscal policies in a situation of deficit financing and rehabilitation and restructuring of the financial sector have been far reaching, thereby reinforcing the need for strong policy coordination. In Jamaica, the coordination of debt management, fiscal, and monetary policies is undertaken within the context of a clear and consistent macroeconomic framework designed to lower inflation and achieve economic stability and sustainable growth and development.

The transfer of the shared debt management function from the BOJ to the ministry of finance and planning has also resulted in greater coordination of fiscal policy and debt management objectives. It also allows for a more clearly defined set of debt management objectives determined independently from monetary policy considerations. Despite these separate objectives, there is a high degree of coordination between the fiscal and monetary authorities.

At the policy level, there are regular meetings between senior officials of the planning authorities—the ministry of finance and planning, the BOJ, the Planning Institute of Jamaica, and the Statistical Institute of Jamaica—to ensure consistency in the government's economic and financial program. At the technical level, there are regular meetings where information is shared on the government's cash-flow requirements and financing program, as well as on current monetary conditions and developments within the money and foreign exchange markets. There are weekly meetings within the ministry of the DMU, fiscal policy management unit, cash management unit, and the accountant general department, as well as between the ministry and the BOJ.

Legal framework

A well-developed legal and institutional framework exists for the execution of debt management. Under Jamaica's Constitution, all loans charged on the consolidated fund, including all external and domestic debt payments, represent a statutory charge on the revenue and assets of Jamaica. This provision allows for debt payments to be made without any requirement of parliamentary approval, and before funds are available for other policies and programs. In addition, the constitution and the Financial Administration and Audit (FAA) Act give the ministry of finance and planning overall responsibility for the management of Jamaica's public debt.

The government's borrowing requirements for each financial year are determined by the ministry of finance and planning and set out in the budget presented to parliament at the beginning of the financial year.

The authority to borrow is established by statutes. The Loan Act, 1964, and subsequent amendments provide the government with the authority to borrow from the domestic and external markets. The Loan Act establishes overall quantitative limits on the amount the government can borrow. Increases in the ceiling have to be obtained by parliamentary approval.

For domestic borrowings, there are specific acts that govern the issuance of the various debt instruments. These are the Treasury Bill, Local Registered Stock, Debenture, Land Bond, and Saving Bonds Acts.

The borrowing powers of public sector entities are set out in the FAA Act and the legislation governing the corporations and are complemented by the new Public Bodies Management and Accountability Act. The board of directors of the public entity determines the extent of borrowing, and the ministry responsible for the entity must approve the borrowing plan. However, the approval of the ministry of finance and planning has to be obtained by all public sector entities needing to finance their operations through debt financing.

Transparency

Considerable efforts have been made to increase transparency and accountability in debt management operations in recent years.

The government's debt management strategy is presented to parliament at the start of the financial year. Since fiscal year 1999/2000, this strategy has been published in the form of a ministry paper that has widespread public distribution. The document is available through the Internet on the web site of the ministry of finance and planning, www.mof.gov.jm.

Comprehensive information on Jamaica's debt is published on the ministry's web site and routinely updated. In addition to information on past debt activity, including debt outstanding, debt-service payments, and debt structure and composition, the web site is also used as a vehicle to announce future debt operations especially as they relate to debt issuance in the domestic market.

The rules for participating in primary debt issues, specifically the auction of medium-term government securities, have also been widely disclosed. Notices for future domestic debt issues are also published in the print media. Similarly, the results of government debt issues are widely reported through the print and electronic media and on the ministry's web site.

There is also regular dissemination of information to players in the international capital markets, credit-rating agencies, and international and regional financial institutions.

Establishing a Capacity to Assess and Manage Cost and Risk

Debt management strategy

The primary aim of Jamaica's debt management strategy is to ensure that overall borrowing is kept within prudent levels and secured on the best terms available. Over the medium term, it is envisaged that debt management strategies will be supported by a continual fall in interest rates, a relatively stable exchange rate environment, a reduction of the fiscal deficit, and a return to fiscal surplus.

Jamaica's public debt management strategy is defined within the context of a macroeconomic framework of fiscal balance, price stability, and growth. Consistent with this, the strategic objective is to bring total debt to sustainable levels over the medium term. Achieving sustainable levels of debt has necessitated the design and implementation of a comprehensive debt management strategy.

The government's debt management strategy is intended to achieve five broad objectives over the medium term:

- satisfying the government's annual borrowing requirements,
- minimizing borrowing and debt service costs,
- achieving a balanced maturity structure,
- building and promoting a liquid and efficient market for government securities, and
- ensuring continued or wider access to markets, both domestic and external.

Risk management framework

Increased attention has been given to managing the government's exposures to unexpected interest rate and currency movements in relation to both the domestic and external debt portfolios. At the end fiscal year 2001/02, more than 57 percent of Jamaica's domestic debt portfolio was composed of floating-rate instruments. This has left the government vulnerable to increases in interest rates with the attendant increases in debt-servicing costs. To reduce interest rate risk, the current debt strategy has been to increase the proportion of fixed-rate debt in the domestic debt portfolio. Progress has been made in this direction, because all local registered stocks issued through auction have been issued on a fixed-rate basis. Fixed-rate debt will continue to be issued over the medium term, thereby redistributing the balance between fixed- and floating-rate debt to more prudent levels. Over the medium term, the government will seek to maintain the fixed-rate target of 60 percent of the domestic debt portfolio, in keeping with international best practice.

The management of the Jamaican debt portfolio's currency exposure will include limiting the share of U.S. dollar exposure in the domestic debt portfolio. Jamaica's issuance of U.S. dollar-denominated and U.S. dollar–indexed securities in the domestic market has led to an increasing share of the domestic debt portfolio exposed to U.S.-dollar currency risk. At the end of fiscal year 2001/02, these categories together made up 15.5 percent of the domestic debt, compared with 8.1 percent at the end of fiscal year 2000/01. Although the government is committed to providing an array of instruments to the domestic markets, maintaining a prudent domestic debt structure requires that the U.S. dollar exposure of the portfolio remain low. Consistent with this, the strategic objective will be to reduce the exposure over the medium term.

External debt

The currency composition of Jamaica's external debt is changing after years of holding steady. The advent of the euro and the replacement of multiple European currencies by a single currency have significantly altered the composition of Jamaica's external debt portfolio. In addition, success in diversifying the portfolio by raising funds in the international capital markets has influenced the currency composition of the debt. Although more than 75 percent of the external debt portfolio is denominated in U.S. dollars, a growing portion of the debt is denominated in euros. The euro is now the second largest currency component of Jamaica's external debt, accounting for 14 percent of the external debt at the end of March 2002.

The seeming complexity of hedging instruments (swaps and options), with its specialized knowledge required to use such instruments effectively, and the costs of using such tools have tended to make Jamaica, like many other developing countries, shy away from actively employing these mechanisms. The notable shift in the currency composition of the public external debt makes it prudent for the government to adopt strategies to manage the currency risk associated with this exposure, because unhedged

exposures can lead to significant increases in debt-service costs. As a result, steps will be taken to minimize the portfolio's vulnerability to adverse movements in the euro by using hedging mechanisms, where appropriate, to minimize the portfolio's foreign currency exposure.

Contingent liabilities

The need to record and assess the impact of the government's contingent liabilities has become increasingly important in recent years. The government is concerned not only with limiting the total face value of contingent liabilities, but also minimizing both the likelihood of contingent liabilities being called and the size of public outlays in the event that a call is made. In assessing the appropriateness of contingent liabilities, consideration is given to how these resources will be used to ensure that they will be used for developmental purposes and are in keeping with government's economic strategy.

A number of measures to minimize the government's risk exposure associated with contingent liabilities are being implemented. Foremost among these is the strengthening of the monitoring and analysis of contingent liabilities so that the potential future impact for debt servicing can be fully evaluated. Legislation designed to enhance accountability and transparency in public sector bodies has been enacted. Work is also under way to ensure the comprehensive data capture of contingent liabilities and the development of a proper risk management framework. Another means of limiting government's risk exposure is to require some level of risk sharing in the issue of government guarantees.

Development and Maintenance of an Efficient Market for Government Securities

Primary market

A core debt management objective is to ensure that funds are raised as cost-effectively as possible. One step in this direction, within the domestic market, has been to adopt a market-based mechanism for selling local registered stocks (LRS),[2] the medium- to long-term instrument. A multiple-price auction system was introduced in October 1999. Previously, the government set rates on these instruments. This often created price distortions in the domestic market, which at times manifested itself in the government's financing needs not being fully met from the market issues, necessitating private placements.

A more competitive pricing of medium- and long-term securities has been achieved through the use of the auction system. This mechanism has resulted in a significant narrowing of interest differentials between long-term and short-term domestic securities. Since the introduction of the auction system, LRS issues have been significantly oversubscribed. Over time, the price range for bids has narrowed. This policy shift has resulted in the government meeting its financing needs at competitive rates. When circumstances make it necessary for the government to raise funds through private placements, it is done through a competitive bidding process.

Another significant development has been the increased ability of the government to extend the maturity structure of its debt since the introduction of the auction system. As of March 2002, 35.1 percent of total domestic debt was scheduled to mature after five years. This compares favorably with the position one year earlier, when 23.3 percent of the total domestic debt was scheduled to mature after five years. At the same time, 17.5 percent of the domestic debt was scheduled to mature after 10 years, compared with 6.6 percent at the end of March 2001.

The appetite for longer-term securities has resulted in a positive shift in the maturity profile of the domestic debt. A milestone was reached in August 2000, when the first 10-year LRS instrument was successfully auctioned. Of the new debt issued in fiscal year 2001/02, some 86.4 percent of LRS issued through the auction system had maturities of five years or more, compared with 53.5 percent of new issues through the same process in the previous fiscal year. In fiscal year 2001/02, 15.5 percent of new domestic debt issued has maturities of 10 years or more. With continued improvement in macroeconomic conditions and renewed investor confidence, the government has been able to successfully auction LRS with maturities as long as 30 years.

The market's appetite for longer-term securities is also reflected in the successful issuance of government-guaranteed, 30-year, inflation-indexed infrastructure bonds for the financing of Jamaica's first toll road.

The conversion of the contingent liabilities associated with the rehabilitation and restructuring of the financial sector into tradable government securities provided an opportunity for further lengthening the maturity profile of the domestic debt. These obligations were converted into securities with maturities of up to 25 years.

Announcements

To facilitate the development of an orderly and well-functioning domestic securities market, the approach has been to not only regularly access the market, but also to inform the market of upcoming issues. Considerable progress has been made in informing the market and increasing the predictability of the government's debt operations. In addition to the publication of a calendar of treasury bill tenders and issue dates at the start of each fiscal year, announcements have been extended to include the publication of an issuance calendar for LRS auctions. This dissemination of information and the regular consultations with primary dealers have allowed for greater transparency and predictability in the domestic capital market.

Portfolio diversification

The domestic debt portfolio comprises short-term treasury bills, fixed- and floating-rate medium- to long-term LRS, medium-term debentures, fixed-rate foreign currency domestic bonds, indexed bonds, savings and developmental bonds, and commercial loans.

Although a significant proportion of the domestic debt portfolio is made up of floating-rate instruments, the use of the auction mechanism to price the government's primary debt-raising instruments, the LRS, has meant that over the medium term, an increasing share of the debt will be on a fixed-rate basis. This will insulate the portfolio from interest rate shocks and rollover risks.

The principal holders of government securities are the central bank, commercial banks, insurance companies, pension funds, and the money market fund managers. In recent years, the government's debt issuance program has tried to meet the needs of the market players. A priority has been to introduce new instruments that are more closely tailored to meet the needs of different market segments. In addition to overall capital market development, the benefit to the government is a larger pool of resources from which financing can be tapped on improved terms.

The introduction of new instruments began in 1999, when, on a small-scale, Jamaica offered U.S. dollar–indexed bonds to the domestic market. These instruments have proven to be attractive to those institutional and retail investors uncertain about the future movements in the exchange rate and who are desirous of maintaining the value of their assets. It is intended to reintroduce savings bonds, which because of their structure and method of distribution are attractive to a wider cross section of investors, including household savers. In January 2002, Jamaica introduced 30-year, inflation-linked bonds in the domestic market for financing of the first toll road. These were purchased mainly by pension funds.

Portfolio diversification has also occurred with the external debt. Renewed access to funding from the international capital markets since 1997 has helped to broaden Jamaica's investor base in terms of the geographic distribution and the type of investors participating in Jamaica's international bond issues. In addition to the 1.375 billion in Eurobonds issued mainly to U.S. investors, Jamaica gained successful entry into the European capital markets in February 2000 and February 2001, issuing euro-denominated bonds totaling €375 million. This market has provided an excellent alternative and a relatively cheaper source of financing for the government of Jamaica and created greater flexibility and choice in meeting its financing needs. The U.S. dollar–denominated bonds were purchased mainly by institutions and fund managers, but the euro-denominated transactions involved widespread participation by retail investors. The registration of future Eurobond offerings with the U.S. Securities and Exchange Commission in February 2002 will also enable Jamaica to further broaden its investor base, because the registration allows for greater access to U.S. investors.

Secondary market

Primary dealers have played a critical role in building the securities market in Jamaica. In 1994, the BOJ created a new financial market arrangement involving primary dealers. The dealers were to be the medium through which the central bank conducts its open market operations. They were also expected to provide continuous underwriting support for new issues of government securities, thereby providing secondary market liquidity. Though not mandatory, dealers—currently numbering 14—are required to take up a total of 45 percent of all primary issues.

Secondary market development in Jamaica is constrained by the absence of exchange trading in securities. The Jamaica Central Securities Depository Ltd. (JCSD), a subsidiary of the Jamaica Stock Exchange, began operation in 1998. However, the depository currently trades equities only. The process to reduce the issuance of paper certificates for government securities has been initiated. This dematerialization of securities, which the central securities depositories provides, will increase the efficiency of secondary market trading and reduce the risk associated with the holding, trading, and settlement of securities. As part of the fiscal year 2002/03 debt strategy, steps will be initiated to reduce the issuance of paper certificates for government securities. This will involve, initially, consulting with market participants and the relevant institutions integral to the process involved in the holding of securities in electronic form. The immobilization of government securities will allow for the further development of the domestic capital market by increasing efficiency and reducing the risk associated with the holding, trading, and settlement of securities.

Taxation

Although taxes on interest have been levied at a rate of 33.3 percent for corporations and 25 percent for individuals, before 1999, taxes were withheld only on savings deposits. In 1999, the government increased the number of financial institutions that were required to withhold taxes on interest as well as the range of financial instruments covered. Withholding tax on interest was increased from 15 percent in 1999 to 25 percent in 2000 on all financial instruments. Corporations are liable for the remaining 8.3 percent when tax returns are filed. In addition to the increase in revenue from this source, there has been a reduction in distortions in the domestic market. In an effort to encourage long-term savings by individuals, the government granted tax-free status to approved long-term savings accounts. These are deposits where the principal amounts are held for at least five years. If the deposits are redeemed before the minimum five-year period, then tax is payable at the 25 percent rate.

Technological developments

The introduction of new and improved technologies is also contributing to the development of the domestic capital market. One such development is the introduction of a new system that allows primary dealers and other financial institutions to electronically bid for securities. An immediate benefit is the greater efficiency in conducting auctions of government securities. Similarly, upgrades to debt management, monitoring, and payment systems are contributing to more comprehensive information being recorded, a greater selection of tools available for debt analysis, and speedier processing of debt payments.

Summary

Jamaica has recognized the need to adopt sound debt management practices. Although advances are still to be made, there has been considerable progress in recent years in strengthening the government's debt management capacity. Clear debt management objectives have led to the articulation of a comprehensive debt strategy, and the increased reliance on market mechanisms to sell government securities has led to the issue of longer-term securities at lower interest costs. The availability of information, greater predictability of issues, and more frequent dialogue with the market have increased market confidence.

The imperative for the future is to build on these achievements, so that over time the culmination of sound debt management policies and practices is sustained economic growth and development for Jamaica. There are a number of factors that will facilitate the further development of the market. These include

- The renewed health of the financial sector: Rehabilitation and restructuring efforts have resulted in a consolidation of the sector into fewer institutions with greater critical mass.
- Further improvements in the legislative framework governing the financial sector: A new regulatory authority—the Financial Services Commission (FSC)—was established in April 2001. The FSC is responsible for the efficient regulation and supervision of entities dealing in securities, collective investment funds (e.g., mutual funds and unit trusts), investment advisers, the insurance industry, and pension funds.
- Planned reform of the pension system: This will create a larger pool of funds for long-term investment.
- Plans to reopen government debt issues to create benchmark securities across the yield curve: This will increase the liquidity of the instruments, further extend the maturity profile of the debt, and lower borrowing costs.

Notes

1. The case study was prepared by the Debt Management Unit of the Ministry of Finance and Planning.
2. LRS may be both fixed- and floating-rate securities.

8
Japan[1]

Governance Framework

Debt management objectives

Debt management policies in Japan have two primary objectives: first, to ensure smooth and stable funding for fiscal management; second, to curb costs on medium-to long-term financing, thus alleviating the burden on taxpayers.

Smooth funding aims to ensure that Japanese government bond (JGB) issuance will not have a turbulent impact on the market. This can be accomplished by maintaining high levels of transparency, predictability, and considerations to financial market trends. Stable funding means to issue bonds according to the planned amount of government bond issuance.

Improving the secondary market is also an essential element that needs to be taken into account in formulating debt management policies. The government bond market is the market where credit risk–free interest rates are formed. Thus, it serves as the foundation for the broader financial marketplace. JGBs also account for the majority of securities in the domestic bond and debenture market, both in issue amount and

trading volume. Consequently, efforts to improve liquidity and increase efficiency in the secondary market, instead of improving the primary market alone, are essential to foster the financial market as a whole. In the end, this will help to increase the Japanese market's international competitiveness. Another point is that an improved secondary market will also facilitate a smoother, more stable, and low-cost issuance of government bonds.

Coordination with monetary and fiscal policies

The primary objectives of debt management policies are to ensure smooth and stable funding while curbing financing costs to alleviate the fiscal burden. Accordingly, debt management policies must facilitate fiscal management.

Both debt management policies and monetary policies can affect the economy via interest rates. So, unless consistency is secured between these two areas, appropriate economic policies cannot be implemented. Therefore, it is essential for the government and the central bank to maintain adequate levels of consistency and transparency in their own policies while fully taking into account policy interactions during the process of policymaking.

In the relations with monetary policy, it is essential to prohibit the central bank from underwriting government bonds in the primary market and adhere to the principle of issuing government bonds in the market. This is mandatory in the context of maintaining fiscal restraints and the independence of the central bank, and it is legally set forth in Japan's Finance Law (Article 5). One exception exists. With the approval of the parliament (the Diet), refunding bonds can be issued directly to the Bank of Japan (BoJ) when government bonds held by the BoJ mature. This exception is permitted because such issuance of refunding bonds will not lead to increased money supply.

The government should not be allowed to request the central bank to ease its monetary policy, alleviate the fiscal burden, or purchase government bonds to help absorb JGBs. Requests such as these would be detrimental to debt management policies, because they would undermine investor confidence in government bonds and also could fuel inflationary expectations. Therefore, such requests are never made. Moreover, developing monetary policy is the prerogative of the policy board at the BoJ, and the final decision making concerning the purchase of government bonds lies with the BoJ.

Legal framework of government debt management

Article 85 of the constitution stipulates that no money shall be expended, nor shall the state obligate itself, except as authorized by the Diet. Accordingly, JGBs are, without exception, issued on legal grounds.

Laws that serve as a basis for issuance vary according to the use of funds

In principle, the issue amount of government bonds is determined for each fiscal year, which begins on April 1 and ends on March 31 the following year. At present, four main laws provide the grounds for the issuance of government bonds:

- Construction bonds under the Public Finance Law: Although the Public Finance Law stipulates

that, in principle, government expenditure must be financed by tax revenue (Body, Paragraph 1 of Article 4), it allows for government bond issuance or borrowing only as a means to finance public works (Proviso, Paragraph 1 of Article 4). The maximum issue amount for each fiscal year is specified in the general provisions of the budget and must be approved by the Diet.

- Special deficit-financing bonds under the special laws: As mentioned, the Public Finance Law permits the issuance of government bonds only to finance public works. However, when there is a budgetary deficit, a special law enacted for each fiscal year based on Article 4 of the Public Finance Law authorizes the government to issue special deficit-financing bonds. Also, with special deficit-financing bonds, the maximum issue amount for each fiscal year is specified in the general provisions of the budget and must be approved by the Diet.

- Refunding bonds under the Special Account Law of the Government Debt Consolidation Fund: The government can issue refunding bonds (except for fiscal loan fund special account bonds) up to the amount required for consolidation or redemption of government bonds during a given fiscal year (Article 5 and 5-2 of the Special Account Law of the Government Debt Consolidation Fund). Because refunding bond issues will not affect the outstanding government debt, their maximum issue amount is not subject to approval from the Diet. The actual issue amount is determined according to the so-called 60-year redemption rule (discussed in another section).

- Fiscal loan fund special account bonds under the Fiscal Loan Fund Special Account Act: The government can now issue bonds or borrow to finance fiscal loan programs (Article 11 of the Fiscal Loan Fund Special Account Act) as a result of the reform of the Fiscal Investment and Loan Program (FILP) system that took effect in April 2001. (Under the old system, all postal savings and pension reserves were deposited with the trust fund bureau to finance the FILP. Such a scheme with a compulsory deposit no longer exists. Instead, under the new system, each FILP agency must in principle raise funds from the market by issuing FILP agency bonds. Should circumstances necessitate, however, the funds can be raised in part by issuing government bonds.)

The laws define how the proceeds will be used. However, from the investor's perspective, there is no differentiation between construction bonds, special deficit-financing bonds, refunding bonds, and fiscal loan fund special account bonds.

Law- and ordinance-based handling of government bonds

The minister of finance is granted the authority by the Law Concerning Government Bonds to determine government bond issuance, registration, and other basic procedural matters related to government bonds. Specific procedures are stipulated in the ministry ordinances established by the Law Concerning Government Bonds. The law also specifies the BoJ's role in handling government bonds.

The government debt consolidation fund

Debt reduction in Japan is built around the government debt consolidation fund (GDCF). Fiscal resources for all interest payments and redemption of government bonds are funneled into the GDCF, accumulated, and disbursed from the GDCF.

Funds are transferred from the general account to the special account for the GDCF. Revenue from issuing refunding bonds is also stored at the GDCF, to be used to redeem bonds at maturity. Independent management of the cash flow regarding interest payments and redemption, as such, aims to contribute to investor confidence in the security of interest payments and redemption.

Sixty-year redemption rule

The so-called 60-year redemption rule—meaning each issue of debt should be redeemed over a span of 60 years—plays a central role in the debt reduction system. The concept is based on the average economic depreciation period of the assets purchased by construction bonds and special deficit-financing bonds being about 60 years, so redemption should be completed during that period.

The rule allows calculation of the net amount to be redeemed out of the gross redemption amount for maturing bonds. In other words, the rule is used to determine the amount of fiscal resources to be financed by issuing refunding bonds (for the purpose of net redemption). The 60-year redemption rule is not applied to fiscal loan fund special account bonds, because the fund collected from the FILP investment will be used for their redemption.

The following is an example to show how the rule actually works. A new ¥60 billion, 10-year funding bond is issued. When the bonds become due, ¥10 billion yen—or one-sixth of the original issue amount—will be put toward cash redemption (in the GDCF) and refunding bonds for the remaining ¥50 billion will be issued. Assume these refunding bonds are in five-year bonds. When the refunding bonds become due in five years, ¥5 billion—or five-sixtieths of the original issue amount—of the redeem and refunding bonds for the remaining ¥45 billion will be issued. Repeating this, the entire issue would be redeemed 60 years after the initial issuance.

Organizational structure

The issue amount in JGBs is determined during the budgetary process for each fiscal year. Within the ministry of finance, the following departments are involved in the work related to government borrowing:

- Budget bureau: The budget bureau compiles the amount of new issuance of funding bonds that constitute the revenue of the general account.
- Financial bureau, fiscal investment and loan program division: As the division in charge of the FILP, this section compiles the issue amount of fiscal loan fund special account bonds that constitute the revenue of fiscal loan fund special account.
- Financial bureau, government debt division: As the name suggests, this division plays the central role in debt management policies, which range from compiling a government bond issuance plan and setting terms for each issue, to designing new schemes and programs, such as the separate trading of registered interest and principal of securities ([STRIPS] that were launched in fis-

cal year 2002). The government debt division also calculates the issue amount of refunding bonds based on the 60-year redemption rule.

- Financial bureau, treasury division: This division is responsible for the day-to-day cash-flow management of the general account, based on the circumstances of debt issuance. It also issues financing bills to cover fund shortages in the short term.
- Tax bureau: Government bond–related tax systems fall under the jurisdiction of the tax bureau.

The BOJ handles all the government bond–related procedural work, from issuance to redemption. Serving as the central securities depository for government bonds, the BOJ also provides the financial network system, BOJ-NET, which is an online system in which a number of financial institutions participate to settle both government bonds and funds.

Being responsible for supervision of financial markets, the financial services agency takes the initiative in establishing rules and systems for trading as well as supervising the secondary market.

Debt Management Strategy and the Risk Management Framework

Debt management strategy

As mentioned, the objectives of debt management can be summarized in three points:

- first, to ensure smooth and stable funding for fiscal management;
- second, to curb costs on medium- to long-term financing, thus alleviating the burden on taxpayers; and
- third, to develop a debt market that has high levels of efficiency and liquidity.

To accomplish these objectives as a whole, it is essential that debt management policy be based on two different, yet closely related, perspectives—to be market friendly and to promote market development.

This section outlines the debt management strategy with a focus on the implementation of policies

that are market friendly. Market development is the focus of the next section.

Strengthened communications with the market

To ensure smooth and stable funding, it is essential to fully take into account the trends and needs in the market so as not to cause turbulence. Therefore, to implement policies that are market friendly, an appropriate understanding of market trends and needs is indispensable. It is equally essential to work on market expectations through two-way communications for any major change in policy.

The government debt division within the ministry of finance, in charge of the issuance and maintenance of government bonds, has several monitoring officials who maintain daily contact with bond market participants. Vital information collected through this channel is reported to higher reaches of government. At the time of issue, a number of market participants are interviewed just before the bidding, so that issue terms can be fine tuned to meet market needs.

Although such day-to-day market monitoring by the officials in charge is instrumental to market-based debt management, it was realized that an advisory group, made up of a wide range of participants, would be helpful for a multilateral exchange of views. Thus, in September 2000, the ministry of finance established the Meeting on the Japanese Government Bond Market, a forum of key market participants, scholars, and experts. Although this meeting is not granted policymaking powers, it promotes an active participation of its members by appropriately reflecting the content of discussion on debt management policies. Moreover, through discussion at the meeting, the debt management authority can indicate its policy stance, either explicitly or implicitly. Thus, the subjects discussed at the meeting are diverse, ranging from short-term agenda, such as maturity structure, to longer-term issues, such as institutional improvement of the government bond market.

Meetings of this group take place more or less monthly. Market participants who take part are elected once every six months, based on their bidding performance. However, it is important that participation in a meeting with the debt management authority does not lead to giving special attention to those who participate. Thus, in the case of the Meeting on the Japanese Government Bond Market, the chair holds a press conference immediately after each meeting to announce the content of the discussion. Furthermore, detailed minutes are published before the market opens the following morning, thus eliminating any information gap between members and nonmembers.

Issuance at par value

Japanese investors tend to prefer issues to take place at or near par value. Accordingly, when determining issue terms, the coupon and maturity must be based on the actual market situation so that the issue price comes close to par value. Consequently, an outstanding issue can be reopened only when the market rate immediately before an auction is close to the coupon rate of the outstanding bond. As a result, whether or not the reopening rule will be applied will not be known until the announcement of the issue terms on the bidding day. One consequence is that it is rather difficult to predict the final outstanding amount for each issue. This is a problem that remains to be addressed, for example, by introducing a regular reopening rule, such as those used in some other countries. A change could make the issue price either substantially over par or under par. Thus, it is crucial to see if the par-driven propensity of Japanese investors will change when current value accounting becomes more prevalent.

Bond issuance via auction

To ensure that government bond issuance is market friendly, it is desirable that the primary and secondary markets be linked. Accordingly, an effective approach to market-based issuance of government bonds is to hold auctions among a number of market participants.

In Japan, 10-year bonds—the main tenor since the beginning of the JGB history—are issued exceptionally through syndicate underwriting. At present, however, 60 percent of the issue is distributed to syndicate members via a competitive-price auction, to reflect the market mechanism as much as possible.

The remaining 40 percent are allocated to syndicate members at a fixed price and share. As to the amount offered at a competitive-price auction, when the offered bids amount to less than the scheduled amount, the syndicate members are supposed to undertake the remaining balance according to their fixed shares at a price equivalent to the average contract price in the competitive-price auction.[2]

All other bonds are issued by use of auctions. As a result, 90 percent of the government bonds issued in the financial market during fiscal year 2001 were offered at auctions.

What method of auction to choose—price or yield auction, or whether to issue bonds at a uniform price or each at a bidding price—is another point to be considered. In Japan, a price auction method has been adopted for all government bonds, except for 30-year bonds and 15-year floating-rate bonds,[3] and issues each of them at a contract price.

With 30-year bonds, the current market yield—the basis for determining the coupon rate—is not readily available, because the secondary market for 30-year bonds is not yet fully functioning. These bonds are therefore offered by a yield auction, and the coupon rate is determined afterward based on auction results, a method that ensures the bonds are issued at or near par. All winning bidders can purchase the bonds at the maximum contract yield (i.e., single-price method). This method is regarded as effective for issuing bonds with a long maturity.

Risk management

The largest risks the debt issuing authority can face are interest rate fluctuation risks and refinancing risk. For example, concentrating issues on a specific maturity when determining maturity structure could increase the risk of raising yields, or concentrating redemption on a specific timing could increase refunding risks in the future. Therefore, a priority is to maintain an appropriate balance among different maturity zones in the debt portfolio. This is achieved by assessing the market latitude for each zone, such as short-term, medium-term, long-term, and super-long-term.

In recent years, JGBs with maturity other than 10 years have quickly established themselves as new benchmark bonds with increasing liquidity, which has facilitated risk management. However, as a result, the appropriate balance among different maturity zones has also been in a state of flux. Thus, at present, no fixed standard exists for either maturity-wise ratios or average maturity.

It is also essential to smooth the redemption structure in the debt portfolio as much as possible. In fiscal year 2002, a buyback program with the aim of adjusting the maturity structure in the debt portfolio is expected to be implemented.

When the distribution of debt issuance among maturity zones is subject to change, it could lead to increasing interest rate fluctuation risks. Similarly, a change in debt-related systems (i.e., systems governing debt market activities such as legal systems or settlement systems) could increase interest rate fluctuation risks if it is not expected by the market. Therefore, when making a policy change, it is desirable to create a soft landing by sending signals to the market via various channels to ensure that the change will be a factor already considered in the market expectations. For example, in a government bond issuance plan for each fiscal year, the market is particularly interested in knowing the issue amount for each maturity zone. This is where the Meeting on the Japanese Government Bond Market can prove its worth. An opportunity to have discussions with market participants, which will help us better understand the market needs, together with prompt disclosure of the content of discussions, should help increase the predictability of the yet-to-be-announced maturity structure.

Developing the Government Securities Market

Diversification of government bond maturity and product appeal

To develop an efficient market for government bonds, it is essential to achieve a smooth yield curve by developing a benchmark bond for each maturity zone, thus increasing liquidity across the entire yield curve. In the past, the maturity structure focused on 10-year bonds, making it virtually the only bench-

mark bond in Japan. In recent years, however, introducing new types of government bonds with maturities of other than 10 years has diversified maturity zones.[4] Also, in compiling the issuance plan for each fiscal year, issues have increased in 2-year, 5-year,[5] 10-year, and 20-year bonds to develop them into benchmarks while taking into account the balance among them. When determining the terms of issue based on the market situation, whether or not the reopening rule can be applied depends on the circumstances at the time of issue, as described. But when the reopening rule is applied, it is aimed and expected to increase liquidity of that particular issue.

However, an excessive diversification of maturity zones will be incompatible with the effort to develop benchmarks. At present, it would be inappropriate to add yet other benchmarks by establishing new maturity bonds in addition to 2-year, 5-year, 10-year, and 20-year bonds.

To provide investors with varied investment opportunities focused just on maturities, it is also necessary to consider diversification from the standpoint of implementation of suitable, needs-oriented instruments and from the angle of product appeal. For example, today, 15-year floating-rate bonds, with the semiannual coupon pegged to the interest rate of 10-year bonds, are offered in public auctions, a response to the growing investor needs for products that can allow them to hedge against interest rate fluctuation risks.

In addition, the STRIPS system is expected to be introduced shortly. This introduction should not only increase the number of options available to investors, but also it will help achieve a more precise zero-coupon yield curve, thus increasing the efficiency of the debt market.

Information regarding bond issuance

Issuance plan for each fiscal year

To make debt issuance transparent and predictable, the ministry of finance formulates and announces a government bond issuance plan for the coming fiscal year at the same time as the announcement of the budget. The issuance plan consists of two parts: classification by funding purpose and classification by issuance methods and maturity.

The latter classification is divided into two: the total amount to be distributed in the private sector and the total amount to those in the public sector. The amount to be distributed in the private sector is further broken down by maturity, and the amount to be distributed in the public sector is further classified by public entity.

Because the ministry of finance makes it a rule to level each issue amount for a given maturity, market participants should be able to predict the approximate amount per issue based on the total issue amount by maturity.

Auction calendar

In March 1999, in an effort to make debt issuance more transparent and predictable, the ministry of finance began to publish the auction calendar and offering amount prior to auctions. Previously, the auction calendar for the coming three months was announced quarterly. The shortcoming of this method, however, was that investors had to wait until the last minute to be informed of the first auction in the coming quarter. Thus, in October 2001, the announcing method was changed to a monthly announcement of the auction calendar scheduled for the three months ahead. This has added to the predictability of debt issuance.

Issue terms

The total offering amount for each issue is published approximately one week before each auction. The coupon rate and the date of redemption, however, are announced on each auction date, because these two are determined by referring to the market situation up to the last minute before the auction starts.

Publication of this information is made to market participants at predetermined times via the Internet and news agencies.

Auction results

To minimize the risks on the part of market participants, it is desirable to announce the auction results as promptly as possible. Since May 2001, auction results have been produced within one and one-half hours. However, results used to take as long as two and one-half hours to appear, but by April 2000, the time had been shortened to two hours.

Government bond–related taxation

A 20 percent withholding tax is levied on the interest on coupon-bearing bonds. Those held by designated financial institutions (e.g., banks and securities firms), however, are exempted from withholding tax.

Furthermore, in September 1999, a withholding tax exemption system for interest on government bonds held by nonresident investors was introduced. In April 2001, the tax benefit was expanded even further. Under the expanded scheme, withholding tax exemption is also granted to interest on government bonds deposited by nonresident investors in the BOJ book-entry systems through foreign financial institutions (including so-called global custodians).

Profits on redemption of discount bonds are subject to an 18 percent withholding tax automatically at the time of purchase. However, profits on treasury bills and financing bills are exempted from withholding tax, because they are now held via the transfer settlement system.

Diversified market participants

To develop a debt market with high levels of liquidity, it is essential to diversify market participants as much as possible, thus increasing the depth of the market.

One of the characteristics of the Japanese debt market is that the government sector (including the public financial sector, such as postal savings), together with the private banking and insurance sector, hold a large share of the outstanding JGBs, whereas the share of JGBs held by individual investors and nonresident investors remains at a low level compared with other countries.[6] Perhaps one underlying factor is Japan's indirect finance–oriented structure. Even today, a large amount of household financial assets (totaling ¥1,400 trillion) is invested indirectly in government bonds via bank deposits and postal savings. One of the reasons that have added to this trend has been the deteriorating demand for funds in the private sector because of stagnation in the economy in recent years.

As such, the structure of debt holders in any given country is so deeply rooted in the financial system as a whole that it is impossible to categorically argue how it should take shape. However, when a limited number of institutional investors hold the majority of outstanding JGBs, the debt market is more likely to move more dramatically if there is a shock. Thus, to increase the stability of the debt market, it is far better to diversify debt holders as much as possible.

Also, the introduction of the payoff system in April 2002 (meaning a deposit insurance system that guaranteed term deposits up to ¥10 million, compared with an unlimited amount in the past) is expected to heighten the public awareness of credit risks. As a result, macroeconomic flows of capital may become more risk conscious. If that happens, there should be greater needs for government bonds, because they are credit risk–free financial assets.

In diversifying market participants, the current policy priorities are to promote further participation by individual investors, nonresident investors, and nonfinancial corporations.

Regarding individual investors, various public relations activities have started to communicate the benefits of investing in government bonds. Toward the end of 2001, for example, a public relations media campaign was designed to reach individual investors, using television, radio, newspapers, magazines, and posters. In addition, plans have been set in fiscal year 2002 to introduce nonmarketable government bonds specifically designed for individual investors.

As for nonresident investors, the tax exemption measures have already facilitated their entry into the JGB market, and there are plans to further promote their understanding of Japan's tax system and other related regulatory frameworks. For the overseas audience, the Internet, in particular, is regarded as an effective vehicle to deliver information.

Improved settlement system

The BoJ serves as the central securities depository for government bonds and provides settlement services for JGBs. The platform for settlement of book-entry securities is the BOJ-NET system. Bidding-related procedures in the issuance of these securities are also processed online via the BOJ-NET system.[7]

Book-entry securities are settled on-line on the BOJ-NET Japanese Government Securities Transfer System, a part of the BOJ-NET system. Another part of the BOJ-NET system is the BOJ-NET Funds Transfer System, an on-line system for the electronic transfer of funds across the current accounts at the BoJ. These separate services were linked in April 1999 to allow for the delivery-versus-payment (DVP) method of settlement. To maintain security of the settlement system, the DVP method of settlement is essential, thus avoiding the risks arising from the different timing of settling funds and securities.

Furthermore, in January 2001, a shift in the method of settling government bonds and the current accounts at the BoJ took place—from designated-time net settlement to real-time gross settlement (RTGS). Such a system involves a settlement mode that limits the direct effect of a financial institution's inability to pay (e.g., in the event the institution is unable to transfer funds or government bonds for any reason) to the counter-parties in a transaction. In other words, the changeover to the RTGS system was aimed at reducing the systemic risk inherent in designated-time net settlement.[8]

Introduction of the RTGS system has also solved another problem of the former designated-time net settlement. Under the old settlement system, each payment was interrelated with other payments settled at the same settlement time through the netting process, whereas with RTGS, each payment is settled individually.

In addition, under the RTGS method, settlement of most transactions at the BoJ is now completed early in the day. The earlier timing of settlement has also contributed to the reduction of systemic risk by substantially reducing the amount outstanding of transactions remaining unsettled on the settlement day. However, RTGS is not totally free from delays in settlement and an increase in loop transactions (a situation where, for example, three counter-parties short-sell a security among each other, which will start a loop because no one has the security to transfer) deriving from an increase in settlement work or a chain of transactions. Therefore, the occurrence of fails,[9] up to a certain degree, needs to be permitted.

Previously, designated-time net settlement was the norm for the Japanese bond market. Thus, to avoid the systemic risk inherent in this settlement method, failed transactions were generally not permitted. Accordingly, the so-called good-fail rule (unified business practice for treatment of fails) was not in demand then. However, introduction of the RTGS system has changed the circumstances, prompting the Japan Securities Dealers Association to study and introduce a good-fail rule similar to the ones established in key overseas markets (for explanation, see the Appendix).

Development of related markets

Increased convenience of the futures market and the repo market should facilitate hedged or arbitrated transactions among three markets, including the cash market (i.e., underlying assets market), thus adding to the liquidity of the government bond market as a whole.

Japan's futures market for government bonds opened in 1985 at the Tokyo Stock Exchange. Trading of long-term (10-year) JGB futures, which account for the majority of JGB futures transactions, in the contract month traded most actively has extremely high levels of liquidity.[10] This is due, in part, to the fact that many market participants take part for a variety of purposes, such as arbitrage between contract months or spot versus futures, hedging, and speculations.

The repo market in Japan used to have two types of transactions—old-type repurchase agreement and repo transactions of JGBs using cash as collateral (known as the "JGB repo"). Both types had some problems to be addressed. Previously, repo transactions of JGBs using cash as collateral were employed for coupon-bearing government bonds, and the former repurchase agreement was the norm for short-term government bonds. In other words, Japan's repo market used to be divided by these two different types of transactions.

In July 1998, market participants began studying new guidelines for repurchase agreements. This resulted eventually in the Master Repurchase Agreement[11] compiled by the Japan Securities Dealers Association, paving the way to the April 2001 introduction of a global standard–oriented method (i.e., new-type repurchase agreement), which is safer and more convenient than the previous method of transactions. The main characteristics of the new-type repurchase agreement are

- a nonresident-friendly method based on international standards and legally positioned as a "buy-and-sell" transaction,
- higher levels of safety due to strengthened methods for risk management (including haircut and margin call, also existing in the JGB repo) and incorporated measures for handling the default of a counter-party, and
- a newly incorporated substitution right (the right to substitute a security with another security during the course of the repo transaction) to facilitate term loan and deposit.

From now on, it is expected that all transactions will be consolidated into the new-type repurchase agreement. The new consolidated method of transactions should also help the efficient formulation of short-term benchmark interest rates that are risk free.

Appendix

The Good-Fail Rule

Under the good-fail rule, a party who fails to honor a transaction on a timely basis is subject to neither punishment nor delinquency charges. This is because the rule is based on the understanding that a fail accompanies the economic effect that as such serves as a deterrent to the occurrence of a fail and, should it occur, as an incentive to address it.

The rule can be illustrated by this example. Suppose X (deliverer) failed to deliver the JGBs to Y (receiver) on the contract date. Then, certainly X cannot receive the money for those JGBs. Thus, X may have to bear the extra cost of raising funds needed to keep holding the securities, or X has to abandon the opportunity to invest the money that was supposed to be paid by Y on the contract date. Besides, X will only be entitled to receive the interest payment for the period that ends on the contract date, no matter how long X is going to hold those JGBs. So, simply put, for X, a fail is nothing but bad news. However, Y will be entitled to receive the interest payment for the period from the contract date to the date of actual delivery, even though the JGBs are not yet in Y's possession. Also, Y can keep investing the money Y was supposed to pay on the contract date until the actual receipt of the securities. Thus, Y will gain from a fail on the part of X.

However, under the current situation of prolonged low interest rates, the mentioned economic rationality is less effective in serving as deterrent. Thus, to put an extra drag on fails, a temporary measure has been introduced that allows Y, for the time being, to demand that X pay for the cost Y would need to obtain the equivalent amount of securities by borrowing JGBs against cash collateral.

Notes

1. The case study was prepared by Kunimasa Antoku from the Government Debt Division, the Financial Bureau of the Ministry of Finance.

2. To implement public offering auctions, it is essential that the secondary market be relatively mature and sizable. Thus, when the market is at a relatively early stage of development, introducing a mechanism that ensures stable funding, such as the syndicate underwriting system in Japan, could be a valid policy option.

3. With 15-year floating-rate bonds, auctions are held on the spread from the reference rate (i.e., the yield on 10-year bonds at the most recent bidding).

4. Public offering auctions have begun in recent years for the following government bonds: 1-year treasury bills (in April 1999), 30-year coupon-bearing bonds (in September 1999), 5-year coupon-bearing bonds (in February 2000), 15-year floating-rate bonds (in June 2000), and 3-year discount bonds (in November 2000).

5. Although bonds with maturities of four and six years used to be issued, these bonds were discontinued in fiscal year 2001/02, and five-year bonds were positioned as the benchmark for the medium-term zone. This occurred in response to the increased liquidity of the five-year coupon-bearing bonds introduced in February 2000.

6. At March 31, 2000, individuals held 2.5 percent and non-resident investors 5.2 percent of outstanding JGBs.

7. The BoJ was the first to introduce such an on-line bidding system for government bonds. The system dramatically reduced the time needed for bidding procedural work, enabling the same-day publication of auction results.

8. This risk involves the systemic disruptions posed to financial institutions, and ultimately to the entire financial system, through a chain of settlement failures or delays in settlement.

9. A fail is a situation in which a recipient of government bonds in a transaction does not receive the bonds from the delivering party on the scheduled settlement date.

10. Super-long-term (20-year) JGB futures and medium-term (5-year) JGB futures are also traded, but the actual trading volume is negligible at present.

11. The Master Repurchase Agreement is based on the Global Master Repurchase Agreement, a standard agreement for repurchase agreement used in Europe and the United States that was compiled by the Bond Market Association and the International Securities Market Association.

9
Mexico[1]

Developing a Sound Governance and Institutional Framework

Objectives

Public debt management aims to ensure that the government's financing needs and its payment obligations are met at the lowest possible cost over the medium to long run, consistent with a prudent degree of risk.

The importance of the government's debt management strategy lies in helping generate macroeconomic stability and stronger public finances. The debt policy for 2002 had the objective of adequately managing the government's debt and helping to generate a stable macroeconomic environment as well as stronger public finances. This was even more important during a year in which most economies were encountering difficulties, characterized by low growth rates and uncertainty in the international capital market. In this regard, the government adopted the following debt management policy for 2002:

- As in past years, the fiscal deficit was financed in the domestic market. The uncertainty in the inter-

national market also underlined the need for this strategy during 2002.

- The strategy in the domestic debt was focused on three areas:
  - improving the maturity profile,
  - extending the average life of domestic debt, and
  - developing the long-term yield curve. It is important to note that issuance of the 10-year nominal fixed rate bond dates only to July 2001.
- The external debt strategy is expected to continue to extend the maturity profile and at the same time lower costs by implementing active debt management strategies aiming at reducing market imperfections in the sovereign yield curve. The strategy also intends to avoid refinancing risk due to large concentrations of maturities in any given year.

Legal framework

The legal framework for the debt management is covered by the following articles:

- Article 73, Section VIII of the Political Constitution of the United Mexican States (UMS) empowers the congress to establish the basis upon which the executive may borrow upon the credit of the nation, approve such borrowings, and order the repayment of the national debt.
- Article 89, Section I of the Political Constitution of the UMS empowers and establishes the duty of the president to promulgate and execute the laws enacted by the congress to provide for exact observance of the laws by the government.
- Article 31, Sections V and VI of the Organic Law of the Federal Public Administration provides that the ministry of finance and public credit shall manage the public debt of the federation and perform and authorize all transactions involving the public credit.
- Article 1 of the General Law of Public Debt provides that the following entities are authorized to borrow: (a) The federal executive and its branches, acting through the ministry of finance and public credit; (b) decentralized public agencies as well as public corporations (i.e., corporations with majority government ownership); (c) government credit institutions and auxiliary credit organizations, government insurance and surety companies; and (d) trusts for which the grantor is the federal government or any of the agencies mentioned above.
- Article 4, Section V of the General Law of Public Debt establishes that the federal executive, acting through the ministry of finance and public credit, shall be vested with the power to contract for, and manage, the federal government public debt and provide the guarantee of the federal government in credit transactions.

Coordination with monetary and fiscal policies

Debt management policy is determined by fiscal policy. If fiscal policy is coordinated with monetary policy, debt management policy will be indirectly related to monetary policy. In this regard, borrowing programs are based on the economic and fiscal projections contained in the government budget. The financial projections used in the government budget, such as the inflation rates and interest rates, are con-

sistent with the monetary program of the Bank of Mexico (BOM), the central bank. In addition, as will be described, the BOM acts as financial agent of the federal government for many transactions. This requires a continuous working relationship between the fiscal and monetary authorities regarding debt management policy.

Guidelines for debt management

When the budget is authorized at the end of each year, the congress approves the annual limit for net external and internal borrowing submitted by the government through the ministry of finance and public credit. This limit reflects the debt policy for the coming year, which is also submitted to the congress, which analyzes this information carefully. This institutional framework supports implementation of a prudent government debt management strategy.

In addition, every new administration sets forth a general program for borrowing and debt management, directly related to the fiscal objectives established for the period.

Institutional structure of debt management

Institutional structure of debt management within the government

The principal agency of debt management is the ministry of finance and public credit, acting through the unit general direction of public credit unit. The main powers delegated to the unit are to negotiate and execute all documents related to

- the public credit;
- the authorization and registration of borrowings by public entities, including the development banks; and
- financial transactions and derivatives to which the government is a party.

The President of the UMS appoints the general director of public credit. The senate must ratify the appointment.

The general director of public credit reports to the undersecretary of finance and public credit.

Every quarter, the issuance program for domestic debt is discussed with the undersecretary before its publication. The reporting covers the negotiations related to the authorization of borrowings by public entities and the financial transactions to which the government is a party. This covers, for example, every new operation of the government in the international capital market. The frequency of the reporting depends on when these negotiations take place.

As mentioned, the central bank acts as financial agent of the government in the issuance and service of domestic bonds as well as other liability management operations. The BOM is also in charge of paying the government debt derived from most of the external debt with the funds of the federal government and under the instruction of the general public credit direction. This entails a constant working relationship between the two entities.

Organizational structure within the debt management office

The debt management office is organized as follows:

- The deputy general direction of external credit manages the issuance of securities in the international capital markets and carries out liability and risk management concerning the debt portfolio.
- The deputy general direction of internal credit formulates the policies and manages the programs concerning the financing in the domestic market.
- The deputy general direction of international financial organisms negotiates the conditions of the loans with the World Bank, the Inter-American Development Bank, and other financial organisms.

- The deputy general direction of project financing negotiates and implements the policy regarding the financial operations, special schemes, and infrastructure projects.
- The deputy general direction of legal procedures is in charge of solving issues related to the legal framework applicable to public debt management and provides legal advice to the general direction of public credit and to the other deputy general directions.
- The deputy general direction of public debt negotiates, authorizes, and registers the public debt. This department also gathers and records the statistical information related to the public debt.

Retain qualified staff

Newly hired directors, deputy directors, and heads of departments must have a strong knowledge of at least one of the following subjects: public finances, economics, accounting, public debt management, law, statistics, and any other subject relating to public debt management.

For the staff, there are internal training programs in public finances, law, and accounting. In addition, scholarship programs are offered to the staff according to the specific area where they work.

Excluding the deputy general directors, directors, and deputy directors, the staff turnover within the general direction of public credit is low. The economic benefits are the same for all government employees, thus there are no additional economic incentives for public credit staff. However, because there are opportunities to learn different aspects of debt management—such as policies concerning financing in the international capital markets and the domestic market, knowledge of the legal framework

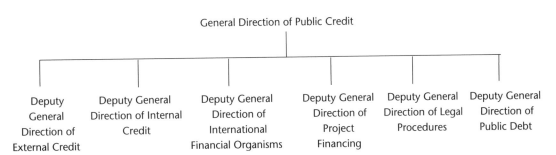

related to public debt management, and risk management of the debt portfolio—the public credit direction is regarded as an attractive place to work.

Transparency and accountability

During the course of each year, a unit of the ministry of the comptroller and administrative development monitors the accounts, financial statements, activities, and operations of the general direction of public credit. Also during each year, the congress, through its auditing organization, reviews the accounts, financial statements, and other specific topics that are of interest to its members. The audit follows generally accepted auditing standards as well as generally accepted accounting principles applicable to government finances and debt management.

In addition, it is important to mention that Mexico belongs to the Data Dissemination Group of the International Monetary Fund. In this regard, historical data on Mexico's public debt from the ministry of finance and public credit is available on its web page (www.shcp.gob.mx).

Debt Management Strategy and Risk Management Framework

The government has been able to reduce the country's vulnerability to contagion of international financial crises mainly through sound macroeconomic policies and fiscal discipline. The fiscal deficit has been decreasing for the past several years, and the government will continue with its medium-term goal of achieving a balanced budget. On the monetary policy front, discipline has contributed to the achievement of the BOM's inflation target for the past two years and, consequently, to more stable domestic financial markets.

A prudent and consistent debt management policy has also been an important tool in the ambition to reduce the country's vulnerability. Since the late 1980s, issues regarding public debt have acquired greater importance in the strategy carried out by Mexican authorities. The focus has been on a strategic debt management that permits control over the debt and, at the same time, improves the debt's terms and conditions.

Since 1995, the public debt as a proportion of GDP has diminished substantially, reaching levels not seen since the mid-1970's (see Figure II.9.1). This has resulted in an important reduction in the debt-service allocation, reducing the vulnerability of the economy to external shocks and also decreasing the pressure on public finance. Furthermore, as a result of the effective transmission of fiscal and monetary policies, a reduction in the interest rates has also been observed.

Naturally, debt policy has to coincide with economic policy. A greater local indebtedness could put pressure on interest rates and increase the financing cost for the private sector, causing a "crowding-out" effect in the domestic market. Furthermore, a greater external indebtedness increases the refinancing risk and could lead the local currency to appreciate, affecting the competitiveness of the private sector and motivating imports of products and services. Therefore, the yearly debt policy approved by the congress establishes what will be the sources of the financing the government requires—whether it will fund itself abroad, in the domestic market, or a combination of both—in accordance with the economic policy. The issuance of debt by both the government and the agencies has to be considered in debt policy to avoid concentration of repayments in the same year. Consolidated reports on this issuance of debt are also presented to the congress.

The government has been very active in promoting the development of the local debt markets by providing new regulations and instruments. This policy has allowed Mexico to fund its budgetary needs with local debt, which in turn also has helped the development of local debt markets and allowed a reduction of the external debt. In this sense, external debt as a percentage of total debt has demonstrated a clear downward trend thanks to declining limits on net external indebtedness.

Internal debt

The Mexican government today faces two different types of risk with respect to domestic debt.

- Interest rate risk: Given that a large amount of floating-rate debt is still outstanding, there is an

Figure II.9.1. Public Debt Evolution, 1971–2001
(In percent of GDP)

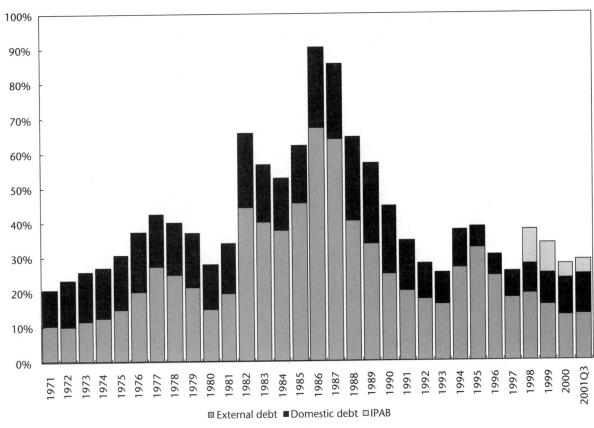

■ External debt ■ Domestic debt □ IPAB

Note: The IPAB (*Instituto de Protección al Ahorro Bancario*) is an institution created by the government to back up credit defaults, thus avoiding banking system failure.

inherent risk that an increase in interest rates will result in higher financial costs. However, as can be seen in Figure II.9.2, the relative importance of floating-rate debt has decreased over recent years.

- Refinancing risk: This risk arises from the possibility of an adverse environment in the global capital market, where the government could face difficulties in rolling over its maturing debt in favorable conditions. Given the improvement of the amortization profile during the past few years (see Figure II.9.3), the refinancing risk is manageable.

To manage the interest rate risk and the refinancing risk, the government has undertaken an issuance strategy based on the following assumptions:

- issuance of long-term floating-rate debt with 3- to 5-year maturities to reduce the refinancing risk started in 1997, and
- gradual issuance of fixed-rate long-term instruments in 3-, 5-, and 10-year maturities to further reduce refinancing risk, at the same time lowering interest rate risks.

Because the market for instruments with long duration is not deep, the Mexican government has continued to issue floating-rate debt. When the market permits, a gradual shift to fixed-rate debt issuance will occur.

This issuing strategy is part of the overall debt management strategy that the government has in place. To guarantee that the current strategy in the

Figure II.9.2. Internal Debt Composition by Type of Instrument

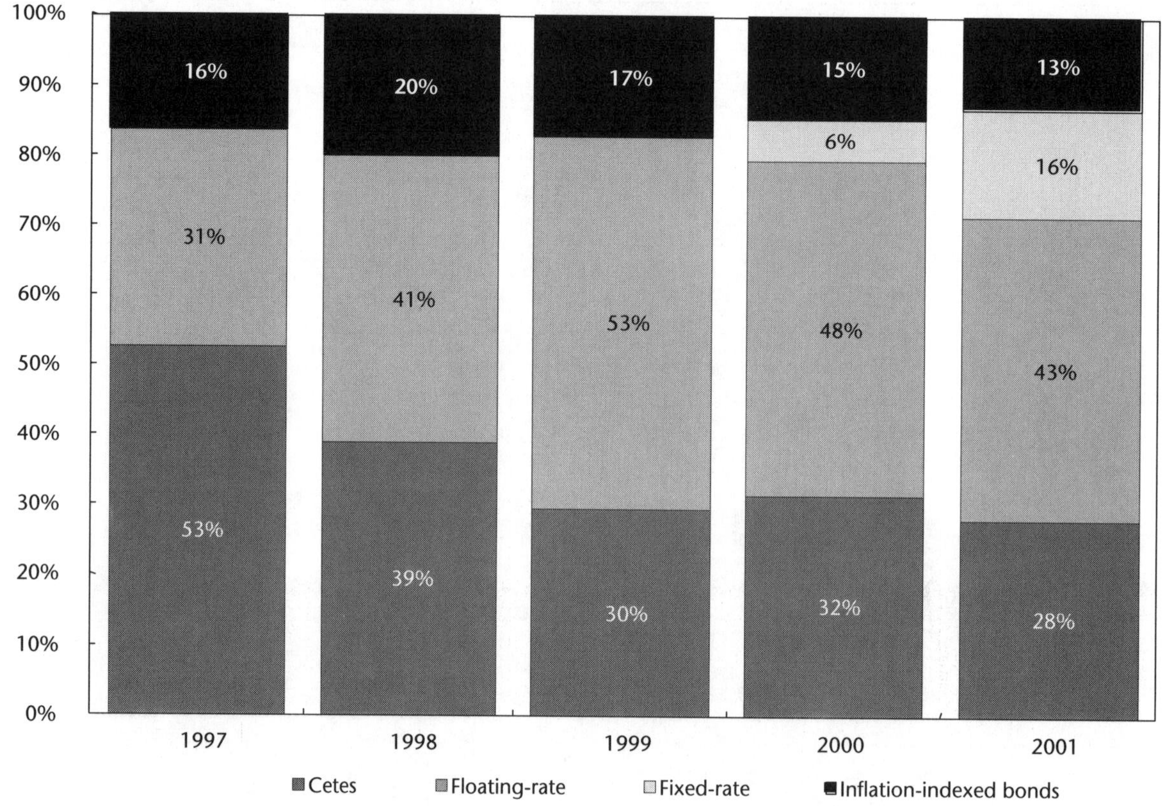

| | Cetes | Floating-rate | Fixed-rate | Inflation-indexed bonds |

Note: Cetes (*certificados de la tesorería*) are short-term zero-coupon instruments with maturities of 1, 3, 6, and 12 months.

local market is sustainable, the government has put special emphasis on macroeconomic policies, both fiscal and monetary, aimed at promoting stability.

External debt

The solid fiscal position registered throughout the most recent years, along with the structural reforms aimed at opening the economy to the external sector, has strengthened the liquidity position of the public sector with its external creditors. This development has led to a reduction in Mexico's vulnerability. Today, the entire stock of public external debt could be covered with a half year's worth of exports, a level not seen since the 1950s. The government regards it as highly important to maintain this situation through prudent management of public finance and external debt. The issuance of external debt by the

government and the agencies is constrained by a ceiling imposed in the budget by the congress at the beginning of the year.

The risk management framework for external debt management is oriented toward covering the government's refinancing needs, servicing existing debt, and improving the maturity profile, as well as lowering the financing cost of debt. The main risks that the government faces with respect to its external debt portfolio are refinancing risk, currency risk, and interest rate risk.

- The refinancing risk is managed by maintaining a prudent maturity profile (see Figures II.9.5 and II.9.6) and not allowing large amounts to mature in a single year.
- The U.S. dollar is the natural source of external funding because of the large inflows of U.S. dol-

Figure II.9.3. Amortization Profile of Domestic Debt (year end)
(In percent of total debt)

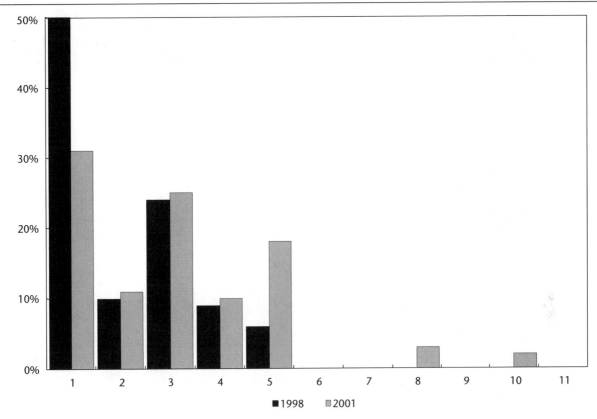

The legend shows ■1998 and □2001.

lars that enter Mexico through foreign direct investment, portfolio investment, and transfers of dollars from Mexicans living in the United States. Consequently, the non-dollar-denominated debt represents greater risk for the government.

- The government has been prudent in selecting the portfolio's composition of floating- and fixed-rate debt, thus it is composed mainly of fixed-rate instruments. To hedge against any risk incurred from any floating-rate debt, the government may use the derivative market. In hedging securities with derivatives, the government mainly uses cross-currency swaps, embedded options, and interest rate forwards.

The government's external debt portfolio consists of both marketable and nonmarketable debt. Collateral deposits guarantee some of the external debt of the government, which are mostly Brady bonds. This guaranteed debt is usually bought back or called whenever there are net present value savings, to monetize the collateral and generate additional resources for the government. The government is currently trying to retire this debt by adding more market debt to its debt stock (see Figure II.9.7), making its portfolio more liquid and qualifying it for more benchmark credit indices as a large and liquid issuer, adding value to the government's bonds.

The government takes advantage of market opportunities as they occur. In the last few years, as a result of favorable market conditions, it has completed its funding early in the year. Because funding requirements have been relatively low, refinancing risk, as such, has not concentrated in any particular month within the year. Once the external funding needs are fulfilled, either in capital markets or from bilateral or multilateral institutions, the government focuses on management of the debt according to the

Figure II.9.4. Ratio of Net Public External Debt to Total Export
(In percent)

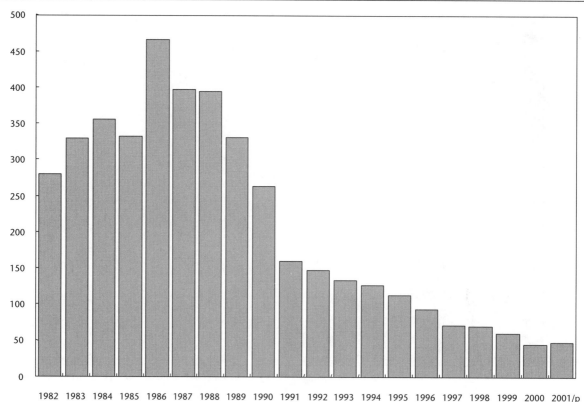

ceiling imposed by the congress. Liability management is mostly used to retire collateralized debt (i.e., Brady bonds) and debt with embedded options, allowing the federal government to benefit from net present value savings.

To assess risk and find an opportunity to lower costs, the government constantly monitors the financial markets, especially markets for securities issued by similarly rated sovereign and corporate borrowers. Nevertheless, the main factors that help the government to reduce the cost and risk of its debt portfolio are without doubt sound fiscal and macroeconomic policies.

Contingent liabilities

The government also guarantees debt issued by the agencies. Every three months, it presents a report to the congress containing all the relevant information about public debt, which includes the public sector's

debt stock, amortizations, new funding, and similar information.

Management information systems

The government's debt managers have the necessary informational tools to analyze the risk profile of the debt portfolio. This is achieved mainly from day-to-day observation of the different financial and economic indicators, taking this information and performing various stress tests using current interest and foreign currency rates, then examining the outcome of each scenario and assessing the probability of an adverse outcome. This is supplemented with periodic reports and databases.

Naturally, any analysis depends on the continuity and reliability of quality information, adding great importance to the various information systems used by the government. It currently uses, through its debt management office, such services as Bloomberg,

Figure II.9.5. Federal Government External Debt Amortization Profile, as of September 30, 2001
(In billions of US$)

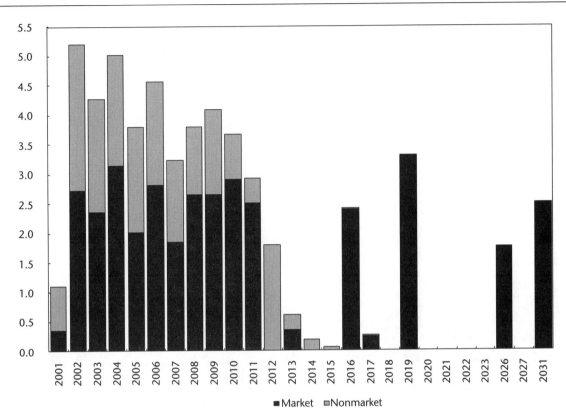

■ Market ▢ Nonmarket

Reuters, and Infosel, as well as having access databases, valuation programs, and on-line quotes from both the local and the external markets.

Developing the Markets for Government Securities

Internal debt

In addition to the strategy followed by the government to develop the domestic debt market, the central authorities have undertaken measures to foster the development of an efficient secondary market.

Extend the yield curve

As can be seen in Figure II.9.8, the average maturity of the debt portfolio has increased substantially dur-

ing recent years. To continue the development of the long-term government securities market, the length of the yield curve has been extended through issuance of longer-term bonds. Instruments of 3-, 5-, and 10-year fixed-rate maturity were introduced in January and May 2000 and July 2001 (see Figure II.9.9). This strategy will be continued to consolidate the yield curve and possibly extend it further. With the development of the yield curve, the government has also paved the way for private sector issuers and has facilitated the development of a liquid derivatives market.

Introduction of market makers (primary dealers)

In October 2000, market makers were introduced to the market to increase liquidity, reduce transaction costs, and facilitate end-buyers' purchases of government securities. Based on their activity in the primary

Figure II.9.6. Agencies External Debt Amortization Profile, as of September 30, 2001
(In billions of US$)

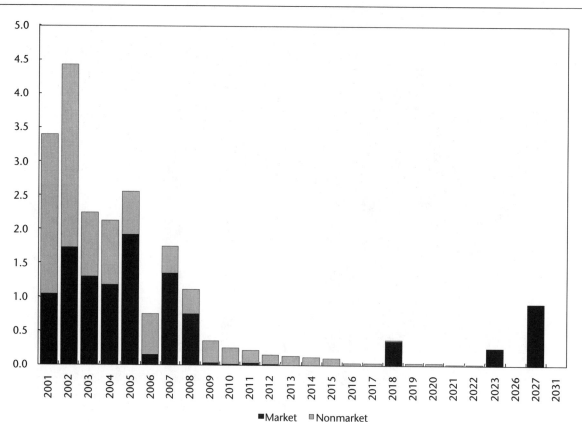

and secondary markets, brokerage firms and financial institutions can be selected as market markers. There is also a continuous evaluation of the market development vis-à-vis the activity of the market makers, to guarantee that they continue to play an important role in the development of the domestic market.

Market makers have the following main obligations:

- place bids in the primary auction for each type of fixed-rate instrument for a minimum amount of 20 percent of the auctioned amount;
- continuously place bid-offer quotes for fixed-rate instruments with authorized brokers for a minimum amount of Mex$20 million and a maximum bid-offer spread of 125 basis points (in terms of yield); and
- provide authorities with all the requested information to quantify their activity.

In exchange for the obligations, market makers have the following privileges:

- The right to buy securities after the primary auction. This call option ("green shoe") has these characteristics:
  - only good for fixed-rate instruments offered in the primary auction,
  - can be exercised only by market makers who offered a competitive rate in the primary auction,
  - additional securities will be assigned at the weighted average rate registered in the primary auction, and
  - the maximum amount that can be exercised through the call option is 20 percent of the auctioned amount.
- The market makers may borrow from the central bank the minimum of the following fixed-rate securities of treasury certificates and bonds:

Figure II.9.7. Percentage of Public External Debt

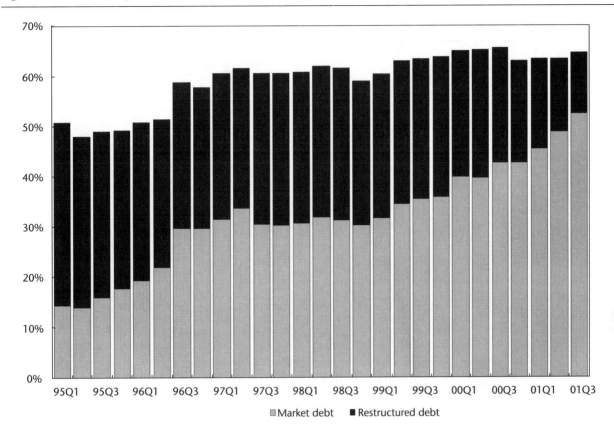

□ Market debt ■ Restructured debt

- 2 percent of the total outstanding amount of each issue of treasury certificates and bonds, and
- 4 percent of the total amount of outstanding treasury certificates and bonds.

With the introduction of market makers, an important increase in secondary market liquidity (see Figure II.9.10) has occurred. As a result, bid-offer spreads for all fixed-rate securities also have tightened substantially. On average, the spreads have decreased from 36 basis points in January 2000 to 27 basis points in November 2001. This has facilitated the distribution of government securities all the way down to end-buyers and smaller clients.

Reopening of outstanding issues to increase size and liquidity

To increase liquidity in the government securities secondary market, the government has been reopening outstanding issues. This has helped to build up issues with a larger outstanding amount and at the same time reduce the number of issues in the market, thereby concentrating liquidity. Currently, the average outstanding amount of long-term securities is Mex$17,000 million per issue, compared with less than Mex$4 billion per issue at 1999.

Securities linked to an inflation index

The government is now regularly issuing 10-year inflation-indexed securities. As a result of the current price stability, the relative importance for this type of instruments has declined (see Figure II.9.2). Nevertheless, because there is a natural demand for inflation-indexed instruments coming from pension funds and insurance companies, it is highly possible that the government will continue to incorporate these instruments into the issuing program.

Figure II.9.8. Average Life
(In days)

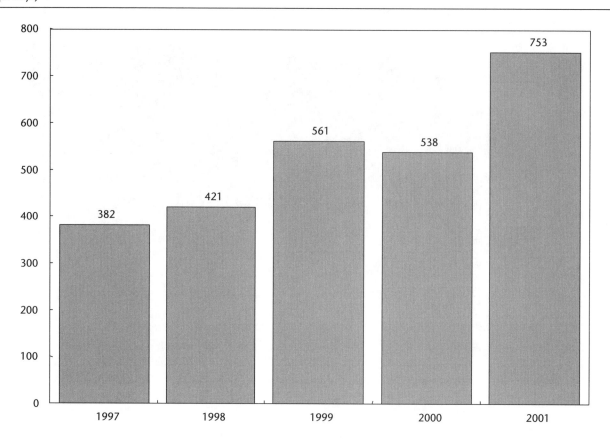

Other measures

In line with the objective of strengthening government securities markets, the government has also been doing the following:

- The government securities auction calendar is announced quarterly.
- Continuous contact with the financial community: There are monthly meetings with market makers to discuss recent developments in the local markets and the overall macroeconomic environment. Moreover, periodic meetings or conference calls are held with other institutional investors to discuss relevant issues and get feedback on the current issuing program of government securities.
- Improvement in the repo market and securities lending regulation: Substantial changes are being discussed on the way the repo market currently operates with the financial community. Some of these changes include the standard documentation by which this market regulates itself (International Swap Dealers Association [ISDA]–type), which is not used currently for repo transactions.

External debt

Mexico is always sensitive to market demands whenever investors are interested in investing in a new issue. Efforts are made wherever possible to satisfy investors who take the risk of providing funding, and in the end motivate good performance in the secondary market. This allows Mexico to better define its yield curve and lower its financing costs. Another step the government has taken to facilitate healthy and well-performing portfolios is to issue new bonds in an amount that is lower compared with the total orders

Figure II.9.9. Evolution of the Interest Rate Curve

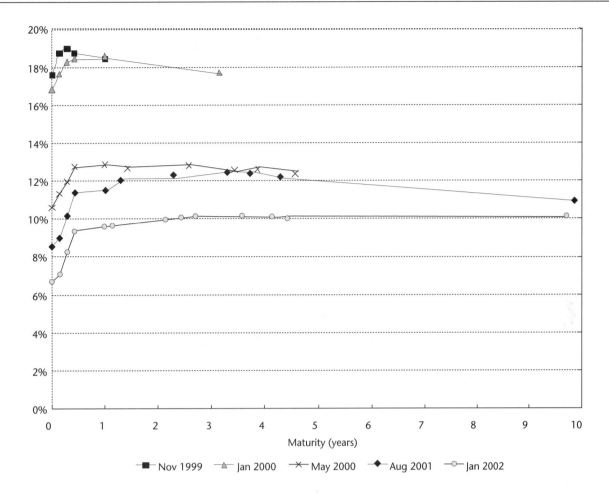

Maturity (years)

—■— Nov 1999   —▲— Jan 2000   —✕— May 2000   —◆— Aug 2001   —○— Jan 2002

made by investors for the new bonds. In this way, the government is able to avoid oversupplying the market with the new issue, which in some ways could affect secondary market performance. The supply-demand information, provided by investment banks, is crucial to better understand the timing and size of a new issue. The government also devotes itself to trying to improve the composition of the debt portfolio by retiring or replacing bonds that cause distortions on the curve. This generates cost savings for the government and satisfies investors.

When selecting the best borrowing alternative in the international market, the government has to consider private sector needs. It does this by trying to choose a tenor that will fill a gap in the sovereign yield curve in the international market and, whenever possible, establish points of reference—in the

form of benchmark issues—for market participants from the private sector. Once the government has established a well-defined yield curve, it will be easier to price a new bond issue for Mexican corporations. Because the sovereign risk component is established and measured with the sovereign yield curve, corporations only have to price their own risk, mainly credit risk. This will achieve a more accurate price of corporate bonds.

To finance itself abroad, the government mainly uses three different markets, which provide different advantages. These are markets for the dollar, the euro, and the yen (see Figure II.9.11).

Because of the large flows of dollars from trade into and out of Mexico, and because some fiscal revenues are also dollar related, the most important foreign market for the government to finance itself

Figure II.9.10. Secondary Market Trading of Bonos
(In millions of pesos)

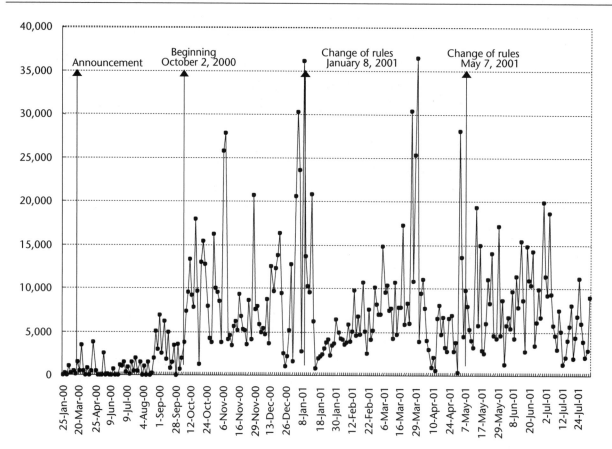

abroad is the dollar market. The yield curve of the debt portfolio in this market is the most complex the government has built in external markets, with securities ranging up to 30 years in maturity and very liquid benchmarks (see Figure II.9.12).

Having a well-defined yield curve in the dollar market allows the government to distribute its debt placements through times when refinancing debt or when new financing is needed. This also helps the private sector to finance itself abroad, by establishing reference points they can compare to, making it easier to value their credit risk. The government has been able to build a yield curve that has provided the market with information and has allowed the government to correctly price its market debt in any given maturity. Although the government has had an important success in the achievement of this goal in

the dollar market, it plans to continue doing so while providing other markets, such as the euro market, with this information.

Even if the euro and yen markets are smaller in proportion compared with the dollar market, they sometimes present arbitrage opportunities in terms of spread over the U.S. Treasury once euros and yen are swapped into dollars, making financing possible at a lower cost compared with that of the dollar market.

Information

Mexico attaches high importance to providing accurate and transparent information to the financial community, whether it is foreign or domestic. Toward this end, senior government officers carry out regular road shows in financial capitals, where they present

Figure II.9.11. UMS Market External Debt Issuance, 1996–2002
(as of January 14, 2002)

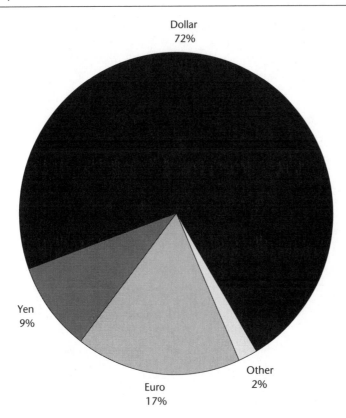

Dollar
72%

Yen
9%

Euro
17%

Other
2%

the most recent economic developments in the economy and projections for the near future. During these presentations, the government also announces any new policies that have been made.

Whenever the government accesses the international market with a new debt issue, it distributes a press bulletin to the media containing the most relevant characteristics of the bond issue with comments on how the issue complies with the debt and economic policy.

The government also makes available relevant investor information on its web site (www.shcp.gob.mx). This information consists of quarterly reports containing debt statistics, tables, and the like. Since 2001, the government has been also publishing monthly debt reports. Even though monthly reports have less detailed information, they are often useful in monitoring public finance and debt.

Tax treatment of government securities

The fiscal treatment for holders of bonds issued by the government also can be attractive for investors, in that any payments of principal or interest are exempt from any withholding tax if they are held by a nonresident of Mexico or through a temporary establishment in Mexico.

Note

1. The case study was prepared by the Mexican Public Debt Department of the Ministry of Finance.

Figure II.9.12. UMS Dollar Yield Curve
(as of February 13, 2002)

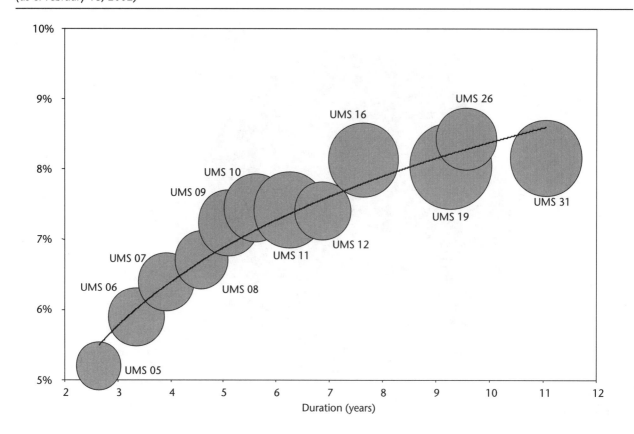

10
Morocco[1]

As an introduction to the description of public debt management in Morocco, it is useful to present some aggregates, illustrating trends in Morocco's public debt burden and associated charges.

At the end of 2000, external public debt (direct and guaranteed debt) amounted to US$16 billion—equivalent to 48 percent of GDP or 121 percent of balance of payments current revenues. External public debt is distributed between the treasury's direct debt and guaranteed debt in the proportions of approximately 70 and 30 percent, respectively. Charges on the external public debt paid during 2000 amounted to more than US$2.5 billion, in other words, 19 percent of balance of payments current revenues.

The treasury's direct debt (domestic and external) at end-2000 amounted to the equivalent of US$25.2 billion, representing 76 percent of GDP, including US$14.1 billion, or 42 percent of GDP, in domestic debt.

The treasury's direct debt service amounted to US$3.7 billion, including US$2 billion in domestic debt and US$1.7 billion in external debt. Interest charges, which amounted to the equivalent of US$1.7 billion, absorbed 22 percent of current budget revenues.

During the period 1983–92, the Moroccan authorities concluded six rescheduling arrangements with the Paris Club and three with the London Club, entailing the rescheduling of US$12.7 billion (US$6.9 billion with the Paris Club and US$5.8 billion with the London Club). Morocco ended the rescheduling cycle in 1993.

Framework for Public Debt Management

Public debt management objectives

The objectives pursued in the area of public debt management have been established in the light of the trends in Morocco's economic and financial situation and the constraints that the country has had to address. Accordingly, until the early 1980s, emphasis was placed primarily on raising the funds required to finance the central government's ambitious investment program. In this context and to offset insufficient domestic saving, the authorities relied substantially on the international financial market, where abundant liquidity was available with favorable interest rates.

With the outbreak of the debt crisis in the early 1980s, debt management objectives shifted substantially to reducing pressure on the balance of payments and the budget by rescheduling of debt charges, mobilizing concessional financing; and relying on domestic resources to cover the treasury's requirements.

Beginning in 1993, as Morocco's macroeconomic viability was restored, the authorities adopted a more dynamic approach to debt management, with the objectives of

- financing the treasury's requirements with optimized costs and risks through arbitrage between domestic and external resources, and
- reducing the burden and cost of existing public debt to sustainable levels.

Legal framework for debt management

Public debt operations, in terms of borrowing (domestic borrowing issues and external loan arrangements) as well as debt expenditure (payment of principal, interest, and commissions), are, like government revenue and expenditure, subject to the principle of prior authorization incorporated each year into the budget law.

The annual budget law voted by parliament therefore includes specific provisions authorizing the government to borrow externally within the ceiling of the programmed overall amount and borrow domestically to cover the treasury's deficit and cash requirements. Parliament also approves the budget appropriations required to honor payments of principal in connection with medium- and long-term debt and interest on all debt.

On the revenue side, the authorization to borrow is covered by two decrees accompanying the budget law, under which the prime minister delegates power for that purpose to the minister of economy and finance or his or her authorized representative to arrange external borrowing and provide government guarantees under the first decree and issue domestic debt under the second decree.

On the expenditure side, the minister of finance, who is the authorizing officer for settlement of domestic and external debt service, delegates powers to make scheduled debt payments to the managing units' officers.

Institutional framework for debt management

Public debt management is the responsibility of the treasury and external finance department of the ministry of economy and finance. This department is responsible for

- meeting the treasury's financing requirements through mobilization of the required domestic and external resources,
- borrowing and payment of debt service,
- dynamic management of existing debt, and
- proposing legislative and regulatory texts and reforms relating to the treasury financing and the financial market in general.

At the external level, the treasury and external finance department establishes the external finance strategy and coordinates the tasks of negotiating and mobilizing the resources involved. The department is therefore responsible for negotiating financial protocols, mobilizing borrowing in connection with the balance of payments and structural adjustment loans, addressing issues related to on-lending, and providing guarantees for external borrowing. It also centralizes external debt data relating to the public and private sectors.

At the domestic level, this department's tasks consist of

- initiating domestic borrowing issues by supervising operations to issue treasury instruments and establishing the needed amounts to be borrowed, issue conditions, and redemption modalities;
- monitoring debt stock and repaying debt charges;
- processing records related to domestic central government guarantees; and
- supervising the program to modernize and reform the financial sector and initiate the relevant legislative and regulatory texts.

The role of Bank Al-Maghrib (BAM), the central bank, acting as financial agent of the government, consists of

- collecting drawings in foreign currencies in connection with external borrowing and supervising treasury instruments auctions (domestic issues), by crediting the treasury's current account for the dirham equivalents of external drawings and the amounts subscribed through the auction market; and
- making settlements on the basis of payment orders received from the treasury and external finance department for debt service in foreign currencies to foreign creditors, and in dirhams to local subscribers, by debiting the treasury's current account.

Last, a central depository, known as Maroclear, was established after the dematerialization of certificates of indebtedness (including treasury instruments). Maroclear is responsible for custody of treasury instruments and supervising settlement and delivery operations in connection with buying and selling of treasury notes on the secondary market.

Organizational framework for debt management

Debt management is the responsibility of the treasury and external finance department, primarily through three divisions:

- Treasury operations division, whose tasks are to (a) prepare budget projections, monitor government finance equilibria, and determine the treasury's financing requirements; (b) mobilize domestic resources needed to cover financing requirements by conducting treasury instruments auctions; (c) propose reforms and measures to stimulate the market; and (d) process and monitor on-lending of external loans.
- External debt management division is responsible for (a) covering public external borrowing and settling central government debt service; (b) preparing debt statistics and analyses on debt, on a sectoral basis and in aggregate form (by country, sector, currency, and so forth); (c) analyzing debt and financial conditions for loans and formulating proposals to reduce debt service, debt stock, or both; and (d) implementing debt relief

activities, such as refinancing onerous debt and renegotiating interest rate.
- Debt restructuring and international financial market division is responsible for (a) implementing debt relief and restructuring operations, such as conversion of debt into public and private investment; (b) preparing for Morocco's return to the international financial market and initiating issuance operations in that market; and (c) executing swap operations involving existing debt.

The treasury and external finance department also has a subdepartment responsible for mobilizing and coordinating traditional external financing, a division responsible for bank regulation and monetary research, and a balance of payments division responsible for, among other things, regulating external financial and commercial operations.

In terms of human resources, the debt management units have a team of 30 professionals highly trained in the areas of economics, finance, law, computer science, and statistics, among others. These professionals have developed sound expertise in debt management through their acquired experience in this area and through targeted continuing education—internally (study days, workshops, and training seminars) and externally (in-service training and courses organized by international banks and institutions).

Budget and monetary policy coordination

Coordination of debt management policy with central government budget policy and the monetary policy implemented by the central bank poses no particular problems.

In this connection, the treasury and external finance department, which is responsible for debt management, participates actively in defining the orientations of the budget law, particularly at the level of the budget deficit and the resources to cover it, budget execution, and rectification of any overruns that may occur. It also prepares government cash projections generated during the budget execution and identifies and implements financing mechanisms.

At the monetary level, coordination with the central bank is the task of an oversight joint committee that is responsible for, among other things, defining monetary and inflation objectives, monitoring their execution, and proposing reforms and measures to be enacted. Guidelines and measures to be applied are presented to participants at meetings of the national committee on money and saving, which is held at the central bank and is chaired jointly by the minister of economy and finance and the governor of BAM.

Further, as the main borrower on the domestic market, the treasury enhances the stability of the money market, primarily through its constant presence on the auction market and the announcement of its financing requirements to provide maximum visibility on that market. This is increasingly important as the interest rate curve on government bonds has become a reference for Morocco's financial market in general, particularly for remuneration of saving and financial instruments.

Transparency and communication

During the annual press conference on financing policy held after adoption of the budget law, the minister of economy and finance assesses indebtedness by presenting the key results and statistics on debt for the year ended and announces the objectives established to cover the treasury's financing requirements for the current fiscal year and the measures and actions to be implemented in the area of financing.

Some statistical data on treasury debt such as drawings, amortization, and outstanding balances are published on the Internet (www.mfie.gov.ma/dtfe/tbstat.htm) in a *note de conjoncture* (economic brief) produced monthly by the treasury and external finance department.

The Moroccan authorities also report external public debt data annually to the World Bank (Report Forms I and II) for publication in the form of summary statements and intend to subscribe to the IMF Special Data Dissemination Standard.

In addition, the treasury and external finance department organizes meetings from time to time among various participants in the domestic market and, in particular, the central bank and transactors (treasury securities dealers, mutual funds, stock brokerage firms, and so forth) to enhance communication and transparency in indebtedness policy. Topics discussed are mainly related to macroeconomic fundamentals, financial market developments (such as the liquidity in the market and the interest rate curve), and reform proposals.

In addition, while working toward achieving the adopted objectives, the treasury and external finance department issues monthly announcements of the amounts to be raised on the auction market and the results of subscriptions in terms of volume, interest rates, and maturities.

Collection of debt data

The treasury and external finance department is responsible for collection and centralization of public debt data. The data available to the department are supplemented and cross-checked regularly with information provided by

- various departments of the ministry of economy and finance and, in particular, the budget department, central guarantee fund and foreign exchange office;
- the central bank for credit and debit notices relating to drawings and reimbursements of treasury debt;
- public enterprises benefiting from a government guarantee, for data on their external borrowing; and
- creditors.

Where government debt is concerned, data collection does not pose any particular problem as the channels for systematic data reporting are well established and the indebtedness processes—external (commitment, disbursement, and repayment) and domestic (subscription and repayment)—are centralized within the ministry of economy and finance.

For external debt guaranteed by the central government, data collection problems were solved by recording information upstream upon the issue of guarantees and by disseminating a circular from the minister of economy and finance instituting the requirement for public enterprises to register their external financing agreements with the external debt management division and file monthly or quarterly reports with the division, containing the data on their external debt, using standard reporting forms provided for that purpose.

For domestic guaranteed debt, data collection poses no problems because guarantees are granted by a decree of the prime minister and decision of the minister of economy and finance establishing the maximum amount of each issue. In addition, guarantee operations have so far involved only a few public institutions, and securities issues have been subscribed by government agencies and insurance companies.

Private debt statistics are collected by the foreign exchange office based on information collected at the level of the banking system, in which a form must be completed for each customer's external borrowing operations and the relevant movements. Similarly, an awareness campaign was conducted with the banking system, and major enterprises were informed that they should report this information directly to the foreign exchange office.

Computerization of debt management

A debt management computer system designed by a Moroccan research firm for public external debt (both central government and public enterprises) became operational in mid-1993 and was later extended to domestic debt and on-lending activities. This system, developed on the basis of a relational database management system known as Informix, operates in a Unix multitask, multiuser environment. A program generator is used to facilitate maintenance and development of the management system, which are the responsibility of the computer unit of the treasury and external finance department.

The system was audited in 1997 by an expert from the United Nations Conference on Trade and Development (UNCTAD), who deemed it satisfactory from the standpoints of design, functioning, and functionalities. In fact, it meets the requirements for current management, including establishment of a comprehensive debt database, calculation and generation of repayment schedules, issue of payment orders, and coverage of payments. It also can be used to produce a full complement of statistical statements required for management, analysis, and preparation of reports to be used as decision-making aids.

This system was recently updated to

- incorporate active debt management operations implemented, such as conversion of debt into investment, prepayment, and cancellations;
- reflect the introduction of the euro while maintaining all prior transactions in the original currency; and
- register swap transactions, particularly currency and interest rate swaps to be initiated in connection with risk management.

In the area of statistical processing, the system produces standard statistical reports on debt—theoretical (based on initial schedules and conditions), actual, or projected—and on outstanding balances, debt service (principal, interest, and commissions), and drawings, broken down by lender, borrower, currency, interest rate, and so on. The system can also be used to produce World Bank Report Forms I and II and generate treasury debt charges to be incorporated into the budget law.

Debt Management Strategy

After a decade of structural adjustment and external debt rescheduling, the Moroccan authorities have managed to reduce the country's vulnerability through significantly enhanced economic and financial equilibria and by ending Morocco's rescheduling cycle in 1993.

The external debt burden, however, has remained high, and the balance of transactions induced by the public external debt (amortization plus interest less drawings) during the period 1993–97 led to significant net outward transfers, which exceeded US$1.5 billion per annum. These transfers were expected to increase sharply with the beginning of principal repayments of rescheduled debt from 1999 for the London Club arrangement and the Paris Club's fifth arrangement, as well as from 2001 for the Paris Club's sixth arrangement.

As a result of this debt trend and considering the macroeconomic framework improvement, Morocco has undertaken an active management strategy for its debt with three main thrusts, described in the following.

Treatment of the treasury's external debt

Since 1996, treatment of the treasury's external debt involved a stock of more than US$2 billion (20 percent of the treasury's external debt). In this connection, the following two mechanisms were used.

Conversion of debts into investment

This mechanism is applied as provided in the Paris Club proceedings. The last two rescheduling arrangements (the fifth and sixth) concluded with the Paris Club provided that the lenders may sell or exchange—in the framework of debt-for-nature, debt-for-aid, or debt-for-equity swaps or other local currency debt swaps—the amounts of outstanding loans rescheduled and eligible for rescheduling with a ceiling of 100 percent for governmental debt and 10 percent or US$10 million for commercial debt. The latter ceiling was increased to 20 percent in 1997 and subsequently to 30 percent or US$40 million in 1999.

Implementation of these provisions has required identification of (a) potential rescheduled debts suitable for conversion operations classified by lender country and (b) actions to be undertaken to convince these countries of the advantage of the debt conversion mechanism to both the lender and the debtor.

Two types of conversions were implemented in this connection:

- Conversion of debts into public investment: The creditor cancels an agreed amount of the rescheduled debt, and Morocco uses the countervalue of the canceled amount to carry out public investment projects.
- Conversion of debt into private investment: After debt conversion agreement, the foreign investor presents an investment project to Moroccan authorities for approval. This approval sets a redemption price of a given amount of the debt. After that, the investor purchases the said amount of debt from the creditor country at a lower price. Then, the investor transfers this debt to Morocco and receives the agreed price after committing to carry out the investment project.

Treatment of onerous debt

This treatment is carried out through prepayment of onerous debts using domestic or external resources associated with more favorable terms or by renegotiating interest rates on onerous loans to align them with the rates prevailing on the financial market.

Implementation of this mechanism requires preliminary work in these areas:

- use of the debt database and use of actuarial techniques to determine onerous debt potential and to identify onerous loans;
- analysis of legal clauses in loan agreements to determine the conditionality of prepayment, refinancing, or interest rate revision;
- identification and selection of refinancing resources that can be mobilized with relevant financial conditions; and
- assessment of the present value of the gain—debt service to be saved—and potential for annual reduction of the interest charges generated by the operation.

For operations involving treatment of guaranteed debt of government institutions, the initiative may come from the treasury and external finance department or from the debtor institution. In both cases, the department, in consultation with other departments of the ministry of economy and finance, issues an opinion on the prepayment operation envisaged based on an assessment of the institution's financial situation and the budget implications that may be involved.

Policy to mobilize financing

Since rescheduling ended, domestic financing has been relied upon substantially to cover the budget deficit and negative net transfers associated with external borrowing. Despite low levels of the budget deficit, this situation has led to an increase in the stock of domestic debt, which amounted to US$14.1 billion (representing 42 percent of GDP) at end-2000, compared with the equivalent of US$12.5 billion (35 percent of GDP) at end-1996 and US$8.8 billion (31 percent of GDP) at end-1993.

This policy, which is explained by the prudent stance of the authorities in the area of external financing, was fostered by availability of resources on the domestic market at favorable rates and the authorities' concern to develop an efficient, modern domestic market to meet the requirements of all transactors in connection with the overall reform of the domestic financial market undertaken in 1993.

For external financing, a highly selective approach was established, characterized by

- selection of new commitments according to the degree of concessionality,
- enhanced selection of investment projects to benefit from financing from bilateral sources or multilateral financial institutions, and
- improved performance in executing financed projects.

In addition, a process to enable Morocco to reaccess the international financial markets was undertaken with the establishment of an international rating by Standard and Poor's and Moody's to allow investors to assess Morocco's risk, and through a familiarization with risk management instruments by developing technical skills for ongoing monitoring of the exposure of Morocco's debt to market risks, as well as the use of appropriate swap operations, as required.

Framework for risk management

The process of implementing a risk management framework, undertaken in 1996, primarily involves three factors, described in the following.

Institutional framework

A study of the legal environment has revealed that Morocco's legal system does not contain any provision opposing dynamic debt management and that the government is authorized under the current legislation to use hedging instruments only for the purpose of stabilizing or lowering debt-service costs.

Accordingly, a decree of the prime minister has since 1998 been appended to the texts accompanying the budget law, delegating authority to the minister of economy and finance, or his/her authorized representative, to contract external borrowing to repay onerous debt and enter into foreign exchange and interest rate swap arrangements to stabilize debt service.

Further, with a permanent budget law provision, a special treasury account was established to reflect foreign exchange and interest rate swaps separately and on a multiyear basis, as well as to cover the charges generated by these operations.

Management of risks related to external debt

Analysis of the treasury's external debt structure shows that this debt is substantially sensitive to exchange rate and interest rate fluctuations and that the liquidity risk is limited because the debt is amortizable and arranged exclusively in the medium and long terms.

Where the exchange risk is concerned, debt exposure exists because the foreign exchange structure of the debt is still inadequate to accommodate Morocco's foreign trade structure. As for interest rates, the risk is attributable to the substantial share of debt associated with floating interest rates, which represents more than 36 percent of the debt.

Accordingly, a benchmark portfolio was identified for external debt, with which the treasury's current debt structure must converge, and to guide external debt financing and management policies. The foreign exchange structure of this benchmark is 60 percent euros, 35 percent U.S. dollars, and 5 percent yen, and the interest rate component entails 20 percent floating-rate debt.

In this connection, the conversion into euros of World Bank currency pool loans denominated in U.S. dollars and yen was undertaken in the amount of US$1.3 billion to increase the euro-denominated debt's share.

Management of risks associated with domestic debt

After the establishment of an auction market with the key features of a modern financial market, analysis of the debt portfolio has brought to light certain risks related to maturities and interest rates, and a risk management program was implemented to manage risks related to repayment, financing, and interest rates.

- To address the repayment risk, debt managers try to smooth the debt schedule as much as possible to avoid excessive concentrations of maturities.
- To offset potential financing risk and enable the treasury to raise the required funds in a timely manner, in addition to smoothing of the debt schedule, the treasury ensures, in connection with government cash management, that the rate of revenue collection is commensurate with the rate of expenditure execution.
- Concerning the interest rate risk, first, it should be borne in mind that treasury instruments are issued at fixed rates. The risk therefore appears when rates decline and remain below the rate of the issue. To address this risk, then, the treasury and external finance department has established the objective of adopting a level of 25 percent, which is deemed sustainable, for short-term debt. The treasury is also now focusing on indexing medium- and long-term maturities to shorter ones. The treasury, accordingly, has already proceeded with two 10-year borrowing operations indexed on 52-week treasury bills and is now studying the possibility of issuing 5-year indexed bonds.

Information system

Debt managers are provided direct access to the debt database by use of client Windows stations with Graphical Query Language, making it possible to use customized queries to perform data analysis and generate various reports and graphics. In addition, these data can be exported to other applications or software (Excel spreadsheets, for example) for other types of processing, as required.

This flexibility also makes it possible to prepare medium- and long-term projections based on different assumptions of trends in interest rates, exchange rates, or both. Similarly, different indebtedness or refinancing strategy scenarios are prepared with arbitrage between use of domestic or external resources and the choice of currency and interest rates.

In addition, managers of the treasury and external finance department were introduced, with support from international financial institutions and with a management system used by banks, to techniques for managing different types of risks inherent in external debt, mainly interest rate risk and exchange rate risk, and a model for managing domestic debt is being prepared.

Development of an Efficient Domestic Market

Concurrently with the vast program to modernize the financial sector and institutional reforms of the Moroccan financial system in the area of mobilization and allocation of resources, it was necessary to review the policy in place for domestic financing, which is characterized by

- mandatory holdings in the form of floors on government instruments that the banking system was required to subscribe at low interest rates, which had amounted to 35 percent of deposits;
- issue of government borrowing at widely attractive interest rates and long-term bonds subscribed by institutional investors;
- total exemption of interest accrued on instruments subscribed by individuals; and
- recourse to the BAM for additional financings.

To end this situation, the treasury's financing method was thoroughly reformed so that the required domestic resources could be mobilized at market terms by instituting the treasury instruments auction market as a sole source of financing, and measures were implemented to eliminate distortion and stimulate the market.

Elimination of the treasury's privileges

The privileges from which the treasury benefited, compared with other borrowers, were eliminated by

- a gradual reduction of mandatory holdings in the form of a floor on government instruments until their total elimination in 1997;

- subjecting interest generated by treasury instruments subscribed by individuals to the corporate tax or the general income tax; and
- abandonment of different types of issues, such as bond issues at attractive rates, national borrowing operations, and so on, that promote segmentation of the market and limit the liquidity of those instruments.

Institution of the treasury instruments auction market

The treasury instruments auction market, which has become the main financing source for the treasury, is governed by a decree of the minister of economy and finance and a set of joint circulars issued by the treasury and external finance department and BAM.

The treasury and external finance department informs investors of the monthly schedule of auctions to be held with the following periodicity, by maturity:

- every Tuesday for 13-, 26-, and 52-week bills;
- the second and last Tuesday of the month for 2-, 5-, 10-, and 15-year bonds; and
- the last Tuesday of the quarter for 20-year bonds.

The department reserves the right, however, to cancel scheduled sessions or to hold additional auctions. These changes are announced one week in advance.

The auctions, held according to the Dutch auction method, proceed as follows: Institutions authorized to submit bids transmit them by fax to the BAM no later than 10:30 a.m. on Tuesday. The BAM then submits the bids to the treasury and external finance department in ordered, anonymous form. The department selects the interest rate or limit price for the auction, which it reports to the BAM. The latter in turn individually informs the bidding institutions of the status of their bids. The results are also disseminated through Reuters. For the successful bids, the equivalent amounts are paid on the Monday following the auction.

Finally, only issues of six-month bills have been maintained to assist in mobilizing small savers. These bills, reserved for nonfinancial institutions and individuals, are issued below par, with a coupon. They are issued on a continuous basis, with small face values,

redeemable after three months by surrendering the coupon. These securities are dematerialized.

Stimulating the auction market

Action has been taken to stimulate the auction market and enhance the liquidity of securities through the following.

Designation of treasury securities dealers

To stimulate the auction market and contribute to its well-functioning, certain institutions have been designated as treasury securities dealers. To that end, these dealers agree to report periodically to the treasury and external finance department on their assessment of overall market demand on the domestic treasury securities and subscribe to at least securities.

In return, treasury securities dealers may submit noncompetitive bids within the limit of an approved maximum based on an award coefficient calculated to reflect their participation in the past three weeks in competitive auctions involving securities in the same category.

To encourage treasury securities dealers to contribute effectively to stimulating the secondary market, these operators committed, in connection with an agreement between themselves and the treasury and external finance department, to quote a certain number of lines covering all maturities.

Introduction of issues by assimilation

The treasury and external finance department introduced the technique of issues by assimilation to develop the secondary market for treasury securities and enhance their liquidity. This technique consists of announcing the coupon in advance, associating new issues with existing lines to establish substantial resources, and reducing the number of lines issued.

Introduction of enhanced communication with partners

The treasury and external finance department opted to establish permanent contact with the financial community to keep it abreast of its interventions in the market.

To this end, periodic meetings are held between the various participants—the treasury department, the BAM, Treasury securities dealers, and secondary market transactors (mutual funds, brokerage firms, and so on)—for more effective communications.

Further, in connection with the agreement between the treasury department and treasury securities dealers, meetings are organized regularly with these dealers to discuss the market situation and any problems that the different institutions may encounter. The treasury department also coordinates with treasury securities dealers in connection with the implementation of new measures aimed to develop the auction market.

Note

1. The case study was prepared by Lahbib El Idrissi Lalami and Ahmed Zoubaine from the Treasury and External Finances Department of the Ministry of Economy, Finance, Privatization, and Tourism.

11
New Zealand[1]

The New Zealand Debt Management Office (NZDMO) was established in 1988 with the aim of improving the management of risk associated with the government's debt portfolio. It is responsible for managing the government's debt, overall net cash flows, and some of its interest-bearing assets within an appropriate risk management framework.

This chapter outlines the evolution of public debt management in New Zealand, the portfolio and risk management framework in which the NZDMO operates, and the development of the market for government securities.

Developing a Sound Governance and Institutional Framework

Objective of the NZDMO

The objective of the NZDMO is to maximize the long-term economic return on the government's financial assets and debt in the context of the government's fiscal strategy, particularly its aversion to risk. That objective requires the NZDMO to balance the likely risks incurred in minimizing cost.

In terms of managing the government's debt portfolio, the NZDMO adopts a risk-averse approach for a number of reasons. For instance:

- Evidence suggests that individuals tend to be risk averse in their decision making and expect the government to reflect that preference in managing its interests.
- Losses incurred in the government's portfolio impose costs that taxpayers are unable to avoid.
- The government does not have a competitive advantage over other market participants in attempting to derive excess returns from its portfolio management, except for its privilege as an institution exempt from taxation and regulation, which the NZDMO does not consider ethical to exploit.

The debt management objective has changed through time, with earlier versions placing an emphasis on risk reduction. That position reflected the significantly higher net debt levels in the late 1980s and early 1990s and the fact that nearly half of the debt was denominated in foreign currencies. Since then, net

153

debt has been reduced by 65 percent, and foreign-currency exposure has been eliminated.

Responsibilities of the NZDMO

The NZDMO's major responsibilities involve

- developing and maintaining a portfolio management framework that promotes the government's debt management objectives;
- financing the government's gross borrowing requirement, managing foreign currency assets required to meet net foreign currency interest and principal payments, and settling and accounting for all debt transactions;
- managing the six principal types of risk—market, credit, liquidity, funding, operational, and concentration—in a manner consistent with the government's fiscal strategy and the NZDMO's internal policies;
- determining a portfolio structure in terms of currency, maturity, and credit exposures consistent with the government's risk aversion and having regard for costs;
- implementing a sound framework for measuring performance on a risk-adjusted basis;
- maximizing the value added to the portfolio, on a risk-adjusted basis, subject to limits set in respect of market, credit, and liquidity exposure;
- disbursing cash to government departments and facilitating departmental cash management;
- undertaking lending to government organizations and state-owned enterprises and facilitating and executing derivatives transactions in accordance with government policy;
- providing capital markets advice for other areas of the New Zealand Treasury, other government departments, and government organizations;
- providing debt-servicing estimates and accounting reports for fiscal forecasting and reporting purposes; and
- maintaining and enhancing, where appropriate, relationships with investors who hold, or are potential holders of, New Zealand government securities, financial intermediaries, and the international credit-rating agencies.

Establishment of the NZDMO

The NZDMO was established because a large volume of government debt created considerable risks for the taxpayer, and those risks needed to be managed in a comprehensive manner.

Beginning in the 1970s, large fiscal deficits became the norm in New Zealand, and ineffective monetary policy led to one of the highest rates of inflation in the Organization for Economic Cooperation and Development (OECD). By the early 1980s, a price and wage freeze had been introduced, and monetary policy was exercised primarily through direct controls and regulation. At the same time, to limit the rate of monetary growth, financial institutions were subject to lending-growth guidelines, which in practice were largely ineffective. Increasingly restrictive measures were introduced by tightening reserve-ratio requirements for banks and raising the government-securities ratios for finance companies and building societies. An attempt was made in 1983 to absorb excess liquidity through auctions of government securities. The effectiveness of the auction program to neutralize the fiscal injection through higher voluntary holdings of government securities was severely constrained by a requirement that upward pressure was not be exerted on interest rates. In that environment, most of the government's borrowing was in foreign currencies, which also served to finance the country's persistent balance of payments deficits.

Following the election of a new government in 1984, dramatic changes occurred in economic management through a series of macroeconomic and microeconomic reforms that enabled the price system to emerge as the dominant signal for investment, production, and consumption decisions. Major changes included

- the removal of controls on prices, interest rates, and wages;
- a free float of the New Zealand dollar and the removal of capital controls;
- a reduction in marginal tax rates and a broadening of the tax base;
- the elimination of subsidies and price supports;
- the removal of reserve-asset requirements for financial institutions;

- extensive deregulation; and
- substantial reforms of the public sector.

Transparency around fiscal policy improved, and deficits were reduced. As was typical of most OECD countries at the time, New Zealand had no separate objective regarding debt management. There was a growing view, however, that a more professional approach to portfolio and risk management was required to manage the stock of public sector debt, particularly the large foreign currency component. Against that backdrop, the NZDMO was formed in 1988 to manage the public debt denominated in both foreign currency and New Zealand dollars under the authority of the minister of finance.

The NZDMO was established as a self-contained unit within the New Zealand Treasury, rather than as a separate entity, because at the time it was thought that important linkages would otherwise be lost. In addition to debt-servicing forecasts for the budget and other fiscal releases, the NZDMO provides a range of capital markets advice to other sections of the treasury. Location within the treasury also allows close monitoring of the NZDMO's development and its effectiveness in managing the government's asset and liability portfolios.

Later restructuring of the treasury, prompted by a heightened emphasis on the government's aggregate balance sheet, led to the NZDMO being folded more closely into the treasury's branch structure. Since 1997, the NZDMO has formed part of the asset and liability management branch. Activities of the branch that are not the responsibility of the NZDMO include managing the government's contingent liabilities and advising on the financial management of departments, state-owned enterprises, and other institutions in which the government has an ownership or balance-sheet interest.

Structure of the NZDMO

The secretary of the treasury is directly responsible to the minister of finance for the actions of the NZDMO. The head of the NZDMO is the treasurer, who reports to the asset and liability management branch manager, who is a deputy secretary.

In addition to normal accountability arrangements, the NZDMO's operations are also overseen by an advisory board, which provides the secretary of the treasury with quality assurance on the NZDMO's activities, risk management framework, and business plan. Members of the advisory board are selected on the basis of their experience in supervising portfolio management, payments, and banking activities; finance and risk management theory; and operational risk and reporting requirements. The advisory board currently includes a senior partner with a major accounting firm, the director of a corporate treasury and risk management advisory firm, and a finance academic.

By design, the structure of the NZDMO resembles that of a private sector financial-markets institution, with separate front, middle, and back offices. That structure leads to clearly defined responsibilities and accountabilities, procedural controls, and the segregation of duties, which is consistent with best practice. The portfolio management group is responsible for portfolio analysis, developing and negotiating transactions, managing the government's liquidity and cash disbursement system, and relationship management with international investors and rating agencies. The risk policy and technology group is responsible for measuring the NZDMO's performance in adding value, measuring risk, monitoring compliance with the approved policies for managing the government's net debt portfolio, maintaining the NZDMO's portfolio and risk management framework consistently with international best practice, and maintaining the NZDMO's information technology (IT) systems. The accounting and transactional services group is responsible for the NZDMO's accounting and forecasting functions and ensuring that transactions are settled in a timely, efficient, and secure manner.

When the government had a significant proportion of its debt in foreign currencies, the NZDMO maintained an office in London. It was responsible for a range of foreign currency transactions, including commercial paper issuance, and for relationship management with financial institutions in the European and North American capital markets. This enabled the NZDMO to maintain a 24-hour transacting capacity, mitigating the effects of the time-zone differences between New Zealand and major financial markets. The London office was closed in 1997, after the elimination of net foreign currency debt.

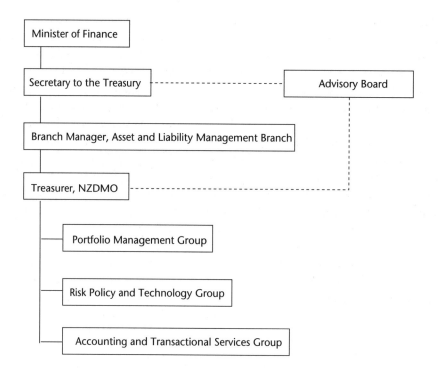

The NZDMO's staff currently numbers 24, with legal and some administrative services provided by other personnel within the treasury.

Legal framework for borrowing

The legal framework in which the NZDMO carries out its functions includes the Public Finance Act, 1989, and the State Sector Act, 1988. In general, the powers in those acts are vested in the minister of finance, but many of them have been delegated to the secretary to the treasury and then subdelegated to specified personnel within the NZDMO. One power that cannot be delegated is the power to borrow in the name of the government, and the NZDMO recommends and obtains approval for its borrowing activities.

The NZDMO must operate within the strategic parameters approved by the minister of finance, but much of the discretion over day-to-day operations has been delegated to the treasurer of the NZDMO.

Coordination with fiscal policy

The NZDMO coordinates with other parts of the treasury that advise the minister of finance on the content of the government's annual budget and prepare budget documents and the government's financial statements.

The Fiscal Responsibility Act, 1994, requires the government to act in accordance with the principles of responsible fiscal management. The act establishes five principles:

- reducing debt to a prudent level,
- maintaining debt at a prudent level,
- achieving and maintaining the government's net worth at a level that provides a buffer against adverse future events,
- prudent management of fiscal risk, and
- reasonably predictable tax rates.

The act does not define a prudent level of debt. Rather, each government determines and publicly discloses what it regards as prudent. However, the current official gross debt target is 30 percent of GDP on average over the economic cycle.

Coordination with monetary policy

During the mid-1980s, debt management was secondary to monetary policy. The priority at the time was to stabilize the economy. By the end of the decade, the NZDMO was established and the Reserve Bank, the central bank, was made independent in the implementation of monetary policy. Under the Reserve Bank Act, 1989, the objective of maintaining price stability was identified as the central bank's primary role.

The NZDMO is responsible for managing the government's debt and ensuring that the government's cash management is conducted efficiently. The Reserve Bank is responsible for the formulation and implementation of monetary policy. The two organizations have a close working relationship, which is formalized in agency agreements.

The NZDMO manages the government's liabilities. Financial assets, in the form of bank deposits and high-grade marketable securities, are held to enable the NZDMO to meet that function. The Reserve Bank manages the government's foreign currency reserves of about $NZ 4.9 billion as of July 2002, which are maintained to mitigate serious liquidity problems in the New Zealand foreign exchange market, should they ever occur. Although these reserves are available to the Reserve Bank for intervention when needed, the Reserve Bank has not intervened in the foreign exchange market since the New Zealand dollar was floated in March 1985. The foreign currency reserves are funded by loans to the Reserve Bank from the NZDMO. An agency agreement clarifies the responsibilities of both organizations, including in the event of foreign exchange intervention.

Another agency agreement between the NZDMO and the Reserve Bank clarifies the central bank's roles where it provides services for the NZDMO. The Reserve Bank acts as the NZDMO's issuing agent, registrar, and paying agent in the domestic market. It conducts auctions of treasury bills and government bonds on the NZDMO's behalf, but the NZDMO retains responsibility for all pricing decisions on these instruments. In addition, the Reserve Bank publishes information on domestic government securities that supports the market in those securities.

The Reserve Bank offers advice to the NZDMO on the structure of the government's domestic borrowing program. The NZDMO, however, has sole responsibility for advising the minister of finance on the size and structure of the domestic borrowing program.

An important provision in the agency agreement on cash and wholesale debt management is that all functions carried out by the Reserve Bank as agent for the NZDMO are conducted without reference to monetary policy considerations.

Transparency and accountability

The Fiscal Responsibility Act requires the government to be explicit about its objectives and explain any changes to them and ensures the provision of comprehensive financial information for informed and focused debate about fiscal policy. Two documents called for in the act are the Budget Policy Statement and the Fiscal Strategy Report. The government is required to table them in parliament to show that its actions are fiscally responsible. They outline the government's short-term fiscal intentions and long-term fiscal objectives, including those regarding gross and net debt, and explain the consistency of those intentions and objectives with the four-year forecasts in the Economic and Fiscal Updates, which are published with the budget and at midyear.

The government's monthly financial statements are prepared according to generally accepted accounting practice and are made public. They show how public resources have been used and report the government's assets and liabilities, revenues and expenses, cash flows, borrowings, contingent liabilities, and commitments. The annual financial statements, in particular, provide detailed information on the stock of outstanding New Zealand dollar and foreign currency debt, the maturity profile and interest rate structure of that debt, and cash flows during the year associated with issuance, redemption, and servicing of debt. The notes disclose information on the NZDMO's risk management practices and the extent of off-balance-sheet positions. The Public Finance Act requires the audit office, an office of parliament, to audit the annual financial statements presented by the government and express an independent opinion on them.

The NZDMO's responsibilities are not codified in legislation. For the past decade, it has operated at arm's length from the minister of finance, but that is a matter of custom and practice as opposed to statutory independence. Nothing in the Public Finance Act or the Fiscal Responsibility Act explicitly constrains the minister of finance in his or her relations with, or power to direct, the NZDMO.

Management of internal operations

The basis of operation, strategic objective, risk management framework, and performance measurement framework for the NZDMO are specified in its portfolio management policy, and the NZDMO's activities are audited for compliance with it. Internal operations are managed through a body of policies, reporting and performance management requirements, procedural manuals, established processes, limits, formal delegations, and segregated duties. Managers within the NZDMO warrant compliance with those controls.

The NZDMO has in place procedures and resources to mitigate risk to its operations caused by natural disasters, infrastructure failures, or other disruptions. Live tests of the business continuity plan are routinely conducted.

The State Sector Act establishes the standards and general obligations of the public service, and the treasury's corporate policies and code of conduct establish the guidelines for behavior expected of treasury personnel. Additional guidelines for ethical behavior apply to NZDMO personnel to ensure that they are free from real, potential, or apparent conflicts of interest and that the NZDMO conforms to the practices and conduct expected of a participant in the financial markets.

The NZDMO recruits successfully from the private sector and places a strong emphasis on staff training and professional development within the organization. Among other reforms of the public sector in the late 1980s was the decentralization of remuneration to departmental chief executives. As a result, the NZDMO is able to offer terms and conditions of employment that are competitive with private sector financial institutions, in the context of the unique opportunities that can be offered.

Information management systems

An information management system that integrates the front, middle, and back offices underpins the NZDMO's operations.

The information management systems used by the NZDMO have evolved through the years. Until 1987, prior to the establishment of the NZDMO, the official recording of outstanding debt and interest payments was contained in manual ledgers and informal spreadsheet tools that lacked adequate control and verification. Innovations in the financial markets during the 1980s also gave urgency to the development of an effective information management system. At the time, no commercially available product could satisfy the most pressing needs for valuation, performance measurement, and sensitivity analysis, owing in large part to the diversity of instruments in the government's debt portfolio. Consequently, a custom-built information management system was developed that, with near continuous development, served the NZDMO through 1997.

By the mid-1990s, however, it was apparent that the closed design of that system would be inadequate in the long run. By that time, as well, commercial systems had advanced to the point where they could accommodate most of the NZDMO's requirements. In 1995, contracts for the purchase and maintenance of a commercial system were signed. Implementation was completed on time and within budget in 1998. Although the new system adequately met front office needs, significant customization, accomplished in-house, was necessary to satisfy requirements of the back and middle offices. That said, the new system provided tangible benefits in terms of

- enhanced pricing, reference benchmarking, and risk management functionality;
- greater system integrity; and
- reductions in in-house development costs, system maintenance overhead, and key person dependency.

Over the years, the system has been continually developed to meet the NZDMO's ongoing requirements. That development has taken place outside the commercial system. Although it generally meets the NZDMO's current requirements, the commercial system lacks the flexibility for the agency's increasingly sophisticated requirements. The NZDMO is currently considering its IT strategy for the next three to five years. The preferred approach is likely to be a series of incremental solutions rather than an entirely new system, with the high cost and risk that would entail.

Debt Management Strategy and Risk Management Framework

Strategy for debt management

Over the past decade, the NZDMO has undertaken a considerable amount of work to analyze the structure of the government's liabilities within an asset-liability framework. There are several points of departure for such a framework.

One approach is to argue that the government should concern itself with constructing a debt portfolio with the aim of hedging the economy as a whole against shocks to national income or net worth. Under such an analysis, domestic debt is regarded as an internal transfer, and the objective is to determine a configuration of net external liabilities that would fall in value if a shock negatively affected the collective economic balance sheet of residents.

A second, narrower approach is to consider the assets and liabilities that relate to only the government as an entity. Even if public accounting conventions do not extend to the publication of a balance sheet, it can be constructed in a notional manner.

A third way to define the relevant assets and liabilities is to adopt definitions that accord with generally accepted accounting practice. In such a manner, the asset side comprises physical infrastructure, lending by government, securities, receivables, and so on. In addition to debt, liabilities include payables, provisions, and unfunded pension liabilities.

To help identify the characteristics of a low-risk portfolio of liabilities, the NZDMO researched private sector best practice and the academic literature. It was concluded that decisions on the government's asset and liability management should be taken with reference to the government's balance sheet. In particular, the risk characteristics of the government's liabilities should match as closely as possible the risk characteristics of the government's assets.

With that principle in mind, the NZDMO commissioned specialists in duration theory to quantify the risk characteristics of the assets in the govern-

ment's balance sheet. Although there were sizable standard errors around the estimates of the interest rate sensitivity of the assets, three important recommendations emerged, which were implemented over the course of the 1990s:

- The duration of the assets tends to be quite long, implying that the debt portfolio should also have a long duration.
- The assets are sensitive to changes in real interest rates, implying that there is a case for issuing some inflation-indexed debt.
- The asset values are not sensitive to exchange rate movements, implying that there is little reason to hold foreign currency debt in the government's debt portfolio.

Tax-smoothing considerations support those conclusions as well. The objective there is to structure total public debt to hedge against fluctuations in the tax base, with a view to stabilizing tax rates over time and reducing deadweight costs. The government's revenue flows exhibit little sensitivity to the exchange rate, implying that the level of foreign currency debt should be reduced. Similarly, the susceptibility of New Zealand to negative supply shocks, which have the effect of increasing inflation and reducing real income, leading to a deteriorating fiscal position, favors a debt portfolio of predominantly nominal long-term debt.

Recently, the NZDMO developed a stochastic simulation model to improve understanding of the trade-off between financial cost and risk associated with the composition of the portfolio of domestic borrowing. The NZDMO is using the model to identify opportunities to reduce the cost or risk of the portfolio, stress-test alternative strategies, and inform decision making when establishing the borrowing program for the coming years.

Going forward, debt strategy is likely to be influenced by analysis that is under way in the treasury aimed at understanding financial risks across the government from a whole-of-government perspective and how the government's balance sheet is likely to change through time. Financial assets will increasingly dominate other assets, allowing more flexibility in terms of implementing a desired composition to meet net worth–related and other objectives, while necessitating new approaches to government-wide financial risk management.

Management of domestic currency debt

Within the asset-liability framework, the domestic debt portfolio is shaped by a set of subobjectives, or principles, that support the NZDMO's debt management objective, rather than one strategic benchmark. They are used to manage the risks and costs of the domestic debt portfolio and help the NZDMO issue debt cost-effectively.

At the highest level, the issue of debt composition has been tackled by thinking about the government's balance sheet. The conclusions from that work have helped identify the rationale for holding nominal and inflation-indexed debt. Underlying that work, however, are differences in theoretical opinion and considerable empirical challenges. To date, it has not been possible to identify with any precision the proportions of each type of debt that should be held.

An additional reason for using a set of subobjectives to manage the domestic debt portfolio is because existing risk-pricing models do not address the trade-offs between different types of risk. In addition, they do not help the NZDMO understand the risk preferences of a sovereign, a sovereign's appropriate level of indebtedness and creditworthiness, the implications for the New Zealand economy as a whole, or intergenerational equity issues.

The principles for managing the New Zealand–dollar debt portfolio include the following:

- To manage risk with respect to refinancing, the NZDMO maintains a relatively even maturity profile for term debt across the yield curve to reduce pressure on the domestic bond market when supply increases unexpectedly and provide the government with greater flexibility in an environment of fiscal surpluses.
- The funding program is calculated on the basis of the cash required within one financial year.
- The NZDMO builds benchmark bonds of around $NZ 3 billion to improve liquidity in the market and, consequently, reduce the government's cost of borrowing.

- When deciding which benchmarks to build up in the current financial year, the NZDMO trades off the size and number of benchmarks to be offered.
- To diversify interest rate risk and lower the cost of the portfolio, the NZDMO maintains a mix of fixed-rate and floating-rate debt and uses interest rate swaps. Inflation-indexed debt makes up a component of the portfolio and is issued when it is cost effective to do so.
- When issuing debt, the NZDMO samples interest rates throughout the year by conducting about 10 tenders of government bonds.
- The NZDMO is committed to transparency, predictability, and evenhandedness.

The NZDMO seeks to lower the government's cost of funds by reducing price uncertainty and encouraging competitive bidding through an efficient auction program. The NZDMO issues all domestic debt securities through auctions. Reserve pricing is used only in very exceptional circumstances, on only two occasions since 1993, to encourage investors to cover the government's borrowing requirements.

Nominal bonds and treasury bills are auctioned through a multiple-price system. Inflation-indexed bonds have not been issued since 1999, because it has not been cost effective to do so. They had been auctioned through a uniform-price system to reduce the potential "winner's curse" problem, which is viewed to be greater for a less liquid instrument that is more difficult to price.

Transparency surrounding the government's domestic borrowing intentions is enhanced by the publication of the details of the borrowing program when the annual budget and midyear fiscal updates are released. For instance, the NZDMO issues a press release that states the financing arithmetic for domestic currency borrowing and sets out the schedule for bond auctions. It states the parameters of the treasury bill program and notes whether the NZDMO intends to undertake New Zealand–dollar interest rate swap transactions. Similarly, the NZDMO consults the market before introducing new policies and practices, which reduces uncertainty around the process of policy change. That predictability enables market participants to plan with confidence, helping the market absorb sizable amounts of government securities.

Although these principles limit the NZDMO's ability to borrow opportunistically or engage in secondary market intervention, the possible opportunistic gains are outweighed by the benefits of being transparent.

This debt management framework also assists other public policy objectives. It seeks to enhance the development of the domestic capital market, including a derivatives market for managing risk, and reduce the cost of capital for private sector borrowers by improving New Zealand's sovereign creditworthiness.

Management of foreign currency debt

Since the float of the New Zealand dollar in 1985, the government has borrowed externally only to finance foreign exchange reserves. All other borrowing has been in the domestic market. At the same time, more than $NZ 18 billion of foreign currency debt has been retired, largely through the proceeds from asset sales and, since 1994, sizable fiscal surpluses. Net foreign currency debt was eliminated in 1996.

Unless otherwise directed by the minister of finance, net foreign currency debt is kept close to zero. The NZDMO aims to

- maintain a foreign-currency liquidity buffer;
- hedge the remaining foreign currency debt in a low-risk and efficient manner, having regard for the government's overall balance sheet;
- fund the Reserve Bank in a low-risk and efficient manner, having regard for the government's overall balance sheet; and
- manage funding risk through the maintenance of adequate reserves and diversified and long-term funding.

The decision to reduce net foreign currency debt to zero was an outcome of the analysis of the government's debt in an asset-liability framework, which indicated that the value of the government's assets are sensitive to movements in domestic interest rates but not movements in the exchange rate. Other considerations were the volatility of New Zealand's terms of trade and susceptibility to exchange rate shocks, which could not be effectively hedged, given the magnitude of the overall external debt portfolio and the capacity of the New Zealand foreign exchange market.

Prior to the elimination of net foreign currency debt, the strategy for the foreign-currency debt portfolio drew insights from mean-variance modeling that consistently showed that the U.S. dollar represented the dominant currency when attempting to reduce risk. The mix between yen and European currencies was unstable, and rebalancing costs were prohibitive. Consequently, the NZDMO adopted a benchmark for the net liability of 50 percent in U.S. dollars, 25 percent in yen, and 25 percent in European currencies. Those allocations corresponded approximately to relative GDP weights of the currency blocs, and so were also consistent with a "sell the market" strategy. For the target duration for each currency subportfolio, the NZDMO adopted the duration of the government bond market in each currency.

Strategic and tactical portfolio management

The portfolio is managed at both a strategic and a tactical level. Strategic management refers to the management of the overall parameters of the portfolio, in terms of currency mix and interest rate sensitivity, within the constraints established from time to time in respect of the mix of New Zealand dollar and foreign currency debt. The strategic parameters are disclosed in the government's annual financial statements. The minister of finance approves the strategic parameters of the portfolio and the annual New Zealand dollar borrowing program on the recommendation of the NZDMO.

Tactical management refers to the discretionary management of the net debt portfolio within established limits around the strategic portfolio. Within those limits, portfolio managers have discretion as to the use of instruments and timing of transactions to effect movements in the portfolio. Arguments in favor of providing the NZDMO with the flexibility to manage tactical positions within established limits, as opposed to adhering to the strategic parameters, include the following:

- Temporary pricing imperfections do sometimes occur, making it possible to generate profit from tactical decision making.

- Tactical trading brings with it knowledge of how various markets operate under a variety of circumstances, which improves the NZDMO's understanding in managing the overall portfolio. It is important, for instance, to maintain high-quality information flows about markets or sectors where intermediation transactions occur but are infrequent. Intermediation transactions occur when a substantial proportion of the value of tactical management is realized.

- Tactical trading enables the NZDMO to develop and maintain skills in analysis, decision making under uncertainty, negotiations, and deal closure. The immediate benefit is a reduced risk of mistakes when transacting and the projection of a more professional image to counter-parties.

Consistent with its commitment to transparency, predictability, and evenhandedness, the NZDMO does not engage in tactical trading with respect to the domestic debt portfolio.

Risk management

With ministerial approval, the NZDMO maintains a portfolio and risk management framework within which it operates. That includes the NZDMO's strategic objective, objectives for New Zealand dollar–denominated and foreign currency debt, the instruments in which the NZDMO may transact, limits regarding market and credit risk use, and composition requirements for the liquidity asset portfolio.

The NZDMO manages six principal types of risk: market, credit, liquidity, funding, operational, and concentration.

The NZDMO manages market risk associated with tactical trading through the use of value-at-risk (VaR) limits and stop-loss limits. It maintains a VaR limit for the overall tactical portfolio and also VaR limits for individual currency subportfolios. The limits are expressed over daily, monthly, and annual time horizons at a 95 percent confidence level and reflect the risk tolerance of the government in respect of tactical activity undertaken by the NZDMO. The limits are set so that the NZDMO

- can efficiently operate its daily business activities within the limits,

- has sufficient capacity to intermediate transactions on behalf of departments and other government organizations and manage the funding requirements for the Reserve Bank, and

- can absorb increases in market risk as a result of changes in global volatilities and correlations within the risk tolerance of the NZDMO.

The limits have evolved with the reduction of the foreign currency portfolio to a net zero position and in step with the evolution of international best practice. When the tactical trading limits were first approved by the minister of finance in the early 1990s, interest rate exposure and exchange rate exposure were managed separately, whereas the current VaR-based limits recognize diversification benefits.

Stop-loss limits are in place to protect the NZDMO from further losses once actual losses reach a certain point. They reflect the tolerance of the government in respect of maximum acceptable losses over monthly, quarterly, and annual time horizons.

The NZDMO uses back-testing to evaluate the performance of its VaR model. Actual profit and loss are compared with the market risk estimates calculated using the VaR model to determine its integrity and performance. Consistent with industry best practice, the NZDMO supplements VaR with stress-testing to understand how extreme or unusual events would affect the portfolio.

The NZDMO manages credit risk associated with transaction counter-parties and security issuers through the use of credit exposure limits. Because the NZDMO maintains credit exposures only with highly rated institutions, for which the probability of default is low, it is primarily concerned with losses arising from downgrade. Credit risk is further controlled by incorporating credit support annexes into the NZDMO's master swap agreements with swap and foreign exchange counter-parties.

The nature of the NZDMO's business is such that large amounts may be settled on one day. For that reason, monetary limits are not placed on the NZDMO's exposure to transaction banks, custodians, fiscal agents, and clearing brokers. The NZDMO manages risk with respect to those institutions through its procedures for selecting and monitoring its transaction settlement agents.

The NZDMO measures credit risk using an in-house credit model, because no suitable external product was available when it was developed in 1996. The model has been reviewed, and inputs to it have been updated, periodically since then. The model can be characterized as a mark-to-market model, which allows for credit losses as a result of changes in credit quality; a multiyear time horizon model, which spans the entire life of each transaction; and a bottom-up model, which calculates the credit risk for each individual transaction and then aggregates those individual credit risks at a portfolio level.

The objective for managing the NZDMO's foreign-currency liquidity portfolio is to have sufficient liquid assets available to meet all the government's obligations as they fall due. Liquidity risk is managed through policies that require the NZDMO to hold assets of appropriate quantity and quality.

To manage funding risk associated with New Zealand dollar borrowing, NZDMO establishes a relatively even maturity profile for term debt across the yield curve to manage the funding requirement, and the uncertainty around it arising from fiscal shocks, flexibly and without putting undue pressure on interest rates. With respect to foreign currency borrowing, the NZDMO establishes a maturity profile for term debt that reduces the likelihood of the government being unable to access markets in a timely manner or raise funds at an acceptable cost.

Operational risks in the NZDMO are managed in a number of ways. Operational risk policies span, for instance, transaction processing, legal and regulatory issues, ethical standards, physical and systems security, and business continuity. They are supported by close communications and regular management meetings that, in turn, reinforce a strong team ethic. Independent experts, such as external auditors, and specific initiatives provide additional support in managing operational risk. The combination of soft and hard practices provides the basis by which operational risks are managed and serves to heighten awareness of relevant risk events.

The NZDMO manages concentration risk as a second-order risk that forms part of the other risks that are managed. The NZDMO's approach is to ensure that risk concentrations are managed prudently within the context of the other individual risks.

The NZDMO's risk management framework has been in place since the NZDMO was established. However, the specifics of implementation have been, and are, subject to continuous improvement as resources allow and as IT capability and analytical techniques have improved. Careful prioritization has been required to ensure that scarce resources are allocated to managing the most significant risks first and fundamental risks are covered. In addition, the NZDMO periodically commissions reviews of its risk management framework and practices, including the strategic parameters of the portfolio, by external experts.

Performance measurement

The NZDMO measures performance on a risk-adjusted basis. The performance measurement regime provides these benefits:

- NZDMO management has information regarding the magnitude of risk associated with discretionary decisions, which assists thinking on alternative financing or investment strategies.
- Portfolio managers have information to assist them in managing the controllable risks for which they are responsible and feedback on the quality of their decisions.
- Information necessary to generate incentive structures that ensure staff incentives are aligned with those of the NZDMO.

The NZDMO undertakes performance measurement as a tool for internal management purposes, including the allocation of resources and the assessment of performance of individuals. It is not a requirement under generally accepted accounting practice, which establishes the framework for the NZDMO's public reporting. For that reason, the performance out-turn is not publicly disclosed.

As noted previously, the overall portfolio managed by the NZDMO is divided into strategic and tactical portfolios. Performance measurement applies to only the tactical portfolios, which are considered "performance" portfolios, whereas strategic portfolios are considered "nonperformance." All activity with respect to domestic currency borrowing is strategic. The daily profit or loss for each tactical portfolio is calculated as the difference in the present value of the portfolio from one day to the next.

In 1999, the NZDMO implemented a transfer-pricing regime (TPR) to allocate the change in the end-of-day valuation from one period to the next. The TPR enables transactions and risk positions to be transferred under agreed-upon rules from one sub-portfolio to another and better track the attribution of value added by activity. Prior to the implementation of that program, performance was measured relative to a shadow, or benchmark, portfolio. It was also measured on a cost basis alone with respect to liquidity management, investment, and foreign exchange transactions. The introduction of the TPR made it possible to measure performance on a risk-adjusted basis.

Value added—that is, profit or loss—is measured for each day, month, quarter, and financial year by the tactical portfolio and also by currency. Risk positions are measured against the net zero foreign-currency debt strategic benchmark. Risk use is calculated for the total tactical portfolio and also by currency.

Risk-adjusted performance measurement (RAPM) refers to the return of tactical management relative to the risk undertaken to achieve that return. RAPM provides information, in addition to simple profit and loss or risk use, that NZDMO management can use to assess the performance of tactical portfolio management activity. The practical effect of RAPM is to encourage portfolio managers to take on risk only when the potential upside is high compared with the size of the risk.

The risk-adjusted performance return is defined as net value added divided by notional risk capital. Net value added accounts for profit or loss and recognizes the expenses incurred in tactical management. It is defined as gross value added, less expenses attributable to tactical management. Notional risk capital accounts for market, credit, and operational risk use. Market risk is measured relative to the strategic net zero foreign-currency debt position and is based on the average total monthly VaR. Credit risk is measured relative to a credit risk–free position, which the NZDMO defines as a portfolio with exposure to only AAA-rated entities, and is based on the average monthly deviation from that AAA benchmark. It is

estimated using the NZDMO credit risk model. Operational risk is assumed to be either zero or the maximum of market or credit risk, because the NZDMO does not have a model to quantify that risk.

Risk-adjusted performance is calculated monthly. The NZDMO compares current risk-adjusted performance against historical performance, instead of a static benchmark. Annual risk-adjusted performance is measured as a moving average of the monthly returns in the previous 12 months.

Developing the Markets for Government Securities

In 1989, net foreign currency debt was $NZ 13 billion, equivalent to 19 percent of GDP and 43 percent of total net debt. Given the government's borrowing requirements at the time, the scope for reduction in the foreign currency exposure of the public debt to meet the NZDMO's balance sheet objectives was limited by the capacity of the New Zealand market to absorb additional borrowing. That encouraged the NZDMO to give a high priority to the development of the domestic debt market.

The preconditions with respect to securities market regulation and market infrastructure were already in place. There was a long-standing, sound legal framework, as well as appropriate accounting and auditing practices. Banking, clearing, and settlement systems were efficient. An independent central bank was able to implement monetary policy and manage market liquidity.

To develop the primary market for government securities, the NZDMO established a commitment to the principles of transparency, predictability, and evenhandedness in its activities, as described before.

In 1988, the minister of finance agreed to concentrate the issuance of bonds in benchmarks of large-volume, standardized securities. The aim of that approach is to reduce debt-servicing costs by achieving greater liquidity in the market, thereby attracting investors for whom liquidity is a major requirement. The domestic debt market until that time consisted of many tranches of relatively small volumes. By 1993, it had been transformed into eight benchmark maturities, each with up to $NZ 2.5 billion in outstanding volume. That pattern has continued through today, although the maximum outstanding volume is now around $NZ 3 billion.

A major consideration when first establishing benchmark bonds was that the maturity of a bond with a large outstanding volume involves a major outflow from the government to the private sector, which requires careful handling through the Reserve Bank's liquidity management operations. In New Zealand, benchmark bonds are large relative to the size of the economy, at about 3 percent of GDP, so their redemption represents a major flow through the financial system. That has been mitigated by buying back bonds in the final six months of life. The Reserve Bank also undertakes reverse repos in open market operations with maturity dates that coincide with the maturity date of a benchmark bond. A number of benchmark bonds have matured since 1993, and those processes have worked well, without distortion to the cash market.

To accelerate the building of benchmark bonds, the NZDMO introduced bond switches in 1989. They involved the issuance of new benchmark bonds in exchange for existing illiquid bonds. The process that was used included both reverse auctions, typically when a switch window was first opened, and negotiations with individual investors. The pricing for those negotiations was framed as a spread to the benchmark bond curve, on a duration-adjusted basis. At times, the savings to the government were substantial, of up to 30 basis points per year.

A further development was the lengthening of the maturity of government securities to reduce funding risk. The original benchmark was for 5 years. A 7-year benchmark was introduced in 1990 and a 10-year benchmark in 1991. The timing of each successive extension was a judgment about the level of demand in the market and, in New Zealand, it was closely associated with disinflation. The 10-year maturity has become an important pricing point in the market for international investors, because it is a common point of comparison across markets.

The NZDMO has not found it necessary to introduce primary dealers or officially appointed market makers to assist with the distribution of securities. Instead, the NZDMO considers that a better outcome is market making in government securities on the basis of commercial decisions by market participants themselves. New Zealand's banking system is efficient and open to new entrants, and this was also the case when a liquid government bond market was developed in the late 1980s and early 1990s. The banking system has been characterized by a high degree of foreign ownership for more than a century, and financial market reforms beginning in the mid-1980s included the removal of any limit to the number of registered banks. It has been comparatively easy for New Zealand banks to develop the necessary skills and systems required for a domestic bond market.

All market participants, including end-investors, may bid in auctions, subject to criteria related to creditworthiness. The arrangement has worked well, with a core group of about six to eight market makers at any one time, who agree among themselves on secondary market standards for liquidity, such as ticket size and spread. A similar approach applies in the New Zealand–dollar foreign exchange market.

A further development that was important for the expansion of the market was the effective removal of nonresident withholding tax. The NZDMO had been aware for some time that this was an issue with international investors, but earlier action had not been possible because of a number of considerations relating to tax policy. Although investors were able to avoid the tax by not holding securities on coupon payment dates, that procedure imposed costs and inconvenience, and many international investors were not prepared to take those measures for ethical reasons.

Holdings by nonresidents of New Zealand government securities increased markedly from 1993. According to surveys by the Reserve Bank, nonresident holdings peaked at 62 percent in 1997, slipping back to 33 percent in 2000. The reduction has been orderly and has occurred for a number of reasons, including a fall in differential interest rates between New Zealand and major markets and a depreciation in the New Zealand dollar as an adjustment process to a weak external position.

One potential concern about high levels of nonresident participation is the threat that those investors could attempt to exit the market all at once. Over the years, there have been periods of divestment, but they have tended to be orderly. Part of the reason is that the number of foreign investors participating in the market has increased over time, so the exit and entry of individual investors is based on their individual views, which tend to vary over time. Another reason is that successive governments have adhered to transparent and prudent fiscal and monetary policies, which provide an anchor of stability for the market.

Another feature of the maturity of the market has been its ability to weather a number of crises in international markets. Events such as the 1994 international bond market sell-off saw yields adjust upward, but the market continued to function continuously and prices generally adjusted smoothly.

One development in recent years that has improved the efficiency of the secondary market has been the increased use of repos. The NZDMO, along with the Reserve Bank, encouraged the development and use of standardized repo documentation, which assisted in that process. The increased use of swap transactions, by both residents and nonresidents, has also had spin-offs for the liquidity of the bond market.

Conclusion

Over the last 13 years, the NZDMO has undertaken continuous improvement in all aspects of its management of the government's debt. The latter half of that period has seen a considerable improvement in the government's finances and a reduction in debt levels. That has created its own technical challenges in relation to debt defeasance and management of uncertainty surrounding asset-sale proceeds and the size of surpluses. Changes in government policy and other initiatives have seen the NZDMO's role expand in the areas of intermediation and risk management. That is likely to continue in the future and, combined with finance industry–driven improvements to risk management techniques, will lead to further evolution of government debt management in New Zealand.

Note

1. The case study was prepared by Greg Horman from the New Zealand Debt Management Office.

12

Poland[1]

Developing a Sound Governance and Institutional Framework

Objectives

In 2001, the evaluation of the existing objectives and changes in macroeconomic conditions led to revision of the existing objectives.[2] The new objectives were incorporated in the strategy of debt management for the years 2002–04. The major change in comparison with the previous strategy was a shift in emphasis regarding the goal of cost minimization, from reducing the cost burden in the three-year time horizon to long-term cost minimization. The objectives are divided into two groups with three main objectives and four complementary (conditional) objectives. The fulfillment of the conditional goals will depend on the situation in the financial markets.

The main objectives are:

- Minimization of debt service costs: This is to be achieved through an optimal selection of debt management instruments, their structure, and issue dates. The time horizon is determined by the maturities of debt management instruments with the longest maturity.
- Limitation of the exchange rate risk and the risk of refinancing in foreign currencies: This objective is to be met mainly through reducing the share of foreign debt.
- Optimization of state budget liquidity management.

The complementary (conditional) objectives are:

- Limitation of the refinancing risk in the domestic currency is to be mainly achieved through the rise in the average maturity of domestic debt.
- Limitation of the interest rate risk is to be met through increasing the share of long-term fixed-rate instruments in total debt.
- Increasing flexibility of debt structure is to be achieved mainly through conversion of nonmarketable debt into marketable instruments.
- Decrease in debt monetization is to be met through increased share of the nonbanking sector in total debt.

167

Scope

The debt management policy pursued by the central government encompasses all activities involving the management of state budget debt. This includes the issuance, management, and service of treasury securities as well as the management and monitoring of other liabilities of the state budget. The influence on the central government debt, other than state budget debt, as well as on the local government debt, is indirect only (unless special procedures of recovering sound financial policies are executed) and includes imposing legal and formal regulations.

Coordination with monetary and fiscal policies

To coordinate the debt management policy with monetary and fiscal policies, the committee of public debt management was founded in 1994. The committee comprises members from the ministry of finance (MoF), the National Bank of Poland (NBP), and the ministry of state treasury. The meetings of the committee are held monthly and have an advisory character. However, the participation of directors of crucial departments of the MoF and the NBP, responsible for implementing and executing the policies, ensures a strong informal authority of the conclusions drawn by the committee. The main fields discussed by the committee include monthly plans for financing the state budget borrowing needs, the budgetary situation, and the situation of the money market.

The management of liquidity is coordinated on an interdepartmental level within the MoF. Under the constraint of a predetermined safe level of the balance of the account (excluding the risk of losing liquidity), the coordination ensures the minimization of alternative costs of holding cash on the central government account. The main instruments of the liquidity management are short-term deposits of surplus cash and issuance of short-term treasury bills.

Legal framework

The Constitution of the Republic of Poland, Article 216 forbids the acceptance of loans and grant guarantees and sureties, as a result of which the relation between public debt augmented by the amount of the anticipated disbursements on sureties and guarantees to the annual gross domestic product would exceed 60 percent. With the purpose of not exceeding the limit referred to in the principal rule, a provision of similar content was included in Article 37 of the Public Finance Act and reinforced in Article 45 by the definition of the so-called prudence and recovery procedures that come into play if the 50 and 55 percent thresholds are exceeded. The minister of finance must control the public finance sector in general and, to ensure the principal rule, the state treasury debt.

The basic legislation governing the conditions of the government debt managers is the Public Finance Act. Under this act, only the minister of finance is authorized to draw financial commitment on behalf of the state treasury, repay the drawn commitment, and carry out other financial transactions connected with debt management, including transactions related to derivative financial instruments.

The Public Finance Act requires the minister of finance to develop a three-year strategy of public finance sector debt management. At the same time, the minister of finance also presents a strategy for influencing public sector debt. These two topics are presented in one document. The need for these regulations was a consequence of the provisions of the Constitution of the Republic of Poland.

To govern the general conditions of issuing bonds, in 1999, the minister of finance issued five ordinances under the delegation laid down in the Public Finance Act.

Institutional structure

Institutional structure within the government

The debt management unit in Poland is situated within the MoF. As one of the units of the ministry, the public debt department (PDD) manages day-to-day debt policy, prepares the strategy of debt management, and cooperates with the Polish and international financial markets in the fields of borrowing and development of the treasury securities market.

The position of the PDD as a part of the MoF has advantages and disadvantages. At the very early stage of development of the domestic financial market, when the transition to the free market economy had just begun, the PDD (the unit with administrative power) had more instruments to support development of the market, cooperate with other regulatory institutions, and prepare efficient legal and infrastructure environments.

Along with the development of the market in Poland, the situation has changed. The number of sophisticated market participants has increased, the base of securities is well developed, and hedging instruments are available. Together with challenges in the risk management of the debt, a more flexible and active approach to debt management is required. The bureaucratic structure in the MoF, subjected to long procedures, hampers the flexibility of debt management. The tendency in Organisation for Economic Co-operation and Development (OECD) countries to separate debt management offices from the MoF is based on experience of being a unit of the MoF, which makes it hard to avoid the conflict between short-term objectives of the fiscal policy and the longer-term ones for debt management. Lessons learned from the yearly meetings of the OECD working group indicate that acting outside the MoF as a separate debt office makes it possible to avoid direct intervention in the borrowing policy, the structure of offered instruments, and the policy of minimization of debt-servicing costs on the medium- and long-term horizon.

Organizational structure in the debt management office

In 1998, domestic and foreign debt management were concentrated in the PDD and divided into four functional units: front office, middle office, back office, and the foreign debt unit. The decision to develop a separate unit for foreign debt was the result of the sizable percentage of foreign debt within total debt. However, external financial institutions perform a large part of the traditional front and back offices operations, and the work of the PDD retains a rather analytical character. Currently, 49 people work at the PDD.

The framework and the point of reference for daily debt management will be described in the next section, where objectives and tasks of debt manage-ment are clearly defined. The formal procedures of daily management are still a work in progress.

The main operating risk of debt management is the lack of an integrated information system for debt management, because the databases are fragmented and not fully compatible with each other. The integrated debt management system was implemented by the end of 2002.

Auditing

The financial accounts of the public debt, as well as other parts of the state budget, are subject to annual audit by the supreme audit office, reporting to parliament. Regardless of that reporting structure, the supreme audit office has the authority to carry out additional control in any area of public finances. Thee minister of finance submits the report on execution of debt-servicing costs quarterly to parliament's commission of the public finance.

Debt Management Strategy and the Risk Management Framework

Policies are implemented to ensure that the public debt management is carried out in a prudent and predictable way, with the aim of minimizing any possible threats to public finances and the country's economy.

Public debt management is one of the crucial areas where the accountability of applied policies and macroeconomic prospects of the economy are subject to scrutiny. To prevent excessive levels of debt by legal measures, the limits of the public debt to GDP ratio were imposed, including special procedures if the debt exceeds 50 percent and 55 percent. As mentioned, these rules and regulations were set forth in the Public Finance Act, and an upper limit of 60 percent was set by the Constitution of the Republic of Poland.

To increase the credibility of public debt management, each year the council of ministers submits to parliament the debt management strategy for the coming three years, which includes a set of clear goals of debt management, the assessment of executing the objectives of previous strategies, and analysis of possible scenarios regarding public debt.

The main risks that the government faces with respect to its foreign currency debt portfolio are the refinancing risk and the exchange rate risk. For the domestic currency debt portfolio, the main risks are the refinancing risk and the interest rate risk.

The policy of reducing the foreign debt outstanding and financing mainly in the domestic market results in the development of a large and stable domestic debt market, which reduces the country's exposure to foreign currency crises and adverse external shocks.

Strategy for managing the costs and risks

Foreign currency debt portfolio

Despite considerably higher service costs of the domestic debt, limitation of the exchange rate risk and the refinancing risk in foreign currencies is among the primary goals in the public finance sector debt management strategy for 2002–04. The basic measure of these two types of risk is the share of foreign debt in total debt. Hence, the main means of reducing the exposure to both these risks is decreasing this foreign debt share.

Consequently, the overall strategy states that the borrowing needs of the government should be satisfied to the greatest possible extent in the domestic market. Funds raised in the foreign market should not be higher than the amount of principal of the foreign debt due in the given fiscal year. However, additional borrowing can be executed in the foreign market to facilitate early repayment of the foreign currency debt. The maturity of the newly issued debt should avoid the years with the highest foreign debt repayments, namely 2004–09. Furthermore, proceeds from privatization obtained in foreign currencies are used for foreign debt service and repayment.

The percentage of foreign debt (according to the place of issue) as part of total debt decreased from 49 percent in 1999 to 35 percent at the end of November 2001. During the same period, the debt expressed in terms of U.S. dollars fell from US$31.3 billion to US$24.7 billion in November 2001. These significant declines were mainly the result of the early redemption of Brady bonds. In addition, Poland signed an agreement with Brazil in October 2001,

under which, by exception and approval of the Paris Club, debt with nominal value of $US3.32 billion was repaid early for the amount of $US2.46 billion.

Currently, an important issue is the preparation of the foreign debt refinancing for the period of peak payments to the Paris Club in the years 2004–09. Owing to the very strong dependence of the debt repayment manner on Poland's political and economic situation, the actions undertaken should be geared to the current situation. Poland's entry into the European Union (EU) will strengthen the country's credibility and broaden its access to international markets, and subsequently joining the European Economic and Monetary Union will mean a substantial decrease in the share of foreign debt.

The strategy of establishing and maintaining access to the most important segments of the international capital market is continuing because of the possible necessity of having to refinance most or all of the maturing foreign debt in the period under consideration. This will be conducted through the placement of issues of treasury securities in the key market segments. Moreover, to upgrade its credit rating, the state treasury conducts operations, within its current capabilities, of early repayment of some debt aimed at reducing foreign debt, minimizing service costs, and reducing principal repayments in the years 2004–09.

In the future, when zlotys will be replaced with euros, the situation will change. Because 43 percent of the external debt consists of euros, the exchange rate risk connected with foreign debt will be reduced substantially. The possibilities of raising funds in financial markets will also change greatly. Poland's entry into the EU will have a considerable influence on the country's credit rating, which will enable financing costs to be reduced. The inflow of the EU funds could also help lower foreign refinancing by allocating the EU funds for repayment of the foreign debt and enlarging domestic debt to raise money to finance goals for which the EU funds were originally intended.

To avoid distorting the exchange rate resulting from large inflows of foreign currency to the market, the privatization proceeds in foreign currencies are put into the special account used for foreign debt servicing.

Domestic currency debt portfolio

The refinancing risk is most often measured by the average term to maturity. Hence, limiting refinancing risk in domestic currency can be achieved by increasing the average maturity of domestic debt. The average term to maturity of domestic market debt in February 2002 was 2.52 years; at the same time, the duration of the market debt denominated in zlotys amounted to 1.90 years. These maturities do not guarantee the appropriate level of safety in the medium term. Extension of the average maturity of domestic debt should be done gradually, along with the development of financial market in Poland, increase in demand for long-term instruments, and fall in long-term interest rates.

The refinancing risk can also be assessed by the time structure of the future redemptions. The policy of reduction of debt in treasury bills in favor of increased debt in medium- to long-term bonds results in the smoothing of a redemption profile or a reduction of redemptions in the next few years (increasing simultaneously the redemptions in the years afterward). This same policy of increased debt in fixed-rate bonds and a decline of debt in treasury bills caused a reduction in interest rate risk. The share of fixed-rate marketable bonds in the domestic debt of the state treasury grew from 39 percent in 1999 to 53 percent at the end of February 2002. The increase was mainly a result of increased sales and the effects of conversion of the nonmarketable securities into fixed-rate marketable securities. The share of treasury bills in domestic debt amounted to 20 percent in February 2002 and has not changed since 1999.

These measures have led to a decreased sensitivity of debt-service costs to the fluctuations of interest rates on the financial market, as well as an increase in the rate of predictability of these costs, in both the current years and future years.

Risk analysis undertaken

When the debt management strategy and the budget act were formulated, different scenarios were considered. Several included the possible macroeconomic and market risks of adverse events, as well as the budget environment. Possible threats to the realization of the strategy were also taken into account.

The main concern in applying the debt management strategy involved a trade-off between minimizing costs and reducing risks. The risks are especially interest rate risk, refinancing risk and exchange rate risk, as well as liquidity management. This requires a dynamic approach, taking current market and budget conditions into consideration. The process of decision making is heuristic, rather than involving the use of formal procedures, although some quantitative measures and formalized models are used as a support (a system of formal procedures is still a work in progress).

The risk measures are computed historically, and forecasts are made. The desired characteristics concerning foreign/domestic and fixed/floating ratios, as well as duration, are modified according to the market situation and financing needs. Currently, these measures of risk are used:

- the debt-to-GDP ratio and the ratio of debt-service costs to GDP—the most general measures, summarizing the overall ability to service public debt;
- the share of foreign debt in total debt—mainly as a measure of exchange rate risk;
- the average maturity of the domestic debt—as a measure of refinancing risk;
- duration of the domestic market debt—as a measure of refinancing and interest rate risk; and
- other measures, mainly descriptive statistics, such as the share of floating- and fixed-rate debt, maturity profile by months and years, and similar data.

Econometric and other quantitative[3] models, developed within the PDD, are also used. Formalized optimization problems solved periodically are also used to support various decisions made. However, the results derived from these models depend heavily on the assumptions regarding future interest rates and other forecasted variables, which can be subjective at times.

The quantification of risks is subject to further methodological research. A breakthrough in this area is expected after the implementation of the integrated debt management system. Currently, information systems used to assess and monitor risk are highly fragmented and are not automated. The input data are manually collected from different databases. The tools of risk monitoring also are not integrated.

The quality of risk assessment and monitoring, as well as other aspects of data management, are expected to improve significantly when the integrated debt management system, financed by PHARE 2000 program funds, is introduced, as well as a loan from the World Bank. The objective of the project is to prepare (in cooperation with the Finnish Ministry of Finance) for a more effective and efficient debt management through an integrated information technology (IT) system in conformity with standards in place in the EU member countries. The system will support the public debt management and the budget process, including defining financing needs and debt-service costs. It will also reduce debt-service costs by using sophisticated analytical tools provided by the system. Furthermore, it will improve the knowledge of the development in the capital markets and strengthen the market approach to debt management. The system will also enhance risk management and control.

Currently, no benchmark portfolio is in use. The comparison of the actual portfolio and forecasts is often informative because of high market volatility and frequent changes of long-term assumptions concerning budget deficits and market conditions.

Active debt management

Public debt management does not encompass activity in the domestic secondary market. The primary concern is cost minimization over the long term, and the current policy is subordinated to it. Active debt management includes actions undertaken besides the regular calendar of debt issuance and servicing, aimed at executing the goals of the debt management strategy. These include occasional buybacks of the domestic and foreign debt before its maturity, regular switch auctions of treasury bonds, swap transactions, and use of other derivative instruments. The last two options are planned.

Active debt management is not used to generate returns in foreign currency debt. The only exception involves buybacks of collateralized Brady bonds, which generate proceeds from sold collateral.

Management-contingent liabilities

A separate department within the MoF coordinates the management of contingent liabilities, especially granting sureties and guaranties by the state treasury. The disbursements effected under this department constitute a service cost of public debt as a whole. The anticipated amount is important for the debt management process.

The management of risks associated with embedded options

A put option (the possibility for an investor to receive an early redemption) is used only in savings bonds, namely the two-year fixed-rate bonds and the four-year inflation-indexed savings bonds. The relatively small share of these instruments in total debt, as well as historical data on the share of bonds where the option was executed, shows that the risk involved was insignificant. Early redemption accounts for about 4 percent of the total value of bonds with this option. One of reasons for this low percentage is the relatively low sensitivity of retail investors to changes in market conditions. However, the potential threats connected with the options are taken into account, and suitable precautions are made to reduce the liquidity risk.

Early redemption is financed by the interest accrued from not taking back funds by bondholders, which is then placed in a bank account maintained by the issue agent. In addition, the issuer has a one week to submit cash to the bondholder executing the options.

Developing the Markets for Government Securities

Borrowing instruments

According to the public finance sector debt management strategy for the years 2002–04, government borrowing should be realized mainly in the domestic market. Borrowing in the foreign market is limited to refinancing maturing debt. In the future, the funds raised in the foreign market will gradually increase along with the increasing repayments of the debt to the creditors associated within the Paris Club.

The increasing significance of minimizing costs, over a time determined by the maturities of debt management instruments with the longest maturity, affected the structure of sales of treasury securities, especially in 2001. Decisions concerning the choice between the issuance of short- and long-term instruments was determined by market conditions and the predicted future shape of the yield curve. The increase in the average term to maturity is acknowledged to be the main means of reducing the refinancing risk of domestic debt.

Marketable and savings treasury securities issued on the domestic market in 2001 included these instruments:

- treasury bills with maturities ranging from 1 to 52 weeks;
- Treasury bonds offered at auction ("wholesale bonds"):
  - 2-year zero-coupon bonds,
  - 5-year fixed-rate bonds,
  - 10-year fixed-rate bonds, and
  - 10-year floating-rate bonds;[4]
- treasury bonds offered in the retail network ("retail bonds"):
  - 2-year fixed-rate savings bonds
  - 3-year floating-rate bonds
  - 4-year savings bonds indexed to inflation, and
  - 5-year fixed-rate bonds.

In 2002, a 20-year fixed-rate bond was introduced. The first auction took place on April 17, 2002.

Retail instruments are used to back up the sales of wholesale instruments, widen the investor base, and promote the propensity for saving. The tasks within this area will include the diversification of instruments offered and the increase in their accessibility to potential investors through the implementation of the new IT. The sale of retail indexed bonds accounted for about 1.0 percent of the total value of all bonds sold by the MoF and approximately 5.8 percent of retail bonds.

The maturity of bonds issued on international capital markets is constrained by the existing foreign debt redemption profile. Until 2001, because of very low funding needs, the MoF executed only one benchmark transaction a year in the international market, not exceeding the amount of principal payments. The main reasons for issuing bonds in the international market are to maintain access to the most important segments of the international capital market because of the possible necessity of refinancing most or all of the foreign debt in the years 2004–09 and to create a benchmark for issues of Polish corporate bonds.

Consolidation of public debt

Data on Polish public debt (debt of units included in the sector of public finance)[5] have been available since 1999 (since 2001 in a consolidated form). Since then, based on the Public Finance Act, two ordinances regulating the recording of debt have been issued. The first ordinance regulates the recording of debt of units included in budgetary entities. The second regulates the recording of debt of the rest of the units of the public finance sector. These regulations make it possible for the MoF (which has the obligation of publishing data on public debt twice a year) to calculate the entire amount of debt of the public sector after consolidation. The regulations also aim to obtain the data needed to meet the requirements of international reporting (e.g., reports prepared for the EUROSTAT, IMF, and OECD).

Mechanisms used to issue debt

Treasury bills and treasury bonds

Treasury bills and treasury bonds are offered for sale in the primary market at auctions organized and held by the NBP. Bids are submitted to the NBP by 11:00 a.m. on the auction day. Upon receipt of a bid summary, the MoF makes a decision on the minimum price with a given maturity. Bids with prices that are higher than the minimum price are accepted in their entirety, and bids with the minimum price can be reduced or accepted in whole. Each bidder buys bonds at the proposed price.

Dates of auctions are announced at the beginning of each year in a calendar of issuance, published on the MoF's web site.[6] The detailed information on forthcoming auction is published on the MoF's web site and on Reuter's two days before the date of the tender. The announcement contains the type and maturity of the instrument offered, value of the offer, a brief description of terms of issue, and the time and place for submitting bids.

Treasury bills are sold at a discount at auctions, which are held on the first business day of each week (i.e., usually on Mondays). However, extra auctions can be held on other days. Participants allowed to submit bids in the auctions are entities that purchased at least 0.2 percent of all bills sold in the primary market in the previous quarter. They are verified every quarter according to this criterion. Other investors can participate through their intermediation. Payment for bills purchased and redemption of maturing bills are usually effected on the second day after the auction through banks' current accounts maintained by the NBP payment system department.

Treasury bonds auctions are usually held on Wednesday.[7] Additional auctions can be held on other days. Entities allowed to submit bids in the auctions are direct participants of the national depository for securities (NDS); other interested parties can participate through their intermediation. Auctions of treasury bonds are settled in cash and in securities through the NDS; cash settlements of bonds auctions are handled directly by the NDS through its account with the NBP.

Retail bonds

The sale and management of retail bonds intended for small investors is handled by the central brokerage house of Bank Pekao S.A. (CDM Pekao S.A.) under agreements signed with the minister of finance. CDM Pekao S.A. is the issuing agent and also the organizer of a consortium of the largest banking and nonbanking brokerage houses, a total of 21. Bonds are offered through a network of customer service outlets—at the beginning of 2000, about 550 units throughout the country—and via the Internet.

The marketable bonds (three-year floating-rate and five-year fixed-rate bonds) are sold at the issue price published before the commencement of sale. The sales price contains, in addition to the issue price, interest accrued from the sale commencement date to the purchase date. There are four series issued every year, with distribution taking place in the following three months. The sales price for five-year bonds is settled monthly. The savings bonds (the two-year fixed-rate and the four-year indexed) are sold at Zl 100 polish on every business day. During each month, the issuer introduces a new series for each type of savings bond.

Disbursement of interest and repurchase of bonds take place at the point of purchase or via the bank account indicated. It is also possible to deposit the three-year floating rate and five-year fixed-rate bonds in an investment account at any stock brokerage house, wherethe servicing and redemption of the bonds takes place via the same account. Both types of bonds are admitted to official listing on the regulated market (the Warsaw Stock Exchange).

Foreign debt

The standard mechanism of foreign bond issuance is used, including a syndicate of international investment banks. Each transaction in the international market is carefully prepared, using the public debt management's and investment banks' expertise to select the best timing and segment of the market. The pricing of bonds is based on market conditions and takes into account the secondary market performance of the bonds.

Development of the secondary market

The main actions taken to increase the liquidity, effectiveness, and transparency of the treasury securities in the secondary market are

- elimination or reduction of restrictions in the settlement infrastructure—for example, the implementation of the real-time gross settlement (RTGS) system and securities borrowing, the reduction of transaction fees and commissions, and the development of the repo market;[8]
- support of trading on the electronic platform for debt instruments and their smooth incorporation into the registration and settlement system;

- continuation of the policy to increase the depth of the treasury securities market through sizable issues of different series, which means fewer maturity dates for different types of treasury securities and an increase in their value in the individual series;
- support of the activity toward elimination of regulations aimed to subject repo transactions to the system of mandatory reserves; and
- introduction of switch operations.

The introduction of a primary dealer system is a work in progress. In 2001, the rules of governing, selecting, and properly assessing primary dealers, and an evaluation of the scope of their rights and duties, were prepared, and then verified during meetings with the banks. The cooperation with primary dealers will also lead to the identification of risks for public debt management and the development of the treasury securities market. The process of monitoring and evaluating the candidates began on April 26, 2002.

Contacts with the financial community

A proper relationship between debt managers and investors is crucial to the effective management of public debt. To achieve this, regular meetings with groups of domestic investors such as banks, brokerage houses, pension funds, investment funds, and insurance companies are held. Individual meetings with important domestic and foreign participant in the treasury securities market are also held.

Relation to the private sector market

The debt market in Poland is dominated by government securities (treasury bonds and treasury bills account for about 90 percent of the total debt outstanding). The issues of nontreasury bonds are mainly private placements. The modest significance of private sector debt makes public debt management independent of considerations regarding the current situation in the private debt market. On the contrary, the development of the public debt market constitutes a key condition of the development of private debt markets.

Rules of taxation

Taxation of residents

Legal entities

Interest and discount income as well as income from the sale of treasury securities were subject to income tax under general principles, that is, at the rate of income tax applicable to income realized by legal entities in the year in which the income was obtained (in 2001, the rate amounted to 28 percent).

Private persons

Interest or discount on securities issued by the state treasury and acquired by private persons before December 1, 2001, was exempt from tax. Interest or discount on securities issued by the state treasury and acquired by taxpayers after November 31, 2001, are subject to withholding tax of 20 percent.

Income from the sale of domestic treasury bonds (issued after January 1, 1989, and acquired before January 1, 2003) received by December 31, 2003, is not subject to income tax unless the sale is the object of business activity. Income from the sale of securities other than bonds issued by the state treasury is subject to personal income tax.

Taxation of Nonresidents

Persons realizing income from treasury securities purchased on the domestic market were subject to the provisions of treaties on the avoidance of double taxation between Poland and the country of residence or domicile of the nonresident earning income in Poland. Where no such treaty existed, the following principles applied.

Legal entities

Interest and discount were subject to withholding tax of 20 percent. Income from the sale of treasury bonds or bills was subject to income tax under general principles, that is, at the rate of income tax applicable to income realized by legal entities in the year in which the income was obtained (in 2001, the rate amounted to 28 percent).

Income realized by legal entities based abroad from the sale, conversion, or other legal transaction transferring rights in bonds issued by the State Treasury of the Republic of Poland on foreign markets since the year 1995 has been exempt from tax.

Private persons

Foreign private persons with a domicile other than Poland or those with no right of permanent or temporary residence in the territory of Poland (temporary residence being a sojourn with a duration of not more than 183 days in a tax year) were liable to tax only on income from work performed in the territory of Poland under a service-based relationship or employment relationship, irrespective of where the remuneration is paid, and on other income realized in Poland.

Interest and discounts on securities issued by the state treasury in the domestic market acquired by taxpayers before December 1, 2001, were exempt from tax. Interest or discounts on securities issued by the state treasury and acquired by taxpayers after November 31, 2001, are subject to withholding tax of 20 percent.

Income from the sale of domestic treasury bonds (issued after January 1, 1989, and acquired before January 1, 2003) received by December 31, 2003, is not liable to income tax unless such sale was the object of business activity. Income from the sale of other domestic securities issued by the state treasury was liable to personal income tax.

Income realized by foreign private persons having their domicile abroad from the sale, conversion, or other legal transaction transferring rights in bonds issued by the State Treasury of the Republic of Poland on foreign markets in the years 1995–01 was exempt from tax.

Effect of tax on trading of government securities

Currently, the sale of government securities is not affected by taxation because of the relief from the tax on civil actions, which has been in force since 1998.

Therefore, it is difficult to give an estimate of the effect of taxation on private persons' trading because of the short period of tax law that is binding. At the same time, income from all kinds of bank deposits was taxed; therefore both of these forms of investment are treated equally. This pattern is also applied in the EU.

Appendix

Development and Changes in Debt Management Objectives Before 2001

The debt management strategy was first prepared in 1999, as a document submitted to parliament with justification of the draft State Budget Act. Long- and short-term objectives were formulated. The long-term horizon of the strategy corresponded to the maturity profile of most of Poland's external debt (to the Paris Club), and it coincided with the horizon adopted for the *Public Finance and Economic Development Strategy: Poland 2000–2010.* The primary objectives of the debt management strategy for the period were:

- reduce the share of external debt in total debt by refinancing part of the debt due with internal debt and early redemption of certain external liabilities;
- achieve the desirable value of the indicators describing the debt maturity structure—average maturity, duration, and the ratio of debt due in a given year to total debt;
- ensure even distribution of debt repayments and debt-servicing costs over time—in particular, to eliminate peaks of payments;
- reduce the risk related to variability of debt-servicing costs (increase their predictability) by increasing the share of fixed-income instruments in total debt; and
- make the external debt structure more flexible.

The following objectives were set forth in the strategy for the three-year horizon:

- Minimize the debt servicing costs under constraints on
  - the borrowing needs of the state budget (net cash requirements);
  - the level of risk involved in debt financing, including exchange risk, refinancing risk, and interest rate risk;
  - the ability of the domestic market to absorb medium- and long-term instruments, given that the national budget does not displace credit for the economy);

  - the conditions prevailing on the international financial market related to a country credit rating; and
  - compliance with the monetary policy of the central bank.
- Develop an optimum schedule of external debt payments for the years 2004–09 (i.e., during the period of high intensity of the payments).
- Reduce the degree of debt monetization by increasing the nonbanking sector's share in total debt.

The goals presented in the first strategy were modified in 2000 as a result of conditions that arose in relation to the need to lay greater emphasis on the minimization of the burden of debt-service costs for public finance in the period of the next two to three years.

Goals formulated in the strategy were as follows:

- Minimization of the debt service costs over the adopted horizon—understood as
  - minimization of the burden of debt-service costs for public finance in 2001–03, mainly through the rising share of the fixed-rate bonds in total debt and the limitation of the share of treasury bills and floating-rate bonds;
  - costs minimization over a time limit determined by the maturities of debt management instruments with the longest maturity and with the preset parameters (including those arising from the need to minimize the costs in the period between 2001 and 2003)— through an optimal selection of debt management instruments and their structure and issue dates;
  - minimization of the service costs to eliminate the reasons causing fixing of debt interest rates at a level higher than the minimal one, which can be attained on the market through increased liquidity and depth of the secondary market for treasury securities, increase in the transparency and safety of trade in debt instruments, and actions aimed at elimination of the technical hindrances in the trade in treasury securities (fees, settlement system, and so forth).

- Limitation of the exchange rate risk and the risk of refinancing in foreign currencies as a result of the lowering of the foreign debt share.
- Limitation of the refinancing risk, mainly through the rise in the average maturity of domestic debt.
- Limitation of the interest rate risk through an increase in the share of medium- and long-term fixed-rate instruments in total debt.
- Increasing flexibility of debt structure as a result of the conversion of nonmarketable debt into marketable instruments.
- Decrease in the debt monetization through an increased share of the nonbanking sector in total debt.
- Optimization of the foreign debt amortization schedule for years 2004–09.

- Optimization of state budget liquidity management.

Notes

1. The case study was prepared by the Public Debt Department of the Ministry of Finance.

2. See Appendix for a detailed description of the previous objectives.

3. The models use applications of mathematical programming, game theory, and neural networks, among others.

4. The sales of DZ were suspended in 2002.

5. The NBP is not included in the sector of public finance.

6. www.mofnet.gov.pl.

7. Specifically, the auctions are held on the first Wednesday of every month for 2- and 5-year fixed-rate and zero-coupon bonds, the second Wednesday of the even months for 10-year floating-rate bonds, and the third Wednesday of the odd months for 10-year fixed-rate bonds.

8. The RTGS system was launched on April 26, 2002.

13
Portugal[1]

As a result of Portugal's entry into the European Economic and Monetary Union (EMU), the environment underlying the management of the Portuguese government debt has gone through very important changes in the last few years. By adopting the euro as its currency, the country now benefits from both the credibility of a monetary policy that is defined at the level of the European Union (EU) and the fiscal discipline that EU members have to comply with. Furthermore, the constraints on government debt management resulting from the execution of the monetary policy have been greatly diminished with EU membership, because Portugal has gained access to a much larger "domestic" financial market—the euro debt market. The challenge the country faces with this new position is the loss of being the reference issuer of the Portuguese escudo and becoming a small borrower in a large market, where one has to compete with other sovereign issuers for the same base of investors.

In the second half of the 1990s, and in anticipation of these changes, a series of important reforms took place that aimed to develop conditions for a more efficient management of public debt in this new environment. These reforms included, at the institutional

level, the creation of an autonomous debt agency, the Instituto de Gestão do Credito Publico ([IGCP] Portuguese Government Debt Agency), in 1996; the publication of a new Public Debt Law approved by parliament in 1998, and government approval of formal guidelines for debt management in 1999.

Developing a Sound Governance and Institutional Framework

Debt management objectives

The strategic objectives to be pursued in government debt management and state financing were made explicit by the new Public Debt Law, which states that these activities should aim to guarantee the financial resources required for the execution of the state budget and be conducted in such a way as to

- minimize the direct and indirect cost of public debt in a long-term perspective,
- guarantee a balanced distribution of debt costs through the several annual budgets,

- prevent an excessive temporal concentration of redemptions,
- avoid excessive risks, and
- promote an efficient and balanced functioning of financial markets.

Minimizing the cost of debt was already an implicit objective of debt management before the approval of the new Public Debt Law. Nevertheless, its enactment has been an important step in that it has formalized these objectives, clarifying the issue of the minimization of cost so that it would be pursued in a long-term perspective and introducing an explicit reference to risk limitation, that is, how to reduce refinancing risk and the volatility of debt cost over time.

The objective of promoting an efficient and balanced functioning of the domestic financial market was particularly important before the creation of the EMU, in a context where most of the debt was denominated in escudos and placed on the domestic market. The relevance of creating and maintaining a benchmark yield curve to support the escudo capital market vanished as the escudo was integrated into the euro.

The guidelines for debt management, approved by the minister of finance in late 1998 and in force since 1999, adopted a model for risk management and translated the strategic objective of minimizing debt costs into the definition of a benchmark that, since then, has been the reference point for debt management. The risk management approach has four basic components:

- adoption of a consistent model for the development of primary and secondary markets for Portuguese public debt;
- development and implementation of clear debt management guidelines and risk/performance evaluation (benchmark);
- investment in information technology (IT) systems to support well-informed management decisions, reduce operational risk, and increase transparency by improving availability and quality of all transaction data; and
- development and implementation of a comprehensive manual of operational procedures to reduce operational risk and support external and internal auditing.

The scope of debt management activity

Debt management includes the issuing of debt instruments, the execution of repo transactions, and the completion of other financial transactions with the purpose of adjusting the structure of the debt portfolio.

There is no limitation in the Public Debt Law as to the nature of the financing instruments that can be used for funding. However, concerns about the liquidity of the government debt led to a progressive concentration of the financing activity into the issuance of a restricted number of standard fixed-rate treasury bonds (*obrigações do tesouro* [OTs]) and euro commercial paper (ECP). The issuance of savings certificates, a retail instrument sold to individuals on a continuous basis, remains an important funding source.

As a facility of last resort, repo transactions are made available to market makers. The objective is to support the market-making obligations of the primary dealers in the secondary market of the OTs. Repos are provided in a range of amounts for each security. Taking into account market conditions, the price is fixed at a rate below the average posted euro overnight interest rate (euro overnight index average [EONIA]).

To adjust the redemption profile of the government debt, the Public Debt Law includes the early redemption and buyback of existing debt and the direct exchange of securities within the scope of operations allowed to debt managers. Since 2001, this practice has also been used more intensively for the purpose of promoting liquidity in the treasury bond market through the concentration of existing debt into larger and more liquid issues.

The Public Debt Law also includes within the scope of debt management the trading of derivatives, namely interest rate and currency swaps, forwards, futures, and options. Those transactions must be linked to the underlying instrument in the debt portfolio. Swaps and foreign currency forwards have been the instruments most used for this purpose.

Although contingent liabilities are not now taken into account in debt management decisions, it is planned to analyze them in the future with a view to including them in the risk management framework. The debt agency, IGCP, is responsible only for the management of the direct public debt of the central government, even though it is required to appraise the financial terms of guaranteed debt and debt issued by (public sector) services and funds with administrative and financial autonomy.[2] Within the ministry of finance, the treasury department follows, quantifies, and reports explicit contingent liabilities in a systematic way.

For the time being, the scope of the IGCP's activity does not include the investment of surpluses that may exist in the state central cash accounts, which are also under the responsibility of the treasury department.[3] The permanent exchange of information on policies and forecasted treasury flows between the two entities is carried out to coordinate funding and surplus investment effectively.

Legal framework

The main legal framework that regulates the issuance of central government debt and the management of public debt includes

- the Public Debt Law, which states that state financing has to be authorized by parliament;
- the annual Budget Law, which establishes limits for the amounts that the government is authorized to borrow during the year in terms of net borrowing (The annual Budget Law may also define maximum terms for the debt to be issued and limits to the currency exposure and to the floating rate debt.); and
- the decree-law that regulates the activity of the IGCP.

According to the legal framework, the IGCP's responsibility is to negotiate and execute all financial transactions related to the issuing of central government debt and the management of the debt. The minister of finance is empowered to define specific guidelines to be followed by the IGCP in the execution of the financing policy.

Permanent guidelines from the minister of finance were formalized through the adoption of a long-term benchmark structure for the composition of the debt portfolio. The benchmark reflects selected targets concerning the duration, interest rate risk, currency risk, and refinancing risk and sets

the reference for the evaluation of the cost and performance of the actual debt portfolio.

The government approves annually, through a council of ministers resolution, the debt instruments that should to be used in state financing for the year and their respective gross borrowing limits. The minister of finance annually approves specific guidelines for the IGCP. The guidelines include broad lines for the management of the debt portfolio (e.g., buyback of debt and repo transactions) and the issuing strategy in terms of instruments, maturities, timing, and placement procedures. The guidelines also cover measures to be implemented regarding the marketing of the debt and the relationship with the primary dealers and other financial intermediaries. These guidelines are made public.

Organization

Previously, two departments inside the ministry of finance were in charge of central government debt management. The treasury department was responsible for the external debt and the issuance of treasury bills, and the public credit department was responsible for domestic debt (excluding treasury bills). Since 1997, operational activities associated with central government debt management, including the servicing of the debt, have been centralized in the IGCP. The IGCP is empowered to negotiate and carry out all financial transactions related to the issuing of central government debt and the active management of the debt portfolio, in compliance with the guidelines approved by the minister of finance.

The IGCP is organized to allow the flexible use of its resources, namely with recourse to project teams. The organizational structure comprises the board of directors, two departments, and five technical and four operational units, with a total staff of 65 people.

The agency is governed by a board of three directors, appointed by the council of ministers for a term of three years. The board reports to the minister of finance. An advisory board, composed of the chairman of the board of directors, a member of the central bank's board of directors, and four experts in economic and financial matters, appointed by the council of ministers, provides recommendations on strategic matters.

The debt management department is responsible for all the aspects related to the definition of issuing and portfolio management policies, follow-up of the secondary market, relationships with the primary dealers and other financial intermediaries, negotiation and placement of nonretail debt, and active management of trading. The department comprises two units, the trading room and a markets unit.

The operations department is responsible for matters related to the confirmation and settlement of the wholesale transactions executed by the trading room, debt accounting, and procedures related to withholding tax on the debt interest. The department is also responsible for the issuance and amortization of savings certificates and the debt service of other retail instruments. The operations department is in charge of the post office, which acts as an agent for the selling and redemption of savings certificates. It includes three operational units, a documentation and settlements unit, a debt accounting and budgeting unit, and a retail debt unit.

Four other units report directly to the board of directors:

- the financial control unit, which is responsible for all aspects related to risk and performance evaluation, internal control, procedures definition, and internal auditing;
- the research and statistics unit, which produces economic analysis, definition of scenarios, and external reporting;
- the IT systems unit; and
- the administration unit, which is in charge of all internal matters, including personnel, acquisitions, and on-site premises.

A markets committee meets weekly to analyze market developments, treasury forecasts, and the position of the debt portfolio against the benchmark and define guidelines for the activity during the week. The committee includes the directors and heads of the debt department, operations department, financial control unit, research and statistics unit, trading room, and markets unit.

There has been a strong concern with transparency since the IGCP began to operate in 1997. Key functions are now covered by written internal procedures, which include delegation of powers and the role of each unit inside the organizational structure.

A detailed quarterly report is submitted to the minister of finance, which describes all the transactions executed during the period and presents the figures for cost and risk of the debt portfolio relative to the benchmark. A report describing the activities carried out throughout the year and presenting the financial accounts of the debt is published annually.

To allow the IGCP to hire and retain qualified staff, some aspects were legally provided for, including a high degree of administrative and financial autonomy within an annual budget approved by the minister of finance and the possibility of hiring personnel under the general labor law, that is, not as civil servants. The guidelines for personnel compensation—approved by the minister of finance—are based on the need to maintain competence in competition with the private banking sector. Budgeting was also adequate in providing the financial resources necessary to acquire and update the information systems.

Auditing

An audit committee is responsible for following up and controlling the financial management of the IGCP as well as supervising its accounting procedures. The audit committee is composed of a chairman nominated by the inspectorate-general of finances and two permanent members (one being an official chartered accountant) appointed by the minister of finance.

The audit court (public sector audit body) is responsible for overseeing the activity of the IGCP, covering the financial accounts of the debt and the compliance with the guidelines and limits established by parliament and the government. This audit has been recently extended to the internal procedures and to the quarterly report presented to the minister of finance.

Risk Management Framework

Main risk variables

Since the inception of the IGCP, a significant effort was made to formulate and, whenever possible, quantify the types of risk relevant to public debt management.[4]

The main priority for the IGCP is to guarantee the fulfillment of Portugal's yearly borrowing requirements. To minimize the risk of not being able to meet this requirement, the focus has been on two key areas—first, the development of an efficient market for the public debt and, second, smoothing the redemption profile of the debt portfolio.

Consequently, a high priority was given to the minimization of refinancing risk[5] in spite of the comfort derived from the depth and liquidity of the euro capital market. The constraints imposed at this level are increasingly important, given the market's constant demand for liquid bonds, basically meaning large outstanding volumes. The reconciliation between these two conflicting requirements has been partially achieved by investing both on the efficiency of the primary and secondary markets (basically trying to compensate lack of size with extra efficiency) and on the set-up of other methods of managing the redemption profile (besides issuance), namely buy-back programs. Subject to that, the debt manager has the overall objective to minimize the long-term cost of debt without incurring any excessive risks. In this context, the IGCP assessed the major risk for a public debt manager as being the extent to which the volatility of financial variables affects the budgets' volatility (through changes in debt-servicing costs), thus reducing the range of maneuvering of the fiscal policymaker. Therefore, in management of the debt, risk is more accurately measured on a cash-flow basis, in contrast to a value-at-risk basis commonly used by asset managers. As a result and like several other public debt managers, the IGCP is working on the development and implementation of an integrated budget-at-risk (BaR) indicator for the debt portfolio.

Until the process to implement the BaR model is finished and tested, cash-flow risk is measured through a combination of indicators, namely duration, refixing profile,[6] and currency exposure. Duration works as a proxy for the degree of cash-flow cost immunization to interest rate movements and has the advantage of being a standard market measure. To give a more comprehensive picture of total interest rate risk, the duration indicator is complemented with the refixing profile. Since 1999 and the introduction of the euro, the foreign exchange risk, measured as the percentage of the portfolio denomi-

nated in foreign currency, has been significantly reduced, so that now it is almost negligible.

In a pure liability management framework,[7] only the use of derivatives causes credit risk. Derivatives are used when the desired portfolio structure is impossible to obtain, for whatever reason, through funding transactions. The IGCP measures this type of risk with an adapted version of the Bank of Internal Settlement (BIS) model,[8] and controls it through tight procedures for counter-party approval, including credit scoring, limits attribution, and International Swap Dealers Association (ISDA) agreement negotiation. The use of collateral as a means of partially covering credit risk has been approved by the minister of finance and was implemented during 2002.

Finally, the IGCP incurs operational risk in its debt management activities. This last type of risk is not measured explicitly, but underlies several policy measures. It was first addressed when the IGCP was created, leading to the choice of an organizational structure based on the financial industry standard of front, middle, and back offices with clearly segregated functions and responsibilities. The operational risk has since been a focus of attention by means of three main initiatives: a significant investment in IT (e.g., the purchase of a management information system), followed by the development of a manual of internal operating procedures, and finally investment in qualified and experienced human resources. In the future, these measures will be complemented with internal auditing, besides the external auditing that is already done by the audit court.

Management guidelines and benchmark portfolio

The debt portfolio management mandate given by the minister of finance to the IGCP was further formalized in 1998 with the approval of management guidelines and a reference portfolio in the form of a benchmark.

The management guidelines aim to describe the main types of risks associated with the debt portfolio, specify whether they are measured on an absolute (e.g., refinancing and credit risk) or a relative[9] basis (cash-flow risk), and, where appropriate, impose limits on the risk variables. The maximum divergence that the debt portfolio can show relative to the benchmark for the relevant risk variables (i.e., the maximum level of additional risk the debt manager can take) is also established in the guidelines.

The main purpose behind the adoption of a benchmark by the IGCP was to have a measurable reference of the long-term target portfolio structure, based on the conviction that this type of guidance would improve consistency between day-to-day debt management decisions and long-term goals. Furthermore, the fact that the IGCP was created as an independent entity raised the need for a tool that allowed an objective evaluation of management results (accountability). This influenced the decision to adopt the benchmark as well for performance measurement purposes.

No standard exists for how to establish and follow a benchmark for public debt management. The IGCP's approach is to create a management instrument, which incorporates the governments' preference concerning the trade-off between short- and long-term risks and costs. The benchmark is therefore deemed to incorporate the long-term objectives of the portfolio owner—that is, the minister of finance, acting on behalf of the tax payers in terms of risk profile and expected level of cost—embodied in a financing strategy and the resulting portfolio structure.

The determination of this benchmark portfolio was based on a mixed simulation-optimization model, in which the key decision variables were cash-flow cost and risk, with a restriction to address explicitly refinancing risk (other risk components were analyzed for every possible solution, but no limits were imposed on them in the model). A short list was then made of the model's solutions, not only in terms of efficiency, but also in terms of robustness to the model's main assumptions (macroeconomic and interest rate scenarios).[10] The final choice of a solution among the subset of efficient and robust possibilities was determined by the conjunction of three factors:

- The trade-off between cash-flow risk and costs: The shape of the efficient frontier given by the model showed a clear reduction in cash-flow risk for portfolio durations of up to 2–2.5 years, justifying the increase in expected cost. For durations

longer than 3.5–4 years, the marginal decrease in cash-flow risk was low, compared with the expected increase in cost. This analysis led to the choice of a first subgroup of possible solutions.
- Comparison of the resulting risk figures (especially interest rate risk) with the equivalent values for other euro-area sovereigns: Consideration of the relevant framework in which fiscal policy operates in Portugal, namely the existence of the stability pact and of a single monetary policy, led to the conviction that the Portuguese debt portfolio should not take on excessive *relative* interest rate risks when compared to the other sovereigns in the euro area. A survey done at that time on the durations of the public debt portfolios in other countries showed durations varying between three and five years. Based on this, it was then decided that the benchmark portfolio should have an expected duration close to the three-to-four years range.
- Finally, the financing strategy associated with each possible solution was analyzed, because the funding strategy associated with the benchmark portfolio had to be a feasible strategy for a euro-area sovereign issuer.

These factors ended up determining the choice of the portfolio that should be taken as a benchmark for the debt management at the IGCP and associated financing strategy.

Formally, the management guidelines approved by the minister of finance are divided into five sections, containing

- a list of relevant definitions (of scope and risk/cost variables),
- the set of authorized instruments and transactions,
- limits for the key risk variables (namely refinancing profile, modified duration, refixing profile, and currency exposure) and reporting requirements (timing and content),
- composition and dynamics of the benchmark portfolio, and
- credit risk.

Of these, the first three were published. The theoretical model behind the definition of the benchmark was also published in the IGCP's *Annual Report 1999*, even though the approved benchmark portfolio is not publicly disclosed (neither are the credit risk guidelines).

To use the benchmark as a fair basis for performance measurement, conditions that allow a separation of funding and market development decisions from portfolio management decisions must be in place. For Portugal, this possibility came about in 1999, with the first stage of the EMU. Since then, the euro capital market became the relevant "domestic" market, in which Portugal is a sufficiently small player for its derivatives transactions to have no major impact and subject to no other interpretation from market participants than pure portfolio management decisions.

In this type of framework, debt management decisions performed through the combination of financing and derivative transactions aim at a certain relative positioning versus this benchmark, in terms of both interest rate and foreign exchange risk, expected by the debt managers to outperform the benchmark. However, when the benchmark model was first developed and analyzed, it was done with a strong emphasis on the strategic objectives, meaning that the main purpose of that reference portfolio was to improve the consistency between the day-to-day management decisions and the long-term portfolio goals. For reasons of accountability, the IGCP decided to also propose its use for evaluation purposes, and this led naturally to the expectation of outperformance. However, there is no formal or informal policy statement (from either the minister of finance or the IGCP) transforming that expectation into a debt management objective, as such.

The benchmarking process in the IGCP had an experimental year in 1999 and has since been in place formally. Even though the overall assessment of its usefulness is positive, it has to be said that it is, in a liability management context, a less straightforward process than asset management, for several reasons. First, not only is it very difficult to quantify all the restrictions and objectives of a sovereign debt manager, but also these change in time, which leads to either the nonduplicability of the benchmark (i.e. the possibility to replicate the benchmark, making it unfair as a performance measurement tool) or to the need to make frequent changes in the benchmark

itself, a situation that goes against the desired nature of such a tool.

Another specific problem is that, even in a small player–big market situation like Portugal's in the euro market, the funding policy adopted by the IGCP has an influence on the credit spreads of Portuguese government bonds, which, however, is very difficult to quantify. This circumstance makes it even harder to estimate the cost levels associated with different funding policies (e.g., the cost of the benchmark-simulated financing strategy), turning the operational maintenance of that reference portfolio into a relatively complex exercise.

The IGCP is continuously improving the model for determining the benchmark portfolio and the methodology for its implementation. However, the project is still in an early phase, and the benchmark has therefore not been made public. In addition, the disclosure of the benchmark may be negative for the debt manager, because it may allow the market to anticipate its position. This problem could occur when the debt manager is asking for quotes on derivatives, such as interest rate swaps. This is a risk that should be analyzed carefully, even in the context of the large euro market. This question will be reassessed during the next revision of the guidelines (including the benchmark), which is scheduled for the end of 2002.

Finally, a performance benchmark in sovereign liability management should always be taken with a high degree of pragmatism and discernment by both the portfolio manager and the portfolio owner (in this case, the government).

Management information systems

At the end of 1999, the IGCP bought a standard treasury system[11] to support its debt management transactions. The choice of a user-friendly front, middle, and back office–integrated system[12] was made not only to mitigate operational risk, but also because of the conviction that, by increasing the use and share of information across the IGCP, it would lead to better data quality. Having one robust database of all debt transactions was one of the selection process's main priorities. The system was initially developed and designed for corporations, thus it had a strong cash-flow focus with a good fit to the risk management policy at the IGCP.

Moreover, a system was developed to handle retail debt transactions, which are then registered monthly in the new treasury system only in aggregate form for position-keeping, accounting, and reporting purposes.

Operational procedures manual

The implementation of these two systems had a considerable impact on the internal processes at the IGCP, increasing the need for the development of a written manual of operating procedures, including the new tools for operational control. This is an ambitious project, which started in 2001 with aims not only to optimize the internal processing circuits at the IGCP, but also and in that process, to develop a new culture regarding operational risk matters and associated control procedures (including internal auditing).

Debt Management Strategy and Government Securities Markets

Debt management strategy

Portuguese debt management follows a market-oriented funding strategy. It acknowledges the importance of issuing marketable instruments at market prices and building up a government yield curve with liquid bonds along different maturities. The new euro environment did not change this target. However, this goal now exists in a different environment. The former role of developing a benchmark yield curve to support the development of the domestic capital market disappeared. Instead, the new competitive environment in the euro area has been driving the funding strategy. A much larger domestic market, where the 12 euro countries compete, replaced the protected Portuguese escudo market. As a consequence, the market participants require higher liquidity and more efficient markets.

Liquidity became, in fact, one of the most important factors behind the spreads displayed by sovereign debt in the euro area. An outstanding amount of no less than 5 billion is commonly accepted as a first cri-

terion of liquidity. Therefore, the target size for Portuguese treasury bonds was increased to this new threshold.[13] Because of the relatively low level of the Portuguese gross annual borrowing needs, a gradual approach to achieving this goal has been followed. Since 1999, every year, priority is given, first, to the introduction of a new 10-year issue and, second, to a new 5-year issue. These two maturities, backed by an efficient derivatives market, reflect the market's preference. In support of this strategy, most of the funding through marketable instruments has been channeled to the euro-denominated treasury bond market. To accelerate this strategy, since 2001, the IGCP has also been relying on an active buyback program aimed at refinancing old issues (with small outstanding sizes and coupons not in line with current market yields) with on-the-run issues.

Feeding liquidity into the OTs market[14] reduced the variety of instruments used to standard and "plain-vanilla" fixed-rate bonds. The issuance of floating-rate bonds has been suspended, and index-linked securities have been ruled out so far. Moreover, in the meantime, the access to the Eurobond market, which was regular before 1999, has been excluded. A global medium-term notes program, in place since 1994, now plays the role of a safety-net funding alternative, with no new issue placed after September 1999.

Although not always cost-efficient in a short-term perspective, the priority given to the issuance of medium- and long-term bonds, putting aside "opportunistic" funding alternatives, is conceived as a medium-term strategy to reduce country vulnerability. Simultaneously, priority has been given to the development of efficient primary and secondary treasury debt markets, making use of advanced technical infrastructures. Foreign and domestic financial intermediaries and final investors were all granted equal access to these markets. This strategy is being rewarded by the increasingly widespread geographic distribution of the OT in the euro area and by its dispersion between buy-and-hold investors and active traders.

Government securities issuance and primary market structure

Credibility is a decisive feature whenever a market-driven funding strategy is followed. Transparency and predictability are, therefore, important pillars of Portuguese debt management.

The strategic guidelines are regularly explained to market participants, financial intermediaries, and, in particular, institutional investors.

At the beginning of the year, the components of the annual funding program are publicly announced, with particular emphasis on the issuance of medium- and long-term tradable debt securities. The market is informed of the estimate of the annual gross borrowing requirements and the amount to be funded through the issuance of Portuguese treasury bonds (OTs). The amounts to be placed, the maturity and final size of the new lines, the mechanisms for placing the OT (syndication and auction), and the financial intermediaries to be involved are also announced. A more precise calendar is published quarterly. The auctions have been kept fixed at the second Wednesday of each month, whenever there is room for such a placement.

About 75–80 percent of the gross borrowing requirements are funded through the placement of OTs.[15] Short-term market instruments and nontradable debt (savings certificates), issued on demand from private investors, account for the remaining 20 percent. The issuance of ECP is a backup alternative supporting the implementation of the treasury bond program.

For liquidity reasons, the initial size of a new treasury bond line corresponds to about 40 percent of the targeted final amount. Therefore, the IGCP is using syndication when launching a new OT line. This option aims to achieve better control of the issue price and, at the same time, further diversify the investors' base. The preference given to the placement of the initial tranche through syndication is due to the belief that it is the most effective way to simultaneously achieve significant size (more than 10 times the indicative amount of auctions held in 1998) and efficient and controlled pricing. Moreover, it helps to achieve a wide and diversified investors' distribution, particularly within the euro area, and increases the visibility of the issuer's name and its debt instruments.

Furthermore, a syndicated structure makes it possible to target specific groups of investors and countries. The IGCP has been closely monitoring the book-building process in all syndicated issues, demanding the investors' identity disclosure from the underwriters. New syndicated structures have been developed, giving increasing importance to the book-building process. More recently, the pot system was studied and has been used. In the pot system, all orders are centralized and collected to a single order book shared by the joint lead banks in the syndicate, in contrast to traditional syndication, in which the joint lead banks are managing separate order books. This gives the IGCP possibility of allocating the distribution after certain desired targets for the investor base are reached. The fees to the banks are set in advance and are not affected by the final distribution.

Only the primary dealers (13 banks) can be invited to be underwriters of the syndicated issues. This is a privilege that not only rewards their commitment to the OT market, but also recognizes that they are the financial intermediaries who know best the OT base of investors.

After the initial OT tranche is issued through syndication, the amount is increased through auctions.[16] Multiple-price electronic auctions are normally conducted once a month (but not every month). In 2000, the technical support for the auctions was radically changed. The fax system previously used for bidding was replaced by an electronic system, the Bloomberg Auction System . This system allows the auction participants to introduce and update bids until the cutoff time (strictly controlled) and have faster access to auction results, thus incurring fewer risks. The possibility of monitoring the reception of bids in real time enables the issuer to reduce the time needed for a decision on the allotment of each auction. Currently, the average time from the bid cutoff time to the release of the auction results to the participants is less than five minutes.[17]

The settlement of primary market transactions is carried out through efficient and internationally recognized central securities depository (Euroclear and Clearstream), making the fulfillment of standard settlement cycles possible for both domestic and foreign investors.

Secondary market for government securities

The development of an efficient primary market for treasury bonds has to be supported by an efficient secondary market. In 1999, a special market for public debt was created, the MEDIP (the Portuguese acronym for "special market for public debt"), which was designed to be a regulated market under the investment services directive. To ensure an efficient and competitive environment, an electronic trading platform (MTS-Portugal) was chosen, based on the MTS platform.[18] After the creation of MEDIP, three segments coexist in the secondary market:

- the exchange market, whose trading structure is mainly directed at the retail segment and the trading of small lots (this segment is traded in the Euronext Lisbon), and participants are those who have access to this market;
- the over-the-counter market, which should offer maximum flexibility in terms of trading and registration of transactions; and
- MEDIP, which aims to centralize wholesale trading by offering the most efficient conditions for this type of transaction where the most important players are the primary dealers.

The creation of MEDIP and the adoption of electronic trading were decisions that fostered financial integration while preserving the national "location" of the wholesale treasury debt market. The setting-up of MEDIP–MTS-Portugal therefore marked an important and decisive step in the modernization of the Portuguese government debt market, a step promoting its efficient integration into the euro financial market and the vast global market. This step, taken by the issuer and the primary dealers together, was the culminating point of a strategy that took almost three years to unfold. This ongoing dialogue, acknowledging the critical role of the primary dealers in developing the secondary market, was an outstanding feature of this process, which led to the selection of the best electronic trading platform to be used.

As a regulated market, MEDIP's access and listing conditions, its governing rules, and its code of conduct are nondiscriminatory and subject to the approval of the Portuguese Securities Market Commission. This market aims at wholesale proprietary trading among specialists. It uses a blind trading platform based on the electronic platform MTS-Telemático, managed by MTS-Portugal (which is a joint-stock company incorporated under Portuguese

law and supervised by the Portuguese Securities Market Commission).[19]

The MEDIP market is driven by market-making obligations, and it settles with Euroclear/Clearstream and has access to repo trading facilities in EuroMTS/MTS-Italy. Real-time prices are disclosed to nonparticipants on the Reuters wire, and a daily market bulletin is published via the Internet. The market makers have the obligation to quote firm bid and ask prices for a set of liquid securities according to maximum spreads—ranging between 5 and 10 basis points, depending of type of security and maturity—and minimum lot sizes. The market dealers can only take prices from market makers. The primary dealers must participate as market makers, and other participants can act either as market makers or market dealers. Prices formed on MEDIP are used as a reference for mark-to-market purposes.

The primary dealers' strategic role

Portuguese debt management relies on the critical role of the primary dealers. The primary dealer system was introduced in Portugal in 1993, but only in 1998 did the role of the primary dealers gain a new strategic dimension. By then, new selection rules had been defined to limit the participation of each major domestic banking group to only one institution, thus inducing the development of critical mass on domestic operators. Also in 1998, this status was first granted to nonresident banks. After 1999, the primary dealers were defined as the principal channel for distributing Portuguese debt, and a network for the regular distribution of debt within the euro area was created.

Primary dealer status is granted for periods coinciding with calendar years and may be renewed annually, depending on the fulfillment of several duties. To be granted primary dealer status, a bank has to fulfill a certain group of obligations vis-à-vis the market and the issuer,[20] namely minimum quotas in the primary and secondary markets have to be attained. Besides being invited to be underwriters of syndicated issues, primary dealers are also granted exclusive access to noncompetitive auctions.[21] The increasingly important direct contact between the issuer and final investors is also conducted in cooperation with the primary dealers.

Counting on a credible and relatively stable group of primary dealers, with a recognized distribution capability (both within the euro area and worldwide) and committed in the long run to the development of the Portuguese debt market, the IGCP established an ongoing partnership for the continuous distribution of the Portuguese debt and for creating a liquid and efficient wholesale secondary market.

Notes

1. The case study was prepared by Rita Granger, Lucia Leitao, and Vasco Pereira from the Instituto de Gestão do Credito Publico ([IGCP], Portuguese Government Debt Agency).

2. Above a certain threshold, set yearly.

3. The decree-law that created the IGCP recognized the importance of further integration of treasury management and debt management. Formal integration is under consideration.

4. For that purpose, all the learning processes associated with the modeling of a benchmark portfolio made a critical contribution, making that project, as such, a worthwhile investment.

5. For instance, such risk involves not being able to roll over the maturing debt close to previous market prices or, in the extreme, at any price.

6. The refixing profile indicates, in nominal terms, the percentage of the portfolio that will either be refixed or have to be refinanced in the future, aggregated in yearly time buckets. It aims to indicate the sensitivity of cash-flow cost to future changes in interest rates.

7. Not considering the cash management function or the "credit" component of settlement risk.

8. In this model, the credit risk is assessed by calculating the current market value of the contract and then adding a factor to reflect the potential future exposure over the remaining life of the contract.

9. Measured as a deviation from the benchmark portfolio equivalent figures.

10. Given the context in which Portuguese debt management is performed, this reference portfolio was built so as not to have any net foreign exchange risk.

11. Finance Kit by Trema

12. This was done at the loss of a more specialized risk management software.

13. The a5 billion standard corresponds to almost twice the average size of the treasury bond lines issued before 1999.

14. Since 1999, the final size of each new OT line has on average been twice that of those issued up to that date.

15. The features of the OTs have been kept stable, and the conventions used are in line with the standards of the euro debt market.

16. The 1999 auctions were already three times larger than the previous ones; in 2000, the average size increased fivefold,

and when compared with 1998 and between 1998 and 2001, the increase was sixfold.

17. Portuguese OT auctions include a competitive phase (in which participation is open to all primary dealers and other auction participants) as well as a noncompetitive phase. Before every quarter, the IGCP releases a calendar of the auctions, although the indicative amount of the auctions is confirmed only slightly before it takes place. A predefined day of the month tends to be used. Each institution can make up to five bids, whose total value may never exceed the amount announced for the competitive phase of the auction. Participating institutions are informed of the bids that were accepted and of the overall results immediately after the close of the auction (on average, two to three minutes after the cutoff time). The overall results of the auction are also immediately announced to all market participants via the IGCP pages in Reuters (IGCP04) and Bloomberg (IGCP). The subscription for the noncompetitive phase of the auction is made at the highest yield accepted in the competitive phase. The maximum amount each primary dealer can subscribe in the noncompetitive phase corresponds to the percentage of its participation in the competitive phase of the previous three bond auctions, considering only the amount placed through primary dealers.

18. The platform became active in July 2000.

19. Shareholders in MTS-Portugal are the IGCP, 15 percent; MTS S.p.A., 15 percent; and primary dealers, 70 percent.

20. Duties of primary dealers:

- participate actively in bond auctions by bidding and subscribing a share no less than 2 percent of the amount placed at the competitive phase of the auctions;
- participate actively on the secondary market for Portuguese government debt securities, ensuring the liquidity of these instruments;
- participate in the wholesale electronic market (MEDIP–MTS-Portugal) as market maker, maintaining a share not lower than 2 percent of this market's turnover in the previous two years;
- participate as shareholder in the managing company of MEDIP–MTS-Portugal; and
- operate as privileged consultant to the issuer in the monitoring of financial markets.

Rights of the primary dealers:

- participation in the competitive phase of the bond auctions and exclusive access to the noncompetitive phase;
- preference in the formation of syndicates;
- access to the facilities created by the IGCP to support the market, namely the "last resort" repo window facility;
- preferential counterpart in the active management of the public debt; and
- privileged hearing in matters of common interest.

21. Another group of banks can also have access to the auctions—the other market participants—but they are not allowed to participate in the noncompetitive auctions.

14

Slovenia[1]

After attaining independence in 1991 and throughout the first half of the 1990s, efforts were devoted to the reestablishment of Slovenia's access to international financial markets, which involved Slovenia's assumption of a share in the external debt of the former Yugoslavia. It also involved a smooth execution of the process of rehabilitating the banking system and restructuring various enterprises. Given the fact that the budget remained in surplus until 1997, debt management operations focused on establishing access for borrowing in different financial markets. Borrowing operations started in the domestic market through short-term borrowing to manage liquidity, continued in 1996 with the first Eurobond issue in the euro market, and, in 1997, with issuance of inflation-indexed bonds and loans in the domestic market.

When relatively small budget deficits emerged, the main objective was to develop a domestic market for debt, primarily for bonds, to finance the budget and any debt obligations incurred before 1996 in the succession process to the former Socialist Federal Republic of Yugoslavia and cover programs of real and banking sector rehabilitation.

Developing the domestic market for debt has become a priority to ensure timely financing in domestic currency and reduce macroeconomic risk associated with financing the deficit with external debt. This task has been eased recently by the lifting of capital controls and increase of foreign direct investment. A growing market capacity for government borrowing has just recently allowed undertaking of active debt management operations to reduce the overall cost of the portfolio. Efforts have also been devoted to enhancing the transparency and tradability of instruments, with the aim of deepening and enhancing liquidity of the secondary market. Similarly, building up a yield curve to price other instruments in the market has also been a priority.

Developing a Sound Governance and Institutional Framework

Objective

The basic principle underlying debt management activities is harmonization of the goals of (a) minimizing borrowing costs over the long term with a maturity structure that ensures a sustainable level of risk in refinancing the debt and (b) a currency and interest rate structure that minimizes the exposure to exchange rate, interest rate, and other risks.

In 1998, for the first time, an annual program of financing the central government budget (financing program) was adopted, stating the main objectives—both strategic and operational—and targets for debt management. These main guidelines were supported by the Public Finance Act, which was enacted in October 1999.

Strategic objectives include, next to provision of sufficient and timely financing of the budget, cost minimization; maximum reliance on financing in the domestic market, pending the crowding out or distorted effects on the market; broadening both the domestic and the foreign investors' base; minimizing interest rate risk; minimizing foreign currency risk through continued increase of euros in the currency structure of foreign debt; and minimizing the risk of inflation in the debt in domestic currency by pursuing interest rate nominalism.

Operational objectives include determination of the short-term versus long-term financing mix consistent with a view on the term structure of the portfolio; determination of the external/foreign currency borrowing mix in total borrowing consistent with the strategy of prioritizing the domestic market; determination of the structure of the instruments, including the shares of fixed-rate, variable-rate, and foreign currency–indexed debt consistent with the strategy toward nominalism and cost and risk considerations.

Scope

Debt management encompasses all direct financial obligations of the central government. The annual financing program includes the amount to finance, which is determined by the annual budget and is the sum of the deficit and debt repayment obligations in the given fiscal year. It sets the amounts for both domestic and foreign currency borrowings, which are coordinated within the program. The choice of market is given in the form of minimal domestic and maximum foreign borrowing amounts and as maximum short-term and minimal long-term financing.

The public debt management department (PDMD) within the ministry of finance (MoF) also exercises central administrative and control functions over debt of public sector entities, whose debt represents contingent liabilities of the central government and issuance of government guarantees.

Coordination with monetary and fiscal policies

There is a clear legal, regulatory, and actual separation of debt management and monetary policy objectives and accountabilities. The Bank of Slovenia (BOS), the central bank, is an independent institution and not a part of the executive government. The government is legally banned from borrowing from the BOS, which, however, manages the foreign currency reserves and is the government's paying agent for foreign currency payments, the depositary for foreign currency cash deposits, and, together with commercial banks, a depositary for domestic currency deposits.

On completion of the proposal of the annual financing program, it is discussed within the scope of fiscal policy documents and also shown to the BOS for (nonbinding) commentary and suggestions. The coordination takes place within the framework of a medium-term fiscal scenario.

The MoF and the BOS also discuss general liquidity conditions in the economy at the time of preparation of the annual financing program. Debt managers share information on the government's current and future financing requirements as well as their dynamics during the year. The MoF informs the BOS of borrowing intentions in advance, whereupon the BoS provides information on market conditions.

There are regular meetings of MoF and central bank officials to discuss, without formal arrangements, the technical scope of their respective policies' execution.

According to a formal agreement between the MoF and the BOS, the former provides two types of monthly forecasts. The first, for three months in advance, consists of day-by-day cash flows of all revenues and expenditures for all items to be received or paid by the government. The second forecast provides the same information one month in advance, but the information is updated and thus more accurate. The three-month forecast provides an indication of future developments in the government's account movements, and the second forecast contains updated and reviewed information.

Within the MoF, a committee on liquidity meets weekly, monitoring monthly liquidity situations and determining necessary activity versus financing and versus budget expenditure management. Budget, tax and customs, debt management, and liquidity management departments are permanent members of the committee. The MoF notifies the central bank about budget liquidity projections and monthly changes, and the BOS provides the MoF with necessary information on market liquidity conditions.

Transparency and accountability

The financing program's objectives and accomplishments are regularly announced. The format of reports contains a separation of objectives and, for every objective where possible, statements of development. Documents are available to the financial community, as well as to the general public. The objectives and instruments of the debt management policy are made public through the annual financing program and other policy documents, including the macroeconomic and fiscal scenarios. These documents are permanently available on the MoF's web site (http://www.sigov.si/mf/angl/apredmf1.html) and other government web sites. The public finance bulletin is also permanently available on the MoF web site and is updated monthly. It includes data on general and central government finance accounts, government debt, and outstanding guarantees.

The annual report on debt management is made public once the government has accepted it. The report includes information pertaining to the execution of strategic objectives of debt management; a description of the debt instruments issued and costs with a cost analysis; an analysis of developments of the central government debt portfolio and dynamics; information on general government and public debt and debt with central government guarantees; data on debt stock, flows, and instruments; and a brief international comparison of debt. In the form of a public finance bulletin, the MoF also publishes monthly information on the structure of the debt portfolio.

Slovenia has a practice of enacting budgets for the current year and the following year and releasing a midterm fiscal strategy paper to parliament and the general public. The amount of debt and debt-servicing projections are regular parts of policy papers. Monthly, the BOS reports a service schedule for total external debt.

The domestic market provides transparency of operations through a choice of standardized instruments, which are offered in a calendar of issuance of bonds and bills supported by publicly accessible auction results. Auction results are displayed on the MoF web site. Issues are quoted on the Ljubljana Stock Exchange. Quotes on treasury bills that are traded over the counter (OTC) are available through market makers. Further efforts to reduce the uncertainty of players in the domestic market are being made through contacts with all the important investors in the domestic financial market. To stabilize and deepen the market for government securities, transparency in domestic issuance is a strategic objective.

The MoF is striving to maintain the awareness of the international investment community by making available the maximum rating information on bonds and through contacts with the investment community within the scope of its resources. Transparency, accountability, and reliability in debt issues, as well as market approach, have been the prime policy objectives of Slovenia since the start of the dissolution of the former Socialist Federal Republic of Yugoslavia.

The tax treatment of public securities is clearly disclosed in the prospectus of each of the securities, which, besides being available to investors, are being publicly disseminated.

Debt management activities are audited annually by the court of accounts, an independent auditing institution that audits the government and public sector entities. Audit reviews of financing are made public through parliamentary procedure as part of the regular budget audit. Audit of the budget is legally required for parliament to approve the annual government budget execution report.

Legal framework

The legal basis for government borrowing and issuance of guarantees is based on Article 149 of the

Slovenian Constitution, which states, "The state shall only be permitted to borrow monies or to guarantee credit on such conditions as are determined by law."

The framework for central government borrowing is determined by the Public Finance Act,[2] which sets out the basis for

- a definition of central government borrowing and liquidity borrowing,
- the method of determining the ceilings on its borrowing,
- the elements of debt management,
- the documents underlying the execution of borrowing transactions or programs, and
- The rules on borrowing by local governments, extrabudgetary funds, and public sector entities.

The annual Budget Execution Law displays nominal ceilings (quotas) for borrowing and issuance of guarantees by the central government and borrowing by public entities.

Once the annual Budget Execution Law is adopted, the government approves the annual financing program submitted by the MoF, in which major policy guidelines and borrowing strategy are stated. This includes objectives, operations, choice of instruments, dynamics, and market choices. If there is any serious digression from the anticipated market movements or other unexpected events, the program can be amended by the same procedure established for the financing program. In preparing the program, which includes the dynamics of borrowing, consideration is given to currency structure and domestic market capacity, where the goal is to fund the bulk of the borrowing requirement domestically and develop the domestic market to minimize macroeconomic risk and risk of funding. The financing program also aims toward monetary neutrality while optimizing currency risk.

The policy guidelines, included in annual financing programs, have evolved with time from being a document that identified only the type of instrument and dynamics of borrowing, to a more strategic document that states and blends policy goals and policy actions. This development is explained to a great extent by the fact that the existing legal framework governing debt management operations does not specify the debt management policy objectives. Therefore, the yearly borrowing program currently aims at filling the legal vacuum and avoiding undesirable trade-offs between cost and risks. However, given the time span of the financial program (one year), only consistent policy actions can ensure that the cost dimension gets preeminence over risk dimension and an appropriate mix is preserved.

Institutional framework and internal organization

According to the Public Finance Act, the MoF is exclusively responsible for the areas of borrowing and debt management for the central government.

For debt management, the organizational framework is determined within a government decree that states functions, responsibilities, departmental organization, and description of basic tasks for every central government employee. Within the MoF, there are three departments responsible for contracting or managing debt or both:

- The international department is responsible for borrowing from international financial institutions (such as the World Bank, European Investment Bank, and the European Bank for Reconstruction and Development). The importance of this source of financing is diminishing steadily and in 2002 represent about 1.5 percent of total financing.
- The liquidity management department is responsible for contracting and managing short-term domestic debt and cash management.
- The PDMD is responsible for executing the annual borrowing program and managing central government debt (long-term domestic and foreign debt). The PDMD also provides back office functions with record-keeping and payment instructions. Another task is to maintain debt statistics and provide long-term and short-term projections on debt service for budgetary and liquidity management uses. The PDMD prepares regular debt reports and reports on the execution of the borrowing program (financing program). Moreover, the PDMD and liquidity management department maintain MoF Internet information

on their respective portions of debt and debt instruments, and the PDMD maintains contacts and provides data in regular format to rating agencies. It also cooperates with these agencies and receives their reports. Finally, the PDMD is in charge of approving and monitoring all public sector borrowing and government guarantees entered into by the minister of finance.

The PDMD is organized into different units with distinct functions and accountabilities, as well as separate reporting lines. The front office is responsible for executing transactions in financial markets, including the management of auctions and other forms of borrowing, and all other funding operations. The back office handles the settlement of transactions and the maintenance of the financial records. A separate middle, or risk management, office has been established to undertake risk analysis and monitor and report on portfolio-related risks, as well as assess the performance of debt managers against strategic benchmarks, but it is not yet in operation. A statistics unit provides reporting service and necessary projections, including debt management–related, short-term liquidity projections and projections for budget preparation, and manages the debt database used by the back office for both settlement and maintenance of debt items records. The liquidity management department is organized into two units, the budget liquidity forecasting unit and the money market unit. The department executes issuance and repayment of treasury bills and other short-term instruments and keeps records on them.

Internally, the PDMD management is carried out along instrument lines in both the debt management (front office) and the transaction management unit (back office). The lines are domestic bonds, foreign bonds, domestic loans, foreign loans, and issuing of guarantees. Except for guarantees, where there is frequent cooperation with line ministries, cooperation operates in the department from front office to back office to statistics and analysis.

Coordination and information sharing between debt management departments and other departments within the MoF take place in various forms: in the formal and internal (committees) organization of the MoF and through common work, organized by

project, on establishing and upgrading information, budget execution, debt management, and accounting software systems. Connection with budget preparation follows the budget preparation schedule. Connection to general accounting is permanent and is based on a generic software application connecting accounting with budget execution and budget users. Also, the software provides a basis for monitoring the budget execution with respect to further budget planning.

Within the ministry, the PDMD and the liquidity management, budget execution, and taxation and customs departments of the MoF survey the short-term (monthly) liquidity situation every week and decide on precise liquidity management tactics. In monthly meetings, these departments analyze the three-month projections and possible developments and propose necessary action(s).

The current division and organization of work are based on the historical development and growth of the MoF. Despite the fact that borrowing functions are located in three units of the MoF, there is a reasonable degree of coordination among them and their mandates are fairly clear. Nevertheless, a drawback of the current institutional arrangement is the absence of a centralized decision-making authority, which to some extent encumbers the process of debt planning, the process of debt management, and implementation of the operations necessary for debt management.

Establishment of a separate debt management agency to take over all central government debt management is being contemplated, and the MoF is studying the suitability of setting up an independent agency or an office within the ministry to manage public debt with the following goals:

- centralization of borrowing and debt management operations;
- increase in responsibility for the execution of operations;
- establishment of a clear and measurable debt management goal, which would become the basis for the delegation of competencies and responsibilities;
- isolation of the debt management function from political and other institutions' interference;

- simplification of procedures for the provision of modern information technologies and human resources with specific knowledge necessary for a progressive stage of debt management and minimizing the operational risk; and increased flexibility of the agency to ensure a response to changes in the market and market participants.

There is no formal coordination with the BOS. The MoF has observer status with the BOS board. On the department (technical) level, both the debt and liquidity management functions hold regular working meetings with appropriate central bank officials—ideally, meetings are held monthly.

Information systems

In Slovenia, the MoF has since 1995 been developing a custom-made database for debt. At present, the base provides for a safe and reliable debt service and is an accurate tool for registering and managing debt items and a solid basis for statistics and organization of data for analysis. The initial building-up of the database has been cosponsored by the World Bank. Plans for upgrading the base—with cash-flow generation, a projections engine, and capabilities for portfolio simulation—are progressing relatively slowly, mainly because of funding constraints. The database will be fully integrated into the government's system of budget execution and accounting system.

Electronic data preservation is supported by storage of hard-copy legal and accounting documentation. The computer system is running a continuous backup procedure. CD storage of documents, as well as data, has been made possible and is in partial use. The system has been under scrutiny at every due diligence proceeding for issuance of international bonds. Operations of the back office are separate from those of the front office, and a fixed internal procedure is in place for document delivery on business items.

Staff

Within the framework of the general administration staff and salary policies and regulations, the MoF and the department are trying to alleviate the problem of low salary incentive mainly through the extra appeal of functional education available on-site for senior staff. In addition, there are a promotional value for a debt management professional, an active policy of and support to postgraduate education through a time-off allowance, and, in most cases, payment of tuition fees. The MoF and the department are also doing their best to provide case-specific education through domestic and international seminars, workshops, and similar events. In 2001, participation of the PDMD staff in off-site educational activities was 84 days, or about 30 percent above the average of the MoF, which is not inconsiderable when taking into account an ongoing technical training for the European Union (EU) accession process. We are also working toward development of professional responsibility in junior staff through a mentor system. Nevertheless, the turnover of trained staff, specifically the front office staff, presents a permanent operational and, above all, development deterrent.

Staff involved in debt management is subject to a general government employees' code of conduct, which includes conflict-of-interest rules. These are further detailed for MoF employees in internal rules on specific conditions applicable to activities of MoF employees. These detail the rules for management of employees' personal financial affairs. Within the department, an unwritten code of conduct applicable for contacts with financial organizations and media is practiced.

Assessment and Management of Cost and Risk

The bulk of central government debt in Slovenia is the result of the assumption of a share in the external debt of the former Yugoslavia, bank rehabilitation, and enterprise restructuring operations. Autonomous growth of debt as a result of indexation of the principal is the second most important factor underlying growth, followed by the exchange rate changes and the budget deficit financing, contributing the least to the growth of debt.

Concerning external debt, early recognition of sovereign succession obligations by the government allowed reestablishment of the country's access to international capital markets and the possibility of managing and reducing the risks embedded in the external debt portfolio. Reestablishing links with international financial markets was critical in ensuring a normal functioning of the economy (i.e., trade financing and access of the private sector to international credit).

External debt operations were targeted to restructure the assumed and nonmarketable, expensive debt by issuance of long-term securities (10 years) denominated in euros, the eventual domestic currency of Slovenia after joining the European Monetary Union. These operations were aimed primarily at reducing the refinancing risk of total debt profile (public and private sector debt) and the risk of a possible balance of payments crisis. They also aimed at setting a benchmark for Slovenian borrowers in international market(s).

On the internal side, most of the initially issued debt was bond issues linked to bank rehabilitation and enterprise restructuring. The government administratively issued inflation- and foreign currency–indexed bonds with a maturity schedule ranging from 5 to 22 years. This strategy, which reduced the refinancing risk and resort to foreign borrowing, took into account the evolving conditions of the small internal financial market.

Debt management strategies

Respecting the size of financing set by the annual budget, the basic principle underlying the debt management activities is harmonization of the goals of (a) minimizing borrowing costs over the long term with a maturity structure that ensures a sustainable level of risk of refinancing the debt and (b) a currency and interest rate structure that minimizes the exposure to exchange rate, interest rate, and other risks.

In deciding on annual financing programs, the MoF takes into account minimizing the rollover risk as well as the optimization of market risk, giving consideration to the desired foreign exchange neutrality of borrowing. In foreign borrowing, the MoF is striving to establish a high degree of market presence and a broadening of investor base, primarily through the Euromarket, which has the deepest knowledge of Slovenia as issuer and socioeconomic entity. At the

same time, with two-thirds of Slovenia's foreign trade in Europe, and with the euro becoming Slovenia's prospective currency, it is the most exchange risk–neutral market.

In deciding where to borrow, the main consideration has been to give priority to the domestic market without disrupting market conditions and crowding out the private sector. External borrowing has also been restricted, to the maximum possible degree, to the rollover of foreign debt and payments of interest in foreign currency.

The risks inherent in the government's debt structure are always being carefully monitored and evaluated. Organizational and legal steps are being taken, in line with the development of the Slovenian legal and economic system in the transition to the EU, to eliminate or hedge different risks. The MoF is continuously moving toward a degree of standardization of domestic issues that will provide the market with necessary supply. Currently, it is running a series of 3- and 5-year variable bonds in Slovenian tolars (where the inflation is the variable part of variable interest rate) and 10-year euro-denominated bonds, as well as 3-, 6-, and 12-month nominal fixed-rate treasury bills in a proportion agreed to by the annual financing program and under a fixed auction calendar, thus adding transparency and predictability to the supply. In 2002, the MoF started issuing 15-year euro-denominated bonds and 3-year tolar-denominated bonds with a nominal fixed rate to replace the present 3-year variable issue. In both the foreign and domestic markets, the MoF is using the reopening device when appropriate for benchmark or cost purposes or both.

Domestic financial capacity has been constrained by the limited depth of the financial market and, until recently, by capital controls (gradually lifted between1999 and January 1, 2002). Portfolio inflows were subject to prohibitive costs, which applied to long- and short-term securities without exception. Thus, capital controls limited foreign investors' participation in the government securities market. It is within these limits that operations were aimed at financing the borrowing requirement without resorting to a significant increase in external debt and monetization, which could have hampered the central bank's meeting its monetary targets (M1 until 1997, and then from thereon, M3). In 2002, the central bank began following a "two-pillar" approach to conducting monetary policy. The first pillar still emphasizes control of broad money and its components, and the second pillar includes various real and financial indicators, both domestic and external.

Nonmarket financing channels are being used for a smaller portion of the short-term borrowing; the legal arrangement allows the MoF to request public institutions to place their cash surpluses, at market rates at a given time, at government disposal through accepting promissory notes, rather than the general market. Borrowing from the BOS is not permitted.

The MoF prepares annual, quarterly, monthly, and weekly liquidity forecasts. Liquidity managers and debt managers form, with the budget execution and taxation department representatives, a permanent working body in the ministry, a committee on liquidity that monitors the constantly adjusted forecasts and decides on appropriate actions. In constant consultation with the IMF resident adviser, the MoF is improving its liquidity and budget management technologies and its revenues and expenditure forecasting.

The MoF policy is to provide a steady supply of long-term and, in proportion, short-term paper, but there is no requirement anywhere in financial, fiscal, or other regulations for buying or holding government paper.

The main risks in the debt portfolio

In the past, the share of external debt has grown slowly but constantly. This is primarily due to the fact that in the succession process, Slovenia assumed part of the debt of the former Yugoslavia, whose structure (in terms of currency, maturity, and interest rate) had no influence over debt expansion. However, the ratio also increased because of the limited size of the domestic financial market, which until 2002 did not offer the possibility of budget deficit financing and refinancing the repayment of principal in tolars in full by borrowing in the domestic financial market.

Within the structure of instruments, there has been a steady increase in the share of securities and a drop in the share of loans. The share of debt to foreign governments and international organizations is also declining, but debt to commercial banks and other creditors is rising. Both of these steady trends

derive from a change in the strategy and conditions of financing. These tend to result from the fact that, since 1996–97, Slovenia has been financing itself primarily in financial markets by use of market mechanisms and instruments.

The structure of the debt is predominantly long term. By the end of 2000, the long-term debt represented 95.5 percent (term-at-issue) and 91.7 percent (term-to-maturity) of total debt. The structure is showing a low exposure to refinancing risk, but domestic short-term debt is growing rapidly.

The main focus of attention is market risk. In particular, this means the reduction of volatility of debt service in domestic currency and reduction of the effect of indexation in debt stock dynamics. The aim and the policy have been to gradually shift the composition of the debt portfolio from inflation-indexed debt (by ceasing to issue such debt from 2000 onward) and foreign currency–indexed debt to nominal instruments. A gradual strategy involving introduction of fixed-rate debt instruments and shifting foreign currency debt to the currency with less volatility (the euro) has taken place.

Most of the risk in the internal portfolio is due to the predominance of debt instruments whose cost in domestic currency varies. The most risky instruments are those indexed to inflation. Because of the high volatility of inflation and its relatively high, single-digit level, they have substantially influenced debt increase.

In the structure of interest rates and types of instruments, there has been a clear trend, since 1997 in particular, toward a fall in the share of index-linked instruments, as well as growth in the share of instruments with a fixed interest rate. The currency structure reveals rapid growth in the share of the euro against a rapid fall in the share of the U.S. dollar. The trends revealed in movements in the structure of debt are primarily a consequence of implementation of the strategic orientations and goals in borrowing and debt management, and it is expected that they will continue in the future.

Risk analysis undertaken to develop the strategy

The MoF relies on a comprehensive definition of cost, which is the basis upon which risk is measured. Cost is measured as the present value of debt service (principal and interest) valued in domestic currency. Risk is measured by the difference between the present value of the baseline scenario and alternate present value scenarios based on possible different behavior of underlying variables affecting debt service.

The ministry relies on periodic assessment of risk based on the impact of changes of exogenous variables on the debt portfolio's structure and cost. The cost of instruments—with the exception of treasury bills, which are short-term fixed instruments—depends on the evolution of different price variables (inflation, interest rate, or exchange rate). Therefore, the analysis of past and future evolution of different prices and its impact on the debt portfolio structure and cost is important to assess the exposure of the portfolio. The MoF relies on its own forecast and on external forecasts of main price variables and interest rates.

Market risk and refinancing risk are periodically quantified. The elasticity of the cost of the portfolio with regard to changes in various variables is calculated and serves as an input in executing the annual borrowing strategy to reduce market risk. Similarly, various issuing strategies are evaluated against the desired maturity profile in both the domestic and international markets. Buybacks are also part of the operations executed to reduce market risk and achieve the desired maturity profile. These operations are discretional and can be executed throughout the year. Debt sustainability analysis is carried out, as well as assessment of the impact of external debt service on current account sustainability.

The evolution of the borrowing requirement and the maturity profile in a dynamic setting (taking into account redemption and new issuance strategies) is important for the assessment of medium-term cost, refinancing risk, and strategy for instrument issuance. Currently, the existing software does not allow for sophisticated statistical and simulation techniques. The analysis consists mainly of simple scenario analysis. The MoF is in the process of upgrading the database applications for assessing risk. Currently, it relies on simple models on spreadsheets.

Assessments of domestic market capacity and its evolution and of international market access are also a critical part in determining cost and risk of the financing program.

Operational risk is not assessed, but it is taken into account as part of the ongoing process of aiming to avoid errors or failures in the various stages of executing and recording transactions. Efforts to reduce operational risk are being done through legal unification of responsibilities in budget execution and regulation of procedures. Responsibility for debt management within the PDMD is separated into front and back offices, with distinct functions and accountabilities and separate reporting lines.

Benchmarks for domestic debt

Currently, there are no performance benchmarks. The MoF does not have an explicit benchmark portfolio with targets. However, long-term policy actions follow policy guidelines targeted toward achieving a portfolio composition that ensures low cost and limits risks. The annual financing program sets the actions in conformity with long-term goals, and the annual debt report discusses whether the result of policy actions was consistent.

Active debt management strategies

Buyback operations and execution of call options are part of MoF operations to reduce debt-service cost. Until 2002, buyback operations have been conducted mainly in international markets, because the relatively small actions of the MoF did not disturb market conditions there. In the domestic market, the main instrument has been the execution of call options, taking into account the overall borrowing capacity of the MoF. Buybacks were not executed in the domestic market, given its relatively modest stage of development. The law strictly regulates active debt management operations. There are criteria for their execution, which include evidencing of cost savings or improvements in the debt portfolio structure without increases in the amount of debt outstanding.

Contingent liabilities

Explicit contingent liabilities are monitored in the same framework as the central debt. They can be incurred only on the basis of law; the entities that would incur them (e.g., borrowing with government guarantee) are monitored throughout the process by the MoF.

The guarantees that are forecasted to be executed (because of liquidation, bankruptcy, and so forth of beneficiaries) are a matter of definite budgetary provisioning, and a set of recovery procedures is in place. Consistent use of short-term rollover projections prevents occurrence of large unpaid liabilities at any point in the system.

Development of the market for private sector debt

The MoF is aware of the importance of the government securities and a benchmark yield curve as the basic reference for pricing private sector debt. In the international market, continued effort is placed on expanding the investor base and keeping a representative yield curve for enhancing the access of domestic investors to those markets, with a clear price reference available for pricing of their transactions. In the domestic market, to build a domestic yield curve, the target has been shifting from issuance of indexed debt to fixed-rate instruments. The process has been gradual. It consisted first of introducing variable instruments as an intermediate step toward fixed-rate instruments, standardizing maturities, and introducing short-term fixed-rate instruments. The next step consists of issuing long-term fixed-rate instruments and extending their maturities. A 10-year euro-denominated bond is issued in the domestic market and will be followed by a 15-year, euro-denominated bond, which helps to price other long-term instruments.

Developing the Markets for Government Securities

Slovenia's government securities market is framed on the background of a hyperinflationary environment inherited from the former Yugoslavia and a strong policy stance until 1997, where the budget was either balanced or in surplus. As a consequence of the hyperinflation scenario inherited from the former Yugoslavia, all financial contracts in the economy were indexed to inflation, the index expressed as the basic interest rate (the average of the last three months of inflation and, later, the last 12 months) calculated by the BOS. Only in 1998 did treasury bills with maturities of 6 and 12 months appear as the first nominal instruments denominated in domestic currency. Issuance of treasury bills before 1997 was only sporadic because of the relatively comfortable fiscal position. The bulk of domestic debt corresponds to the bank rehabilitation and enterprise restructuring that followed independence in 1991. The instruments issued for these purposes were inflation-indexed bonds or foreign currency–indexed bonds with different maturities. These instruments were issued administratively (not in the market) and were the only long-term instruments available until 1997.

In 1997, as the budget deficit emerged, inflation-indexed bonds started to be issued sporadically without a preannounced calendar. Sporadic issuance of indexed bonds continued in 1998 and 1999 without standardized maturities. Since 2000, bonds have been regularly issued according to a preannounced calendar. Maturities were standardized as 3- and 5-year variable-rate bonds (where indexation is the variable part of variable interest rate) as part of the strategy to move toward introduction of fixed-rate instruments denominated in domestic currency, and a 10-year fixed-rate foreign currency–denominated bond. The bonds aimed at spreading the stock of debt across the yield curve to minimize rollover risk. Different interest calculation formulas used earlier were unified to enhance secondary trading and transparency. Enhancement of the market structure—including improvements in the auction mechanism, standardization and issuance of simple instruments, and announcement and calendar of funding needs—contributes to developing the market and helps to broaden the investor base.

The 10- and 15-year bonds were introduced to satisfy the demand of institutional investors. They are denominated in foreign currency and payable in domestic currency as an intermediate step toward nominal rates. In the event Slovenia becomes an EU country, the euro-denominated bonds will be repaid in euros.

In 2002, the MoF issued, for the first time, a three-year fixed-rate bond denominated in domestic currency, and the ministry will gradually shift other maturities to fixed-rate instruments. The shift to fixed-rate instruments not only aims at reducing market risk, but also at developing an identifiable yield curve and enhancement of trading. The MoF also believes that a liquid secondary market in government securities can be built only by means of fixed-rate instruments. When investors buy variable or inflation-indexed instruments, they are hedged against inflation risk, which deters trading of inflationary expectations. Inflation-indexed bonds are the least traded instrument in the secondary market.

The MoF reopens on-the-run issues several times during the year, according to a preannounced calendar, until it reaches a desired level (benchmark). The MoF has resorted to such a technique because of limited subscription in a single auction.

The issuance of treasury bills also became systematic in 1998. First, a three-month bill was introduced in May 1998, then a 6-month bill in October 1999, and a one-year bill in May 2000. These bills aim at establishing a flexible and cost-effective source of short-term borrowing to finance liquidity shortages, and they have contributed decisively to the move toward nominal rates in the economy and creation of a money market yield curve.

The MoF and the BOS issue their respective instruments. The MoF issues treasury bills and bonds, and the central bank issues its central bank bills. The MoF issues securities through an auction mechanism and accepts the market price, and the BOS, by means of a tap and recently through the use of auctions. There is no conflict in issuing different instruments and pricing them differently. However, there might be competition of securities in the secondary market.

Auctions

Securities are issued through auctions. Bonds are issued by means of a multiple-price auction, and treasury bills, through a fixed-price auction. Auctions are, in legal form, public auctions. The MoF executes the auctions.

For short-term paper, all sectors except the BOS can participate. All participants bid through primary dealers, the commercial banks that are registered security dealers.

In auctions of long-term paper, banks, securities dealers and other firms, and funds, including public and government agencies—all sectors except the central bank—can participate; interested entities that possess adequate technical and other means can participate in the auctions directly by agreement with the MoF (the PDMD). Other market participants, including households, participate through those commercial banks that are registered securities dealers.

Secondary market

To develop an efficient secondary market of government securities, the first task has been to provide instruments that can be easily marketable and will have simple features and clearly identifiable cash flow. To achieve this goal, the MoF is implementing a strategy toward nominalization of the main borrowing instruments. This includes the introduction of treasury bills with different maturities and a shift from inflation-indexed instruments, first, toward variable-rate instruments and, then, to fixed-rate instruments. Changing to variable-rate bonds also involved a gradual simplification of bond formulas in an effort to avoid disrupting the market. This development has also fostered similar development in the products offered by the domestic banking system.

In Slovenia, the central bank conducts open market operations exclusively with central bank bills, which can deter secondary trading of government securities. However, the BOS had a catalytic role in contributing to establishment of OTC trading in short-term government securities in November 2001. In particular, the BOS designed its regulatory framework. OTC transactions in government bonds also started recently, in August 2001, and activity has increased steadily in both types of instruments. The BOS is also contributing to the design of the regulatory framework for repo operations with short-term government securities in the OTC market. The rapid increase in OTC transactions is due to lower costs resulting from the absence of brokerage fees and low commissions charged by the Depository and Settlement Company.

Keeping access to domestic and international financial markets

To keep access to domestic and international financial markets, the MoF maintains frequent contact with investors and monitors financial markets' developments and investors' preferences. There has also been a strategy to issue debt instruments with standard maturities and, within the limits of borrowing needs, a size that enhances investors' appetite. In the international market, the PDMD has aimed at establishing a yield curve, which helps to price transactions. The PDMD strives to establish a size that ensures a certain degree of liquidity for investors but at the same time does not represent a refinancing risk for the portfolio. In the domestic market, investors are informed in advance about the issuing plans, to avoid any surprises or advantage. The PDMD aims at being reliable in its strategy and pricing of transactions. The investors' preference for particular instruments is also taken into account in preparation of the annual financing program.

Clearing and settlement

Slovenia uses an electronic system to settle and clear all security transactions occurring on the Ljubljana Stock Exchange. All trades conducted on that exchange are automatically transmitted to the Depository and Settlement Company, a clearing and settlement corporation. Settlement is T+2 on a delivery-versus-payment basis. Depository and Settlement Company rules comply with the Group of 30 international standards and all nine recommended actions in 1989 for clearing houses. Compliance with the CPSS-IOSCO recommendations adopted in November 2001 is under assessment.

Taxation

Interest income and capital gains from government securities is at present taxed under the broad category of corporate income tax. Interest income from government securities is tax exempt for personal income tax purposes. Any profit arising from appreciation in the price of the security, when a security is sold within three years of the date of its acquisition, is treated as a capital gain for personal income tax purposes. There are no differences between financial and nonfinancial corporations in the treatment of government securities for taxation purposes. There is also no distinction between current income and capital gains for corporate income tax purposes. No withholding tax is applied on income derived from government securities for residents and nonresidents. Primary and secondary transactions with securities and shares are exempt from value-added tax.

Appendix

Legal Framework

The outlines of the legal framework, given in Articles 81 through 84 of the Public Finance Act, are as follows:

The central government may incur debt both locally and abroad and up to the level stipulated by law (i.e., to the sum necessary for financing the deficit and for repayments of debt in the current year). During a period of temporary financing, the central government may incur debt up to the amount necessary for current debt repayments.

If, because of mismatches in flows, budget expenditures cannot be covered with current budget receipts, the central government may borrow for liquidity purposes, however not in excess of 5 percent of the last regular budget.

By drawing loans and issuing securities, the central government may raise funds necessary either to repay the public debt before falling due or to purchase its own securities, provided that:

1. Measures to establish economic stability are supported;
2. Cost of central government debt is reduced; or
3. The quality of debt portfolio is improved without increasing the central government debt.

The central or local government may also enter into other debt transactions in order to manage exchange and interest risks related to the central and/or local government debt (transactions with derivatives). The central government may buy and sell its own securities either on or outside the organized securities market. The funds for the purchase of securities shall be included in the central government budget.

Decisions regarding transactions in relation to central government borrowing, central government debt management, and interventions in securities markets are made by the minister responsible for finance on the basis of the annual Financing Program adopted by the Government.

The debt operations are concluded by the minister responsible for finance or another person authorized by the minister in writing.

Decisions regarding liquidity borrowing are made and executed by the minister responsible for finance or another person authorized in writing by the minister.

Article 85 specifies financing rules for local governments:

Local governments may borrow and manage debt on the basis of prior approval of the minister responsible for finance and under the terms and conditions laid down by the act regulating the financing of local governments. Borrowing transactions for which no prior approval has been given by the ministry responsible for finance shall be deemed null and void. Should it be impossible to balance the implementation of the budget due to uneven inflow of receipts, local governments may borrow for liquidity, however no more than 5 percent of the last regular budget. Unless otherwise stipulated in a special law, incomes from cash management are budget revenues, whereas the expenses of liquidity borrowing of the budget are budget expenditures. Local governments are obliged to report to the ministry responsible for finance on the borrowing and repayments of debt in a manner determined by the minister responsible for finance.

Note

1. The case study was prepared by Stanislava Zadravec C., Gonzalo Caprirolo, and Andrej Klemenčič from the Public Debt Management Department of the Ministry of Finance.

2. A more detailed outline of the framework is described in the Appendix to this report.

15

South Africa[1]

The South African government securities market has gone through various phases since the late 1970s. No formal and prevailing market rate existed before this period. The government periodically issued bonds at par, when needed. As the market started to develop, the government realized the importance of creating benchmark bonds across the yield curve to increase liquidity. By the early 1990s, a debt trap was looming, and the government intensified its focus on debt management. The government's macroeconomic framework under the growth, employment, and redistribution program was designed to, among other economic challenges, bring the total debt to manageable levels. As a result, the department of finance developed a framework of philosophies and principles to manage its debt. This led to guidelines and strategies to manage debt more actively.

Today the central government, state-owned entities, and local governments in South Africa are responsible for issuing more than 95 percent of the total fixed-interest-rate securities in the market. The government has taken great care to prove itself a reliable and responsible borrower, domestically as well as abroad. The funding is concentrated in large, liquid benchmark bonds to provide liquidity to the market.

Currently, the government is able to finance the total funding requirement in a sophisticated, liquid, and well-regulated domestic market. Much attention has been paid to the structural, legal, and infrastructural sides of supporting market development. There is regular interaction with the Bond Exchange of South Africa (BESA), the Financial Services Board, and the South African Reserve Bank (SARB) to help with the proper control of the domestic market. The government has also maintained a transparent relationship with the market. Quality information has been made available, particularly on key budgetary figures and funding strategies. As a result, South Africa's debt management strategy has moved beyond the stage that characterizes most emerging markets, and it is closer to that of developed markets in the industrial countries.

The Domestic Market Before 1990

In the 1970s, new government bond issues were sold as periodic public issues. Typically, the secretary of finance would issue bonds at par three or four times a year, usually to coincide with the date of a maturing bond. There was no active secondary market and, therefore, no prevailing market rate. However, several investigations of and reports on future developments in the capital market of South Africa highlighted the need for changes, among others the De Kock Commission, the Stals report, and the Jacobs report. In 1978, a broad consensus among all market participants was formed, pointing out the real need for market development.

In 1981, Eskom (the Electricity Supply Commission) was the first public entity to issue a bond at a discount to the market. The government soon followed. During the early 1980s, the government issued bonds on an open-ended tap basis until the allotted nominal amount, as specified in the prospectus, was fully issued. For each amount issued, a new bond was introduced to the market. During this period, there was no clear separation between monetary and fiscal policies. Primary issues were used for both financing government spending and open market transactions.

In the mid-1980s, important participants in the capital market established a forum with the South African government to discuss matters of mutual interest. The investment community was partly concerned about the Act on Prescribed Assets. This act was introduced in 1958 to create funds for semigovernmental institutions (such as universities and the South African Broadcasting Corporation) and developments in the former homelands. To fund these institutions, pension funds and insurance companies were obliged to invest part of their funds as prescribed assets in government bonds, government guarantee bonds, and bonds approved and specified by the registrar of pensions (e.g., homeland bonds). Moreover, the investment community was concerned about the small amounts of holdings being kept in a particular bond, some of which were illiquid.

The prescribed assets were a serious stumbling block in the development of financial markets. No prevailing market rate could be determined because of such requirements. The act was finally done away with in October 1989. When prescribed assets were lifted, the scene was set for further market developments in the South African capital market.

In 1989, the then department of finance consolidated several smaller issues to create benchmarks in

5-, 10-, 15-, and 20-year maturities. Furthermore, Eskom and other public entities began making two-way prices (i.e., quoting bid and offer prices) in their bonds.

Developments 1990–98

Developments in the domestic market

Development of the BESA

The development of a formal bond exchange in South Africa originated from recommendations made in the Stals and Jacobs reports. The authorities recognized that self-regulation by the market participants was more desirable and acceptable than imposed control. As a result, bond-trading firms who had run a voluntary association called the Bond Market Association since 1989 were licensed in 1996 as a formal exchange called BESA (the Bond Exchange of South Africa).

To develop the clearing operations, BESA adopted the Group of 30 recommendations on clearing and settlement. The exchange also established a recognized clearinghouse, UNEXcor (Universal Exchange Corporation). Today, BESA members are able to benefit from electronic trade reporting, matching, and settlement. Electronic net settlement takes place each trading day and is facilitated by four settlement agent banks and their Central Depository of South Africa.

Introduction of auctions and market making

In the early 1990s, the SARB had been appointed as the agent to issue, settle, and make a market in government bonds. In September 1996, the department of finance conducted a survey among members of BESA and certain foreign banks to obtain their views on how to improve issuance and secondary market-making activity in government bonds. As a result of the problems experienced with selling primary issues to the market on demand, South Africa decided to adopt the international practice of using regular auctions as a method of selling primary issues of government securities to the market. To ensure efficiency, liquidity, and transparency of the secondary market for government bonds, market participants also agreed with the principle of moving toward formal systems of market making. As a result, primary dealers were appointed, and their main responsibility was to make a market (quoting of two-way prices) and provision of liquidity in the secondary market for government bonds.

Auctions

Since 1998, the responsibilities of the SARB changed from being an issue, settle, and market-making agent in government bonds to conducting auctions of benchmark bonds according to a fixed program on behalf of the national treasury. The treasury, in a timely manner, informs all market participants about the year's public sector borrowing program, including the extent of the borrowing requirement, auction dates through an auction calendar, the maturity structure and size of issues, and the instruments to be issued. Seven days before the weekly auction, an announcement is made on what instrument will be issued. The auctions of benchmark bonds are open only to primary dealers.[2]

Appointment of primary dealers

In 1998, the national treasury appointed a panel of 12 primary dealers, consisting of 6 local banks and 6 foreign banks. The reasons for appointing primary dealers were to reduce refinancing risk for the government, improve the liquidity and efficiency of the government bond market, and create clear and transparent price formation. The introduction of a primary dealer system also supported the development of regulations for trading and investor protection and establishment of a more efficient clearing and settlement procedure. Other benefits of primary dealership include improved market analysis and research.

The criteria to be a primary dealer, set out by the national treasury, require both the local and nonresident market makers to hold a specified minimum amount of rand-denominated capital in South Africa. This held capital is a demonstration by market makers of the capacity to deal with the inherent risks associated with market making. In addition, it shows a firm commitment toward developing the domestic market.

Some requirements were identified to be put in place before the appointment of market makers. It was also decided that a gradual approach to change was necessary to avoid undue disruptions in the market. Two main areas for measures were identified, necessary structural improvements and liquidity enhancing issues.

- Structural improvements included
  - creation of an efficient legal framework,
  - market surveillance of primary dealers by the SARB and the national treasury,
  - introduction of minimum capital requirements of banks wanting to operate as market makers,
  - introduction of an auction system to sell government bonds to formal market makers,
  - dematerialization of bond certificates,
  - shortening of the settlement period to T+3, and
  - introduction of the risk management system in the treasury.
- Liquidity enhancing issues referred to measures aimed to provide sufficient liquidity to the broader market, for example, in ensuring that there is continuous provision of market-related bid and offer prices in appropriate volumes and under all market conditions. These objectives were achieved through introducing benchmark bonds and establishing the repo market.

Other developments

Other developments in the 1990s were, among others, the issuance of the first corporate bond in the South African market by SA Breweries, the establishment of the South African Futures Exchange, and the development of a register, payment, and debt recording system in the debt operation division of the department of finance.

The framework of philosophies and principles

In the early and mid-1990s, an ever-increasing budget deficit, a rising stock of debt, and a rising cost of servicing the debt caused an intensive public debate on the sustainability of the government's debt-servicing costs. Interest rates were high in both nominal and real terms, and the average maturity of the debt portfolio was just below 10 years, about 60 percent of which had to be refinanced within 5 years. This meant that besides the net new deficit that had to be financed, a high percentage of the existing debt also had to be refinanced in an environment of high interest rates. The threat of falling into a debt trap, and the uncertainty of potential liabilities, triggered a focus on prudent debt management.

In March 1996, an announcement was made in the *Budget Review* that the entire debt management policy would be reviewed. Following this measure, a framework of philosophies and principles to manage public debt, cash, and risk was developed and approved by parliament to promote a proper understanding of what was to be achieved and further a broad base of support. The framework identified risk areas, as well as the strategies to follow. Following suggestions in this framework, a public debt office was also established. This office was named the asset and liability management (ALM) branch of the department of finance (the department of finance is today called the national treasury). The following chart illustrates the current structure of the ALM branch.

The Evolving Debt Management Strategy Since 1999

The performance of the South African capital markets during the 1997–98 financial crises proved that the South African government bond market was no longer at a nascent stage. However, at the same time, it was evident that debt management objectives had to change to face new challenges. The willingness of the investors to commit their funds at the long end of the curve (27-year maturity) and the active participation of foreign investors signified the need to change the debt management approach. A research paper titled "Comprehensive Debt Management Framework" identified certain policy gaps that had to be addressed. The paper proposed that debt management objectives should be changed, including recommendations for a tactical debt management approach.

Identifiable policy and instrument gaps

- Design and use of instruments: Although low-cost debt instruments such as inflation-linked bonds were introduced, there was a need to consider introducing the low-coupon, fixed-rate bond. The

ALM Branch Structure

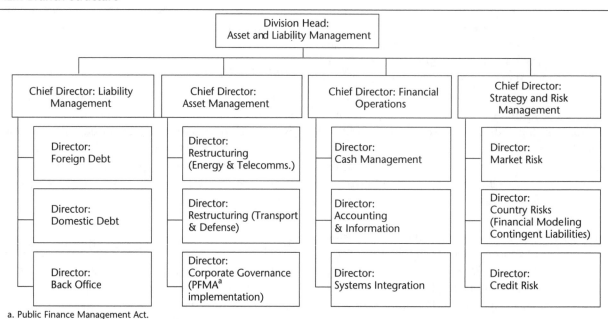

a. Public Finance Management Act.

design and use of low-coupon instruments is in line with the government's policy of introducing inflation targeting, which has helped to reduce unreasonable expectations about the future of the inflation rate. New low-coupon bonds have been successfully used as a destination bond in switches.

- Use of derivatives: Derivatives were not used when South Africa was still developing a risk management framework. However, this could change in the near future. Discussions are going on regarding the use of derivatives, such as separate trading of registered interest and principal of securities (STRIPS)[3] and interest rate swaps.
- Maturities: The capacity at the short end was limited. Switches between different maturities have been offered to the market to restructure the maturity profile of outstanding debt.
- Proper coordination of the funding activities of state-owned enterprises (SOEs): To ensure a smooth, efficient, and predictable securities market, there was a need to harmonize government borrowing with the SOEs. The public sector borrowers forum was launched on May 31, 2001, to organize the funding activities of the public sector issuers. The forum consists of the parastatals, the Financial Services Board, the SARB, and the national treasury.
- Coordination of liability management and monetary policy: There was no coordination between liability management and monetary operations. Consequently, a detailed work plan for the public debt management committee, which consisted of high-level decision makers from the national treasury and the SARB, had to be formulated.

Change in the hierarchy of debt management objectives

Based on the analysis in "Comprehensive Debt Management Framework," debt management objectives were changed. Before 1999, the primary objective of debt management was to develop the domestic capital market, and the secondary objective was to promote a balanced maturity structure. Developments in the domestic market changed the emphasis of these objectives. The primary objective shifted to focusing on the reduction of the cost of debt within

acceptable risk limits, and the secondary objective, to ensuring government access to financial markets and diversifying funding instruments.

A shift from strategic to tactical debt management

The national treasury acknowledged that while the objectives of South African debt management were now prudent; developments in the global sovereign capital markets necessitated a change from strategic to tactical debt management in South Africa. The strategic debt management policy looked at the overall design and implementation of the debt management program. This includes how primary issuance is designed and managed, how debt instruments are designed and traded, and how liquidity is provided. Tactical debt management policies concentrate on actively managing the outstanding stock of debt and its composition to reduce the cost of debt to within acceptable risk limits.

Achievements

Notable achievements in implementing new debt management approach cover improved domestic bond market liquidity. The total South African bond market turnover increased from R 5 trillion in 1997 to about R 11 trillion in 2000. The government bond proportion of total market turnover has also increased, from about 55 percent in 1995 to 91 percent in 2000. Moreover, investor confidence has risen, as has the participation of foreign investors in the domestic bond market. Meanwhile, the perceived risk associated with foreign investment in South Africa has continued to decrease with rising efficiency, sophistication, and openness in the South African capital market. Evidence of this was the fact that South Africa was one of the few countries to issue and fund in the longer-dated bonds during the 1997–98 financial market crises.

The Main Challenge Facing the National Treasury

The government's budget deficit as a percentage of GDP decreased from 5.1 percent in fiscal year

1994/95 to 1.5 percent in the 2001/02 fiscal year. The main challenge facing the national treasury today is to find ways to uphold an efficient, transparent, and liquid government bond market in an environment with declining borrowing needs. The decline in the supply of government paper is often interpreted as a decrease in the liquidity of the bond market, especially in those countries whose securities markets are still at a nascent stage. However, South Africa has reduced its supply of paper in line with the government's lower financing needs, without sacrificing liquidity in the bond market. The country has managed to achieve this by carrying out active debt management strategies with use of tools such as debt consolidation (switches) of bonds and debt buybacks. Inflation-linked bonds have also been introduced, and a facility to strip government bonds has been established. Swap derivatives will be introduced in due course.

Debt consolidation (switches)

Debt consolidation was introduced to reduce the fragmenting of bonds on the yield curve and thereby improve the liquidity of the benchmark issues. Debt consolidation has also helped to smooth out the maturity profile and reduce the refinancing risk, easing the pressure at the short end of the curve. The number of outstanding issues of small amounts and high coupons has been converted (switched) into larger liquid bonds with low coupons. To execute the debt consolidation (switches), exchange auctions have proved to be a powerful tool. Exchange auctions have also been used as a cash management tool. As at the end of 2001/02 fiscal year, a total of R 52 billion in bonds had been switched.

Debt buybacks

With the objective of reducing the government's debt-servicing costs in the medium to long term—and strengthen the integrity of the government securities market—small, illiquid, high-coupon bonds of less than R 1 billion as well as ex-homeland bonds have been bought back from the market. At the end of the 2001/02 fiscal year, R 4.5 billion of illiquid bonds had been bought back.

Inflation-linked bonds

To reduce the long-run cost of debt, the ALM branch has embarked on the design of instruments that can lower the overall cost of debt for the government, such as the issuance of inflation-linked bonds. Inflation-linked bonds give institutional investors a chance to match long-term assets and liabilities, while also providing an objective measure of inflationary expectations and acting as a benchmark for other issuers. These bonds were considered a mechanism for unlocking the liquidity of the long-term fixed-rate bonds, because inflation-linked bonds tend to attract the buy-and-hold investors. By switching into inflation-linked bonds, institutional investors released long-term fixed-rate bonds in the secondary market to trade, thereby increasing liquidity on the long end of the curve for long-term, fixed-rate nominal bonds.

South Africa has developed a full inflation-linked bonds curve with 2008, 2013, and 2023 maturities. These bonds had an average yield of 4percent as of May 20, 2002. However, as in other similar markets, the liquidity in the South African inflation-linked market is low, because these bonds mostly are bought by investors who tend to hold the bonds to maturity. The primary dealers do not have any price-making responsibilities on inflation-linked bonds.

Stripping of government bonds

The ALM branch undertook a project of discovering whether the STRIPS system improves the liquidity of the underlying instruments. The project pointed out that STRIPS could increase demand for the underlying instrument and encourage active portfolio managers to take advantage of arbitrage opportunities through stripping and reconstitution. Under conditions of declining government funding, the project discovered that it was clear that it was necessary to introduce a STRIPS program to maintain the liquidity and integrity of the domestic capital market. Trading in STRIPS began at the end of January 2002 through primary dealers acting as market makers. The Central Depository of South Africa acts as a government agent in stripping government bonds. By introducing a strip facility, the national treasury discouraged investment banks from creating their own special purpose vehicles, whose sole responsibility is to strip government bonds for market participants.

Swaps

To manage the duration of the government's debt portfolio, the national treasury's liability management division is introducing interest rate swaps as instruments for cost and risk management. Moreover, with government participation in the swap market, it is assumed that the liquidity of both the swap market and the underlying bond market will improve.

Foreign Borrowing

Political unrests due to apartheid system in 1984 and 1985 resulted in sizable capital outflows. The fiscal and monetary decision makers were forced to enter into a partial debt standstill.[4] According to a SARB census, South Africa's indebtedness on August 31, 1985 was US$23.7 billion (41.4 percent of GDP), US$13.6 billion of which was deemed to fall under the debt standstill. The repayment of this part of the debt was executed under four debt standstill agreements starting in 1985. The final repayment under these agreements was made in August 2001.

After a period of restricted access, the South African government was able to return to the foreign market in 1994 after the election of the first democratic government. The first issue after this return was a U.S. dollar global bond issue, followed by a yen bond issue in 1995. The government also set up an EMTN (euro medium-term note) program.

Since then, an integrated strategic approach has been followed when entering the foreign market to fund the budget deficit, as stipulated in the *Budget Review* each year. Usually, foreign funding has amounted to US$1 billion per fiscal year. However, the prime focus has not been for funding purposes, but to create benchmarks in specific foreign markets for other South African entities to follow. This is mainly because South Africa is capable of funding its total budget deficit from the domestic capital market only.

The strategy of borrowing in the foreign market so far has been to exploit perceived pricing anomalies to obtain cost-effective funds. Moreover, in the future, the foreign debt management will also focus on promoting the rand market by taking advantage of the South Africa's positive credit-rating development whenever possible.

Risk Management Framework

From 1996 to 1999, three financial risk management objectives drove the ALM branch, namely controlling the quantum of capital, optimizing the return on capital, and managing the cost of capital, each described in the following.

Controlling the quantum of capital

As mentioned before, the debt issued by the state, and the cost of servicing this debt, were at a high level in the mid-1990s. In this light, a distinction was made between two different broad areas of risk:

- Risk of ever-increasing deficit: This risk was not seen as the primary responsibility of the ALM branch. The primary responsibility for managing this risk was guided by the implementation of the government's macroeconomic framework, the growth, employment, and redistribution program.
- Risk of ensuring cash availability to meet the state's expenses: The liability manager was given direct responsibility for
  - ensuring the state's continued access to financial markets, both domestic and foreign;
  - contributing to the absorption capacity of state debt within these markets through ongoing market development, product innovation, and proper coordination of activities with the SARB's monetary management operations;
  - developing efficient secondary markets for its securities; and
  - establishing the state's name as a fair and efficient borrower in the financial markets through the active marketing of its debt instruments.

Optimizing the return on capital

The ALM branch was interested in investments relating to surplus cash arising because of overall funding requirements and ensuring liquidity needs. The level of surplus cash was largely affected by cash management activities. However, from a risk management perspective, a certain level of investment was kept as a liquidity buffer. The return on capital invested in programs and projects through the budgetary process did not concern the ALM branch.

Managing the Cost of Capital

An integrated strategy was followed for domestic and foreign borrowing. It was accepted that savings in the cost of debt service could be achieved from the ongoing development of the depth and width of the domestic financial markets, rather than through efforts to borrow more cheaply in foreign markets. Because of the size of South Africa's domestic debt, limited scope existed for actively managing the debt portfolio and reducing debt-servicing costs. The focus of existing domestic debt management aimed, therefore, at addressing the maturity structure to avoid unwanted bundling across the debt profile. Although funding of the new gross financing need (new issues) was managed actively, cost savings were not achieved by taking interest rate views.

The principles regarding individual risk categories concentrated on these risk areas:

- Liquidity risk: The management of this risk, considered by the ALM branch to be the most important, involved ensuring that the minimum amount of cash was always available to meet the state's expenses. Further explanation of liquidity risk will be covered under the section on cash management.
- Interest rate risk: This risk meant that adverse changes in interest rates could cause an increase in borrowing costs. It was accepted that the state's minimum risk position was in long-term, rand-denominated debt. A duration target was established to control the interest rate risk. No interest rate view was taken as a means of achieving cost savings.

- Credit risk: In the course of managing cash balances and derivatives positions, the guiding philosophy and principle was that the role of the ALM branch, in managing the state's market risk, involved a transfer of that risk to the marketplace in return for the credit risk of the counter-party. The state's size in the financial markets necessitated accepting credit risk from a far wider range of counter-parties. With the exception of liquidity, no counter-party or issuer was exempt from the process of having a credit limit imposed. Transactions could be conducted only after formal limits were set with counter-parties and issuers that satisfied soundly based and acceptable assessment processes.
- Foreign exchange risk: It was accepted that it was not appropriate for the ALM branch to hedge foreign loans raised by the state through the rand, because the foreign currency debt represents just a small part of the total debt. Instead, the national treasury regards controlling the level of foreign currency debt as essential.
- Market-making risk: It was accepted that this risk should be limited and confined to debt markets. Market-making activities in South African bonds were removed from the government (the role that was played by the SARB as an agent of the government) and transferred to the market when primary dealers were introduced in 1998. Thus, the risk of fluctuations in the market was shifted to the market participants, where it was deemed to belong.
- Trading and ethical risk: Primary dealers took responsibility for trading and ethical risk. A code of conduct was drafted, documented, and signed between primary dealers and the ALM branch. The code of conduct addressed the issues of business ethics, relationships, due diligence, confidentiality, controls, and trading rules.

Setting up the capacity to assess and manage cost and risk

In 1999, a risk management project was introduced. Its purpose was to set up a separate section within the

ALM branch that would be solely responsible for managing risks of the government portfolio. In 2000, a risk management team was put in place to run the project. The chief directorate of the strategy and risk management controls and manages risks that are identified and debt it is exposed to. Specific risk management responsibilities within the context of the ALM branch are to

- create and maintain a risk management framework for general government bodies and public enterprises,
- develop an ideal benchmark for government debt, and
- monitor and manage credit risk exposure.

Risk management today

Because of the developments that have taken place in both the domestic and foreign markets, the national treasury has resolved that the risk management framework adopted in 1996 needs to be realigned. This is mainly due to the fact that debt management practices have evolved, and more emphasis is now placed on advanced tactical and quantitative models, rather than just on policies. Although the risks identified are still the same, the new model in each case ensures that policies and procedures to quantify, control, and manage risk exposure are now put in place. Table II.15.1 summarizes the types of risk and the management of these risks.

Table II.15.1. Management of Risk

Type of risk	Management of risk
1. Liquidity and refinancing risk Short-term liquidity	• Monitor exchequer cash balance and flows. • Maintain a certain minimum cash balance. • Maintain access to short-term borrowing. • Limit size of short-term debt. • Prefinance maturing debt.
Long-term liquidity	• Smooth the maturity profile. • Extend portfolio maturity. • Develop liquid benchmarks.
2. Interest rate risk	• Manage ratio of fixed- vs. floating-rate debt. • Manage ratio of short-term vs. long-term debt. • Manage nonparallel yield curve shifts. • Use interest rate swaps.
3. Currency risk	• Domestic vs. foreign debt. • Use of currency swaps. • Manage short-term vs. long-term debt. • Composition of currencies.
4. Budget risk	• Modest short-term borrowing. • Reduce volatility of short-term interest rates. • Monitor actual vs. debt service costs. • Stress-testing (implemented in 2002).
5. Credit risk	• Set overall counter-party credit status, for example, rating (implementation started in 2002). • Set individual counter-party credit limits (implementation started in 2002). • ISDA mitigation clauses (implemented in 2002).
6. Downgrade risk	• Identify key factors that are important in the credit-rating process. • Develop a culture of consistent messages between other departments and the international community.
7. Operational risk	• Put policies and measures in place to control back office operations and payments.

Benchmark for management and performance

To ensure accountability and the delegation of risk, the government has approved a benchmark that should reflect and establish an acceptable level of risk and target costs. The benchmark reflects the defined debt management objectives and acceptable quantifiable risks, and it expresses the government's strategic debt position and aligns debt policy to economic policy. Altogether, the benchmark provides appropriate risk management and control and forms a baseline for measuring the performance of debt managers. The benchmark was formulated under these principles:

- Robustness: A conclusion should rely on few assumptions.
- Efficiency: The government should be able to take the least possible risk for a certain cost.
- Mark-to-market valuation: The government should be able to measure savings and cost over the lifetime of the debt.
- Risk context: Risks should be constrained to the annual debt-service expense.
- Transparency: There should be an open basis for performance measurement.

Cash Management

Both the cabinet memorandum of February 1997 and the Public Finance Management Act require cash management in the ALM branch to provide a framework for creating awareness in all spheres of the government of the need for proper cash-flow management. The responsibility to plan and manage the government's daily cash-flow needs was officially taken over from the SARB in June 1999.

To ensure enough funds are available for the state to meet all expected and unexpected financial commitments, it is necessary and prudent to keep an appropriate level of cash and near-cash. It is therefore important to optimize returns on cash balances. Therefore, the cash manager's responsibilities are to

- manage liquidity by ensuring that the right amount of funds are available in the right currencies, at the right time, and in the right place;

- plot projected flows and monitor the actual flows against projections: Timely and accurate future cash-flow projections are critical to plan the funding of the national revenue fund effectively, minimizing the required liquidity buffer and maximizing returns on surplus cash;
- create an appropriate organizational structure; and
- engineer the required linkages between the tax and loan accounts, the paymaster general accounts, and the departmental accounting systems.

During the early 1990s, the then department of finance introduced a tax and loan account system. It opened four tax and loan accounts with each of the four major domestic banks in South Africa. Surplus funds in the exchequer account, kept at the SARB, are deposited into these accounts daily. When spending occurs, funds flow back via the exchequer account to the various departmental accounts. This establishes daily outflows from the accounts.

Since June 1998, the difference between projected daily cash flows and actual cash flows has been maintained daily. Taking control over cash-flow estimates, and more accurate information on projected monthly and daily cash flows, have made it possible to plan and draw up proposals on financing needs more accurately. Also, the active use of treasury bills, issuing of short-term (one-day) treasury bills to finance cash-flow peaks, and investments by the Corporation for Public Deposits (an organization that manages short-term public funds and is part of the SARB) has contributed to cash-flow management carrying lower cash balances ahead of cash-flow peaks.

Managing Investor Relations

The national treasury also attaches greater significance to managing investor relations and has set up an annual investor relations program, which includes road shows, primary dealer meetings, and one-on-one meetings with investors and other market participants, such as banks, fund managers, and the like.

The annual road shows are intended to promote the exchange of ideas between the national treasury and investors (foreign and domestic) on issues of mutual interest. This could, for example, involve discussions on funding needs, new instruments and projects proposed by the ALM branch, and any concerns about the market.

At the establishment of the primary dealership, the national treasury, the SARB, market makers, and the BESA agreed to coordinate their responsibilities to ensure a transparent and efficient bond market. All new strategies have been discussed with market participants, and they have been encouraged to submit their comments. The national treasury has adhered to its annual funding strategy, and any unplanned events have been avoided. Furthermore, the ALM branch within the national treasury and the money and capital market division of the SARB have had a formal program of meeting primary dealers to discuss their performance in the primary and secondary markets and capital market issues of mutual interest.

The ALM branch and the money and capital market division of the SARB have also held discussions with the top management of various capital market participants.

Legal Framework for Issuing Government Debt Instruments

The Public Finance Management Act forms the basis for financial administration in the South African government. The act

- regulates financial management in the national and provincial governments;
- ensures that all the revenue, spending, assets, and liabilities of those governments are managed efficiently and effectively;
- provides for responsibilities of people entrusted with financial management in those governments; and
- incorporates the regulations on borrowing by public entities (It does not allow provinces to borrow from abroad.).

The act also stipulates the limits on borrowing, guarantees, and other commitments. To improve accountability of debt management, the act settles who should

- borrow for the government;
- issue a guarantee, indemnity, or security; and
- enter into any other transaction that binds the government.

The act also lists the purposes for which the minister of finance, as an executive authority, may borrow money. These are to

- finance the national budget deficit,
- refinance maturing debt or a loan paid before the redemption date,
- buy foreign currency,
- maintain credit balances on a national revenue fund bank account,
- regulate internal monetary conditions should the need arise, and
- for any other purpose approved by the national assembly by special resolution.

Concluding Remarks

South Africa has gained valuable experience and learned important lessons in public debt management. The most significant lesson the government has learned was the importance of having a debt management framework to deal with the mounting debt that was threatening South Africa. The framework identified risk areas, as well as the strategies to follow. Of special importance in the implementation of the framework have been

- the development of liquidity in both financial instruments and the capital market;
- the development of a yield curve and the issuing of bonds over the spectrum of the yield curve;
- the diversification of fixed-income instruments such as floating- and variable-rate bonds, fixed-interest bonds, and inflation-linked bonds;
- market making, trading, and investment risks were transferred to the market through the appointment of primary dealers;
- the opportunity to issue bonds in a proper, well-structured (regulated), and developed market; and
- introduction of cash management, with an emphasis on actively managing cash balances

(This entails the daily monitoring of actual flows against projections.).

Today, the inherent conflict between debt management and monetary policies is now well understood. A clear separation of activities has been introduced, and existing conflicts have now been dealt with in the appropriate manner.

To reduce costs, a gradual approach has been followed, from emphasizing market development to actively taking positions in the market. This enables the government to actively manage its outstanding stock of debt and the composition of this debt. It also has become critical to identify, control, and manage the government's risk exposure. The national treasury's ALM branch has actively managed these risks, guided by a comprehensive risk management framework.

Establishing and maintaining a good relationship with investors, both locally and internationally, has been one of the priorities in promoting the South African bond market. The investor relations program, run by top management in the national treasury and the SARB, has increased the transparency and openness of the bond market and encouraged investor confidence in the government's ability to manage debt.

Although all of these issues are important, it is crucial to note that the South African bond market could not have been so efficient without a prudent macroeconomic framework and a well-constructed legal framework.

Notes

1. The case study was prepared by the National Treasury of the Republic of South Africa.

2. Information is available on the web site, www.treasury.gov.za.

3. The interest and principal components of a security are split into separately tradable instruments.

4. Deferred of government debt.

16

Sweden[1]

Sweden has had a separate agency, Riksgäldskontoret (the Swedish National Debt Office [SNDO]), for government debt management since 1789. Inevitably, the principles and practices of debt management have changed repeatedly over the years. A major reform of the governance system was enacted in 1998. As a result, debt management decisions are made within a more clearly structured framework. There is also a more structured approach to evaluate the decisions after the fact. The outline of this system and the experiences so far are presented in the first section, which also discusses the organization of the debt office.

The new governance system has created a framework for more focused analysis of the debt management strategy and the risks involved. The second section discusses the key features of debt management strategy and the analyses undertaken to get a better understanding of the costs of government debt and the associated risks.

The third section discusses measures for developing the government securities markets.

Developing a Sound Governance and Institutional Framework

Statutory rules

The core principles and rules for central government debt management in Sweden are given in the Act on State Borrowing and Debt Management.[2] The current legislation was enacted by parliament in 1998. The government's right to borrow is based on an annual authorization from parliament, which is given as part of the decision on the state budget for the subsequent fiscal year. There is no fixed limit on the annual amount of borrowing. Instead, the act specifies the purposes for which the government may borrow, in particular, to finance the budget and refinance maturing debt.[3] The government invariably delegates the mandate to borrow to the SNDO.

The objective of debt management is also formulated in the act. It stipulates that the state's debt shall be managed so that the long-term costs are minimized while taking risks into account. Debt management shall also respect the demands of monetary policy. This is basically the same rule that governed debt management before the reform in 1998. The difference is that the objective now is stated in a law enacted by parliament, whereas it previously was set out in documents issued by the government.

Finally, the act contains procedural rules. First, it stipulates that the government each year shall decide guidelines for debt management. This decision shall be based on a proposal submitted by the SNDO. The proposal shall be sent to the Riksbank, the central bank for comments, to ensure that the demands of monetary policy are taken into account. Second, the act instructs the government to submit an annual report to parliament in which it makes an evaluation of the management of the debt. The SNDO's proposal, the Riksbank's comments, and the government's guidelines, as well as the evaluation report, are all public documents.

The statutory rules create a framework for delegation, reporting, and evaluation. Parliament—at the top of the system—has established the objective. On the basis of this objective, the government is mandated to set guidelines. In preparing the guidelines, the SNDO assists the government. This reflects the fact that the SNDO staff work full-time with debt policy, whereas the government (the ministry of finance) has many other obligations and is confronted with debt policy issues infrequently.[4]

The implementation of debt management on the basis of the guidelines is then delegated to the SNDO. The guidelines define in broad terms how the debt should be structured. They typically include ranges around target values, leaving scope for the SNDO to make more detailed decisions on the management of the debt.[5] There are two decision levels within the SNDO. The first level is the board, which is made up of external members (with the exception of the director general).[6] For example, it makes strategic decisions on how to use the ranges given in the government guidelines and benchmark portfolios. The second level is the operative management of the debt within the frame set by the board, which is in the hands of the SNDO's staff, led by the director general.

The governance system also puts emphasis on evaluation. Each decision level is evaluated by its immediate superior body. This means that the board monitors and evaluates operative debt management and reports to the government. At the next level, the government evaluates the overall result of the SNDO's decisions. Finally, parliament evaluates debt management as a whole, including the government's guidelines. This evaluation is in the form of an annual written statement, adopted after a debate and vote in parliament. This statement is published in time for the SNDO to consider comments and recommendations from parliament when preparing the next guideline proposal, closing the loop of delegation and monitoring.

This governance framework applies to central government gross debt, or the debt portfolio managed by the SNDO. The Swedish government sector also has financial assets, for example, in funds in the public pension system and in equity holdings. Indeed, at end-2001, the general government net financial debt was negative, despite a central government debt-to-GDP ratio of about 54 percent. There is no debt management strategy at the level of general government, partly because the public pension funds are managed separately from the state budget, based on objectives derived from their role in securing future pensions, and because local authorities have a significant degree of independence. However, attempts are made to broaden the perspective to include the central government's balance sheet in the analysis of risks relevant to central government debt management.

The governance framework in practice

The first guidelines constructed within the new framework were adopted in 1998, covering debt management in 1999. When the guidelines for 2002 were adopted in November 2001, it was thus the fourth time the exercise was repeated. It was recognized when the new system was put in place that the objective was vague and that further analysis was needed to translate it into a practical framework for debt management. In the preparation of the guideline proposals, emphasis has been put on complementing the statutory target with appropriate definitions of costs and risks. In addition, the SNDO has presented analyses of how the composition of the debt portfolio can be expected to affect costs and risks. The main conclusions and the resulting debt management strategy are summarized in the second section.

The changes in the way debt policy is governed have not, at least so far, altered the practices of debt management. The most significant effect is perhaps that the time perspective in the guidelines has been extended from one year to include tentative plans for rolling three-year periods, consistent with the time frame used in the budget process. However, the importance of the form and structure of governance should not be underestimated.

First, the new system has increased the attention given to debt policy in both the government and parliament. Considering the size of the annual debt costs, this attention is justified.

Second, the procedure surrounding the annual guideline decision has affected the perception of debt policy. All strategic proposals and decisions must be explained to the public in terms of their impact on costs and risks. The decisions are then evaluated in terms of their impact on costs, and the results are made available to the public. The transparency of the system helps to commit the policymakers to the stated objective of long-term cost minimization with due regard to risks. In particular, borrowing strategies that reduce short-term costs, but also significantly raise medium- or long-term costs or the risk of the debt are difficult to implement.

Third, the system provides a clearer distribution of responsibilities between the parties concerned. The government (the ministry of finance) delegates debt management to the SNDO for one year at a time. The government can change the guidelines during the year if the circumstances underlying the decision have changed materially, but this has to be done in the form of an amended guideline, that is, in a public document.

Similarly, the central bank's views are brought into the process in a formalized way when the Riksbank is invited to comment on the annual proposal. This is in contrast to the situation 10 or 15 years ago, when debt management often was used as an instrument of monetary and exchange rate policy. Now it is clear that monetary policy, at most, acts as a constraint on the cost minimization problem, and it is not part of the objective. An objection from the

Riksbank to a proposal from the SNDO must be linked explicitly to "the demands of monetary policy" (i.e., the suggested guidelines would interfere with the Riksbank's ability to reach its statutory objective or price stability). In an economy with well-developed financial markets, this will only rarely be the case. A gradual separation between monetary policy and debt policy had begun before the governance system was reformed, but the new process has contributed to an even clearer decoupling of monetary policy and debt policy.

In summary, the governance framework introduced in 1998 makes it clear that debt management is a policy area in its own right, with its own objective. The government is answerable to parliament for achieving this target, but major responsibilities are delegated to the SNDO, in both the preparation of guideline proposals and operative debt management. As a result of the guideline procedure, the operative independence of the SNDO has increased. However, through the reporting and evaluation mechanisms, there has been a corresponding increase in the possibilities to hold the SNDO accountable for its decisions. As is appropriate, delegation and accountability go hand in hand.

The arguments for delegating the implementation of monetary policy to an independent central bank are well known, and the practice of doing so is wide spread. The Swedish governance framework for debt management illustrates how debt policy can be delegated in a similar fashion to an independent debt office. However, the degree of delegation is less far reaching than in monetary policy.

First, the debt management objective is two-dimensional, in that there may be trade-offs to make between cost and risk. Second, the attitude to risk is presumably not invariant to the overall fiscal position of the country. Debt must be seen as part of the overall balance sheet of the government. It must be assessed in relation to expenditure commitments, defining another class of liabilities, and future tax revenues, which are the most important assets on the balance sheet. It seems inevitable that an optimal debt policy is state contingent in that the attitude to risk will vary depending on the overall outlook for government finances. Strategic decisions on debt management are thus closely linked to fiscal and budget policies, which fall within the realm of the government and parliament. An independent debt office may not have the necessary information to make such assessments. Moreover, and more important, it is not be possible to make a separate debt office accountable for decisions that are ultimately political in nature. It is therefore difficult to delegate strategic decisions to an administrative agency to the same extent as the implementation of monetary policy can be delegated to an independent central bank.

The organization of the SNDO

Background

For the first 200 years, the SNDO was responsible directly to parliament. This meant, for example, that it had an external board appointed directly by parliament. However, in 1989, it was turned into an agency of the government. This reflected primarily the assessment that parliament's influence was secured via the budget process and that the implementation of debt policy was handled more efficiently by an agency reporting to the government.

Internal organization

The operative responsibility for the SNDO is in the hands of the director general and the deputy director general, both appointed by the government. The director general is also the chairman of the board. The government also appoints the other board members, none of whom is employed by the SNDO. Reflecting the previous link to parliament, four of the eight board members are also members of parliament. The board decides on strategic issues related to debt management (e.g., guideline proposals and risk control).

Within the SNDO, there is a clear organizational separation between front, middle, and back office responsibilities. Front office activities, such as auctions, debt, and cash management transactions, are executed within the debt management department. The head of the debt management department reports to the director general.

Debt management is monitored by the risk control department, the middle office. Its responsibilities

include monitoring positions relative to benchmarks and observance of credit limits on counter-parties. The risk control department is also responsible for monitoring operative risks.

Confirmation and settlement of debt management transactions are handled by the back office department. Reports on the results of debt transactions are handled by the accounting department. The heads of risk control, back office, and accounting report to the deputy director general to achieve a further separation between operative debt management and follow-up activities.

In addition, there is the internal auditing department. It reports directly to the board on results of audits of the activities of the SNDO.[7]

Financial and human resources

The SNDO is funded by the state budget. The SNDO submits budget proposals to the government, covering rolling three-year periods, that explain its financing needs. Current expenditures for salaries, rents, and similar expenditures are covered by one budget title, interest payments on the debt by another. Consequently, the SNDO cannot use savings on interest costs, for example, to hire additional staff.

Within the limit set in the budget, the SNDO has considerable flexibility in allocating funds between uses, including hiring decisions. Swedish government agencies, in general, are controlled not by detailed specifications on how they may use their funds, but by whether they manage to achieve the objectives set up for them. The evaluation system for debt management is thus unusual only in that it is more elaborate and formalized than in other areas.

This affects, for example, decisions on salaries. The government appoints the director general and the deputy director general and sets their salaries. The SNDO, ultimately the director general, makes hiring decisions and establishes the salaries of all other employees. There is no fixed salary structure, based on seniority or other set criteria, within the Swedish central government. Instead, merit and degree of competition from the outside for a particular skill are key factors. This means that salaries can be adjusted to the SNDO's need to recruit or retain a particular individual—that is, of course, within the limits in any organization to maintain a wage structure perceived to be fair and reasonable.

Still, the SNDO cannot directly outbid private financial firms in terms of wages. The key to recruiting and retaining staff with appropriate financial market skills is to offer challenging and interesting tasks to work with. In particular, it is important to involve also relatively junior staff in discussion and decisions on policy issues. Even though debt management involves portfolio decisions analogous to those made in private financial institutions, there are connections to broader economic policy issues not present elsewhere. By building on this aspect, a debt office can create an advantage relative to the private sector, offsetting some of the differences in salary levels. In areas such as the back office and information technology, the differences between working in a policymaking institution and a private firm are less pronounced. The SNDO therefore tends to meet tougher competition when it comes to retaining staff in administrative functions than in the core policy areas.

Debt Management Strategy and Risk Management Framework

Background

The statutory objective—long-term cost minimization with due regard to risk—is obviously sound. However, more precise concepts are needed to translate the objective into a strategy for actual debt management. An important element in the analyses conducted within the new governance framework has been to define what one should mean by costs and risks.

The next question is how the debt portfolio should be structured. The SNDO has concluded that the composition of Sweden's current debt portfolio, in particular in terms of the share allocated to foreign currency debt, differs from what is desirable. The discrepancy is so significant in relation to the speed with which the debt composition can be modified that it has been deemed unnecessary at this stage to define a target portfolio in terms of percentage shares. The guidelines have instead pointed out the desired directions in which to move the portfolio. The resulting

debt portfolio strategy is discussed in this section, as are various aspects of active debt management.

The concepts of costs and risks

It was acknowledged when the new law was enacted that additional analyses were required to give the concepts of costs and risks more concrete interpretations. Although much remains to be done, some tentative conclusions have been drawn by the SNDO and confirmed in the government's guideline decisions.

The first step in the process was to consider whether costs (and related risks) should be measured on the basis of a complete mark-to-market of the debt or using interest rates set when bonds were issued. The conclusion was that market value changes do matter. However, the bulk of the debt is not—and indeed cannot be—refinanced at short notice. As a first approximation, therefore, it is reasonable to assume that debt instruments are left outstanding until maturity. This means that short-term fluctuations in market values resulting from changes in market interest rates are of little consequence for the realized costs of the debt. This view is also reflected in the accounting practice of not revaluing the debt on the basis of current market interest rates.

It should be noted, however, that the foreign currency debt is consistently valued in terms of current exchange rates. One reason to treat interest rate and exchange rate movements differently is that the latter can be expected to lead to realized losses or gains even if the bond is left outstanding to maturity, because payments are made in foreign currency. Moreover, the current exchange rate is probably the best available indicator of the rate at maturity.

In the bill presenting the new legislation, the government indicated that real (as opposed to nominal) measures of costs seemed appropriate from a general economic perspective. However, the government noted that the understanding of real measures of financial risk was limited and that nominal costs therefore would be used pending further analysis. A second step in the analysis has dealt with the question of how to go beyond nominal measures of costs and risks.

In its simplest form, a real measure could be obtained by deflating nominal costs with a price index, for example, the Consumer Price Index. This would, for example, make the cost of an inflation-linked bond predetermined and, hence, risk free. It is intuitively clear, however, that there is more to "real risk" than inflation adjustment, and, more concretely, that an inflation-linked bond is not in general risk free for the government. This line of thinking led to a broadening of the perspective beyond the government debt as usually defined. Inspiration also came from the practice, in particular in financial firms, of making risk analyses in terms of the entire balance sheet, leading to a perspective akin to asset and liability management (ALM).

The starting point is to note that debt is just one item on the government's balance sheet, broadly defined. First, there are nondebt obligations of all kinds, including entitlement programs and other future expenditures. Second, the government has assets. The most important of these is the right to charge taxes, which in balance-sheet terms could be measured as the present value of future tax revenues.

Risks arise when assets and liabilities are not perfectly matched. To manage its risks, the government must therefore consider the entire balance sheet and try to limit the mismatch between assets and liabilities.[8] A complete balance-sheet analysis of the government is an inordinately complicated undertaking. An ALM-based approach to debt management can also be helpful if one does not have a complete quantitative picture, however. In particular, it becomes clear that the risk of government debt should be assessed on the basis of whether it exacerbates or mitigates strains on the balance sheet.

One simple measure of the (current) strains on the balance sheet is the budget balance. For example, a debt portfolio that typically has high costs in recessions, that is, when public finances are strained for other reasons, must be considered riskier than a portfolio for which the opposite is true. This translates into treating deficit smoothing as an operative objective of debt management.

An ALM perspective also modifies the assessment of inflation-linked bonds. Debt costs linked to inflation mitigate swings in public finances as long as inflation is high when tax bases are high and expenditures low, that is, if inflation is positively correlated with the business cycle. However, if the economy is hit by a supply shock leading to stagflation—high inflation combined with low growth—inflation-linked debt adds to the strains on public finances.

Acknowledging that ALM provides an appropriate frame for thinking about debt management risks is one thing; translating it into a complete debt management strategy is quite another. The most visible effect so far on Swedish debt management is that in qualitative and quantitative analyses, debt costs are set in relation to GDP. GDP is here seen as a measure of other business cycle–related influences on the budget, or a debt portfolio perceived as having a relatively stable cost-to-GDP ratio is regarded as less risky. Using the cost-to-GDP ratio as the criterion for ranking debt portfolios is a step in the direction of ALM.

The SNDO has built a stochastic simulation model, which is used, jointly with qualitative reasoning, in the work on guidelines for debt management. The model generates paths for interest rates, exchange rates, GDP, and the borrowing requirement for up to 30 years. These time series are then used to simulate the costs of a set of debt portfolios with different characteristics, making it possible to rank portfolios on the basis of their expected costs and the variability of costs. The primary metric used is the cost-to-GDP ratio. Because GDP is generated in the model, it is possible to capture correlations between interest rates, exchange rates, and GDP in an internally consistent manner.[9]

Debt portfolio strategy

Background

For the purpose of discussing debt strategy at the portfolio level, the Swedish central government debt can be broken down into three parts, nominal krona debt, inflation-linked krona debt, and foreign currency debt. Figure II.16.1 shows how the debt and its composition have developed since 1992.[10]

The current debt portfolio is dominated by nominal loans in domestic currency, made up of bonds and bills, but less so than in most Organization for Economic Cooperation and Development countries. First, Sweden has an unusually large share of inflation-linked loans, although still less than 10 percent of total debt. Second, and more significant, more than a third of the debt is in foreign currencies. The

Figure II.16.1. Central Government Debt, 1990–2001
(In billions of Swedish kronor)

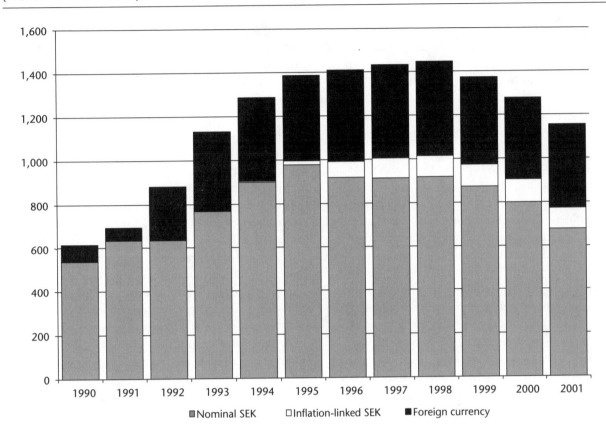

■ Nominal SEK   □ Inflation-linked SEK   ■ Foreign currency

foreign currency debt is largely a legacy from the early 1990s. As can be seen in Figure II.16.1, total debt more than doubled between 1990 and 1995, when Sweden experienced the deepest recession since the 1930s. With an annual net borrowing requirement corresponding to 14 percent of GDP at the peak, it was useful to divert some of the borrowing to foreign capital markets. This reduced the pressure on long-term interest rates in the domestic market and diversified the debt portfolio.

The duration of the combined nominal krona and foreign currency debt is approximately 2.7 years. The inflation-linked debt has a duration (measured in terms of real rates) of close to 10 years.

Conclusions concerning the debt portfolio

The key question in the analyses conducted within the new governance framework has been how a port-

folio consistent with the objective of long-term cost minimization with due regard to risk should be structured. Special attention has been given to foreign currency debt, reflecting that this is the aspect in which the Swedish debt portfolio stands out, and to inflation-linked debt, as a relatively new instrument.

Foreign currency debt

Based on qualitative and quantitative analyses, the SNDO has concluded that it is desirable to reduce the share of foreign currency debt.[11] It adds risk without offering expected long-term cost savings. First, the government has few foreign currency assets (i.e., the foreign exchange exposure is basically unhedged).[12] Second, it is not unlikely that the domestic currency weakens in recessionary periods, because the costs of foreign currency debt would tend to add to swings in the deficit-to-GDP ratio. Third, at a somewhat subtler level, the simulations model illustrates that (under flexible exchange rates) domestic short-term interest rates are negatively correlated with the business cycle, because the central bank will vary short rates in a counter-cyclical manner. This tends to stabilize the ratio of debt costs to GDP. For a small country, foreign interest rates will be unaffected by domestic events, making foreign currency debt less attractive than domestic currency debt, other things being equal.

In the guidelines for 2001, the government decided that the share of foreign currency debt should be reduced.[13] No percentage target was set, partly because the desired share is so far below the current one that a decision on this point was not urgent. Instead, the government established a plan of annual amortizations corresponding to SKr 35 billion. Annual repayments could be varied within an interval of ±SKr 15 billion. The government instructed the SNDO to take account of the value of the krona when deciding the actual rate of repayment. If the krona is seen as significantly undervalued, it is rational—given a cost minimization target—to reduce repayments until the krona exchange rate has returned to more normal levels. In the guidelines for 2002, the government decided to lower the long-term rate of repayment to SKr 25 billion. Moreover, it set the 2002 target rate to SKr 15 billion, citing the weakness of the krona.

Also pointing to the depreciation of the krona, the SNDO used its mandate to hold back amortizations of close to SKr 15 billion in 2001. It has also announced that repayments will be made at a lower pace than the targeted rate from the start of 2002. In combination with a significant reduction in the krona-denominated debt and the depreciation of the krona, this has led to an increase in the foreign currency share during 2001 (Figure II.16.1). The long-term ambition is still to gradually decrease the foreign currency debt to achieve a debt portfolio more in line with the objective of debt management.

Inflation-linked debt

In the guideline proposal for 2002, the SNDO focused on the role of inflation-linked debt.[14] The quantitative results from the simulation model were less clear cut than in the analysis of foreign currency debt. The model indicates that there is little difference in terms of costs and risks between nominal and inflation-linked domestic currency debt. One potential explanation is that the model assumes the economy is not subjected to severe shocks. For example, budgetary and monetary policy targets are met on average in all simulations. The debt portfolios are thus not subjected to any stress-tests, because these are hard to handle in a long-term simulation model. In such an environment, there is little reason to expect inflation-linked debt to differ markedly from nominal debt.

Using qualitative reasoning, the SNDO points to other possibilities. For example, in an environment with low growth and low inflation, perhaps even deflation, inflation-linked bonds are helpful for deficit smoothing. Conversely, during a period of stagflation, having a large inflation-linked debt is undesirable. The observation that neither deflation nor stagflation can be ruled out before the fact. is then sufficient to indicate that a portfolio made up of several types of debt is preferable from the point of view of reducing risk. As long as inflation-linked bonds are not markedly more costly than nominal bonds, this diversification effect thus argues for including inflation-linked debt in the portfolio. The tentative assessment is that the share should be higher than the current 8 percent for inflation-linked debt to make an appreciable difference in an actual stress test.

In the guidelines for 2002, the government instructed the SNDO to increase the share of inflation-linked debt in the long term.[15] However, given the cost minimization objective, the rate of increase must be weighed against the costs of other types of debt. As in other countries, the inflation-linked bond market has periodically been characterized by limited investor demand and high liquidity premiums. An important task for the SNDO is therefore to continue its efforts to improve the functioning of the market so that the benefits in terms of reduced portfolio risks can be achieved at acceptable costs. (See also the third section.)

Duration

The choice of duration involves a trade-off between costs and refinancing risks. Experience indicates that nominal short rates, on average, are lower than long rates. Strict cost minimization would thus argue for having a debt with short duration. As noted before, domestic short rates may also be negatively correlated with the business cycle, which contributes to deficit smoothing. However, a short duration would make debt costs more sensitive to current interest rate levels. Moreover, short rates tend to be more volatile than long rates.

The duration of the nominal part of Swedish debt is 2.7 years, which has been concluded to represent a reasonable trade-off between the considerations discussed. The current guidelines thus indicate unchanged duration over the three-year planning horizon.

The inflation-linked debt is significantly longer, as is appropriate for an instrument aimed at protecting investors from inflation uncertainty. The guidelines state that inflation-linked debt should have at least five years' maturity at the time of issuance and preferably longer. Inflation-linked debt therefore extends average maturity and helps reduce refinancing risks for the debt portfolio as a whole.

Maturity profile

A duration target does not limit refinancing risks. In principle, a mixture of just two maturities can achieve any duration target. In practice, the rollover risk is limited by the SNDO's overall borrowing strategy, based on a set of nominal benchmark bonds extending to at least 10 years and a set of inflation-linked bonds, some of which have an even longer time to maturity. For the purpose of clarity, the guidelines still set a limit on the permissible extent of refinancing over the short term. The stipulation is that the SNDO should plan its borrowing in such a way that no more than 25 percent of the debt matures over the next 12 months.

Summary

Sweden has decided that the concept of risk in the statutory objective shall be interpreted in terms of how debt costs affect the overall stability of government finances. In this regard, Swedish authorities have adopted an ALM approach as the starting point for debt portfolio analysis. Given the time perspec-

tives involved in government debt management, potentially spanning generations, genuine uncertainty will always be a key element in debt management. One should therefore not expect to reach robust, once-and-for-all quantitative conclusions about what is an optimal debt portfolio. The main contribution of the ALM approach is probably as much in the questions it raises as in the formal answers. In particular, the debt manager is forced to address issues related to risk taking in a more consistent manner than if debt costs are seen in isolation from the rest of the government balance sheet.

Active debt management

Background

It is useful to distinguish between two types of active debt management. The first type includes actions allowing a separation between funding decisions, on the one hand, and decisions on the characteristics of the debt portfolio, on the other, achieved primarily through derivatives. Such activities are motivated by a desire to use low-cost methods of funding without necessarily accepting the risks attached to those instruments. The resulting debt portfolio should have lower funding costs or risk or both than an identical portfolio created by direct borrowing. This form of active management is driven by strategic considerations.[16]

The second type of active debt management refers to positions taken on the basis of views on the future paths of interest rates or exchange rates. This requires a defined benchmark. A position is then created by modifying the actual portfolio so that it deviates from the benchmark. The result of the position can be evaluated by comparing the (market) value of the actual portfolio to the value of the benchmark. This form of active management is typically driven by tactical considerations.

The SNDO uses both forms of active debt management. The following explains the motivations and frameworks used in each.

Portfolio management strategies

The separation between funding and portfolio decisions originates from how the foreign currency debt has been managed. Traditionally, the SNDO pursued an opportunistic borrowing strategy, seeking out low-cost funding sources without regard to currency or maturity. To achieve the desired composition of the foreign currency debt portfolio, expressed in a benchmark portfolio, it used derivatives to transform the cash flows.

Given this experience of working with derivatives, it was not a major step when the SNDO in 1996 began borrowing in Swedish krona and converting the debt into synthetic foreign currency obligations by use of foreign currency swaps.[17] This transformation involves several steps. First, the SNDO issues a long-term krona bond. Second, it does an interest-rate swap (IRS) in kronor in which it receives payments based on a fixed interest rate and pays based on a floating interest rate. Third, the floating krona cash flow is converted to euros, say, via a foreign currency swap. Finally, there is an IRS in foreign currency to achieve the desired duration of the foreign currency

exposure. At the end of 2001, about 45 percent of the foreign currency exposure, equivalent to SKr 180 billion, was in the form of krona/currency swaps. As can be seen in Figure II.16.2, annual swap volumes have varied between SKr 20 billion and SKr 40 billion, depending partly on the perceived depth of the market. In recent years, at least half of the krona bonds issued have been swapped.

Krona/currency swaps have for several years been the cheapest method for creating foreign currency exposure. The reason is that the SNDO—as a representative of the state—has a comparative advantage in long-term borrowing in kronor. In other words, the long-term swap rate is higher than the SNDO's long-term funding cost. This swap spread is partly offset by the fact that the floating swap rate is higher than the treasury bill rate, which determines the cost for direct short-term funding. As long as the average short-term spread over the term of the swap is lower than the initial long-term swap spread, the SNDO obtains cheaper

Figure II.16.2. Bond Issuance and Swap Volumes, 1996–2001

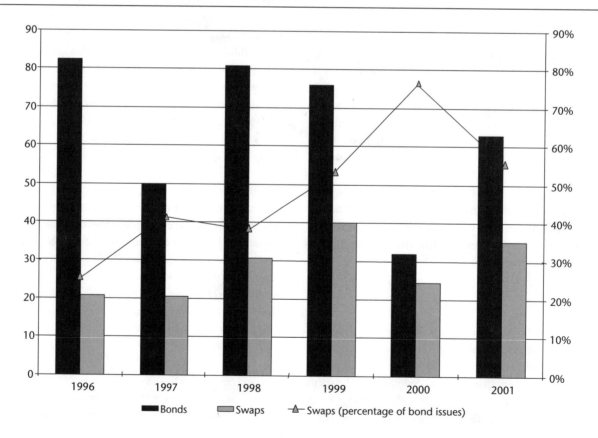

funding by using swaps than by issuing bills. Moreover, it avoids the refinancing risk.[18]

The SNDO has announced that IRSs can be used as an alternative to short-term funding, that is, as a complement to bills. This enables the SNDO to borrow in the long end of the yield curve without increasing the duration of the debt. Swaps thus also result in larger issue volumes in the Swedish bond market, which should support liquidity. This aspect has been important in recent years, when gross borrowing needs, following an improved budget situation, have decreased.

It is important that large-scale derivates transactions are handled in a transparent manner to avoid any confusion in the marketplace about the motives for using them. As in the bond market, the SNDO therefore announces its yearly planned swap activities. The volumes are decided based on previous experiences and following comments from market players. The actual volumes can change depending on market conditions. Moreover, a swaps book of the size built up in Sweden presupposes that swaps markets have sufficient depth, so that shrinking swap spreads do not erode the benefits. A gradual expansion of the program, with due regard to the costs of swaps relative to other funding techniques, is therefore advisable.

Swaps and other derivatives give rise to counterparty risks, which must be carefully managed. The SNDO uses credit support annex agreements as a method for reducing credit risks. This is a system of bilateral exchange of cash based on the current market value of the net position. Such a system limits the credit exposure to the daily changes in market value, allowing the SNDO to transact with the counter-parties that offer the best prices at each point basically without regard to the previous contracts written with those intermediaries.[19]

Tactical debt allocation

Foreign currency debt

The SNDO takes tactical positions to benefit from movements in exchange rates and interest rates only in the management of the foreign currency debt. The framework for this activity is a benchmark portfolio determined by the SNDO's board. The board defines a neutral portfolio in terms of currency and maturity composition and the maximum permissible deviations from this portfolio. Within these boundaries, the SNDO management has the mandate to take positions. The observance of these limits is monitored by the risk control department, which is separate from the debt management department.

The SNDO also engages external portfolio managers (currently five) working with the same mandate, scaled down to a fraction of the total foreign currency debt. This practice gives an additional measuring rod for evaluation of the SNDO's debt allocation decisions.

Domestic currency debt

The SNDO makes no corresponding debt allocation decisions based on views on interest rates in the management of the krona debt. The main reason is that the SNDO is so dominant a player in the krona fixed-income market that its reallocations could move interest rates. Opportunistic behavior by such a borrower will raise the overall level of interest rates as investors demand compensation for the added risks they face. Given its typical dominance of the domestic currency bond market, a predictable and transparent borrowing strategy is a better means to lower debt costs for a sovereign issuer. (See also the third section.)

As noted, the SNDO bases decisions on the rate of repayment of the foreign currency debt partly on exchange rate assessments. This is also a form of active debt management, affecting the composition of the debt, although there is no defined benchmark for the overall debt portfolio.

It should be emphasized that from the point of view of securing low costs and acceptable risks, active debt management relative to a benchmark portfolio is of secondary importance compared with the decision on the benchmark portfolio itself. For example, it is obvious that choosing a duration target of 2 years instead of 5 years affects costs and risks far more than variations within an interval of ±0.3 years around either central value. Still, the savings from successful active debt management can be significant in absolute numbers. Moreover, instruments used for position taking can be applicable also in conventional debt management, for example, on the use of derivatives instruments, thus giving positive side effects.

Cash management and the links to the central bank

The state payment system in Sweden is based on the single-account principle, that is, all payments are channeled through a system with a single top account, managed by the SNDO. Up until 1994, the balance on this account was held with the Riksbank. This meant that the SNDO was not engaged in cash management. Instead, the Riksbank had to sterilize the changes in bank reserves resulting from swings in the balance on the government's account.

In connection with Sweden's entry into the European Union (EU), it was decided that the SNDO should manage the top account outside the Riksbank. One reason was that EU rules prohibit the central bank from lending directly to the government, that is, the SNDO could no longer have a negative balance on its account overnight. Because the government's cash position fluctuates strongly over the month, it would have had to deposit a sizable sum with the Riksbank to create a buffer that would prevent the balance from ever turning negative. This was deemed to be an inefficient form of cash management.

In the current framework, the SNDO uses its Riksbank account for participation in the payment clearing system, but the balance on the account is set to zero at the end of each day. This is achieved via transactions in the short-term interbank market with such instruments as overnight loans and deposits, as well as repos. Typically, the balance is brought to zero by such interbank market transactions. On occasion, there is a remaining balance (positive or negative), rarely exceeding a few million kronor, at the end of the day. This is then transferred automatically to an account held by the SNDO with a commercial bank. In this way, the SNDO has responsibility for all aspects of government debt management, from overnight loans to 30-year inflation-linked bonds.

This arrangement also means that the Riksbank does not have to offset the swings in the government cash position via market operations. Because the SNDO is part of the interbank market, the reserves available to the banking system are not affected by the government's cash position. Separation of government cash management from the central bank thus also simplifies the Riksbank's task of managing its balance sheet to set the overnight interest rate at the target level.

Although the SNDO has been responsible for domestic currency cash management since 1994, it has continued to make all exchanges between kronor and foreign currencies with the Riksbank. The Riksbank makes the exchanges needed to cover the SNDO's purchases of foreign currencies in a predetermined pattern to avoid confusion with interventions for exchange rate policy purposes. Specifically, the bank buys a preannounced sum of foreign currency during a certain period on each trading day.

As of July 1, 2002, the SNDO will also have the right to make such exchanges with other counter-parties. The motivation for the government's decision is that this will allow greater flexibility in the handling of the transactions. Although the SNDO is also instructed to act predictably and transparently in the foreign exchange market—that is, short-term speculative transactions are ruled out—it need not adhere to such a strict calendar as the Riksbank, thus making it possible to also use the timing of purchases of foreign currency as an instrument for reducing the costs of the debt.

Management of contingent liabilities

Contingent liabilities in the form of guarantees can be issued only on the basis of authorization from parliament. Four government agencies are in charge of special guarantee programs related to export credit, housing, international aid, and deposit insurance. The SNDO issues other guarantees based on specific authorizations by parliament in each case. The budget law stipulates that a risk-related fee should be charged for guarantees. If parliament decides that the recipient of the guarantee does not have to pay, budget means must be reserved to cover the fee. The SNDO sets the fee, that is, there is a clear separation between the decision to issue the guarantee and the pricing. The accuracy of the SNDO's pricing decisions can be evaluated after the fact by checking whether the fees accumulated over long periods match the payments made to cover guarantee claims.

With an ALM approach to debt management, it is clear that guarantees (and other contingent liabilities) must be considered in analyses of the risks in public finances. In a consistent risk management framework, it should be possible, for example, to consider whether a risk reduction should be achieved via a change in the government debt portfolio or by transferring a guarantee to a guarantor in the private sector.

Again, this principle is easier to state than to implement. A first step would be to present consistent aggregate information on government guarantees. This should include expected losses on the total guarantee portfolio, but also capture the magnitude of unexpected losses. Reports on the guarantee portfolio should be presented to parliament in connection with the budget proposal. If the expected or unexpected guarantee losses increase, this should be considered before decisions on expenditures and taxes are taken, because this would be equivalent to a weakening of the underlying budget position. Such a framework is not in place in Sweden, but steps in this direction are being taken to improve the analysis and management of contingent liabilities.

Developing the Markets for Government Securities

Introduction

In addition to a well-balanced allocation among types of debt, a smoothly functioning market for government securities is important to achieve the objective of minimizing costs. As a dominant borrower and participant in the Swedish fixed-income market, the SNDO has a responsibility for ensuring the efficiency and development of the market. The SNDO has therefore taken an active role in the discussions and development of the market place. This includes measures to improve the secondary market to enhance liquidity and transparency. Some examples of measures taken in the different market segments are discussed in this section.

Nominal bonds

Primary market

The overall strategy is to concentrate borrowing in a few fairly large issues. Currently, there are around 10 such benchmark bonds. Large issues make trading easier, and the risk of short squeezes in specific issues is lowered. The SNDO previously aimed at ensuring that there were bonds maturing every year. This strategy was slightly changed during 2000, when a new 10-year issue was introduced, maturing in 2011, leaving 2010 without any maturity. Considering the large budget surpluses, it was more important to concentrate borrowing to support liquidity than to have yearly maturities of benchmark bonds. The maturity profile at the end of 2001 is illustrated in Figure II.16.3.

When a new issue is introduced, normally with a 10-year maturity, switches from old issues are carried out to quickly build up the new issue. In addition, a special repo facility of some SKr 20 billion is in place immediately after the first auction of the new bond. The repo rate is typically 15 basis points below the Riksbank's target for the overnight interest rate. This repo facility ensures that no single investors can squeeze the market for a new issue. As a result, the SNDO has not set any limitation on how large a share a single investor may hold of a single bond or on the share allocated to a single dealer in an auction.

Bond auctions are held biweekly. The issue for auction and the volume are announced one week in advance. The authorized dealers are committed to enter bids on behalf of investors and for their own account. The result is presented 15 minutes after the auction is closed.

Secondary market

One important way to enhance liquidity in the secondary market is to offer repo facilities to the authorized dealers. This lowers the risk of shortages and, hence, supports liquidity. To ensure that the SNDO does not assume too dominant a position in the repo market, these activities are limited. The SNDO has set a maximum repo volume of SKr 500 million, which the authorized dealers can use at a penalty rate of 60 basis points below the Riksbank's target for the overnight rate. This spread ensures that the facility is regarded as a "repo of last resort." Although these repo facilities are rarely used, they are important because they make it impossible to create a squeeze. With a penalty rate as high as 60 basis points, supply

Figure II.16.3. Maturity Profile for Nominal Bonds, December 2001

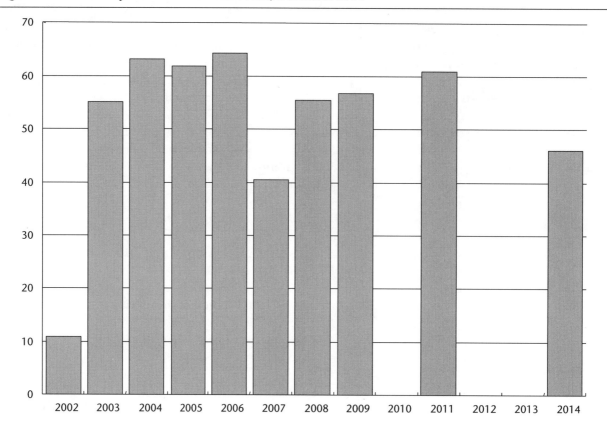

and demand in the market still govern pricing in normal circumstances, without interference from the SNDO.

In addition, repos are a natural instrument in the SNDO's liquidity management. When the SNDO needs to borrow in the short term, it might, for instance, lend a security to an investor in a repo to get short-term funds. In this case, the repo rate is 15–25 basis points below the targeted overnight interest rate. Other alternatives are to borrow directly in the deposit market or issue short-term treasury bills on tap.

Treasury bills

The Swedish treasury bill market is relatively large in an international perspective. About 20 percent of the total debt is in treasury bills. This market is built around the same principles as the bond market. Borrowing is made through biweekly auctions and is concentrated in eight bills, normally of up to 12 months' maturity (see Figure II.16.4). The repo market is less liquid and deep than the bond market, but the SNDO has similar repo facilities as those in the bond market, with slightly more generous conditions.

When a bond has less than one year to maturity, investors are offered opportunities to switch into a package of three or four bills. The package is constructed so that the exchange is duration neutral. The operation leaves the investor with more liquid securities and lowers the refinancing risk of the SNDO, because the redemption is spread over several dates.

Inflation-linked bonds

Inflation-linked bonds were introduced in 1994. The share of the total debt is some 8 percent. This makes the Swedish inflation-linked market one of the largest

Figure II.16.4. Maturity Profile for Treasury Bills, December 2001

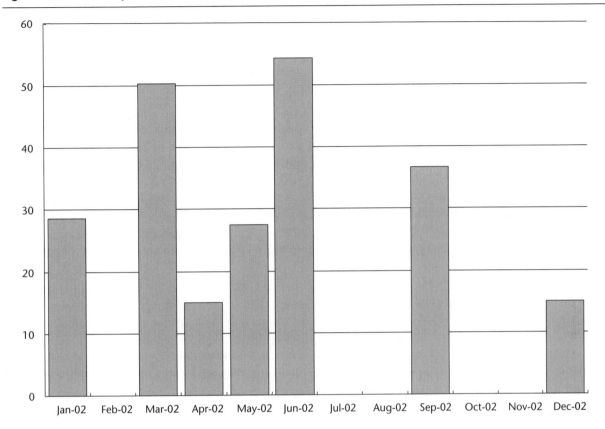

in the world in relative terms. There are currently seven inflation-linked bonds ranging from 2 to 26 years in maturity.

Two main arguments have been put forward to support issuance of inflation-linked bonds. First, the long-term funding cost should be lower, because the state assumes the inflation risk. If the inflation risk premium is higher than other premiums that might work in the other direction, such as liquidity premiums, the funding cost of inflation-linked bonds should be lower than for nominal bonds. The second argument—discussed in the second section—is that inflation-linked bonds contribute to diversification of the debt portfolio.

In the first years of the program, the cost argument seems to have been valid because investors bought inflation-linked bonds at breakeven levels higher than the official inflation target set by the Riksbank. Probably the inflation target at that time did not have full credibility, which made it rational for investors to pay to avoid the inflation risk. Inflation fell below the inflation target, and, as a consequence, the SNDO has calculated that so far the inflation-linked borrowing has saved some SKr 8 billion in accumulated funding cost since 1994. However, in recent years, the credibility for the 2 percent inflation target has been established, and breakeven inflation priced by the market has been below 2 percent. This has raised the question whether issuance of inflation-linked bonds is cost efficient.

The government and the SNDO have concluded that the cost saving might vary substantially over time. When inflation risks are regarded as small, it might be less favorable to issue inflation-linked bonds and vice versa when inflation risks rise. Also, it is important for the SNDO to support an efficient market for inflation-linked bonds to bring down the liquidity premium.

Developing a market for a new type of instrument is a challenge. Theoretical arguments support inclusion of inflation-linked bonds in long-term asset portfolios. However, most large asset portfolios in Sweden still have small shares of inflation-linked assets. There are several reasons behind this. One is probably that many investors use nominal accounting and benchmarking, making inflation-linked instruments appear more, rather than less, risky. Fund managers also have a tendency not to deviate very much from their competitors, implying that there may be thresholds that need to be passed to increase aggregate holdings of inflation-linked bonds.

One lesson from Sweden's experience is that a pragmatic approach is warranted. For example, the SNDO has issued inflation-linked bonds through both auctions and on tap. On-tap issuance—issuance of securities at the request of authorized dealers—worked well when the large domestic investors were building up strategic holdings in inflation-linked bonds. The on-tap method made it possible to meet this demand in a flexible way. As the market grew, auctions were introduced, because this method increased transparency and predictability.

Although inflation-linked bonds are sold through auctions, the SNDO offers authorized dealers an on-tap switching facility in the secondary market, making it possible for authorized dealers to switch between two bonds on a duration-neutral basis. The SNDO sets the price in a way that makes switches expensive for the dealers. Like repo facilities for nominal bonds, the switching facility should be regarded as a "last resort" offer. In addition, the SNDO has repo facilities for inflation-linked bonds. Each authorized dealer can repo SKr 200 million 25 basis points below the Riksbank overnight rate.

Ahead of auctions, the SNDO takes advice from authorized dealers. The SNDO is more inclined to listen to advice in the inflation-linked market than in the nominal bond market; dialogue with investors and dealers is more important in a new market.

Naturally, when deciding what and how much to issue, the SNDO also takes prices into account. In particular, the it tries to avoid funding at breakeven inflation rates, which are too low. However, the SNDO finds it important to support the market by also issuing at least small volumes when funding costs

seem less favorable. In the longer run, this should help bring down liquidity premiums and, hence, make inflation-linked funding less expensive.

Authorized dealers

The SNDO has three separate dealer agreements: one for nominal bonds, one for treasury bills, and one for inflation-linked bonds. The reason for having formal agreements is that it enables the SNDO to form dealer groups committed to take part in both the primary and secondary markets on an ongoing basis. A commitment from dealers is of added importance in Sweden, given its fairly small market.

The agreement for nominal bonds was changed in 2001, when an electronic trading platform was started. The SNDO used the agreements as an instrument to make a uniform change of the market structure possible. According to the new agreement, the authorized dealers will, apart from taking part in the primary market, quote binding two-way prices in 2-, 5-, and 10-year bonds in the electronic system. The agreement specifies minimum volumes and maximum bid-offer spreads. As part of the new agreement, the SNDO began to pay commissions to dealers to encourage participation in the electronic trading system. One part is fixed, and one is related to how active the dealer has been in the primary and secondary markets. In total, commissions amount to between SKr 15 million and SKr 20 million per year (equivalent to less than US$2 million).

An advisory board governs the new electronic trading platform. The authorized dealers, the SNDO, and the exchange are represented on that board.

The SNDO does not pay commissions in the treasury bill market, because the commitment needed—especially in the secondary market—from the dealers is not regarded as important as in the bond market. However, the authorized dealers have the advantage of being the only ones allowed to bid in the auctions and have access to repo facilities.

The agreement for inflation-linked bonds is more extensive in the sense that it requires the candidates to apply once a year and present a business plan for their activities. By requiring business plans, the SNDO wants to stress that it is important that dealers are active in promoting inflation-linked bonds to help broaden the investor base. Commissions are also paid to authorized dealers in the inflation-linked market—in total, about SKr 12 million per year.

Investor relations

As the fixed-income markets become more global and integrated, the importance of investor relations increases. Previously, the debt policy of a country was of interest for only a limited number of mostly domestic investors. Now, investors can and will choose from a number of fixed-income markets. Consequently, sovereign borrowers are in competition with each other and with other large issuers.

The main element in the SNDO's investor relations strategy is to have a transparent and predictable borrowing strategy. When investors understand the framework for debt management and know what variables are important, there will be less uncertainty and risk premiums will be lower. However, transparency and predictability do not exclude changes in borrowing plans or the set of instruments used. The issuer must have the opportunity to adjust its plans, for example, to unforeseen changes in the borrowing requirement. Therefore, the objective should be to communicate strategic principles—for example, duration of the debt and the desired debt composition—and explain what factors are important when formulating policies.

In this respect, the guideline system serves as a good basis. In the guidelines, investors and others can find the motives behind a certain strategy. The fact that all documents in the guideline process are public also allows dealers, investors, and other concerned parties to offer their comments.

The SNDO publishes a report three times a year in which it presents the latest forecast for the borrowing requirement as well as plans for future issuance. In addition, the report discusses different topics related to debt management. This may include articles about swap strategies, proposals for changes of the market structure, and similar topics. The purpose is to provide information and stimulate the debate on debt management. The Internet (www.rgk.se) is used extensively to make information available.

Apart from written material, the SNDO finds it important to be available to investors who want to discuss debt policy. The SNDO also takes initiatives to meet investors both in Sweden and abroad.

Clearing and settlement

All tradable debt instruments used by the SNDO are registered electronically with the Swedish Central Securities Depository and Clearing Organization (VPC), which is a corporation controlled by the major domestic banks. VPC handles the clearing and settlement of all transactions in government securities, as well as interest payments and repayment on maturity. The normal settlement date for treasury bills is T+2, and for bonds, it is T+3.

Clearing in the Swedish system is done on a net basis, making it sensitive to unwinding problems in the event of a major player failing to pay or deliver securities. To cope with this problem, all market players, including the SNDO and the Riksbank, have agreed to support the market through repo arrangements. However, this is not binding, that is, there is still a risk that unwinding problems would occur, which implies that the system does not fully comply with international standards. There is a systemic risk that is implicitly covered by the state. The Riksbank, as responsible for the payment system in Sweden, has demanded that the system be changed. At present, the introduction of a central counterpart seems the most likely solution, but other options, such as gross settlement, have been discussed.

Trends shaping the future market for government securities

Looking ahead, debt management and funding strategy in Sweden will continue to focus on broadening the investor base. This includes attracting new international institutional investors to offset the international diversification by domestic portfolio managers. However, it also involves making government debt instruments available to smaller investors, including retail. In recent years, such a development has to some extent been hindered by the extreme stock market performance; for private individuals in Sweden, fixed-income instruments have not seemed attractive. Following the correction in the stock market, the SNDO has noticed an increased appetite for fixed-income savings.

This raises issues related to how to reach retail investors. More efficient distribution channels might change the role of the authorized dealers and other intermediaries. One scenario could be that investors, retail as well as institutions, enter bids in auctions directly through the SNDO's web site. The advantage from the investors' point of view would be that they could enter bids without intermediaries and without revealing information to other market participants. Moreover, intermediaries might not find it worthwhile to invite retail investors to the primary market for government securities, because this may be less profitable than selling other products.

Therefore, the SNDO believes that to reach smaller investors, it is important to develop direct distribution channels. The drawback with such a strategy is that it might be costly to handle small lots. The trend toward straight-through processing should bring down this cost in the coming years, however. Also, the costs involved need to be valued against costs of using intermediaries, such as commissions and underwriting fees. In the more competitive environment faced by sovereign issuers, the fees required for such services may tend to rise.

It is far from certain what rapid technological change will mean for the distribution of debt instruments. However, the SNDO considers it important to be prepared in the event that new distribution channels, for example, based on Internet solutions, turn out to be attractive to investors. Changes are hard to anticipate, making it all the more important not to rely on only one strategy.

If the primary market changes with more direct selling to investors, what will then happen to the secondary market? Today, the secondary market is built around a market-maker system, with banks quoting two-way prices. With a less central role in the primary market, some intermediaries might not find it profitable to commit resources to secondary market activity. Either such a development will go hand in hand with a trend where debt markets, similar to the equity markets, are primarily order driven and market makers are less important; or the issuers will have to find new ways to get support from intermediaries in the

secondary market. In either case, it is rational to have alternative distribution channels. However, these alternatives should be developed taking into account the effects on the secondary market. Also, for retail investors, it is important that their bond holdings can be converted to cash at reasonable costs.

Continued technical change is bound to change fixed-income markets as it is changing other financial markets. The separation of the primary and secondary markets, and the strong role for intermediaries in both segments, are two areas where new solutions might come up. Therefore, it is advisable for debt managers to make possible changes in the traditional market structure into account when forming strategies for how to improve the functioning of government securities markets.

Notes

1. The case study was prepared by Lars Hörngren and Erik Thedéen from the Swedish National Debt Office.

2. This report deals with central government debt management. For brevity, the term "central" will be left out, unless it is needed to avoid confusion with other aspects of public debt.

3. Expenditures are controlled via the budget, not by ceilings on government borrowing or the size of the debt.

4. This also reflects a long-standing tradition in Sweden of working with small ministries, which are responsible for policy decisions, and delegating operative functions to agencies that have separate management and are at arm's length from the ministries.

5. Concrete illustrations of the contents of the guidelines are presented in the second section.

6. For more on the organization of the SNDO, see the second section.

7. The national audit office, an independent agency for central government auditing, also audits the activities and accounts of the SNDO.

8. The ALM perspective was introduced in the guideline proposal presented in October 2000, available at the SNDO's web site (http://www.rgk.se/files/upl497-Guidelines_2001.pdf).

9. The model and the simulation results are described in papers available at the SNDO's web site (http://www.rgk.se/files/upl553-Teknisk_Rapport.pdf).

10. The SNDO has used derivatives and other debt management instruments actively for a number of years. The numbers in Figure II.16.1 refer to the exposures when account has been taken of derivatives.

11. The analysis is presented in the guideline proposal for 2001, available at the SNDO's web site (http://www.rgk.se/files/upl497-Guidelines_2001.pdf).

12. The foreign exchange reserves are owned and managed by the Riksbank, reflecting its responsibility for implementing foreign exchange policy. Because the foreign exchange reserves are set aside for a special purpose, they give no hedging effect from

the point of view of the central government. The foreign currency debt and the foreign exchange reserves are therefore managed separately.

13. The government's decision for 2001 can be found at the SNDO's web site (http://www.rgk.se/files/upl546-statsskuld_eng.pdf).

14. The guideline proposal for 2002 is available at the SNDO's web site (http://www.rgk.se/files/upl1037-Riktlinjer_Eng.pdf).

15. The government's decision for 2002 can be found at the SNDO's web site (http://www.rgk.se/files/upl1115-riktlinjebeslut_2002_eng.pdf).

16. One could include exchanges and buybacks of outstanding debt in active debt management, because they imply deviations from a plain "issue-and-leave-outstanding" strategy. These instruments are discussed in the third section, because they are also meant to enhance market liquidity.

17. For an in-depth review of the use of swaps by debt managers (including the SNDO), see Gustavo Piga, *Derivatives and Public Debt Management* (Zurich: International Securities Market Association), 2001.

18. A long-term bond combined with an interest-rate swap is equivalent to a (synthetic) floating-rate note.

19. The SNDO works with symmetrical credit support annex agreements, that is, the it also transfers cash if a counter-party has a net claim, in line with market practice.

17

United Kingdom[1]

Developing a Sound Governance and Institutional Framework

Objectives of debt management policy

The government's current debt management policy was first outlined in the *Report of the Debt Management Review* in 1995. The debt management policy objective is: "to minimize over the long term the cost of meeting the government's financing needs, taking into account risk, whilst ensuring that debt management is consistent with the objectives of monetary policy."

This policy objective is achieved by

- pursuing an issuance policy that is open, predictable, and transparent;
- issuing conventional gilts that achieve a benchmark premium;
- adjusting the maturity and nature of the government debt portfolio by means of the maturity and composition of debt issuance and other market operations, including switch auctions, conversion offers, and buybacks;

- developing a liquid and efficient gilts market; and
- offering cost-effective retail savings instruments through national savings.

Before the 1995 review, the formal objective for debt management was to

- support and complement monetary policy;
- subject to this, avoid distorting financial markets; and
- subject to this, fund at least cost and risk.

However, it was felt these objectives were not an appropriate description of the way that debt management policy functioned in practice. In particular:

- Funding at least cost subject to risk is the primary objective of debt management policy.
- An efficient and liquid gilts market lowers yields and, hence, reduces funding costs, thus helping to achieve the primary objective.
- Debt management is not the major tool of monetary policy, nor is monetary policy the main objective of debt management.

- The objective did not mention the important specific roles of the gilts market and national savings.

The current objective focuses on the long term. This avoids the government seeking short-term gain by, say, reducing the debt interest bill over the published forecast period. The long-term nature of many of the instruments used in the debt market plus the importance of maintaining an issuer's reputation mean that it is preferable to focus on long-term aims rather than seek short-run gains.

By taking account of risk, the government does not follow a purely cost-minimizing strategy. Rather, the government seeks to ensure that it is robust against a variety of economic results. The main way of doing this is by considering the effect of issuance on the ensuing government debt portfolio. Broadly speaking, the government will not be able to predict which particular gilt will prove to be cheaper than any other, because they will seldom be any better informed than the market on the future path of key macroeconomic variables. Indeed, the market will price any relevant information into the gilt yield curve. Therefore, it would seem futile for the government to attempt to beat the market systematically by trying to anticipate the future path of the economy that differs from that embodied in market expectations. It is therefore preferable for the government to select a portfolio that would protect it from as wide a range of economic shocks as possible.

In terms of operational delivery of the new debt management objective, the 1995 review heralded a move away from a highly discretionary debt management policy. The review rejected the thesis that discretion benefited the government in that it could sell appropriate debt at advantageous prices. It was felt that under such arrangements, the government would pay an unnecessary premium, because it would be systematically attempting to beat the market and there would be no certainty over or transparency in the path of issuance policy. Therefore, the review advocated a change to a policy that would promote a more efficient, liquid, and transparent market. It recommended a move toward a policy of annual published remits that would set out in advance issuance in terms of type and maturity of gilt, a preannounced

auction calendar, and a movement toward more gilt sales by auction and less by tap.

Institutional framework for debt management

On May 6, 1997, the chancellor of the exchequer announced that he was granting operational control of interest rate policy to the Bank of England. Among the other changes announced were that operational responsibility for debt and cash management should pass to Her Majesty's Treasury. Following a consultation exercise in July 1997, treasury ministers announced the creation of a new executive agency, the United Kingdom Debt Management Office (DMO), which would be charged with carrying out the government's operations in the debt and cash markets. The DMO became officially operational as of April 1, 1998, and took over responsibility for debt management from the Bank of England from that date. Full responsibility for cash management was assumed on April 3, 2000.

Before April 1998, the Bank of England acted as the government's agent in the debt and cash markets. The transfer to Her Majesty's Treasury helped mitigate any perception that the government's debt and cash operations might benefit from inside knowledge over the future path of interest rates and avoided a potential conflict of interest, or perception of conflict, between the objectives of the government's debt and monetary policy operations. This separation of responsibilities allows the setting of clear and separate objectives for monetary policy, debt management, and cash management, with benefits in terms of reduced market uncertainty and, hence, lower financing rates. The Bank of England's monetary policy committee is able to raise any issues about the implications of debt management for monetary policy with the treasury's representative at monetary policy committee meetings.

As with all executive agencies, the DMO's relationship with the treasury is outlined in a framework document.[2] The basic structure for debt management is that treasury ministers advised by officials in the debt and reserves management team will set the policy framework within which the DMO will make operational decisions within the terms of the annual remit is set for them by treasury ministers. The

DMO's business objectives include a requirement for the DMO to advise the treasury about the appropriate policy framework, but strategic decisions rest with the respective ministers. The Bank of England acts as the DMO's agent for gilt settlement and retains responsibility for gilts registration.

Legal framework for borrowing

The government's overall policy on debt management is set out in "The Code for Fiscal Stability," which has statutory effect by virtue of Section 155 of the Finance Act, 1998. Paragraph 12 of the code states that:

> the primary objective of debt management policy shall be to minimize—over the long term—the costs of meeting the Government's financing needs whilst:
> - taking account of risk; and
> - ensuring that policy does not conflict with monetary policy.

All central government borrowing is done through the treasury (including the DMO) or national savings, although the Bank of England acts as agent for foreign currency borrowing for the official reserves. National savings is responsible for providing personal savings products to members of the public (mainly small investors).

The treasury has wide discretion as to how to raise money by borrowing, and it does so through two statutory funds, the National Loans Fund and the debt management account. Its main power to borrow for the National Loans Fund is conferred by Section 12 of the National Loans Act, 1968, which was subsequently amended in 1998 to establish the debt management account. This provides that the treasury can raise any money that it considers expedient to raise for the purpose of promoting sound monetary conditions in the United Kingdom, and this money may be raised in such manner and on such terms and conditions as the treasury thinks fit. Section 12(3) of the same act makes it clear that the treasury's power to raise money extends to raising money either within or outside the United Kingdom, and in other currencies. There are no set limits on the extent to which

the treasury may borrow from outside the United Kingdom. The treasury's power to borrow for the debt management account is conferred by Paragraph 4 of Schedule 5A of the National Loans Act, 1968, and this paragraph, like Section 12 of the act, gives the treasury a wide discretion as to how to raise money. Paragraph 4(3) is similar in terms to Section 12(3) of the act, and it provides that the treasury's power to raise money under Paragraph 4 extends to raising money either within or outside the United Kingdom, and in other currencies. Again, there is nothing in Schedule 5 of the act to limit the amount of money the treasury may borrow from outside the United Kingdom.

In practice, treasury borrowing takes a wide range of forms and ranges from the issuing of long-term securities (gilts) to the issuing of short-term treasury bills (12 months maximum) under the Treasury Bills Act, 1877.

Organizational structure within the DMO[3]

The chancellor of the exchequer, under advice from treasury officials, determines the policy and financial framework within which the DMO operates and delegates to its chief executive operational decisions on debt and cash management and day-to-day management issues. The chief executive is appointed by the treasury and variously reports to the permanent secretary (on expenditure and related issues), treasury Ministers (on policy issues), and parliament (in the formal presentation of accounts). In particular, he/she is responsible to treasury ministers for the overall operation of the agency and delivering the remit (which may include a confidential element that expands on the published remit) in a way that he/she judges will involve the least long-run cost to the exchequer, subject to being compatible with other policy considerations.

The DMO is organized around eight business units (see Appendix) and has a structure of corporate governance in place to assist the chief executive in carrying out his responsibilities. This comprises a high-level advisory board, advising the managing committee, which is the senior decision-making body for the office. The managing committee is in turn supported by a credit and risk committee and strategy groups for each key business area (debt, cash, investments). There are currently two external nonexecutive directors on the advisory board, both of whom are also on the office's audit committee, together with a member of the treasury. The advisory board, however, is an informal arrangement, and its proceedings are not published.

The DMO is an on-vote agency of the treasury, is financed as part of the treasury, and operates under arrangements that control its administrative cost. The DMO is subject to an internal audit function that reviews the systems of internal control, including financial controls, and to external audit by the national audit office. The chief executive is the accounting officer for both the office's administrative accounts and the accounts of the debt management account, through which all its market transactions pass.

The chief executive of the DMO is responsible for setting the DMO's personnel policies and managing staff. The office has delegated authority for pay, pay bargaining, training, and setting terms and conditions to recruit, retain, and motivate staff. Nonetheless, personnel policies are designed to be consistent with wider public sector pay policy and the *Civil Service Management Code*. The DMO achieved Investors in People accreditation in June 2000.

An important issue for debt managers is the need to control operational risk, which can entail large losses for the government and tarnish the reputation of debt managers. The DMO has developed a corporate governance framework to ensure sound risk monitoring and control practices to reduce operational risk (see the DMO's functional structure in the Appendix). The "Statement on Internal Control" in the *DMO's Annual Report and Accounts (ARA) 2001-02* (available on the DMO's web site) describes the DMO's approach to managing its operational risk. A risk management unit has been established within the DMO. A business continuity plan is also being developed with key market participants to mitigate the impact of a severe disruption to the market's infrastructure. The adequacy of the DMO's management of risk and internal controls is regularly reviewed by the DMO's audit committee, which is chaired by an external nonexecutive director.

Debt Management Strategy and the Risk Management Framework

Coordination of debt management and fiscal and monetary policy

The separation of debt management from monetary policy responsibility was part of the changes announced to the operation of monetary policy on May 6,1997. However, the debt management objective still has a reference to monetary policy. It ensures that the Bank of England's monetary policy responsibilities will not be undermined by the DMO or the treasury (e.g., "printing money" to meet the cash requirement or DMO cash market operations interfering with the Bank of England's money market operations).[4] This constraint on debt management reflects the institutional changes made in 1997. However, the *Debt Management Review* in 1995 noted that debt management no longer played a major role in the delivery of monetary policy objectives.[5]

The credibility of the United Kingdom's fiscal policy is underpinned by the government's fiscal framework[6] that was introduced in 1997 as part of the macroeconomic reforms of the current administration. In addition, "The Code for Fiscal Stability" (1998) sets out the principles that guide the formulation and implementation of fiscal policy. The relationship between debt management and fiscal policy is an area where there is an ongoing program of work. The treasury will shortly be producing work that will look at the linkages between fiscal policy and the debt portfolio. This work includes the development of a comprehensive asset and liability risk monitor to aid the quantification of the risks faced by the central government on its balance sheet. A preliminary version was published in the *Debt and Reserves Management Report 2002–03*, as a precursor to the publication of the whole of government accounts in 2005–06. Other risks related to the central government's contingent liabilities are currently being published annually within the "Supplementary Statements" that accompany the publication of the *Consolidated Fund and National Loans Fund Accounts*. A list of contingent liabilities and their maximum values is also available. Quantification and assessment of the risks that give rise to these liabilities will also be further developed.

Risk management framework

As previously noted, the 1995 *Debt Management Review* (as subsequently updated) established the primary objective of U.K. debt management policy as "to minimize over the long term the cost of meeting the government's financing needs, taking account of risk, whilst ensuring that debt management policy is consistent with the objectives of monetary policy." This primary objective has been reaffirmed in subsequent debt management reports, which are published annually with the budget papers. On the cost side, the main elements include nominal/cash-flow costs committed to when borrowing, real interest costs, accrual/net present value costs that include changes in capital costs on redemption, and the cost of issuance, which is relatively small for sovereign issuers.

These costs expose the balance sheet of the government to various risks, which are not as tractable as those of the private sector because governments tend not to match their financial liabilities with financial assets. Risks therefore need to be placed in the context of the overall government balance sheet and include

- default risk: the risk that the government will be unable to meet its nominal cash-flow commitments for interest and redemption payments;
- refinancing risk: the risk that government will be unable to refinance its maturing borrowing through further borrowing (or in doing so, it is faced with a high cost of finance);
- cash-flow risk: the risk that interest rate shocks cause large fluctuations in the debt interest bill; and
- mark-to-market/ex post financing risk: the risk that the government will regret its choice of borrowing instrument after the event because of nominal and real interest rate shocks.

Given the longevity of the government's balance sheet and the long maturity of its potential borrowings, these costs and risks need to be traded off over a relatively long time horizon. The optimal debt portfolio, comprising different types of securities and maturities, will depend primarily on which type of

risk the fiscal authorities are trying to contain and their preferences over any cost implications of a risk mitigation strategy. The focus could be on either variations in the debt-servicing cost alone (cash-smoothing/cost- at-risk) or in government spending as a whole (tax-smoothing). If considering the latter, the relationship among different economic variables and their effect on the level of the government's annual deficit (e.g., on government revenues and the returns on government assets) also needs to be considered.

Debt management strategy

The treasury, with the DMO, determines the desired structure of new issuance over the year ahead, taking into account the financing requirement and considerations of the various costs and risks. This accounting structure is outlined in the annual *Debt and Reserves Management Report* (*DRMR*) and is expressed in terms of the percentage of issuance across each class of gilt and overall financing to be raised through the issuance of treasury bills. In consultation with the treasury and market participants, the DMO makes further decisions about specific issuance instruments and timing during the year in line with the overall target. Significant changes in the public finances forecasts may lead to a revision in the remit. The *Chancellor's Pre-Budget Report* (generally available in November) provides an opportunity to revise this structure, if necessary in light of revised treasury forecasts for the economy.

It is currently the policy of the U.K. government to issue debt across a variety of instruments. At 7.83 years (by end-December 2001), the average modified duration of the gilts portfolio is longer than most of its peers among Organization for Economic Cooperation and Development member governments. This partly reflects the desire to minimize refinancing and cash-flow risks inherent in the high postwar debt-to-GDP ratios. It also prevents government financing from having a major impact on liquidity conditions for monetary policy and latterly has been a response to the high institutional demand for long-maturity paper from U.K. pension funds. Along with a relatively smooth redemption profile, this helps to add additional certainty to projections of future debt-servicing costs. Long duration will also limit the effect of any negative supply-side shock on the government's fiscal position.

By end-December 2001, 24.6 percent of the marketable debt portfolio was made up of index-linked gilts and treasury bills. In the event of a demand shock, this proportion should allow the changes in the debt-servicing cost relating to this particular part of the national debt to mitigate the resulting move in the government's budget balance. Of this, index-linked gilts also provide protection against a "nominal" shock. U.K. governments have not used foreign currency debt to finance the domestic borrowing requirement in peacetime, reflecting the belief that foreign currency risk to the balance sheet was neither desirable nor cost effective.

U.K. issuance of foreign currency debt in recent years has been used to augment the foreign currency reserves rather than for domestic funding reasons. Issuing liabilities in the currency in which the United Kingdom wished to hold foreign currency assets allowed exchange rate exposures to be hedged. However, the development of the swaps market has meant that the currency the debt is issued in, and the currency in which assets are held, do not necessarily have to be the same. Value for money is the primary concern when deciding whether to fund the foreign currency reserves from debt issued in pounds sterling swapped into foreign currency, or from the issuance of foreign currency–denominated debt, with the comparison being made on a swapped basis.

The government is conducting further work on managing risk in the debt portfolio by determining the resilience of cost and tax-smoothing properties of different debt structures to a range of economic conditions and shocks. This should help to quantify a more optimal debt portfolio against which an issuance strategy and long-term performance could be assessed.

The treasury select committee's report on debt and cash management[7] recommended, "that the Treasury considers adopting a benchmark approach to debt management … [that] … would help produce a clear published assessment of the costs and risks faced by the DMO." Responding to the committee, the government accepted that greater transparency in performance measurement would be desirable if it could be achieved without compromis-

ing other strategic debt management objectives, but expressed reservations about the extent to which this was possible. The DMO's aim has not been developed into an all-embracing quantitative target, or set of benchmarks, for four reasons:

- Minimizing debt interest costs over a short period could encourage opportunistic behavior with potential damage to the long run-objective. (A nonopportunistic approach to debt management reduces the long-term risk premium priced into gilt yields.)
- It is not straightforward to decide the interest rate risk that the exchequer should take in its liability portfolio, given that it is not being matched against a portfolio of financial assets.
- Any benchmark is not independent of the DMO's own actions, as monopoly supplier of U.K. government bonds, and so it could be altered to a degree by the DMO's decisions.
- The DMO and the treasury do not want to be considered to be taking short-term views on interest rate changes, to maintain the separation of monetary policy decision making and debt and cash management.

The DMO does not seek to manage the debt portfolio actively to profit from expectations of movements in interest rates and exchange rates, which differ from implicit market prices. This would risk financial loss as well as potentially sending adverse signals to the markets and conflicting with monetary or fiscal policies or both. It would also add to market uncertainty.

However, a target duration for the portfolio is implicit in the financing structure agreed annually with the treasury, in that it sets out clear parameters within which the DMO must operate is.

Developing the markets for government securities

Since the comprehensive review of debt management in 1995, there have been a number of advances in issuance techniques, the range of debt instruments has been refined and expanded, and numerous structural changes to the debt markets have taken place. The overall aim of the reforms has been to help lower the cost of public financing over the long term, responding to both endogenous and exogenous factors that have influenced the U.K. debt market during the period. In recent years, these factors have included budget surpluses, the rapid rise of the U.K. corporate bond sector, institutional changes (particularly those relating to pension funds), increasing technological and other advancements (which have enhanced systems), market structures, and debt instruments around the world.

The process of reform has been continued by the DMO, whose published objectives include "to conduct its market operations, liaising as necessary with regulatory and other bodies, with a view to maintaining orderly and efficient markets and promoting a liquid market for gilts." All the changes to the market have involved considerable consultation with market participants and other stakeholders to develop broad-based support and promote predictability.

Issuance transparency

Although the benefits are difficult to quantify, transparency and predictability should reduce the amount the government is charged for market uncertainty (the "supply uncertainty premium"). Predictability should also allow investors to plan and invest more efficiently (in the knowledge of when and in what maturity band supply will occur) and thus reduce the liquidity risk premium. This is particularly the case in the United Kingdom, where government debt constitutes a relatively significant proportion of fixed-income debt and opportunistic trading on the part of the government would have a significant influence on the market.

The government's borrowing plans for the year ahead are announced before the start of each financial year in the *DRMR* published by the treasury alongside the budget, usually each March.[8] The *DRMR* details the financing requirement, the forecast sales of gilts, their breakdown by maturity and instrument type, and the gilt auction calendar for the coming year, along with planned short-term debt sales, including treasury bills. An auction calendar is also issued at the end of each quarter by the DMO, which confirms auction dates for the coming quarter and states which gilts are to be issued on which date. Normally, eight calendar days before an auction, the

amount of stock to be auctioned is announced (and if it is a new stock, the coupon). At this point, the stock is listed on the London Stock Exchange (LSE) and when-issued trading commences. (This is the forward trading of the stock to be sold at the auction. When-issued trades settle on the auction's settlement date, and the process helps reveal price information in the run-up to the auction.)

Market makers and end-investor groups are consulted during the formulation of these plans (and also quarterly before the DMO announces specific auction stocks for the quarter ahead).

Gilts are now issued entirely by auction unless there are exceptional circumstances. The DMO retains the ability to buy back or issue gilts in smaller quantities (by tap) at short notice for market management reasons only. Buybacks can be done either bilaterally or by reverse auction. The DMO also undertakes a range of market management operations, which are essentially neutral in terms of government financing and include the conversion or switching between specified stocks and repurchase (repo) activities. A gilt repo involves one party selling gilts to a counter-party with an agreement to repurchase equivalent securities at an agreed price on an agreed date. In June 2000, the DMO introduced a nondiscretionary standing repo facility, whereby the DMO may temporarily create upon request a gilt for repo, for the purpose of managing actual or potential dislocations in the gilt repo market. Operational transparency is enhanced through close coordination with market participants and agreed announcement and publication requirements.[9]

Portfolio operations and instruments

The U.K. securities market incorporates a range of debt instruments, including treasury bills, conventional gilts, double-dated gilts, undated gilts, index-linked gilts, and gilt strips.[10] The distribution of the portfolio and the main holders of gilts are detailed in the Tables II.17.1 and II.17.2 and Figure II.17.1.

Treasury bills

The DMO took over full responsibility for exchequer cash management on April 3, 2000.[11] The transfer of

Table II.17.1. Details of the Debt Portfolio at December 31, 2001

Figure II.17.1 Composition of Debt Stock	Gilt portfolio summary statistics	
Conventional 70.3% / T-bills 3.9% / Index-linked 24.6% / Undated 1.1%	Nominal value of the gilt portfolio (including inflation uplift)	£274.92 bn
	Market value of the gilt portfolio	£302.76 bn
	Weighted average market yields:	
	Conventional gilts	4.90%
	Index-linked gilts	2.44%
	Portfolio average maturity	11.28 yrs
	Portfolio average modified duration	7.83 yrs
	Portfolio average convexity	115.35
	Average amount outstanding of largest 20 gilts	£9.80 bn

Source: DMO quarterly review (October–December 2001).

Table II.17.2. Distribution of Gilt Holdings as of end-December 2001
(Market values)

	End-Dec. 2001 £bn	Percentage
Insurance companies and pension funds	183.7	63
Banks and building societies	3.1	1
Other financial institutions	29.6	10
Households	18.8	6
Public sector holdings[a]	4.4	2
Overseas sector	53.4	18
Total	**292.9**	**100**

a. Local authorities, public corporations, and charities. Net of central government holdings.
Source: Office for National Statistics.

cash management to the DMO was delayed from the earliest possible date in October 1998 by technical, capacity, and administrative issues (including concerns over systems during the millennium period).

The DMO's main strategic objective in carrying out its cash management role is to "offset, through its market operations, the expected cash flow into or out of the National Loans Fund (NLF),[12] on every business day; and in a cost effective manner with due regard for credit risk management."[13] An important part of the DMO's approach is to seek to ensure that its actions do not distort market or trading patterns and as such, in its bilateral dealings with the market, the DMO is a price taker. The DMO also has to take account of the operational requirements of the Bank of England for implementing its monetary policy objectives.

The DMO carries out its cash management objectives primarily through a combination of weekly treasury bill tenders conducted on a competitive bidding basis, bilateral operations with DMO counter-parties, and repo or reverse repo transactions.

Treasury bill tenders are currently held on the last business day of each week for settlement on the next working day. Following the final tender at the end of each calendar quarter, the DMO issues a notice broadly outlining the maturities of treasury bills available in each week of the next quarter. The precise quantities of bills on offer and the maturity of bills on offer in each week are announced one week before the relevant tender.

To facilitate a significant increase in the stock of treasury bills, the DMO changed the arrangements relating to the issuance by tender of treasury bills from October 5, 2001. As part of these changes, the DMO recognized a list of primary participants in the treasury bill market. These are banks or financial institutions that have agreed to place bids at treasury bill tenders on behalf of other parties, subject to their own due diligence and controls. On request, the primary participants will also provide their customers with secondary dealing levels for treasury bills. The DMO's cash management counter-parties and a limited number of wholesale market participants who have established a telephone bidding relationship with the DMO are also eligible to bid directly in treasury bill tenders.

The DMO publishes the tender results on the wire services pages. The DMO will announce, at the same time, the amounts on offer at each maturity at the next tender, together with an outline of any planned ad hoc tenders to be held in the following week.

The DMO may also issue shorter-maturity treasury bills (up to 28 days) at ad hoc tenders. The objective of ad hoc tenders will be to provide additional flexibility for the DMO in smoothing the exchequer's cash flows, which the regular tender program may not provide.

Gilts

Conventional gilts are the simplest form of government bond and constituted 70.3 percent of the debt portfolio as of end-December 2001. There are eight undated gilts still in issue, making up about 1 percent of the portfolio. Their redemption is at the discretion of the government, but because of their age, they all have low coupons and there is little current incentive for the government to redeem them. The last floating-rate gilt (whose coupon was set with reference to the three-month Libid [London interbank bid]) rate] was redeemed on maturity in July 2001. To avoid periodic price fluctuations related to coupon payment dates, gilt prices are now quoted clean, that is, without accrued interest, although the "dirty"

price (including accrued interest) is used for conversion offers.

The United Kingdom was one of the earliest governments to introduce index-linked bonds, with the first issue in 1981. Index-linked bonds now account for about 25 percent of the government securities portfolio.

Gilt strips[14]

The U.K. gilt STRIPS market was launched on December 8, 1997. "Stripping" a gilt refers to breaking it down into individual cash flows that can be traded separately as zero-coupon gilts. Not all gilts can be stripped, although it is the DMO's intention to make all new gilts strippable. The STRIPS market was introduced to permit investors to

- closely match the cash flows of their assets (strips) to those of their liabilities (e.g., annuities),
- enable different types of investment risk to be taken, and
- bring the range of products offered in the U.K. market in line with other large markets, such as the United States, Japan, Germany, and France.

From the issuer's perspective, a STRIPS market can result in slightly lower financing costs if the market is willing to pay a premium for "strippable" bonds. As of September 28, 2001, there were 11 strippable gilts in issue, totaling £115.18 billion (nominal). Of these, £2.4 billion of stock was held in stripped form. All issues have aligned coupon payment dates. This means that coupons from different strippable bonds are fungible when traded as strips. However, coupon and principal strips paid on the same day are not fungible, that is, a specific bond cannot be reconstituted by substituting the relevant principal strip with a coupon strip with the same maturity. This feature protects the overall size of any issue and thus maintains the integrity of various benchmarking indices.

The first series of strippable stocks were issued with June 7/December 7 coupon dates; however, in 2001, the DMO issued two new conventional stocks with coupon dates aligned on March 7/September 7. These stocks will become strippable from April 2002.

The second series of coupon dates was introduced to avoid cash flows becoming too concentrated on just two days in the year.

Although anyone can trade or hold strips, only a gilt-edged market maker (GEMM), the DMO, or the Bank of England can strip (or reconstitute) a strippable gilt through the CREST electronic settlement system. GEMMs are obliged to make a market for strips.

The market in gilt strips has grown slowly since its inception. Factors that have contributed to this slow take-off have been the need for pension fund trustees to give appropriate authority to fund managers to invest in strips and the inversion of the yield curve over the period since the inception of strips, which makes strips appear expensive relative to conventional gilts. Retail demand for strips has also been hampered by the necessary tax treatment, whereby securities are taxed each year on their accrued capital gain or loss, even though no income payment has been made. However, the ability to hold strips within some tax-exempt savings products will reduce the tax disincentives to personal investment in strips.

GEMMs

The U.K. government bond market operates as a primary dealer system. As of end-December 2001, there were 16 firms recognized as primary dealers (GEMMs) by the DMO. Each GEMM must be a member of the LSE and must undertake a number of market-making obligations in return for certain benefits.

In broad terms, the obligations of a GEMM are to participate actively in the DMO's gilt issuance program, make effective two-way prices on demand in all nonrump gilts and non-index-linked gilts, and provide information to the DMO on market conditions. As September 28, 2001, 10 of the 16 recognized GEMMs were also recognized as index-linked gilt-edged market makers (IG GEMMs). Their market-making obligations extend to cover index-linked gilts.

The benefits of GEMM status are exclusive rights to competitive telephone bidding at gilt auctions and taps, either for the GEMM's own account or on behalf of clients; exclusive access to a noncompetitive bidding facility at outright auctions; the exclusive facility to trade or switch stocks from the DMO's dealing screens; exclusive facilities to strip and reconstitute gilts; an invitation to a quarterly consultation meeting with the DMO[15] (allowing the GEMMs to advise on the stock(s) to be scheduled for auction in the following quarter and discuss other market-related issues); and exclusive access to gilt interdealer broker (IDB) screens. In addition, any transactions undertaken by the DMO for market management purposes are carried out only with or through the GEMMs.

Since early 2002, the GEMMs have been required to provide firm two-way quotes to other GEMMs in a small set of benchmark gilts. These quotes are to be made on a near-continuous basis on any of the recognized IDB screens. The purpose of this new obligation is to enhance liquidity in the intra-GEMM market for the benefit of the entire secondary market for gilts.

Gilt IDBs

As of end-December 2001, there were three specialist gilt IDBs operating in the gilt market. Their services are limited to the GEMM community. Their main purpose is to support liquidity in the secondary markets by enabling the GEMMs to unwind anonymously any unwanted gilt positions acquired in the course of their market-making activities. All but a few inter-GEMM trades are executed through an IDB. Non-index-linked GEMMs have no access to index-linked screens.

Each IDB is registered with the LSE and endorsed by the DMO. The DMO monitors this segment of the market on an ongoing basis to ensure that an IDB service is available to all GEMMs on an equitable basis and the market-maker structure is effectively supported by the IDB arrangements. The IDBs are also subject to specific conduct-of-business rules promulgated by the LSE. For example, they are prohibited from taking principal positions or from disseminating any market information beyond the GEMM community.

Mechanisms used to issue gilts

Auctions are the exclusive means by which the government issues gilts as part of its scheduled funding operations. However, the government retains the flexibility to tap or repo both index-linked and conventional gilts for market management reasons. The move to reliance on a preannounced auction schedule reflects the government's commitment to transparency and predictability in gilt issuance.

The government uses two different auction formats to issue gilts:

- conventional gilts are issued through a multiple-price auction, and
- index-linked gilts are auctioned on a uniform-price basis.

The two different formats are used because of the different nature of the risks involved to the bidder for the different securities.

Conventional gilts are viewed as having less primary issuance risk. There are often similar gilts already in the market to allow ease of pricing (or, if more of an existing gilt is being issued, there is price information on the existing parent stock); auction positions can be hedged using gilt futures; and the secondary market is relatively liquid. This suggests that participation is not significantly deterred by bidders not knowing the rest of the market's valuation of the gilts on offer. A multiple-price auction format also reduces the risk to the government of implicit collusion by strategic bidding at auctions.

In contrast, positions in index-linked gilts cannot be hedged as easily as conventional gilts. The secondary market for index-linked gilts is also not as liquid as for conventional gilts. Both of these factors increase the uncertainty of index-linked auctions and increase the "winner's curse" for successful bidders—that is, the cost of bidding high when the rest of the market bids low. Uniform price auctions thus reduce this uncertainty for auction participants and encourage participation. In addition, there are fewer index-linked bonds than conventionals in issue, so pricing a new index-linked issue may be harder than for a new conventional.

GEMMs also have access to a noncompetitive bidding facility under both formats. They can submit a noncompetitive bid for up to 0.5 percent of the amount of stock on offer in a conventional gilt auction. The proportion of stock available to each index-linked GEMM in an index-linked auction is linked to their performance in the previous three auctions.

The DMO allots stock to individual bidders at its absolute discretion. In exceptional circumstances, the DMO may choose not to allot all the stock on offer, for example, where the auction was covered only at a level unacceptably below the prevailing market level. In addition, the DMO may decline to allot stock to an individual bidder if it appears that to do so would be likely to lead to a market distortion. As a guideline, successful bidders, either GEMMs or end-investors, should not expect to acquire at the auction for their own account more than 25 percent of the amount on offer (net of the GEMM's short position in the when-issued market or parent stock or both) for conventional gilts and 40 percent for index-linked stock.

Tap issues

The DMO will use taps of both conventional and index-linked gilts only for market management reasons in extreme conditions of temporary excess demand in a particular stock or sector. The last tap was in August 1999.

Conversion offers and switch auctions

In addition, the DMO will occasionally issue stock through a conversion offer or a switch auction, in which stockholders are offered the opportunity to convert or switch their holding of one gilt into another at a rate of conversion related to the market prices of each stock. In both cases, the main purposes of these operations are to

- build up the size of new benchmark gilts more quickly than can be achieved through auctions alone (This is particularly important in a period of low issuance.); and
- concentrate liquidity across the gilt yield curve by reducing the number of small, high-coupon gilts and converting them into larger, current-coupon gilts of broadly similar maturity.

Conversion candidates will not have fewer than about five years to maturity or more than £5.5 billion nominal outstanding. In addition, conversion offers will not be made for a stock that is "cheapest-to-deliver," or has a reasonable likelihood of becoming cheapest-to-deliver, for any gilt futures contracts with any outstanding open interest.

The price terms of any conversion offer will be decided by the DMO, using its own yield-curve model to provide a benchmark ratio for the offer. The DMO will then (at its own discretion) adjust this ratio to take some account of the observed cheap/dear characteristics of the source and destination stocks. Conversion offers remain open for a period of three weeks from the date of the initial announcement of the fixed dirty-price ratio. The appropriate amount of accrued interest on both gilts is incorporated into the calculation of the dirty-price ratio for forward settlement. The conversion itself will involve no exchange of cash flows.

Acceptance of such offers is voluntary, and stockholders are free to retain their existing stock. However, this is likely to become less liquid (i.e., traded less widely, with a possible adverse impact on price) if the bulk of the other holders of the gilt choose to convert their holdings. Should the amount outstanding of a gilt be too small to expect the existence of a two-way market, the DMO is prepared, when asked by a GEMM, to bid a price of its own choosing for the gilt. In addition, the DMO would relax market-making obligations of GEMMs in this "rump" gilt. The DMO would announce if a gilt took on this "rump" status.

In addition to the main purposes identified for conversion offers, switch auctions were introduced in 2000 to

- allow the DMO to smooth the immediate gilt redemption profile by offering switches out of large ultra-short issues into the current five-year benchmark (or other short-term instruments), and
- facilitate switching longer by index-tracking funds as a particular stock is about to fall out of a significant maturity bracket, thus contributing to market stability.

Switch auctions are held only for a proportion of a larger stock that is too large to be considered for an outright conversion offer. The DMO ensures that a sufficient amount of the source stock remains for a viable, liquid market to exist following a switch auction. Hence, the DMO will not hold a switch auction for a conventional stock that would reduce the amount in issue to below £4.5 billion (nominal). Switch auctions

are held only when both the respective stocks are within the same maturity bracket, although here the maturity brackets overlap (short and ultra-short, 0–7 years; medium, 5–15 years; long, 14 years and more). In addition, the DMO will not hold a switch auction out of a stock that is cheapest-to-deliver, or has a reasonable likelihood of becoming cheapest-to-deliver, into any of the "active" gilt futures contracts. The DMO might, however, switch into such a stock.

Switch auctions are open to all holders of the source stock, although non-GEMMs must route their bid through a GEMM. They are conducted on a competitive bid-price basis, where successful competitive bidders are allotted stock at the prices they bid. There is no noncompetitive facility, and the DMO does not set a minimum price.

The same principles apply to index-linked switch auctions with the following exceptions. First, index-linked switches will be held only when both the respective stocks have longer than four and one-half years to maturity and when the source stock has not been auctioned in the previous six months. Second, the (nominal) size of any single index-linked switch auction is limited to £250 million to £750 million of the source stock, and the DMO will not hold a switch auction that would leave an index-linked stock with a resultant amount outstanding of less than a nominal £1.5 billion. Third, the auctions are conducted on a uniform bid-price basis, whereby all successful bidders will receive stock at the same price. Where a GEMM's bids are above this price, it will be allotted in the full amount bid, but allotments for bids at the striking price may be scaled. Published results will include the common allotment price, the pro rata rate at this price, the real yield equivalent to that price and the inflation assumption used in that calculation, and the ratio of bids received to the amount on offer (the cover). Only one index-linked switch auction has been held up until end-2001.

Gilt repo

The gilt repo market was introduced in January 1996. After 1986, a limited market in stock borrowing existed in which GEMMs (and discount houses for short-dated stocks) were allowed to cover *short* positions by borrowing stock in the stock-lending market and approved stock lenders were allowed to lend. However, the introduction of an entirely open trading market in gilt repos has enabled market participants to borrow or lend gilts more easily. This has improved market liquidity and the ease with which gilt positions can be financed. A Bank of England survey put the size of the gilt repo market as of November 2001 at £130 billion (equivalent to one-fourth of the pound sterling money market at that time), with an additional £48 billion of stock lending.

Gilt repos now account for the majority of Bank of England monetary policy operations and a significant proportion of the DMO's dealing to manage the exchequer's cash flow. It is estimated that gilt repos now account for about half of all overnight transactions in the pound sterling money market. Conduct in the gilt repo market is guided by the *Gilt Repo Code of Best Practice*, as published by the stock lending and repo committee chaired by the Bank of England (latest version, August 1998).

The DMO has the ability to create and repo specific stocks to market makers, or other DMO counter-party, under a special repo facility if, for example, a particular stock is in exceptionally short supply and distorting the orderly functioning of the market. In response to a previous consultation exercise, the DMO introduced, in June 2000, a nondiscretionary standing repo facility, for the purpose of managing actual or potential dislocations in the gilt repo market. Any registered GEMM, or other DMO counter-party, may request the temporary creation of any nonrump stock for repo purposes. The DMO charges an overnight penalty rate, and the returned stock is canceled.

Recent Factors Shaping the U.K. Bond Markets

As in other currencies, the pound sterling credit market has seen increased annual private issuance in recent times, at a time when the United Kingdom has been running a budget surplus. Thus, the government's percentage of the overall outstanding pound sterling debt market had been steadily reducing. Decreasing government funding requirements have led to gilts acquiring a scarcity premium, especially in longer-dated stocks, which in turn has lead to a reduction in yields. At the same time, the United Kingdom has enjoyed a low-inflation, low-interest rate environment recently (relative to the 1970s and 1980s), so a need to enhance returns has led investors to increase their appetite for (credit) risk.

As the U.K. government's budgetary position improved, gross issuance of gilts declined from a peak of £54.8 billion in financial year 1993–94, reaching a minimum of £8.1 billion in 1998–99. However, given that the government's borrowing needs are cyclical, there is a benefit in maintaining a minimum level of issuance so that market infrastructure is sustained and the market remains sufficiently liquid and retains the capability to absorb future larger gross issuance. Table II.17.4 summarizes the government's forecast for the central government net cash requirement over the next few years. The medium-term forecasts point to a prudent level of borrowing, reflecting planned investments in public services that are fully consistent with the fiscal rules.

In view of the limited amount of gilt issuance in recent years, the DMO has adopted a number of strategies to concentrate debt issuance into larger benchmark issues, currently at three maturity points, with a 5-, 10-, and 30- year term to maturity. These larger issues allow governments to capture a liquidity premium across the yield curve. The DMO has also used conversion and switch auctions to build up benchmark issues.

The government also decided to launch a structured gilt buyback program in fiscal year 2000/01 to add to gross issuance and thus help to maintain liquidity in the market during a time of strong demand.

Table II.17.3. Changing Levels of Debt
(Absolute terms and relative to GDP)

	2000/01	1999/00	1998/99	1997/98
Market value of debt	£287 bn	£348 bn	£374 bn	£343 bn
Net debt/GDP (percent)	31.8	36.8	40.8	43.3

Table II.17.4. April 2002 Public Borrowing Requirement Forecasts for the Central Government Net Cash Requirement

(£ billion)

2001–02 projection	2002–03 projection	2003–04 projection	2004–05 projection	2005–06 projection	2006–07 projection
3	14	18	16	21	24

Following market consultations, reverse auctions were reintroduced in fiscal year 2000/01 while the DMO bought in, direct from the secondary market, short-dated index-linked gilts and double-dated gilts. The DMO also buys in near-maturity gilts (with less than six months' residual maturity) as part of its regular operations to smooth the cash-flow impact of redemption.

In general, these operations have been very successful. There was more than 90 percent take-up of the conversion offers, apart from the one conducted in November 1998. The switch auctions have all been covered with a comfortable margin, and the three longer-dated switches have secured very attractive forward-dated funding rates. The rates at which the DMO has repurchased stock in the reverse auction was at yields, which were predominantly "cheap" relative to the DMO's fitted yield curve.

During fiscal year 2000/01, the DMO (in consultation with the Bank of England, the treasury, the Radio Communications Agency, and market participants) put in place arrangements to facilitate the smooth handling of much larger than expected receipts from the third-generation mobile phone license auction. Total receipts of £22.5 billion amplified the fiscal surplus in fiscal year 2000/01. The government subsequently decided to maintain a minimum level of gross gilts issuance to sustain gilt market liquidity and investor interest in light of the forecasts of an increase in the financing requirement over the next few years. As a consequence of these policy decisions, the DMO held a short-term net cash position of £11 billion at the end of fiscal year 2001/02. Partly to assist the management of this, the range of high-quality, short-term money market instruments in which the DMO may transact on a bilateral basis for cash management purposes was

extended in October 2000. It is expected that the cash position will be run down over the three financial years to end-March 2004.

As part of its continuing commitment to encourage liquidity and transparency of the gilts market, the DMO consulted widely in 2000 about the possible impact of electronic trading systems on the secondary market for gilts and how the DMO's relationship with the GEMMs might change as a consequence. That work continued during 2001, with a view to introducing early in 2002 inter-GEMM mandatory quote obligations in the more liquid gilts, as outlined in the response document published in June 2000.

To promote further transparency in the gilts market, in September 2000, the DMO introduced a real-time benchmark gilt price screen on its wire services showing indicative midprices for a series of gilts derived from GEMMs' published quotes.

Tax

In 1995–96, the basis for taxation of gilts was reformed. Essentially, this meant that capital gains or losses on gilts experienced by corporate investors would be taxed similarly to income from gilts. This eliminated most of the tax-driven pricing anomalies in the market by making the tax system neutral with regard to holding high- or low-coupon bonds, which was a necessary precondition to launching the STRIPS market to avoid tax-based incentives for stripping all or none of a bond. In addition, since April 1998, all gilt interest has been paid gross, unless the recipient has preferred net, to reduce the compliance obligations for custodians and make the gilt market more accessible and attractive to investors.

Appendix

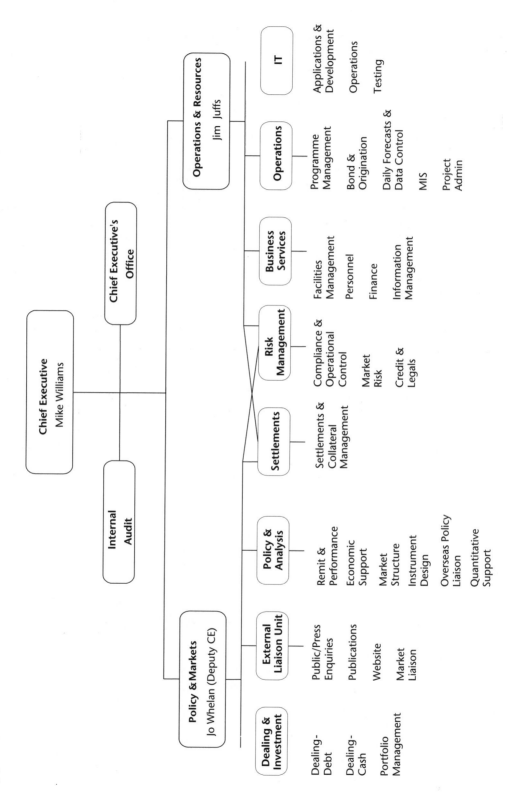

Notes

1. The case study was prepared by the U.K. Debt Management Office and the Debt and Reserves Management Team of the U.K. Treasury.

2. A full description of all the DMO's responsibilities, objectives, and lines of accountability is set out in the current version of its *Framework Document* (July 2001, www.dmo.gov.uk/publication/f2spc.htm). Other relevant documents can be found on the DMO's web site: www.dmo.gov.uk.

3. The following information reflects the situation as of June 30, 2002. However, effective July 1, 2002, the DMO took on two additional business units: the public works loans board and the commissioners for the reduction of the national debt. This led to an increase in the number of staff at the DMO to about 80 employees. Before July 1, 2002, another government department—the national investment and loans office—had carried out the functions of the public works loans board and commissioners for the reduction of the national debt. The staff were transferred from the national investment and loans office, which no longer exists.

4. The *DMO Handbook: Exchequer Cash Management in the United Kingdom* (February 2002) details the interaction of cash management with U.K. monetary policy and can be found on the DMO's web site.

5. Further detailed discussion can be found in K.Alec Chrystal, ed., *Government Debt Structure and Monetary Conditions* (London: Bank of England), 1999.

6. A detailed discussion of the fiscal framework can be found in HM Treasury, *Analysing U.K. Fiscal Policy*, 1999, available at www.hm-treasury.gov.uk/mediastore/otherfiles/90.pdf. A full discussion of recent developments in macroeconomic and financial policy can be found in HM Treasury, *Reforming Britain's Economic and Financial Policy—Toward Greater Economic Stability*, 2001, available at www.palgrave.com/catalogue/catalogue.asp?Title_Id=0333966104.

7. "Government's Cash and Debt Management" (HC 154) (available at www.publications.parliament.uk/pa/cm199900/cmselect/cmtreasy/154/15402.htm) was published on May 22, 2000. It provides a comprehensive guide to the government's cash and debt management arrangements as well as records of the oral evidence provided by officials and expert witnesses.

8. The *Debt Management Report* was first published in 1995–96. It was retitled the *Debt and Reserves Management Report* in 2001–02, when it outlined for the first time the annual framework for the management of official foreign currency reserves.

9. Full details of all these instruments and operations are available in the "Gilt Operational Notice" and "Cash Operational Notice" on the DMO web site.

10. Full details of all these instruments and operations are available in the "Gilt Operational Notice" and "Cash Operational Notice" on the DMO web site.

11. The *DMO Handbook: Exchequer Cash Management in the United Kingdom* (February 2002) details the cash management operations and can be found on the DMO's web site.

12. The National Loans Fund is the account that consolidates all government lending and borrowing.

13. The strategic objective for cash management is contained in a remit "Exchequer Cash Management Remit," published in HM Treasury, *Debt and Reserve Management Report 2002–03* (London), March 2002.

14. A full description of the separate trading of registered interest and principal of securities (STRIPS) market is given in the information memorandum, "Issue, Stripping and Reconstitution of British Government Stock," July 2000, on the DMO web site.

15. The DMO also holds quarterly meetings with the representatives of end-investors. Minutes of these meetings are published shortly afterwards on the DMO's web site. In addition, there are annual meetings with the economic secretary to the treasury for both groups in January as part of the preparations for the annual remit, published in March.

18
United States of America[1]

The U.S. Treasury enjoys several advantages over other countries in managing debt. Federal debt issuance is a relatively small percentage of total domestic debt issuance, so financial markets easily absorb changes in the government's borrowing needs. The depth of private markets also allows the government to borrow solely in domestic currency. The sophistication of domestic financial markets allows the government to rely on the private sector for a range of activities that increase the liquidity of treasury securities. The wide breadth of participation in treasury auctions makes uniform-price auctions feasible. Underlying these advantages is the additional advantage of a large, diverse economy that assures investors that debt will be repaid. Many of these advantages have become self-reinforcing: As market depth and breadth have increased, more market participants have been willing to rely more on treasury securities.

The advantages enjoyed by the United States have influenced the development of the treasury market and U.S. debt management techniques. The result is a system that has unique characteristics and constraints. Consequently, the following outline of U.S. governance, strategy, and market development may have limited applicability to other countries.

Governance Framework

The power of the U.S. government to borrow is authorized by the U.S. Constitution. Congress has delegated the secretary of the treasury the power to issue

- certificates of indebtedness and bills: debt obligations maturing not more than 1 year from the date of issue,
- notes: debt obligations maturing at least 1 year and not more than 10 years from the date of issue,
- bonds: debt obligations of more than 10 years,
- savings bonds: retail debt obligations maturing not more than 20 years from the date of issue, and
- savings certificates: retail debt obligations maturing not more than 10 years from the date of issue.

The secretary of the treasury is authorized to prescribe the terms and conditions of the debt obligations issued by the treasury and the conditions under which the debt obligations will be issued. For this and other duties, the secretary may delegate duties and powers to another officer or employee of the U.S. Department of the Treasury. In practice, this means that a political appointee under the secretary generally makes debt management decisions with the advice of career staff.

The Secretary of the treasury can invest in the treasury's own securities or in commercial bank deposits secured by a broad range of pledged collateral acceptable to the treasury, including obligations of the U.S. government and private issuers. As part of its cash management, the treasury maintains relationships with a large number of commercial banks that help to absorb its large seasonal swings in cash balances.

Congress sets a limit on the total face amount of debt obligations issued by the secretary of the treasury. This limit is changed periodically as provided by law, either through the congressional budget process or otherwise. Until late 1917, congressional approval was required every time the treasury needed to borrow. During World War I, this approach to debt issuance became unduly cumbersome, and congress gave the treasury the authority to borrow, while maintaining authority over the total amount of debt outstanding. This practice has allowed the treasury to issue debt for a period, often one or two years, without having to seek congressional approval.

The secretary of the treasury is required to submit to congress an annual report that includes certain statistics about the treasury's past and projected public debt activities. These reports are based on the administration's annual budget projections and increase the accountability of government debt managers. In addition, the government auditing agency may investigate the treasury department's debt management activities.

Administrative structure

The department of the treasury is organized into two major components: the departmental offices and the operating bureaus. The departmental offices are primarily responsible for the formulation of policy and management of the treasury department as a whole, and the operating bureaus carry out the specific operations assigned to the department.

Within the departmental offices, the secretary of the treasury has primary responsibility for debt management activities of the federal government, is the principal economic adviser to the president, and

plays a critical role in policymaking by bringing an economic and government financial policy perspective to issues facing the federal government. Departmental staff formulate and recommend domestic and international financial, economic, and tax policy. Debt management responsibilities include

- determining the treasury's financing needs, planning schedules of security issues and amounts needed, and analyzing alternative types of securities and sales techniques;
- soliciting private sector advice in carrying out treasury financing and debt management policy, and preparing reports containing such recommendations;
- analyzing current economic and securities market conditions and their potential effects on treasury financing on a regular basis;
- coordinating with the Federal Reserve Bank of New York, part of the central banking system, regarding its fiscal agent responsibilities;
- participating in an interagency market surveillance group; and
- coordinating and approving market borrowing of federal agencies and government-sponsored enterprises.

Debt administration is conducted by the bureau of the public debt (BPD), which reports to the treasury. Specific functions of the BPD include

- borrowing the money necessary to operate the federal government and accounting for the resulting public debt;
- issuing, keeping records of, and redeeming government securities; servicing registered accounts; and paying interest when due;
- maintaining accounting and audit control over public debt transactions and publishing statements;
- processing claims for physical securities that are lost, stolen, or destroyed; and
- promoting the sale and retention of retail instruments, U.S. savings bonds.

Cash is managed by the financial management service (FMS), which also reports to the treasury. The

FMS receives and disburses all public monies, maintains government accounts, and prepares daily and monthly reports on the status of government finances. The FMS is the government's primary disbursing agent, collections agent, accountant and reporter of financial information, and collector of delinquent federal debt.

The FMS manages the collection of federal revenues, such as individual and corporate income tax deposits, customs duties, loan repayments, fines, and proceeds from leases, and maintains a network of about 18,000 financial institutions to collect these revenues. The FMS also oversees the federal government's central accounting and reporting system, keeping track of its monetary assets and liabilities. The FMS works with federal agencies to help them adopt uniform accounting and reporting standards and systems.

In addition to the operating bureaus, the Federal Reserve Bank of New York acts as the treasury' fiscal agent in carrying out debt management activities. Fiscal agency services performed include

- maintaining the treasury's funds account,
- clearing treasury checks drawn on that account,
- conducting auctions of treasury securities,
- maintaining treasury's securities electronic bookkeeping system, and
- issuing, servicing, and redeeming treasury securities.

The Federal Reserve System (the Fed) is an independent government entity. Debt policy and monetary policy are conducted independently. Although the treasury and the Fed have independent policies, the Fed acts as the treasury's fiscal agent, carrying out various operational activities for the treasury, and senior staff meet weekly to discuss policy issues.

The relevant web sites for current information are

- http://www.treas.gov/domfin for treasury debt management,
- http://www.publicdebt.treas.gov for the BPD,
- http://www.fms.treas.gov for the FMS, and
- http://www.newyorkfed.org for the Federal Reserve Bank of New York.

Debt Management Strategy and Risk Management Framework

The treasury's debt management objective is to obtain the lowest possible cost of financing over time. In achieving this goal, the treasury's debt management strategy is guided by five interrelated principles.

The first principle is maintaining the "risk-free" status of treasury securities. This is accomplished through prudent fiscal discipline and timely increases in the debt limit. Ready market access at the lowest cost to the government over time is an essential component of debt management.

The second principle is maintaining consistency and predictability in the financing program. The treasury issues securities on a regular schedule with set auction procedures. This reduces uncertainty in the market and helps minimize overall cost of borrowing. In keeping with this principle, the treasury does not seek to time markets, that is, it does not act opportunistically to issue debt when market conditions appear favorable.

The idea of regular and predictable auction schedules began in the 1970s. Starting in 1970, the federal government began financing generally increasing deficits, and most of the treasury's debt management tools were well-suited for the task. New auction cycles were added, frequencies of issuance increased, and auction sizes rose over time. By the late 1970s, the magnitude of the treasury's financing needs led to the introduction of a "regular and consistent" debt issuance schedule.

The third principle of debt management is the treasury's commitment to ensuring market liquidity. Liquidity promotes efficient capital markets by providing an underlying security for a wide range of financial transactions and lowers borrowing costs for the treasury by increasing demand for its securities.

Fourth, the treasury finances across the yield curve. A balanced maturity structure mitigates refunding risks and appeals to the broadest range of investors. In addition, providing a pricing mechanism for interest rates across the yield curve further promotes efficient capital markets.

Fifth, the treasury employs unitary financing. The government's financing needs are aggregated so that borrowing across agencies is conducted through the treasury. Thus, all programs of the federal government can benefit from the treasury's low borrowing rate. Otherwise, separate programs with smaller, less liquid issues would compete with one another in the market. There are some exceptions to unitary financing, amounting to less than 1 percent of all public debt securities outstanding.

These principles frequently act as constraints on the treasury as it works to meet its objective. Regular issuance across the yield curve may occasionally lead to relatively high short-term borrowing costs—costs that we believe are more than offset by the premium investors are willing to pay for a predictable supply of treasury securities. The most significant constraint, however, is that the future can be seen only imperfectly and, therefore, the treasury constantly works to forecast our likely borrowing needs, anticipate how we should alter our borrowing pattern when the future does not fit our forecast, and anticipate what will prove to be the lowest-cost means of financing in the future.

The treasury's long-term financing decisions are made quarterly after advice is solicited from the private sector through interviews with market participants and advice from a private sector advisory group. The group is composed of about 20 individuals who come from broker/dealer firms and investment firms and who are active participants in the government securities market. They meet at the time of each treasury midquarter refunding to advise the treasury on their recommendations for the current refunding operation and debt management policy matters. The group's formal recommendations and the minutes of the group's meetings are available on the Internet at http://www.treas.gov/domfin. The treasury also solicits advice from individuals through an e-mail address: debt.management@do.treas.gov.

Risk management

Financial liabilities are denominated only in local currency. Domestic currency liabilities are viewed as appropriate for the treasury's balance sheet, given the very high proportion of its domestic currency assets. Aside from appropriate, a portfolio solely of domestic currency liabilities is feasible because of the large size of domestic financial markets that can readily absorb fluctuations in the treasury's borrowing needs.

The treasury issues benchmark securities across a wide range of maturities to reduce refinancing risk. Expected borrowing needs are announced quarterly. Changes in schedules or amounts are announced with sufficient lead-time for price discovery and distribution to investors. Underlying this approach is the treasury's large presence in the market, which means that policy changes are likely to lead to price changes.

Management of liability risk is concentrated on maintaining a stable average maturity through balanced issuance of short-, medium-, and long-term securities and ensuring high liquidity through a regular and predictable issuance of benchmark securities. The average length of privately held, marketable treasury debt at the end of 2001 was 5 years and 6 months, excluding inflation-indexed securities, and 5 years and 10 months, including inflation-indexed securities.

Borrowing programs are based on the fiscal and economic projections contained in the annual budget established by congress. The treasury uses the administration's most recent projections of the federal government's budget position as inputs in these models. New budget projections are made annually and published early in the calendar year. Projections are then revised five or six months later.

Based on the administration's projections, the treasury creates long-term debt projections using internally developed models. These models are used to monitor rollover risk and ensure a relatively smooth maturity profile. Short-term debt issuance patterns are based on cash management projections that incorporate both the administration's long-term forecasts and the most recent estimates of short-term expenditures and revenues.

The treasury ensures a high level of liquidity through a large, regular, and predictable issuance pattern. The Fed's primary dealer system for debt issuance, which helps to ensure the success of treasury auctions, further reduces liquidity risk. The frequency and large scale of treasury operations helps to provide assurances that allow for frequent testing of settlement systems.

The treasury is responsible for the operation and management of the commercial book entry program, which includes the announcement, auction, issuance, and buyback of marketable treasury securities as well as regulating, servicing, and accounting for these securities. The Federal Reserve Bank of New York, working as the treasury's fiscal agent, has the day-to-day responsibility for identifying, monitoring, and mitigating operational risk associated with the national book entry system, a safekeeping and transfer system for the treasury's marketable securities. The identification and monitoring of risks associated with the announcement, auction, issuance, and buyback of marketable treasury securities rests with the BPD. These risks are mitigated by contingency plans and associated with various points of failure throughout the automated systems required to perform these functions.

Operational risk is minimized through the delivery-versus-payment feature of the commercial book entry program and by separate agencies handling auctions and settlements. As an additional assurance, annual audits are conducted by the accounting agency of the legislative branch of government.

Recent policy changes

Because of recent budget surpluses, the treasury had been paying down its outstanding debt by issuing less debt than the amount of maturing debt, decreasing both its short- and long-term debt issuance. Paying down debt is inherently asymmetrical, with the paydown occurring at the short end of the maturity spectrum, leading to an increase in average length.

The treasury instituted policies to help mitigate growth in the average length, including regular, smaller reopenings of longer-term debt and buybacks of outstanding long-term debt. Also, it recently suspended issuance of 30-year bonds. This decision was based, in part, on a need to reduce longer-term debt issuance. It also reflected market experience, which indicates that financing with 30-year bonds is expensive relative to 10-year financing.

Continuing economic sluggishness, reduced tax revenue, and the fiscal response to the tragic events of September 11 have led to an increase in the treasury's near-term financing needs. These needs are expected to be temporary and largely met through increased treasury bill and shorter-term note issuance, which in turn has helped to decrease the average length of the privately held marketable debt.

Asset management

The U.S. government's holdings of financial assets (including foreign reserves) are small compared with its financial liabilities. Cash is largely held in commercial banks that are required to post substantial collateral. The Fed, as fiscal agent for and at the direction of the treasury, has primary operational responsibility for investment of cash in participating commercial banks. These responsibilities include accepting, valuing, safekeeping, monitoring for collateral deficiencies, and releasing collateral. The Fed is also the primary point of contact for the depositary financial institutions that participate in the program.

Cash management operations are reviewed and audited both internally and externally. Operations, including both the Fed and commercial banks participating in cash management, employ coordinated and comprehensive risk management procedures to ensure that processes and operations are available. Such management ensures that the objectives of the program are achieved and safeguarded.

The Government Securities Market

Debt management has evolved as the U.S. financial markets have become more sophisticated. As recently as World War II, retail instruments provided an important role in debt issuance. In the 1950s and 1960s, the dominant bond issuers were corporate rather than government. Regular issuance of all debt instruments did not occur until the 1970s. Rules on participation continue to evolve in response to changes in the number of treasury market participants and changes in technology.

The major increase in government debt issuance in the United States took place in financial markets that were already well developed. However, given that ready market access is essential to the government's debt management program, the treasury does focus on how to broaden the market for its securities. Broad distribution of treasury securities enhances liquidity and efficiency of the market for government debt, while minimizing the impacts of government debt management activities on the economy and money markets and increasing the distribution of the benefits of government borrowing.

Because of the treasury market's size, security, and demand by other investors, treasury securities represent the most liquid capital investment in the world. For investors looking for safety, predictability, and easy liquidity, treasury securities offer a range of benefits suited to those objectives.

The treasury issues fixed-rate nominal and inflation-indexed securities. They are direct obligations of the U.S. government and are known commonly as marketable securities because they can be bought and sold in the secondary market at prevailing market prices through financial institutions, brokers, and dealers in government securities. Except for a few specific issues of treasury bonds that were issued before 1985 that are callable, marketable treasury securities are not redeemable before maturity. All marketable treasury securities are issued only in book-entry form, with a minimum purchase amount of $1,000 and in multiples of $1,000. Since September 1998, customers who have established accounts with the treasury have been able to purchase securities via the Internet at the BPD's web site (www.publicdebt.treas.gov).

The treasury currently offers fixed-rate nominal securities with maturities ranging from 4 weeks to 10 years on a regular basis. Bills with maturities of 4, 13, and 26 weeks are auctioned weekly, with Thursday settlement dates; 2-year notes are offered monthly for settlement at month-end; and 5- and 10-year notes are auctioned quarterly with midmonth settlement dates. This wide range of maturity dates allows an investor to structure a portfolio to specific time horizons.

In an effort to expand the types of securities it offers and broaden the base of direct investors in its securities auctions, the treasury began auctioning inflation-indexed securities in January 1997. These securities help to protect investors from inflation, and their auctions have had broader direct participation relative to treasury fixed-rate nominal security auctions by appealing to investors that have not previously invested in treasury securities and encouraging other portfolios to invest more. This increased participation should help to lower overall financing

costs. The treasury also issues a retail inflation-indexed savings bond.

The treasury initially offered 5- and 10-year inflation-indexed notes and 30-year inflation-indexed bonds, but market interest has largely focused on the 10-year note, so 5-year inflation-indexed notes were last issued in October 1997 and 30-year inflation-indexed bonds were suspended in October 2001. The principal of the security is adjusted daily for inflation. The inflation adjustment is subject to federal income tax in the year it is earned, and the inflation-adjusted principal is paid at maturity. Semiannual interest payments are a fixed percentage of the inflation-adjusted principal. The security uses the nonseasonally adjusted consumer price index for all urban consumers as the inflation index. The treasury currently offers the 10-year inflation-indexed note on a regular, semiannual schedule.

Before the early 1970s, the traditional methods for selling notes and bonds were subscription offerings, exchange offerings, and advance refundings. Subscriptions involved the treasury setting an interest rate on the securities to be sold and then selling (or taking subscriptions for) them at a fixed price. In exchange offerings, the treasury allowed holders of outstanding maturing securities to exchange them for new issues at an announced price and coupon rate. In some cases, new securities were issued only to holders of the specific maturing securities; in others, additional amounts of the new security were issued. Advance refundings differed from exchange offerings in that the outstanding securities could be exchanged before their maturity date.

A fundamental difficulty with fixed-price subscription and exchange offerings was that market yields could change between the announcement of the offering and the deadline for subscriptions. Increased market volatility in the 1970s made fixed-price offerings very risky for the treasury.

A modified auction technique was introduced in 1970, in which the treasury preset the interest rate (coupon rate) and bids were made on the basis of price. The treasury started to auction coupon issues on a yield basis in 1974. Bids were accepted on the basis of an annual percentage yield, with the coupon rate based on the weighted-average yield of accepted competitive tenders received in the auction. Yield auctions free the treasury from having to set the coupon rate before the auction and ensure that the interest costs of new note and bond issues accurately reflect actual market demand and supply conditions at the time of the auction.

Today, all marketable treasury securities are sold in uniform-price auctions, and all treasury auctions are conducted on a yield basis. The terms and conditions for offerings of treasury securities are governed by the terms and conditions set forth in the "Uniform Offering Circular for the Sale and Issue of Marketable Book-Entry Treasury Bills, Notes, and Bonds" (in the *United States Code of Federal Regulations*, available at www.publicdebt.treas.gov/gsr/gsruo-cam.htm). A separate announcement is made for each auction, providing the dates of the auction and settlement, the amount offered for sale, the maturity of the security, and other details. The treasury sells the entire announced amount of each security offered at the yield determined in the auction.

The treasury permits trading during the period between announcement and settlement on a when-issued basis that provides for price discovery and reduces uncertainties surrounding auction pricing. Potential competitive bidders look to when-issued trading levels as a market gauge of demand to determine how to bid at an auction. Noncompetitive bidders, to whom securities are awarded at the auction-determined yield, can use the quotes in the when-issued market to assess the likely auction yield.

Until late 1998, the method for selling marketable treasury securities generally had been multiple-price auctions. In a multiple-price auction, competitive bids were accepted from the lowest yield (discount rates in the case of treasury bills) to the highest yield required to sell the amount offered to the public. Competitive bidders whose tenders were accepted paid the price equivalent to the yield (or discount rate) that they bid. Noncompetitive bidders paid the weighted-average price of accepted competitive bids.

The treasury adopted the use of single-price auctions for all marketable treasury securities in November 1998. All auctions of inflation-indexed notes and bonds have been on a single-price basis since the Treasury began selling inflation-indexed securities. As with multiple-price auctions, single-price auctions are conducted in terms of yield (bank discount rate in the case of treasury bills). Bids are accepted from the lowest yield (or discount rate) to the highest required to sell the amount offered. In contrast to multiple-price auctions, all awards are at the highest yield (or discount rate) of accepted bids.

The treasury has found that single-price auctions have some advantages over multiple-price auctions. First, they tend to distribute auction awards to a greater number of bidders than multiple-price auctions. Second, auction participants may bid more aggressively in single-price auctions. Successful bidders are able to reduce the so-called winner's curse, the risk that a successful bidder will pay more than the common market value of the security and, therefore, will be less likely to realize a profit from selling it. There is evidence that more aggressive bidding has lowered treasury borrowing costs somewhat.

Any entity may submit a bid in a treasury auction directly to a federal reserve bank, which acts as the treasury's fiscal agent, indirectly through a dealer, or directly to the treasury department. The treasury permits all dealers registered with the Securities and Exchange Commission and all federally regulated financial institutions to submit bids in treasury auctions for their own accounts and for the account of customers. All bidders in treasury auctions—not just primary dealers and financial institutions—may bid in treasury auctions without a deposit, provided the bidder has a payment mechanism in place (an "autocharge agreement") with its federal reserve bank.

Primary dealers are firms through which the Federal Reserve Bank of New York conducts its open market operations. They include large diversified securities firms, money center banks, and specialized securities firms, and they are foreign owned and U.S. owned. Over the last decade, the number of primary dealers has declined from 46 to 22. Among their responsibilities, primary dealers are expected to participate meaningfully in treasury auctions, make reasonably good markets in their trading relationships with the Federal Reserve Bank of New York's trading desk, and supply market information to the Fed. Formerly, primary dealers were also required to transact a certain level of trading volume with customers and thereby maintain a liquid secondary market for treasury securities. Customers include nonprimary dealers, other financial institutions (such as banks, insurance companies, pension funds, and mutual funds), nonfinancial institutions, and individuals. Although trading with customers is no longer a requirement, primary dealers remain the predominant market makers in U.S. Treasury securities.

The treasury has facilitated purchases of treasury securities by small investors by awarding securities on a noncompetitive basis for up to $5 million through a book-entry system. Through this system, the investor holds treasury securities directly on the books of the treasury, without using the services of a financial institution or a dealer.

Note

1. The case study was prepared by the Office of Market Finance of the U.S. Treasury.

Appendix

Summary of the Debt Management Guidelines[1]

1. Debt management objectives and coordination

1.1 Objectives

The main objective of public debt management is to ensure that the government's financing needs and its payment obligations are met at the lowest possible cost over the medium to long run, consistent with a prudent degree of risk.

1.2 Scope

Debt management should encompass the main financial obligations over which the central government exercises control.

1.3 Coordination with monetary and fiscal policies

Debt managers, fiscal policy advisers, and central bankers should share an understanding of the objectives of debt management, fiscal, and monetary poli-

cies given the interdependencies between their different policy instruments. Debt managers should convey to fiscal authorities their views on the costs and risks associated with government financing requirements and debt levels.

Where the level of financial development allows, there should be a separation of debt management and monetary policy objectives and accountabilities.

Debt management, fiscal, and monetary authorities should share information on the government's current and future liquidity needs.

2. Transparency and accountability

2.1 Clarity of roles, responsibilities, and objectives of financial agencies responsible for debt management

The allocation of responsibilities among the ministry of finance, the central bank, or a separate debt management agency for debt management policy advice, and for undertaking primary debt issues, secondary market arrangements, depository facilities, and clearing and settlement arrangements for trade in government securities, should be publicly disclosed.

The objectives for debt management should be clearly defined and publicly disclosed, and the measures of cost and risk that are adopted should be explained.

2.2 Open process for formulating and reporting debt management policies

Materially important aspects of debt management operations should be publicly disclosed.

2.3 Public availability of information on debt management policies

The public should be provided with information on the past, current, and projected budgetary activity, including its financing, and the consolidated financial position of the government.

The government should regularly publish information on the stock and composition of its debt and financial assets, including their currency, maturity, and interest rate structure.

2.4 Accountability and assurances of integrity by agencies responsible for debt management

Debt management activities should be audited annually by external auditors.

3. Institutional framework

3.1 Governance

The legal framework should clarify the authority to borrow and issue new debt, invest, and undertake transactions on the government's behalf.

The organizational framework for debt management should be well specified and ensure that mandates and roles are well articulated.

3.2 Management of internal operations

Risks of government losses from inadequate operational controls should be managed according to sound business practices, including well-articulated responsibilities for staff, and clear monitoring and control policies and reporting arrangements.

Debt management activities should be supported by an accurate and comprehensive management information system with proper safeguards.

Staff involved in debt management should be subject to code-of-conduct and conflict-of-interest guidelines regarding the management of their personal financial affairs.

Sound business recovery procedures should be in place to mitigate the risk that debt management activities might be severely disrupted by natural disasters, social unrest, or acts of terrorism.

4. Debt management strategy

The risks inherent in the structure of the government's debt should be carefully monitored and evaluated. These risks should be mitigated to the extent feasible by modifying the debt structure, taking into account the cost of doing so.

In order to help guide borrowing decisions and reduce the government's risk, debt managers should consider the financial and other risk characteristics of the government's cash flows.

Debt managers should carefully assess and manage the risks associated with foreign currency and short-term or floating-rate debt.

There should be cost-effective cash management policies in place to enable the authorities to meet with a high degree of certainty their financial obligations as they fall due.

5. Risk management framework

A framework should be developed to enable debt managers to identify and manage the trade-offs between expected cost and risk in the government debt portfolio.

To assess risk, debt managers should regularly conduct stress tests of the debt portfolio on the basis of the economic and financial shocks to which the government—and the country more generally—are potentially exposed.

5.1 Scope for active management

Debt managers who seek to manage actively the debt portfolio to profit from expectations of movements in interest rates and exchange rates, which differ from those implicit in current market prices, should be aware of the risks involved and accountable for their actions.

5.2 Contingent liabilities

Debt managers should consider the impact that contingent liabilities have on the government's financial position, including its overall liquidity, when making borrowing decisions.

6. Development and maintenance of an efficient market for government securities

In order to minimize cost and risk over the medium to long run, debt managers should ensure that their policies and operations are consistent with the development of an efficient government securities market.

6.1 Portfolio diversification and instruments

The government should strive to achieve a broad investor base for its domestic and foreign obligations, with due regard to cost and risk, and should treat investors equitably.

6.2 Primary market

Debt management operations in the primary market should be transparent and predictable.

To the extent possible, debt issuance should use market-based mechanisms, including competitive auctions and syndications.

6.3 Secondary market

Governments and central banks should promote the development of resilient secondary markets that can function effectively under a wide range of market conditions.

The systems used to settle and clear financial market transactions involving government securities should reflect sound practices.

Note

1. The IMF–World Bank *Guidelines for Public Debt Management* can be found on the IMF and the World Bank web sites in 5 languages:
http://www.imf.org/external/pubs/cat/longres.cfm?sk=15113.0
and
http://www.worldbank.org/pdm/pdf/guidelines_2001_final.pdf.